YOU'RE MAKING that FACE AGAIN

Also by Jerry Scott and Jim Borgman

Zits: Sketchbook 1
Growth Spurt: Zits Sketchbook 2
Don't Roll Your Eyes at Me, Young Man!: Zits Sketchbook 3
Are We an "Us"?: Zits Sketchbook 4
Zits Unzipped: Zits Sketchbook 5
Busted!: Zits Sketchbook 6
Road Trip: Zits Sketchbook 7
Teenage Tales: Zits Sketchbook No. 8
Thrashed: Zits Sketchbook No. 9
Pimp My Lunch: Zits Sketchbook No. 10
Are We Out of the Driveway Yet?: Zits Sketchbook No. 11
Rude, Crude, and Tattooed: Zits Sketchbook No. 12
Jeremy and Mom
Pierced
Lust and Other Uses for Spare Hormones
Jeremy & Dad

Treasuries
Humongous Zits
Big Honkin' Zits
Zits: Supersized
Random Zits
Crack of Noon
Alternative Zits
My Bad

Gift Book
A Zits Guide to Living with Your Teenager

YOU'RE MAKING that FACE AGAIN

Zits® Sketchbook 13

by Jerry Scott and Jim Borgman

Andrews McMeel
Publishing, LLC

Kansas City • Sydney • London

Zits® is syndicated internationally by King Features Syndicate, Inc. For information, write King Features Syndicate, Inc., 300 West Fifty-Seventh Street, New York, New York 10019.

10 11 12 13 14 RR2 10 9 8 7 6 5 4 3 2 1

ISBN: 978-0-7407-9734-7

Library of Congress Control Number: 2010924498

Zits® may be viewed online at
www.kingfeatures.com.

www.andrewsmcmeel.com

─────── **ATTENTION: SCHOOLS AND BUSINESSES** ───────

Andrews McMeel books are available at quantity discounts with bulk purchase for educational, business, or sales promotional use. For information, please write to: Special Sales Department, Andrews McMeel Publishing, LLC, 1130 Walnut Street, Kansas City, Missouri 64106.

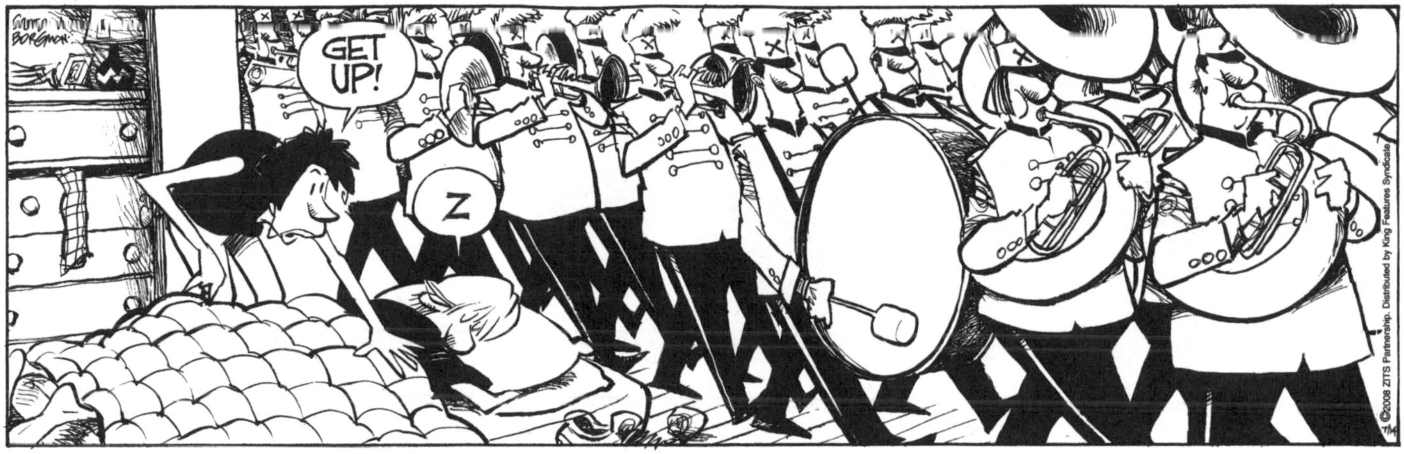
GET UP!
Z
©2008 ZITS Partnership. Distributed by King Features Syndicate

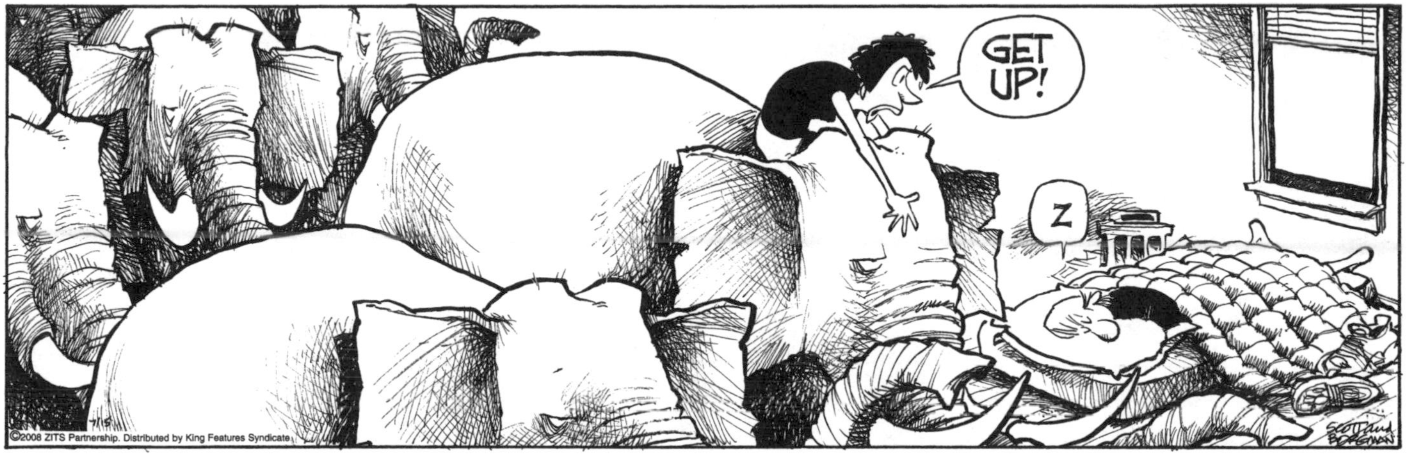
GET UP!
Z
©2008 ZITS Partnership. Distributed by King Features Syndicate

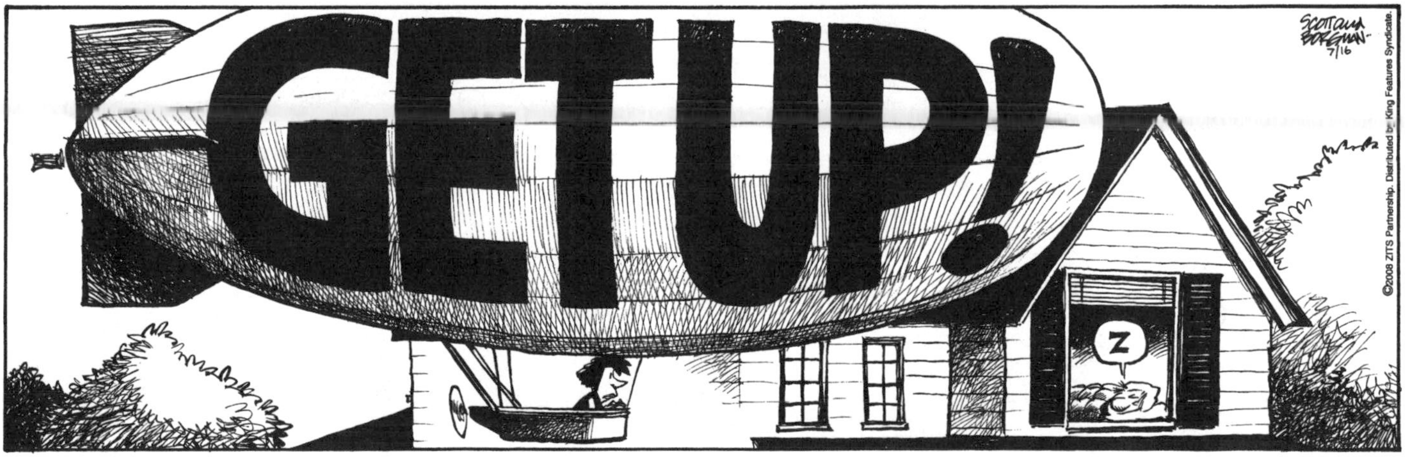
GET UP!
Z
©2008 ZITS Partnership. Distributed by King Features Syndicate.

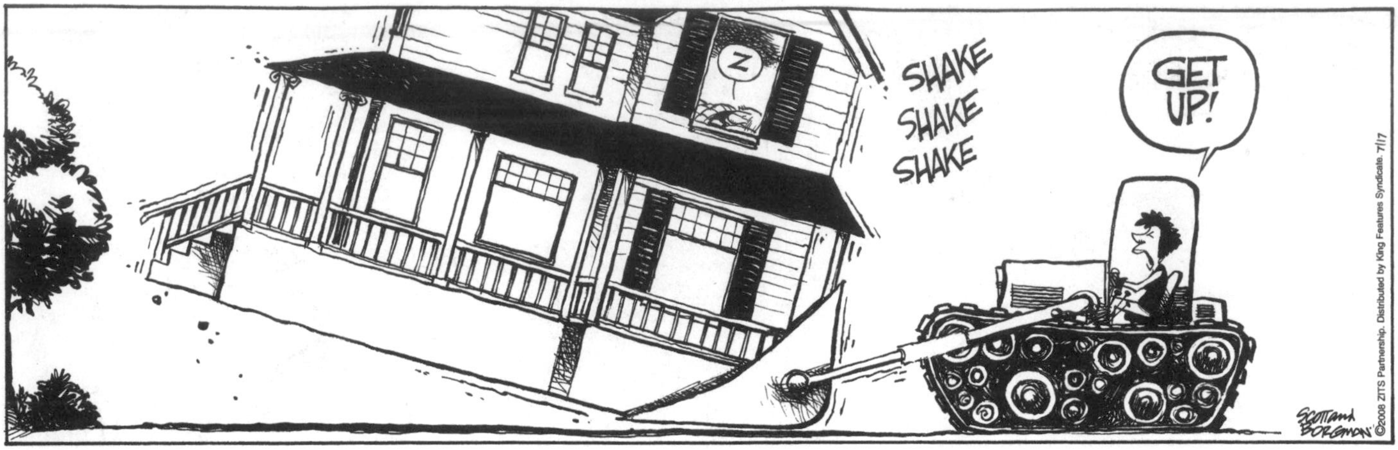
SHAKE
SHAKE
SHAKE
GET UP!
SCOTT and BORGMAN
©2008 ZITS Partnership. Distributed by King Features Syndicate. 7/17

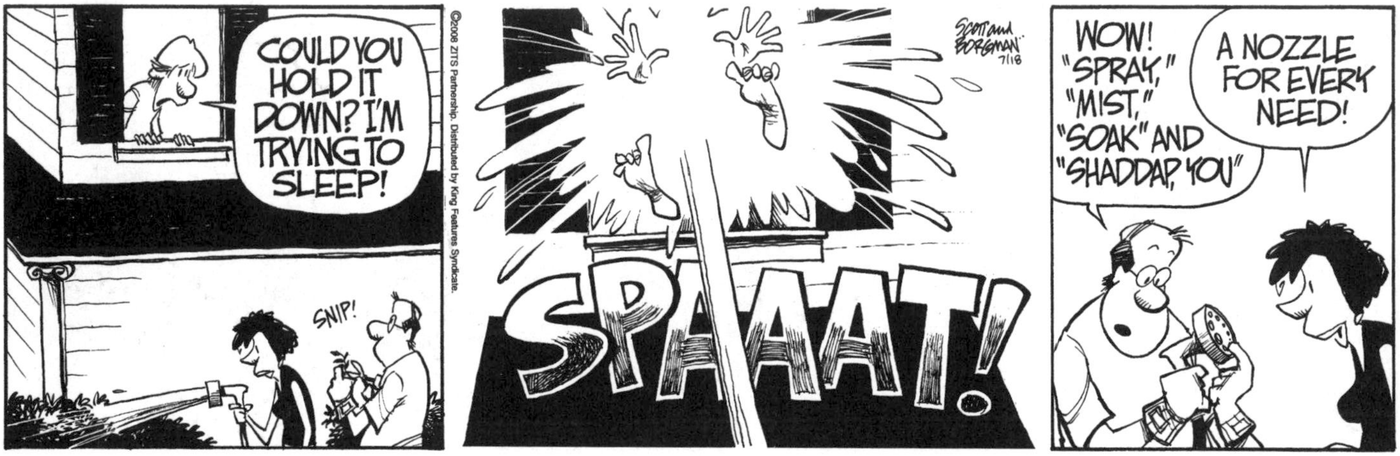
COULD YOU HOLD IT DOWN? I'M TRYING TO SLEEP!
SNIP!
©2008 ZITS Partnership. Distributed by King Features Syndicate.
SCOTT and BORGMAN 7/18
SPAAAT!
WOW! "SPRAY," "MIST," "SOAK" AND "SHADDAP, YOU"
A NOZZLE FOR EVERY NEED!

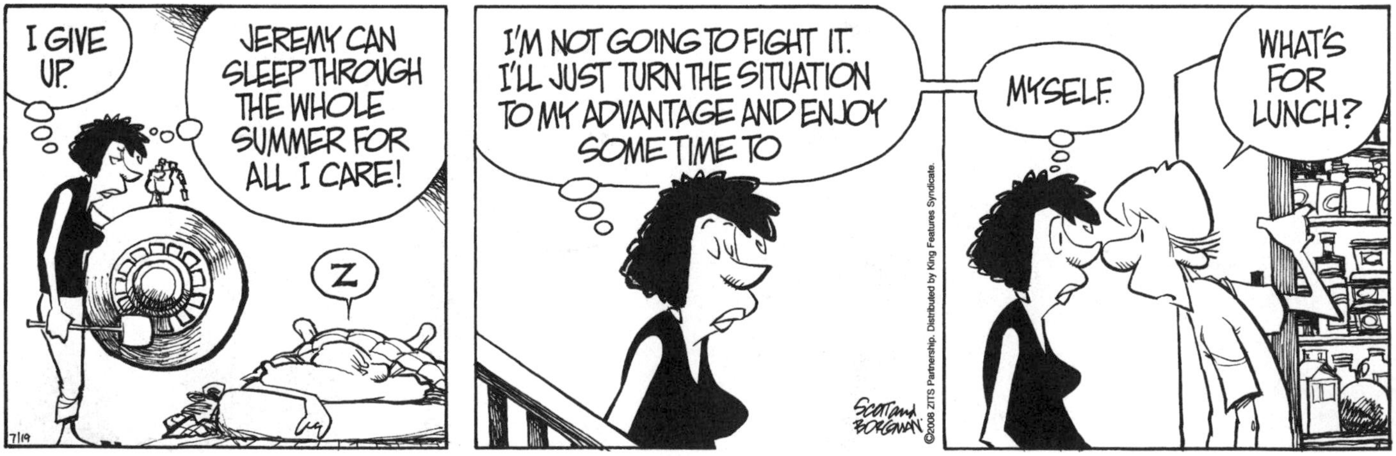
I GIVE UP.
JEREMY CAN SLEEP THROUGH THE WHOLE SUMMER FOR ALL I CARE!
Z
7/19
I'M NOT GOING TO FIGHT IT. I'LL JUST TURN THE SITUATION TO MY ADVANTAGE AND ENJOY SOME TIME TO
©2008 ZITS Partnership. Distributed by King Features Syndicate.
SCOTT and BORGMAN
MYSELF.
WHAT'S FOR LUNCH?

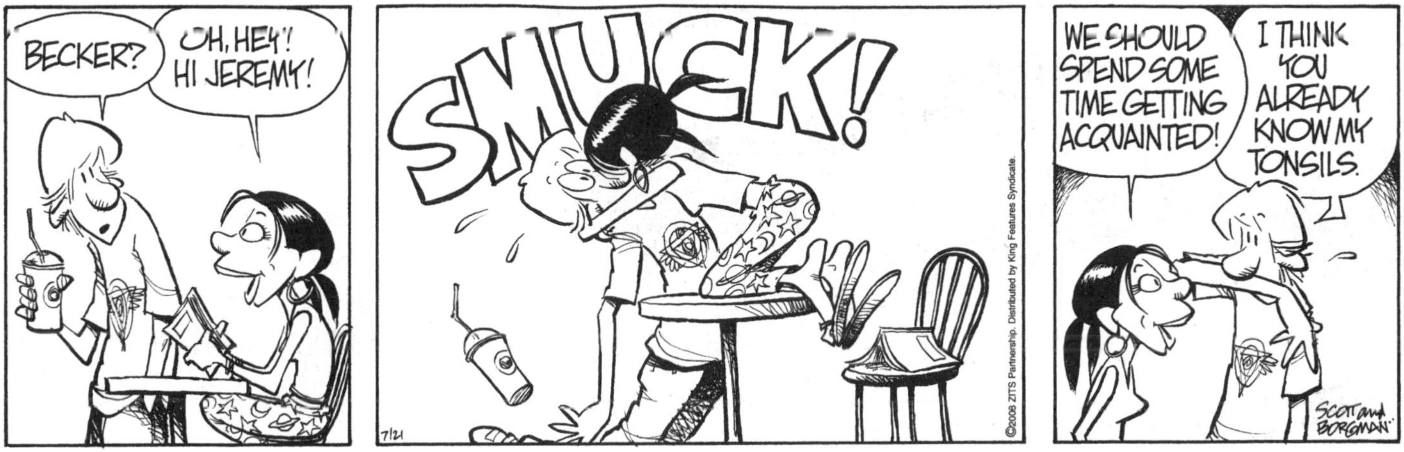
BECKER?
OH, HEY! HI JEREMY!
SMUCK!
7/21
©2008 ZITS Partnership. Distributed by King Features Syndicate.
WE SHOULD SPEND SOME TIME GETTING ACQUAINTED!
I THINK YOU ALREADY KNOW MY TONSILS.
SCOTT and BORGMAN

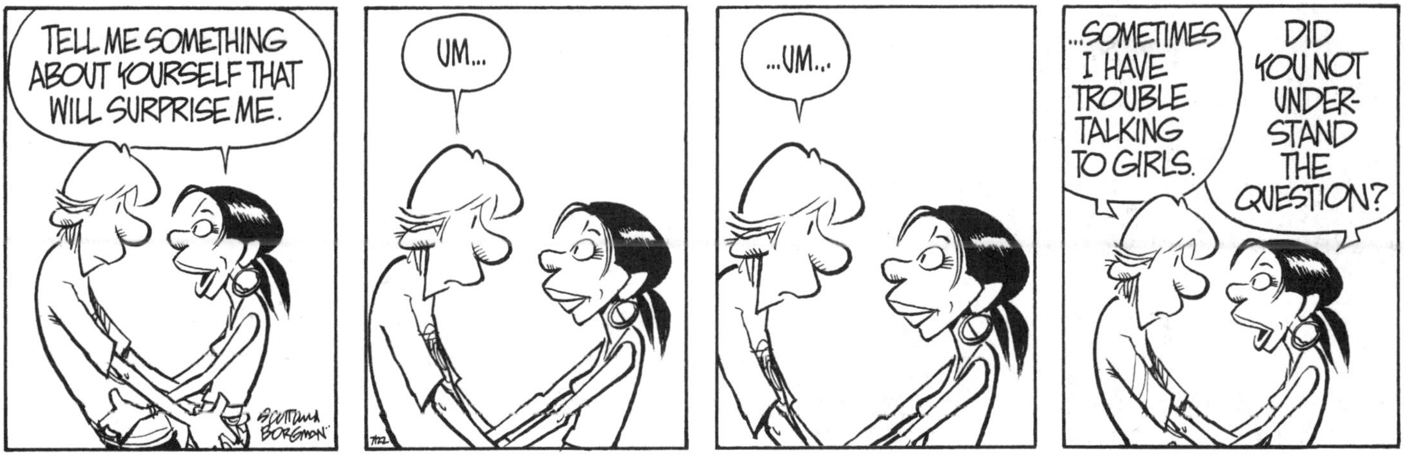
TELL ME SOMETHING ABOUT YOURSELF THAT WILL SURPRISE ME.
SCOTT and BORGMAN
UM...
...UM...
...SOMETIMES I HAVE TROUBLE TALKING TO GIRLS.
DID YOU NOT UNDERSTAND THE QUESTION?

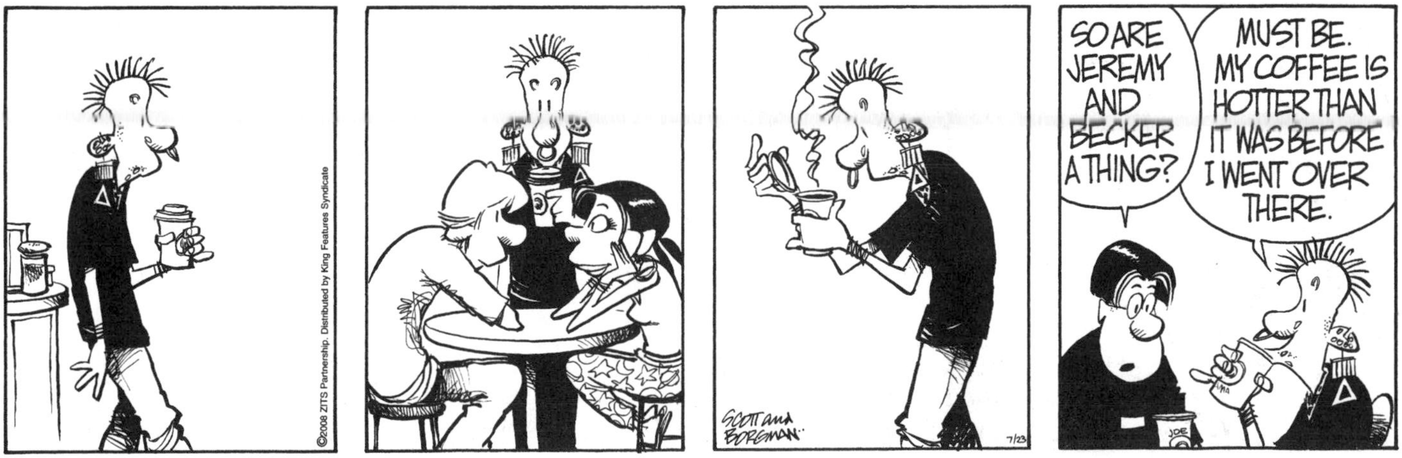
©2008 ZITS Partnership. Distributed by King Features Syndicate
SCOTT and BORGMAN
7/23
SO ARE JEREMY AND BECKER A THING?
MUST BE. MY COFFEE IS HOTTER THAN IT WAS BEFORE I WENT OVER THERE.
JOE

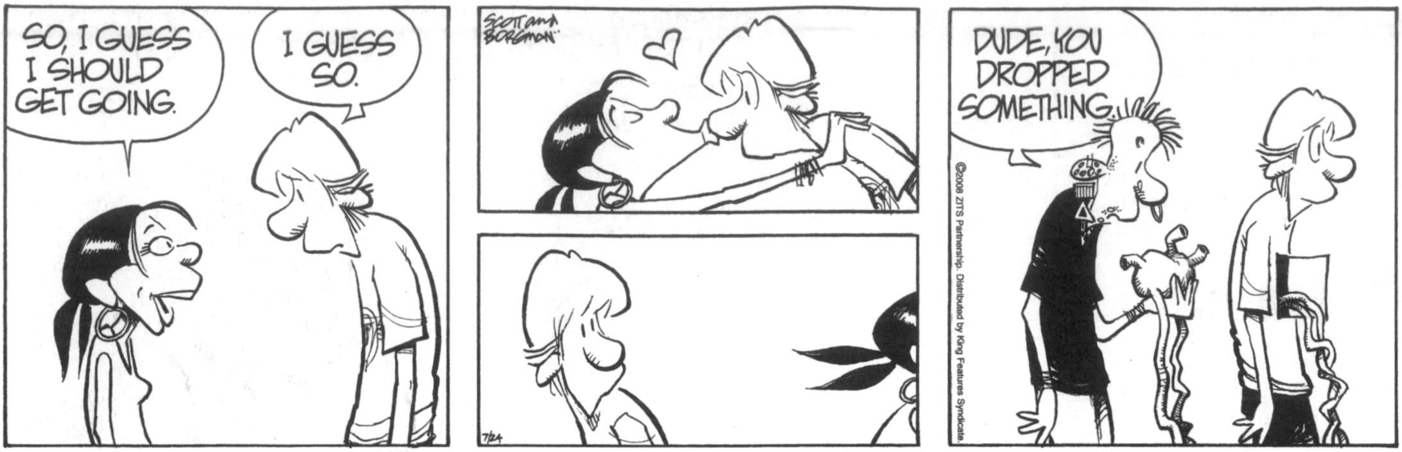
SO, I GUESS I SHOULD GET GOING.
I GUESS SO.
SCOTT and BORGMAN
7/24
DUDE, YOU DROPPED SOMETHING.
©2008 ZITS Partnership. Distributed by King Features Syndicate.

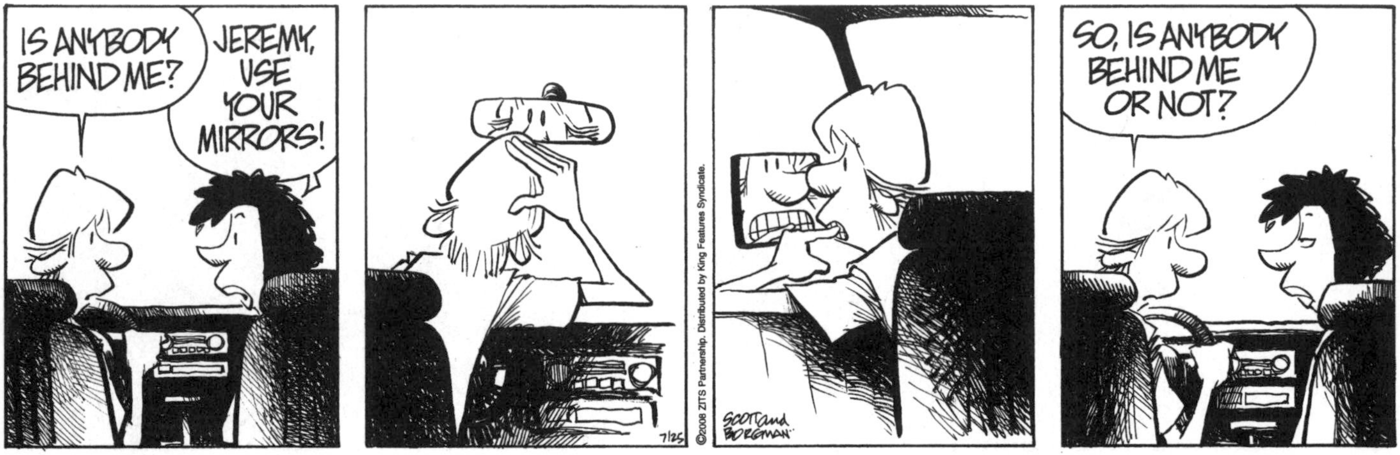
IS ANYBODY BEHIND ME?
JEREMY, USE YOUR MIRRORS!
7/25
©2008 ZITS Partnership. Distributed by King Features Syndicate.
SCOTT and BORGMAN
SO, IS ANYBODY BEHIND ME OR NOT?

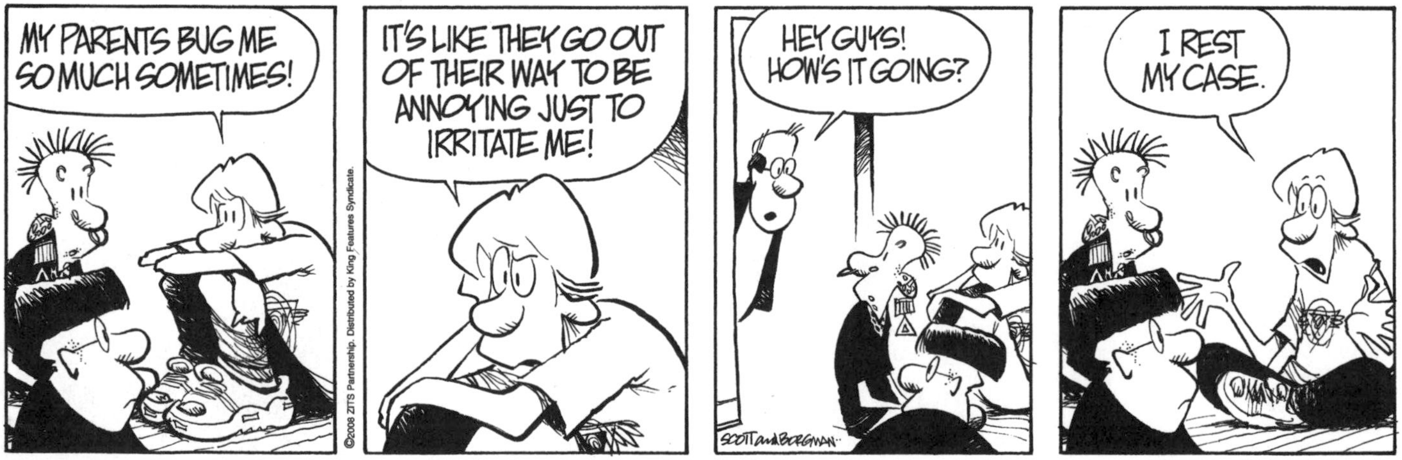
MY PARENTS BUG ME SO MUCH SOMETIMES!
©2008 ZITS Partnership. Distributed by King Features Syndicate.
IT'S LIKE THEY GO OUT OF THEIR WAY TO BE ANNOYING JUST TO IRRITATE ME!
HEY GUYS! HOW'S IT GOING?
SCOTT and BORGMAN
I REST MY CASE.

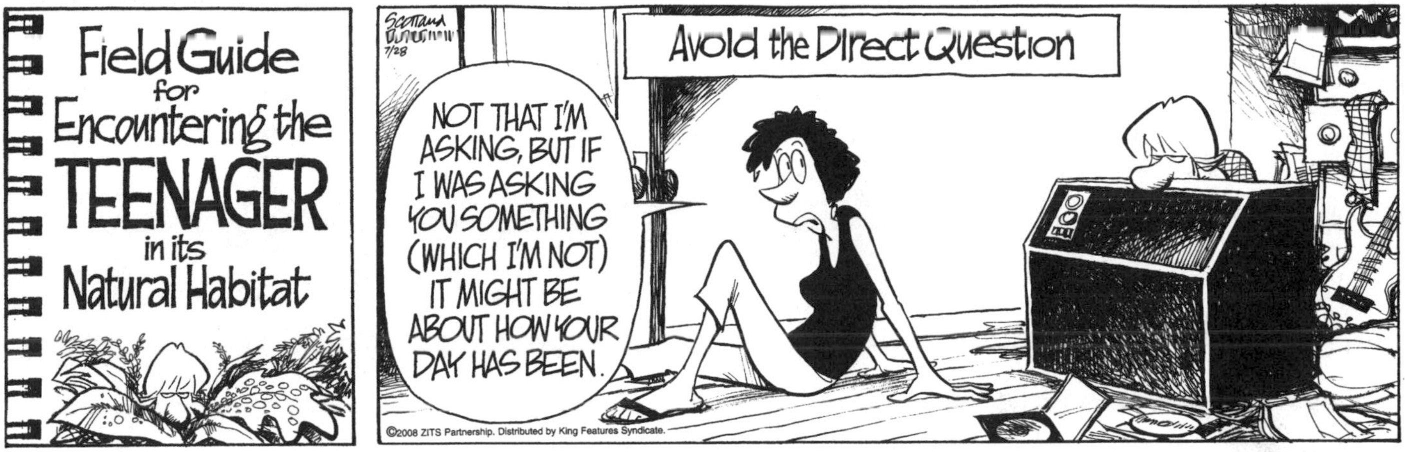
Field Guide for Encountering the TEENAGER in its Natural Habitat
Avoid the Direct Question
NOT THAT I'M ASKING, BUT IF I WAS ASKING YOU SOMETHING (WHICH I'M NOT) IT MIGHT BE ABOUT HOW YOUR DAY HAS BEEN.
©2008 ZITS Partnership. Distributed by King Features Syndicate.

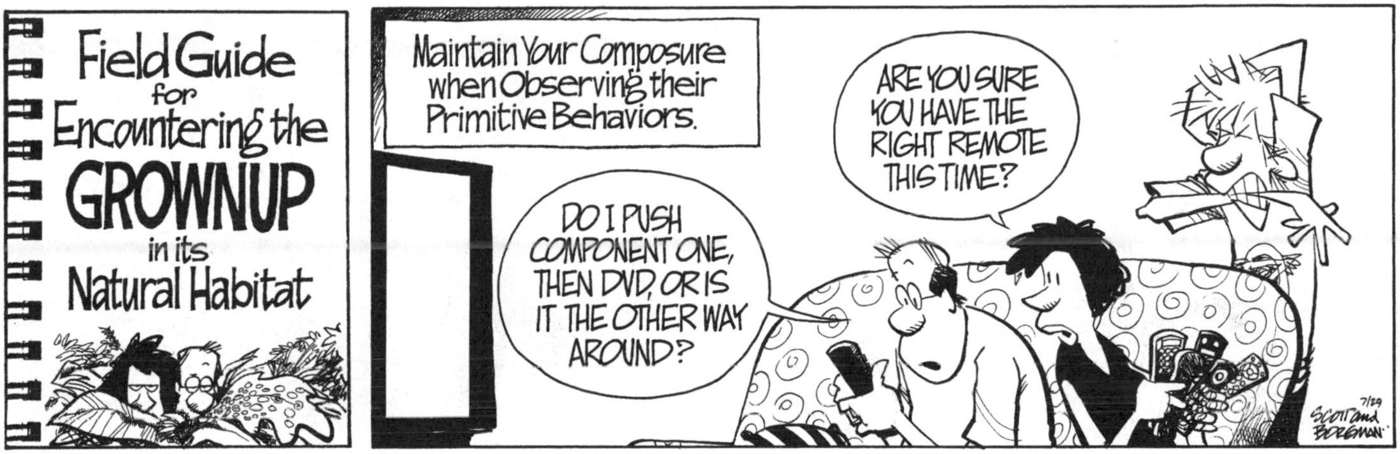
Field Guide for Encountering the GROWNUP in its Natural Habitat
Maintain Your Composure when Observing their Primitive Behaviors.
DO I PUSH COMPONENT ONE, THEN DVD, OR IS IT THE OTHER WAY AROUND?
ARE YOU SURE YOU HAVE THE RIGHT REMOTE THIS TIME?

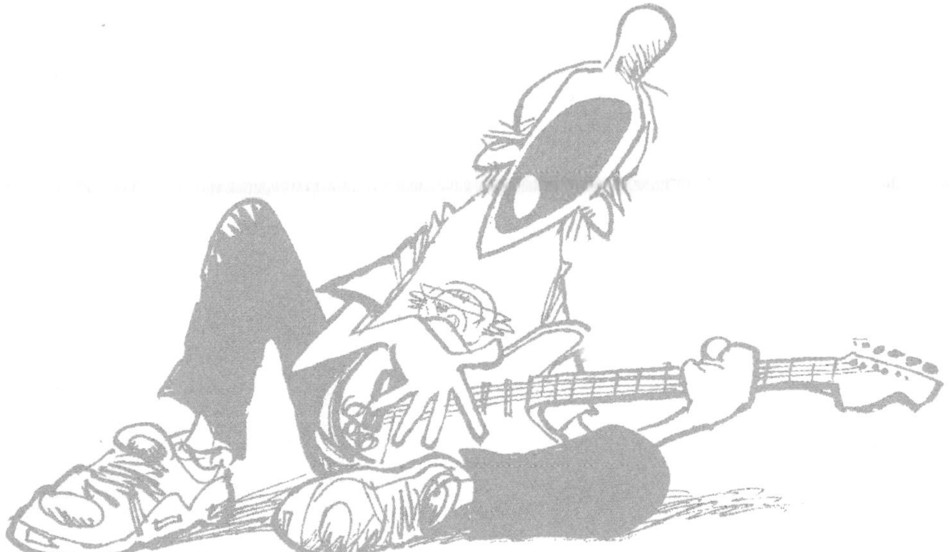

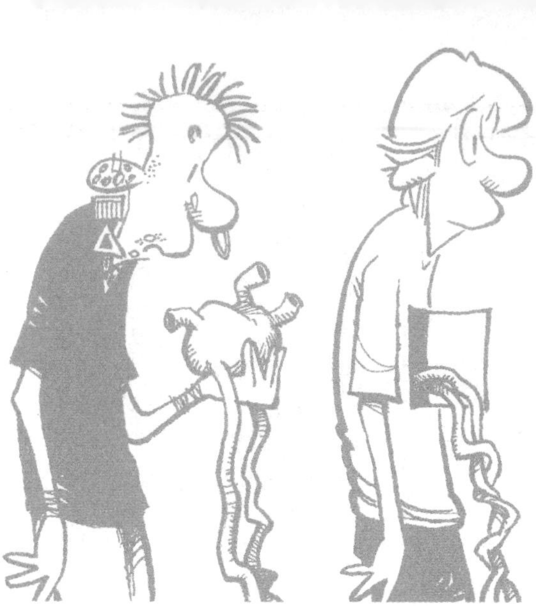

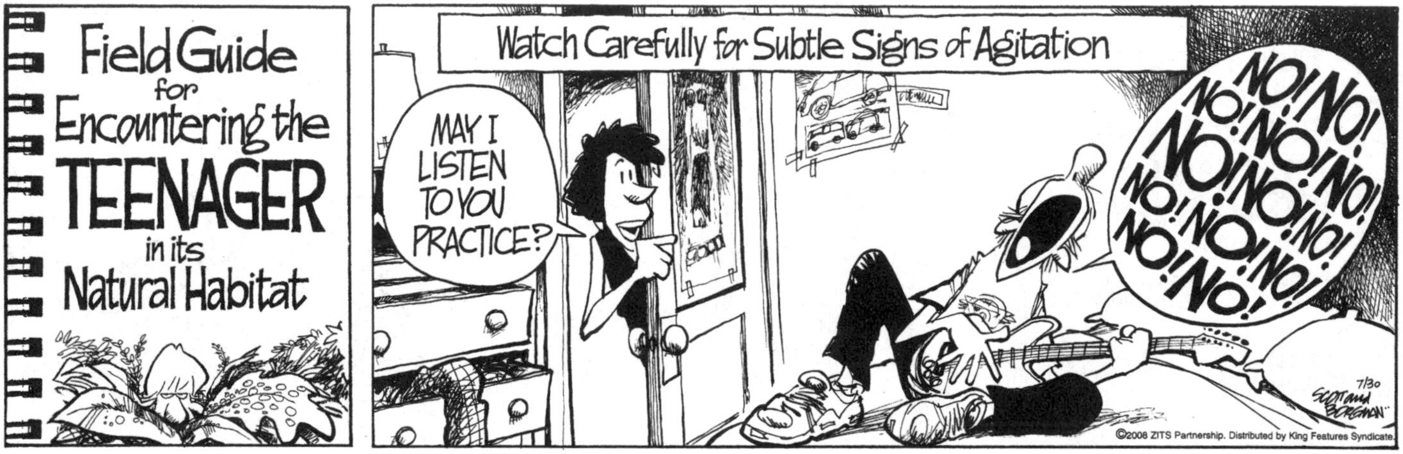
Field Guide for Encountering the TEENAGER in its Natural Habitat
Watch Carefully for Subtle Signs of Agitation
MAY I LISTEN TO YOU PRACTICE?
NO! NO! NO! NO! NO! NO! NO! NO! NO! NO! NO! NO! NO! NO! NO!
7/30 SCOTT and BORGMAN
©2008 ZITS Partnership. Distributed by King Features Syndicate.

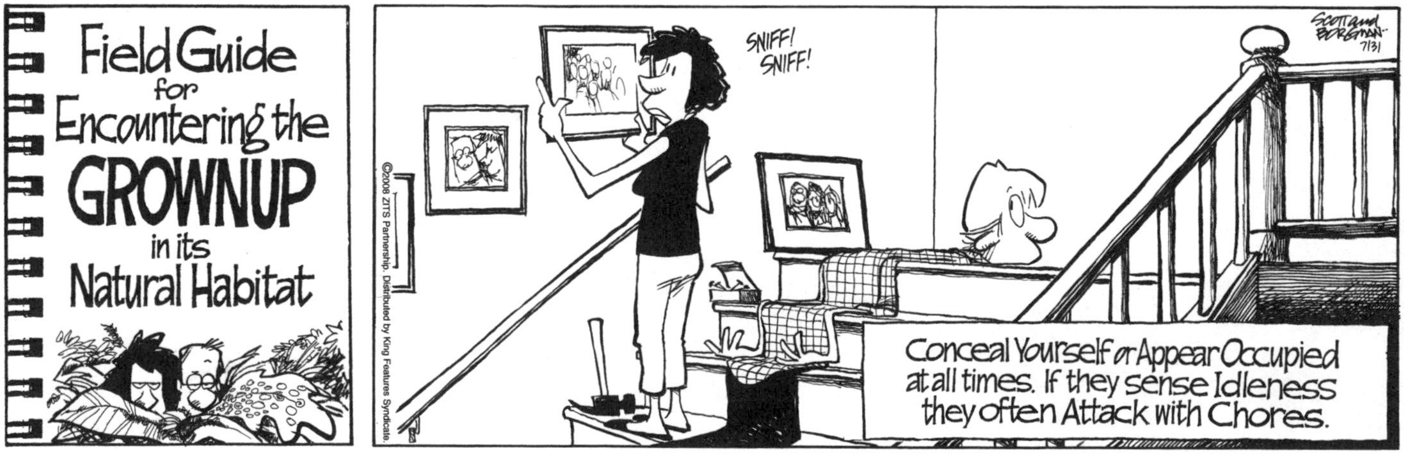
Field Guide for Encountering the GROWNUP in its Natural Habitat
©2008 ZITS Partnership. Distributed by King Features Syndicate.
SNIFF! SNIFF!
SCOTT and BORGMAN 7/31
Conceal Yourself or Appear Occupied at all times. If they sense Idleness they often Attack with Chores.

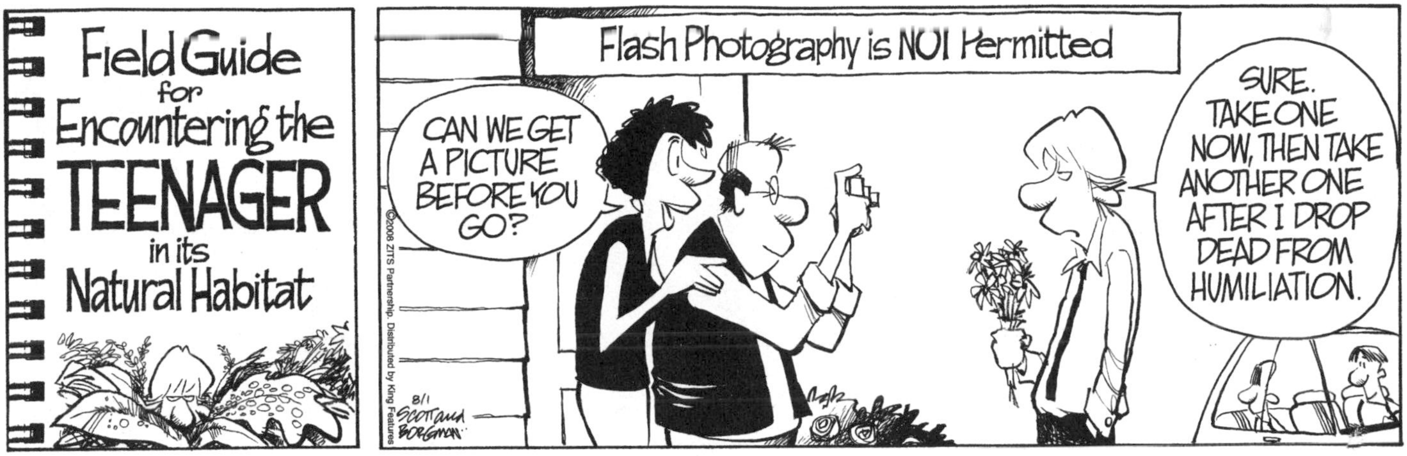
Field Guide for Encountering the TEENAGER in its Natural Habitat
Flash Photography is NOT Permitted
CAN WE GET A PICTURE BEFORE YOU GO?
SURE. TAKE ONE NOW, THEN TAKE ANOTHER ONE AFTER I DROP DEAD FROM HUMILIATION.
©2008 ZITS Partnership. Distributed by King Features
8/1 SCOTT and BORGMAN

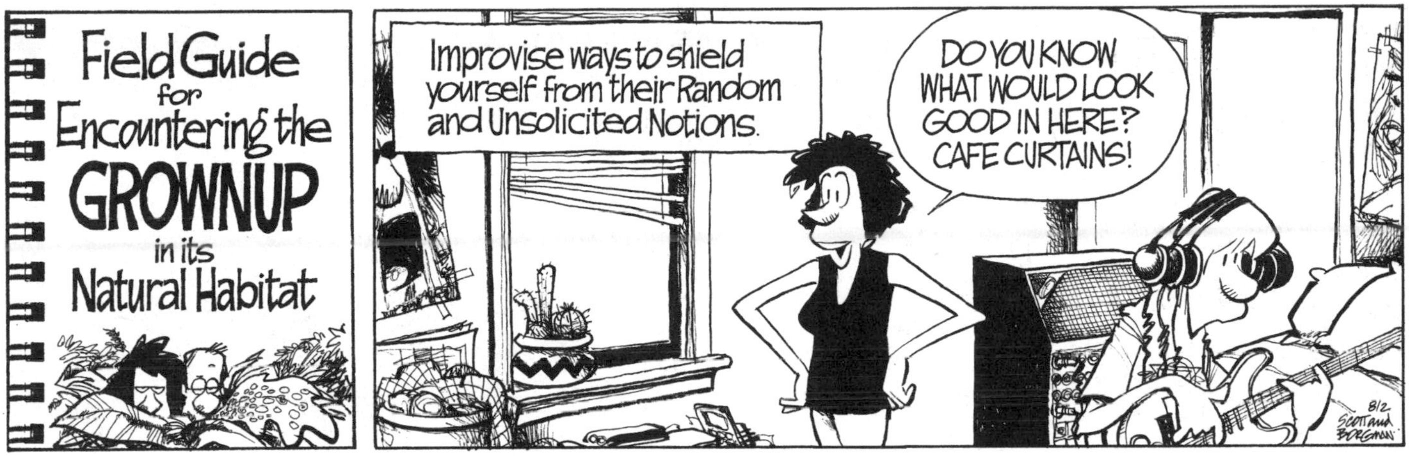
Field Guide for Encountering the GROWNUP in its Natural Habitat
Improvise ways to shield yourself from their Random and Unsolicited Notions.
DO YOU KNOW WHAT WOULD LOOK GOOD IN HERE? CAFE CURTAINS!
8/2 SCOTT and BORGMAN

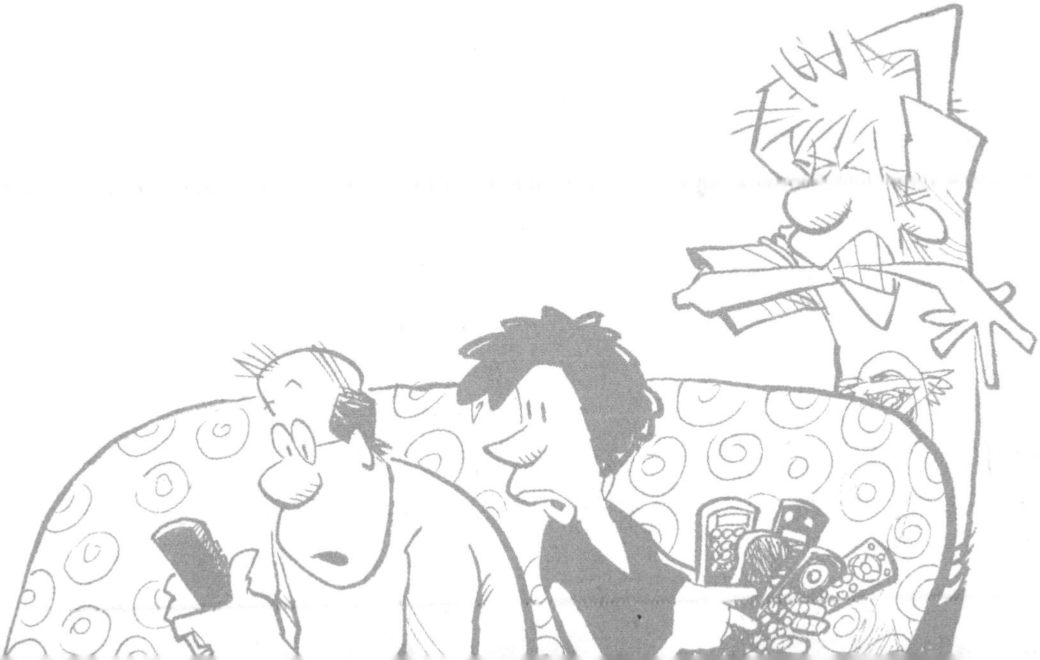

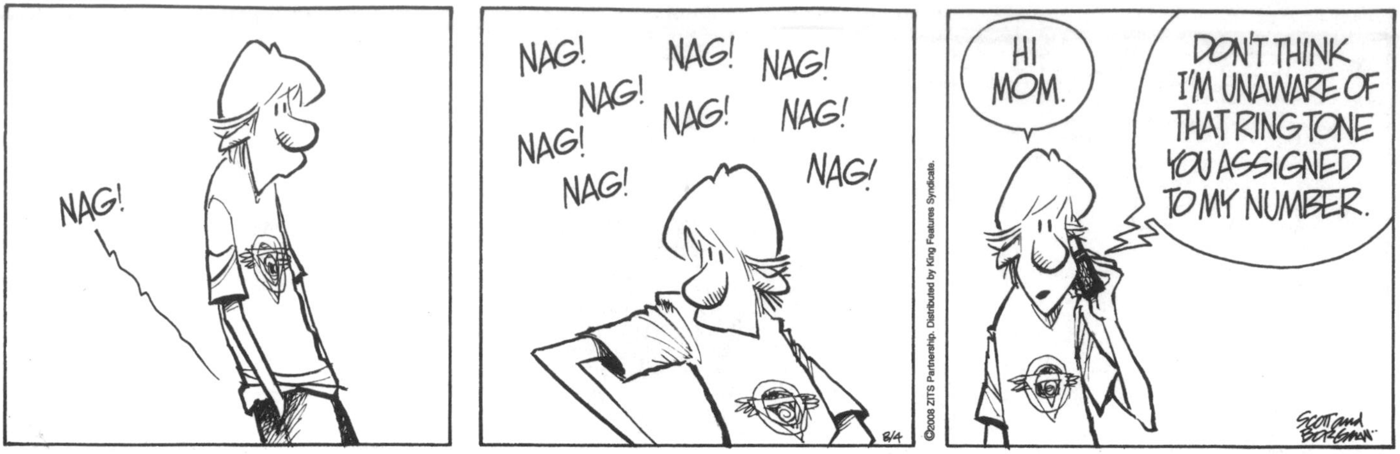
NAG!
NAG! NAG! NAG! NAG! NAG! NAG! NAG! NAG!
8/4
©2008 ZITS Partnership. Distributed by King Features Syndicate.
HI MOM.
DON'T THINK I'M UNAWARE OF THAT RING TONE YOU ASSIGNED TO MY NUMBER.
SCOTT and BORGMAN

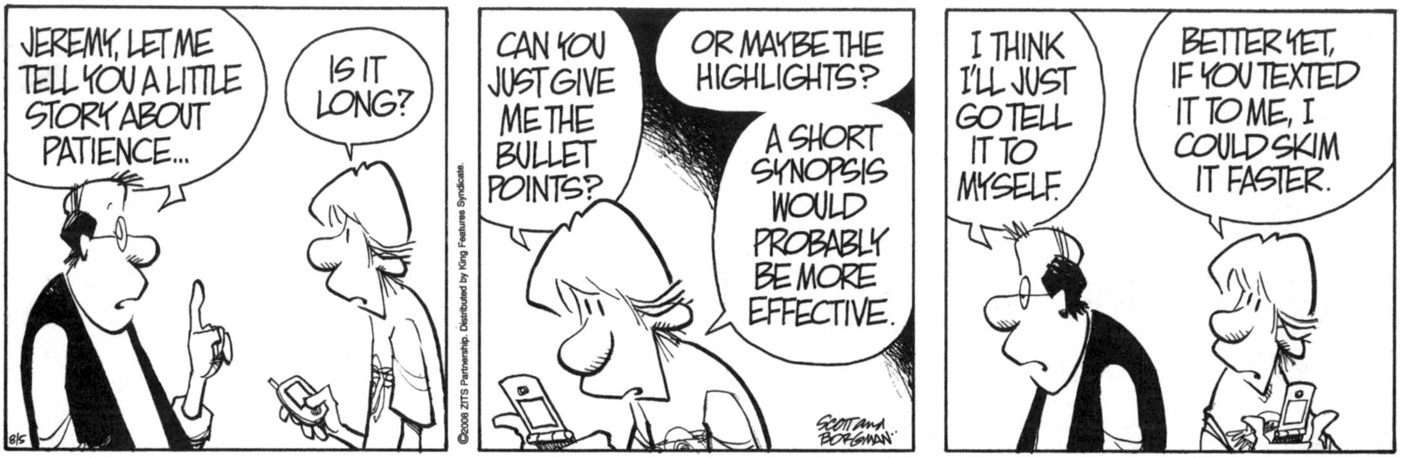
JEREMY, LET ME TELL YOU A LITTLE STORY ABOUT PATIENCE...
IS IT LONG?
8/5
©2008 ZITS Partnership. Distributed by King Features Syndicate.
CAN YOU JUST GIVE ME THE BULLET POINTS?
OR MAYBE THE HIGHLIGHTS?
A SHORT SYNOPSIS WOULD PROBABLY BE MORE EFFECTIVE.
SCOTT and BORGMAN
I THINK I'LL JUST GO TELL IT TO MYSELF.
BETTER YET, IF YOU TEXTED IT TO ME, I COULD SKIM IT FASTER.

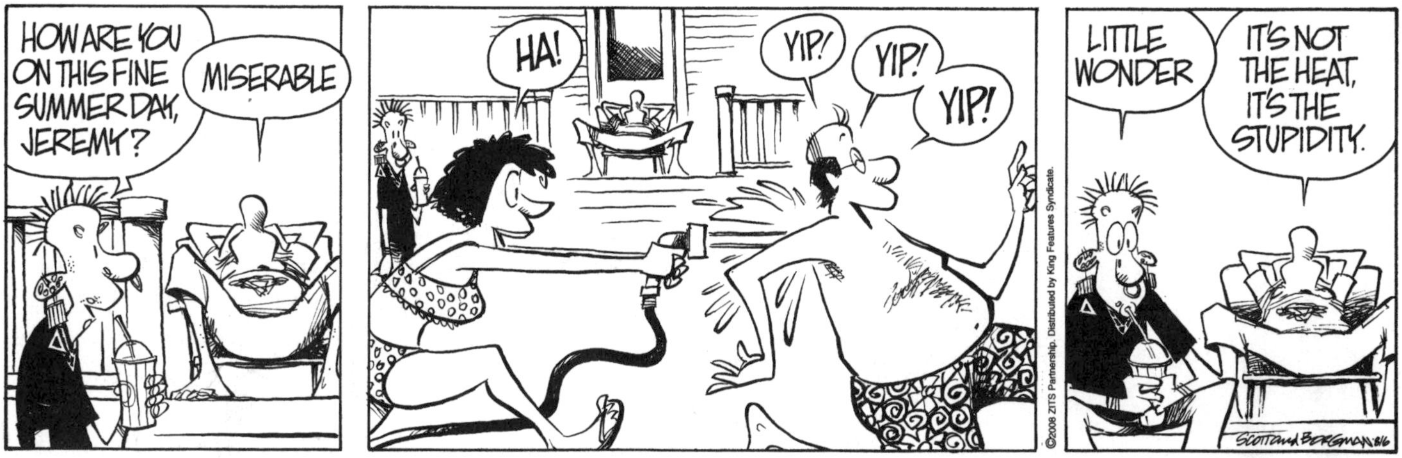
HOW ARE YOU ON THIS FINE SUMMER DAY, JEREMY?
MISERABLE
HA!
YIP!
YIP!
YIP!
©2008 ZITS Partnership. Distributed by King Features Syndicate.
LITTLE WONDER
IT'S NOT THE HEAT, IT'S THE STUPIDITY.
SCOTT and BORGMAN 8/6

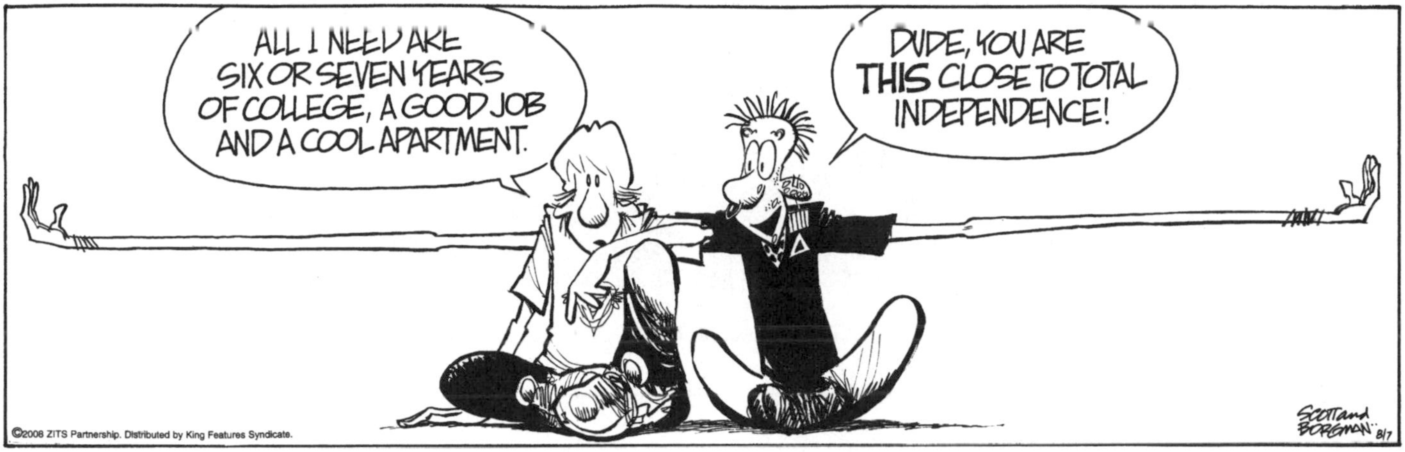
ALL I NEED ARE SIX OR SEVEN YEARS OF COLLEGE, A GOOD JOB AND A COOL APARTMENT.
DUDE, YOU ARE THIS CLOSE TO TOTAL INDEPENDENCE!
©2008 ZITS Partnership. Distributed by King Features Syndicate.
SCOTT and BORGMAN 8/7

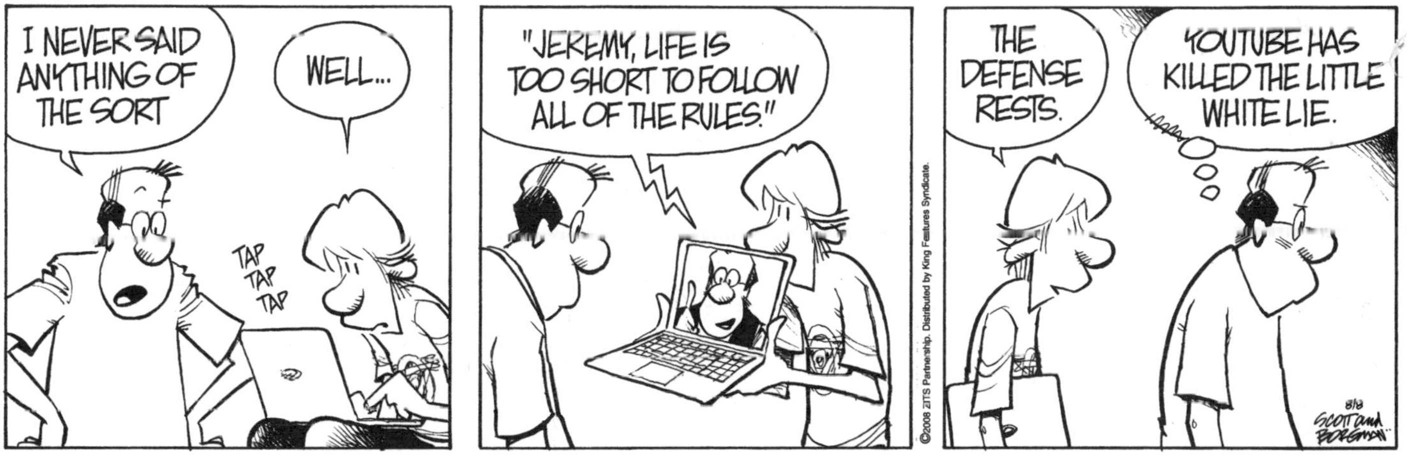
I NEVER SAID ANYTHING OF THE SORT
WELL...
TAP TAP TAP
"JEREMY, LIFE IS TOO SHORT TO FOLLOW ALL OF THE RULES."
©2008 ZITS Partnership. Distributed by King Features Syndicate.
THE DEFENSE RESTS.
YOUTUBE HAS KILLED THE LITTLE WHITE LIE.
8/8 SCOTT and BORGMAN

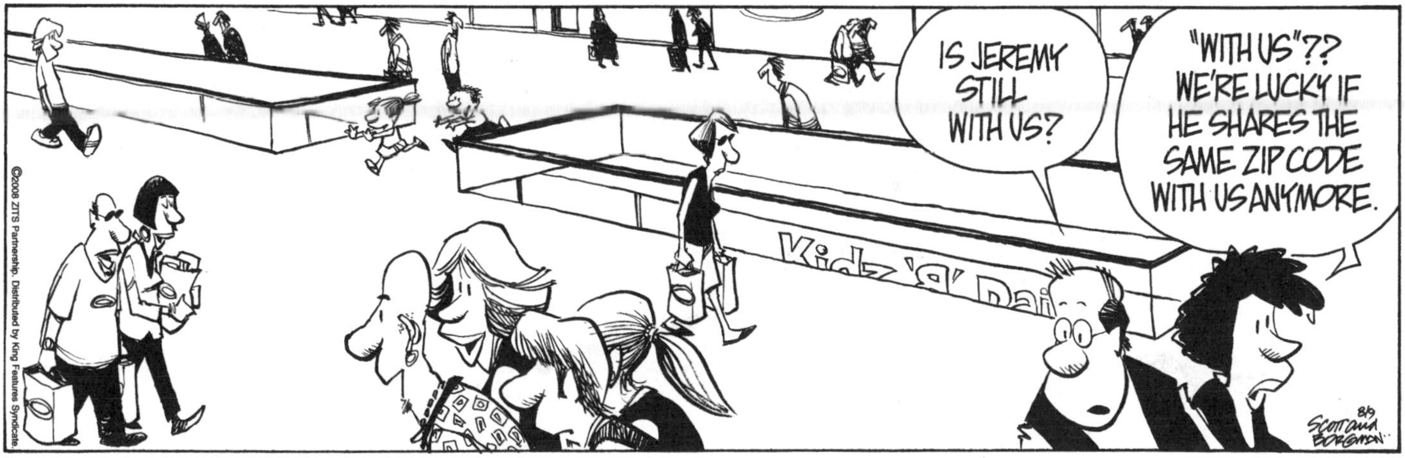
©2008 ZITS Partnership. Distributed by King Features Syndicate.
IS JEREMY STILL WITH US?
"WITH US"?? WE'RE LUCKY IF HE SHARES THE SAME ZIP CODE WITH US ANYMORE.
8/9 SCOTT and BORGMAN

Zits
by
JERRY SCOTT and
JIM BORGMAN

HAIR COLOR
SHAKE
SHAKE
SHAKE
©2008 ZITS Partnership. Distributed by King Features Syndicate
ONE! TWO! THREE! FOUR!
DID I TELL YOU THAT THE BOYS WERE GOING TO HAVE BAND PRACTICE HERE TODAY?

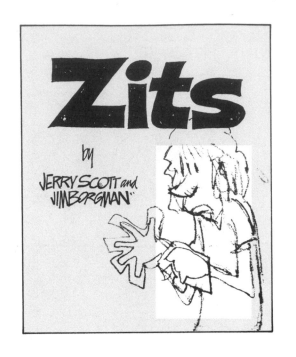

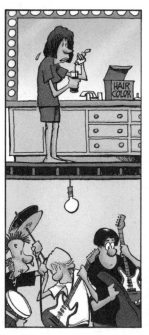

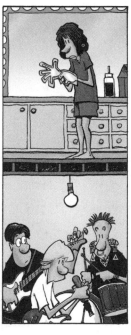

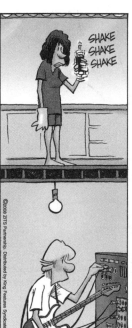

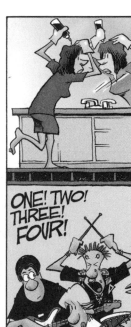

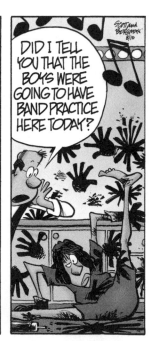

WHAT ARE YOU DOING TODAY, JEREMY?
ABSOLUTELY NOTHING.
8/11
GOOD. I WANT YOU TO CLEAN OUT THE GARAGE.
YOU ALWAYS RUIN MY PLANS!
©2008 ZITS Partnership. Distributed by King Features Syndicate.
SCOTT and BORGMAN

I'M NOT CLEANING OUT THE GARAGE TODAY!
YOU. WILL. CLEAN. THE. GARAGE. TODAY. WITHOUT. ANOTHER. WORD.
GOT IT?
OKAY! OKAY! OKAY!
8/12
©2008 ZITS Partnership. Distributed by King Features Syndicate.
WHY DO YOU ALWAYS TAKE EVERYTHING I SAY OUT OF CONTEXT?
SCOTT and BORGMAN

I KNOW YOUR TIME IS VALUABLE, JEREMY.
IF YOU'LL SPEND A FEW HOURS CLEANING THE GARAGE, I'LL GIVE YOU FORTY BUCKS AND WE WON'T ASK YOU TO DO ANYTHING ELSE FOR THE REST OF THE WEEK.
WHY DOES EVERYBODY ALWAYS PICK ON ME?
©2008 ZITS Partnership. Distributed by King Features Syndicate.
SCOTT and BORGMAN 8/13

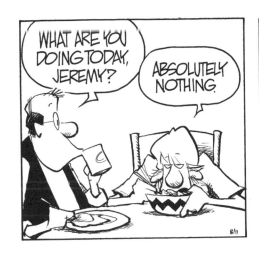

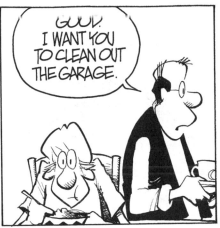

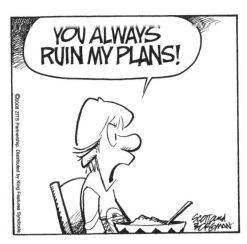

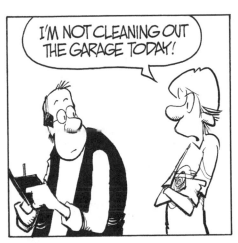

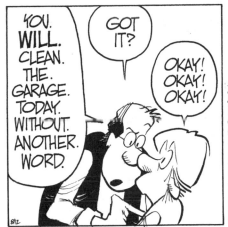

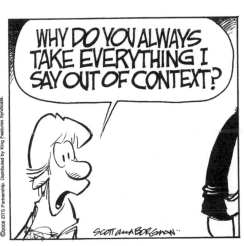

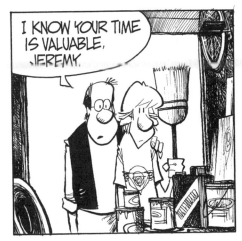

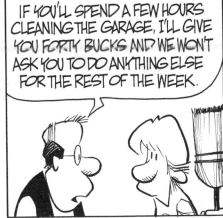

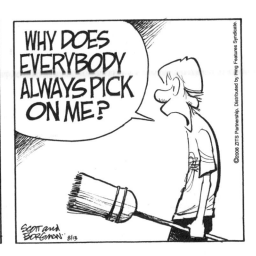

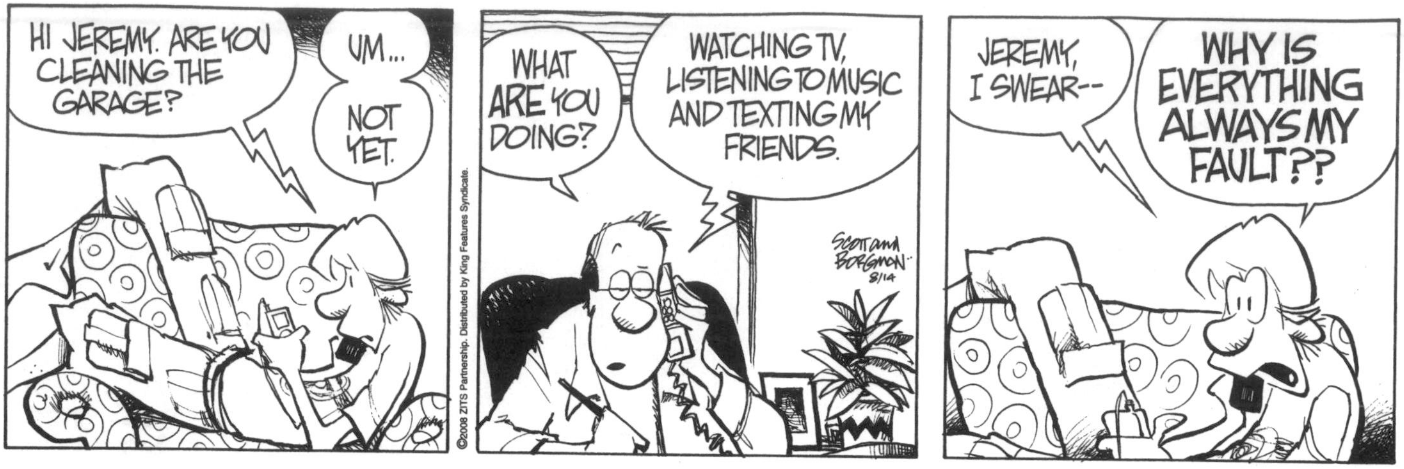
HI JEREMY. ARE YOU CLEANING THE GARAGE?
UM...
NOT YET.
©2008 ZITS Partnership. Distributed by King Features Syndicate.
WHAT ARE YOU DOING?
WATCHING TV, LISTENING TO MUSIC AND TEXTING MY FRIENDS.
SCOTT and BORGMAN 8/14
JEREMY, I SWEAR--
WHY IS EVERYTHING ALWAYS MY FAULT??

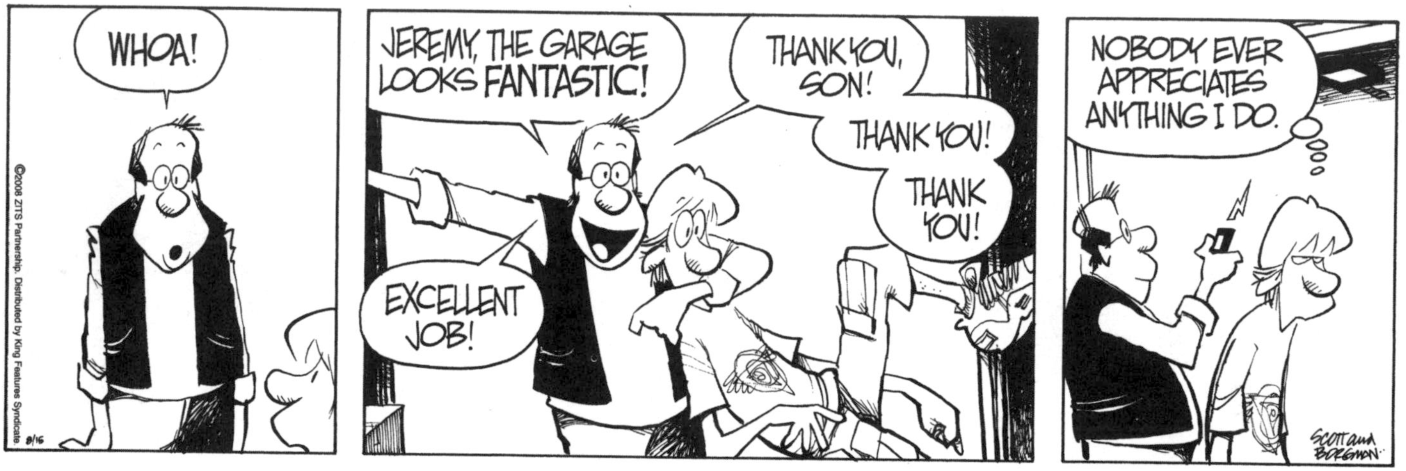
WHOA!
©2008 ZITS Partnership. Distributed by King Features Syndicate.
8/15
JEREMY, THE GARAGE LOOKS FANTASTIC!
EXCELLENT JOB!
THANK YOU, SON!
THANK YOU!
THANK YOU!
NOBODY EVER APPRECIATES ANYTHING I DO.
SCOTT and BORGMAN

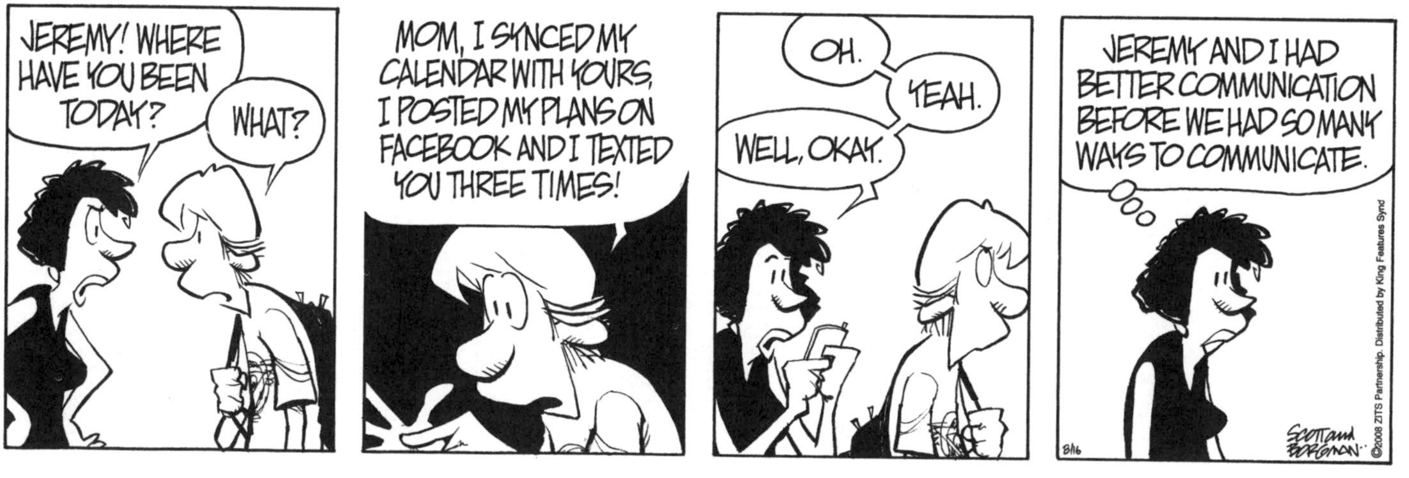
JEREMY! WHERE HAVE YOU BEEN TODAY?
WHAT?
MOM, I SYNCED MY CALENDAR WITH YOURS, I POSTED MY PLANS ON FACEBOOK AND I TEXTED YOU THREE TIMES!
OH.
YEAH.
WELL, OKAY.
JEREMY AND I HAD BETTER COMMUNICATION BEFORE WE HAD SO MANY WAYS TO COMMUNICATE.
8/16
SCOTT and BORGMAN
©2008 ZITS Partnership. Distributed by King Features Synd

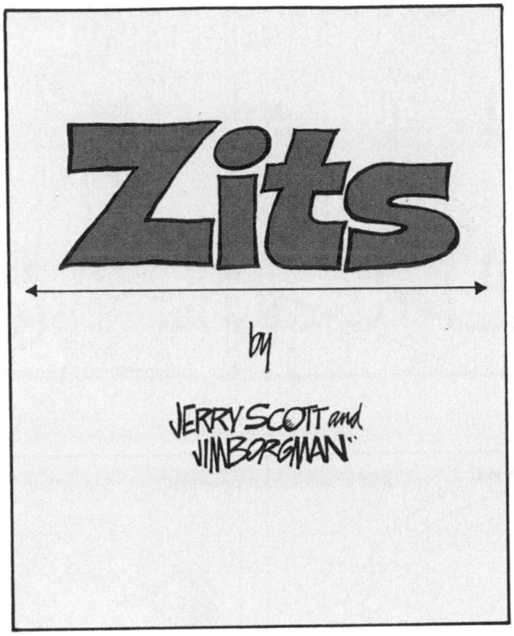
Zits
by
JERRY SCOTT and
JIM BORGMAN

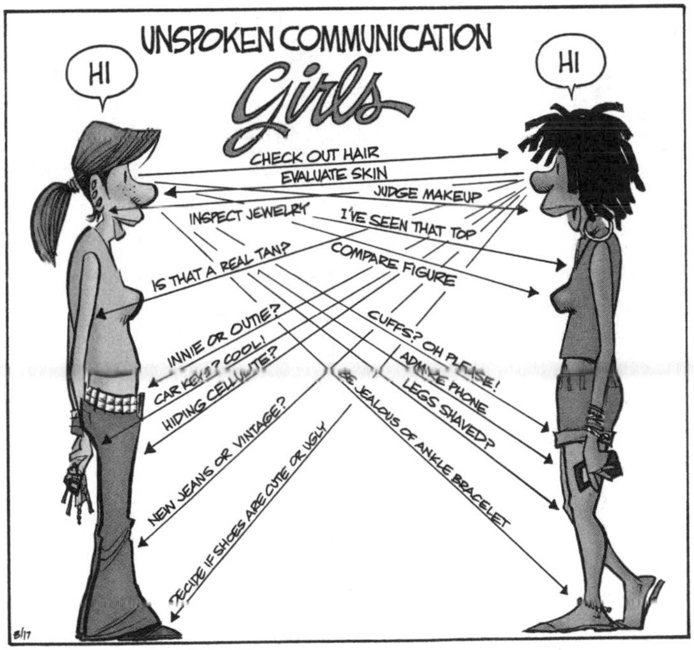
UNSPOKEN COMMUNICATION
Girls
HI
HI
CHECK OUT HAIR
EVALUATE SKIN
JUDGE MAKEUP
INSPECT JEWELRY
I'VE SEEN THAT TOP
IS THAT A REAL TAN?
COMPARE FIGURE
INNIE OR OUTIE?
CAR KEYS? COOL!
HIDING CELLULITE?
CUFFS? OH PLEASE!
ADMIRE PHONE
LEGS SHAVED?
BE JEALOUS OF ANKLE BRACELET
NEW JEANS OR VINTAGE?
DECIDE IF SHOES ARE CUTE OR UGLY
8/17

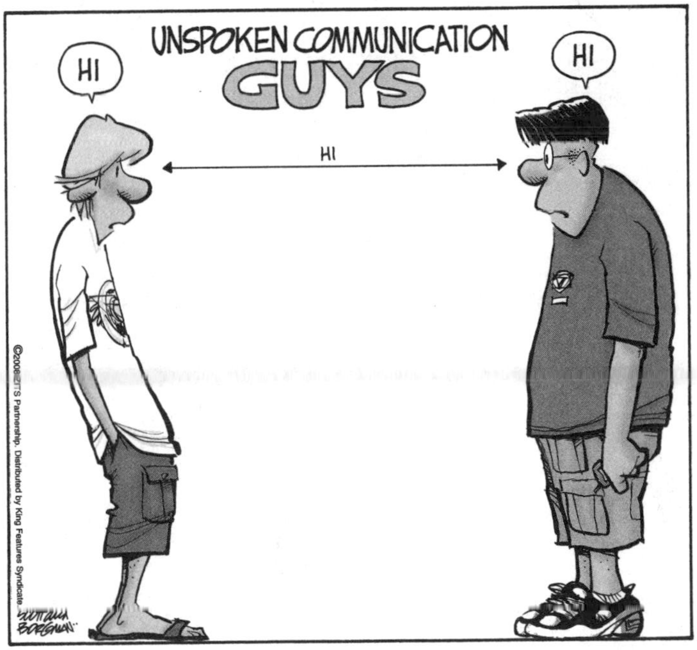
UNSPOKEN COMMUNICATION
GUYS
HI
HI
HI
©2006 ZITS Partnership. Distributed by King Features Syndicate.
SCOTT and BORGMAN

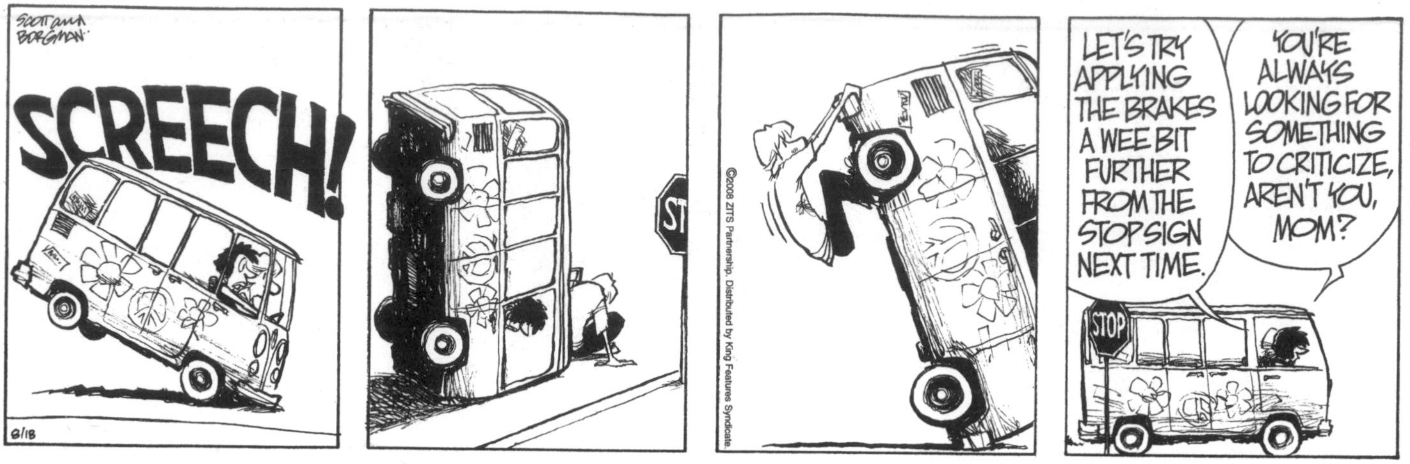
SCREECH!
LET'S TRY APPLYING THE BRAKES A WEE BIT FURTHER FROM THE STOP SIGN NEXT TIME.
YOU'RE ALWAYS LOOKING FOR SOMETHING TO CRITICIZE, AREN'T YOU, MOM?
STOP
©2008 ZITS Partnership. Distributed by King Features Syndicate

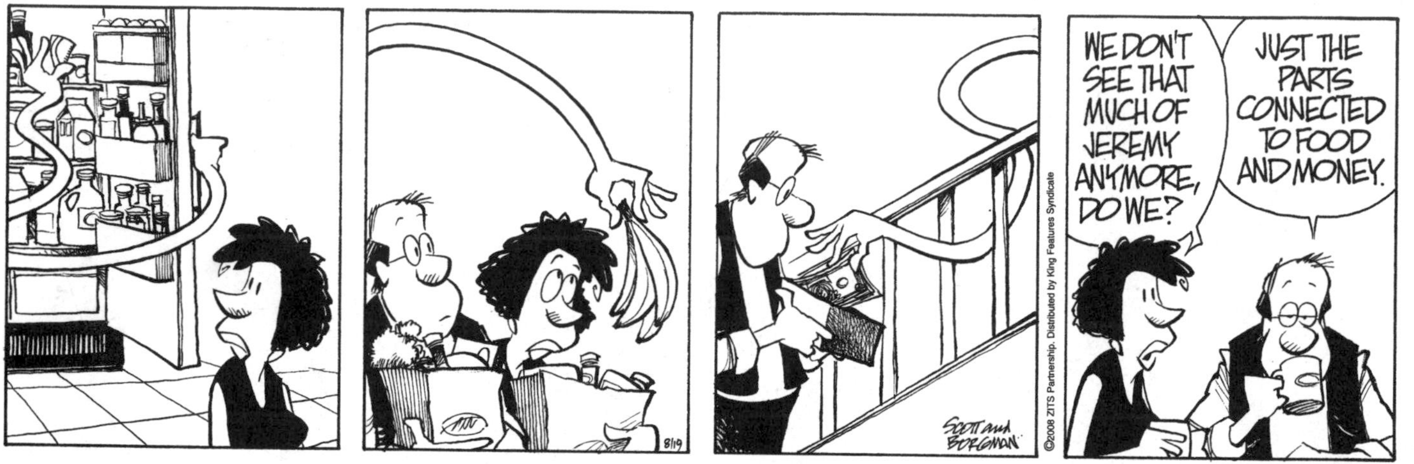
WE DON'T SEE THAT MUCH OF JEREMY ANYMORE, DO WE?
JUST THE PARTS CONNECTED TO FOOD AND MONEY.
©2008 ZITS Partnership. Distributed by King Features Syndicate

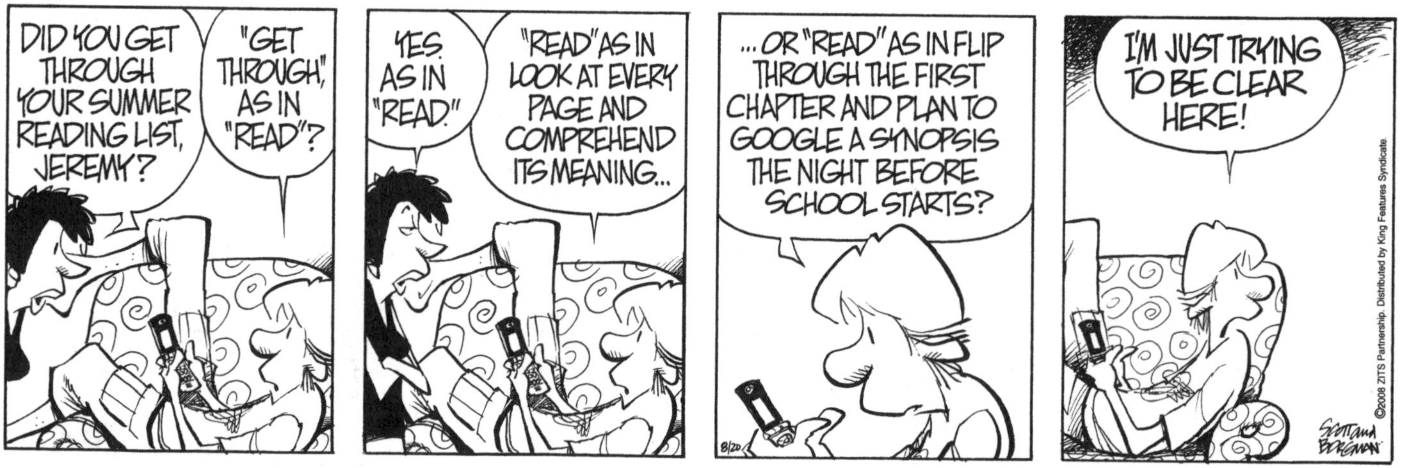
DID YOU GET THROUGH YOUR SUMMER READING LIST, JEREMY?
"GET THROUGH," AS IN "READ"?
YES. AS IN "READ."
"READ" AS IN LOOK AT EVERY PAGE AND COMPREHEND ITS MEANING...
...OR "READ" AS IN FLIP THROUGH THE FIRST CHAPTER AND PLAN TO GOOGLE A SYNOPSIS THE NIGHT BEFORE SCHOOL STARTS?
I'M JUST TRYING TO BE CLEAR HERE!
©2008 ZITS Partnership. Distributed by King Features Syndicate

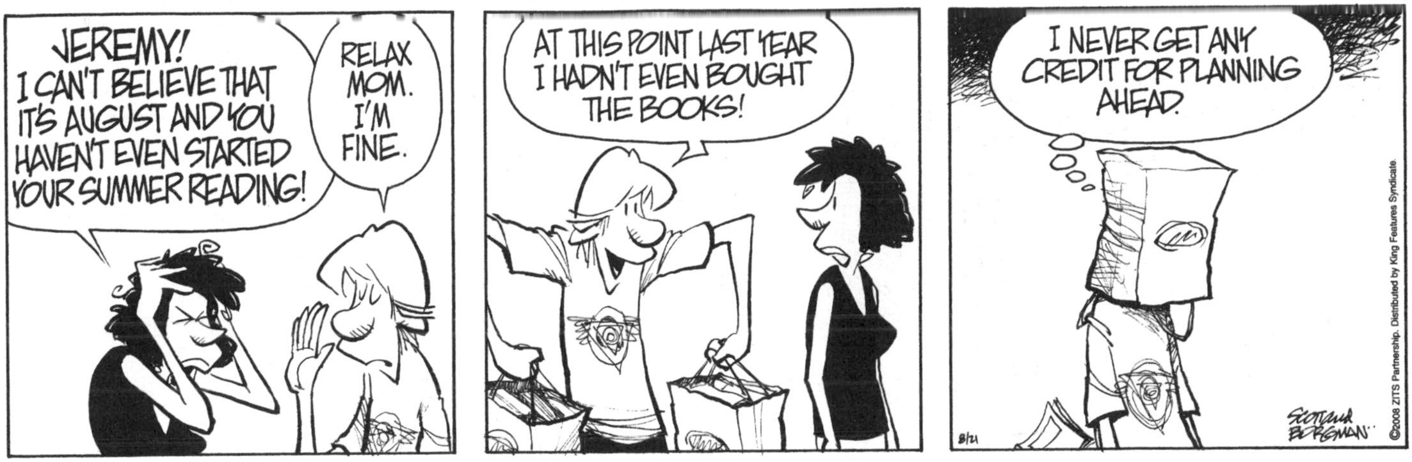
JEREMY! I CAN'T BELIEVE THAT IT'S AUGUST AND YOU HAVEN'T EVEN STARTED YOUR SUMMER READING!
RELAX MOM. I'M FINE.
AT THIS POINT LAST YEAR I HADN'T EVEN BOUGHT THE BOOKS!
I NEVER GET ANY CREDIT FOR PLANNING AHEAD.
©2008 ZITS Partnership. Distributed by King Features Syndicate
SCOTT AND BORGMAN
8/21

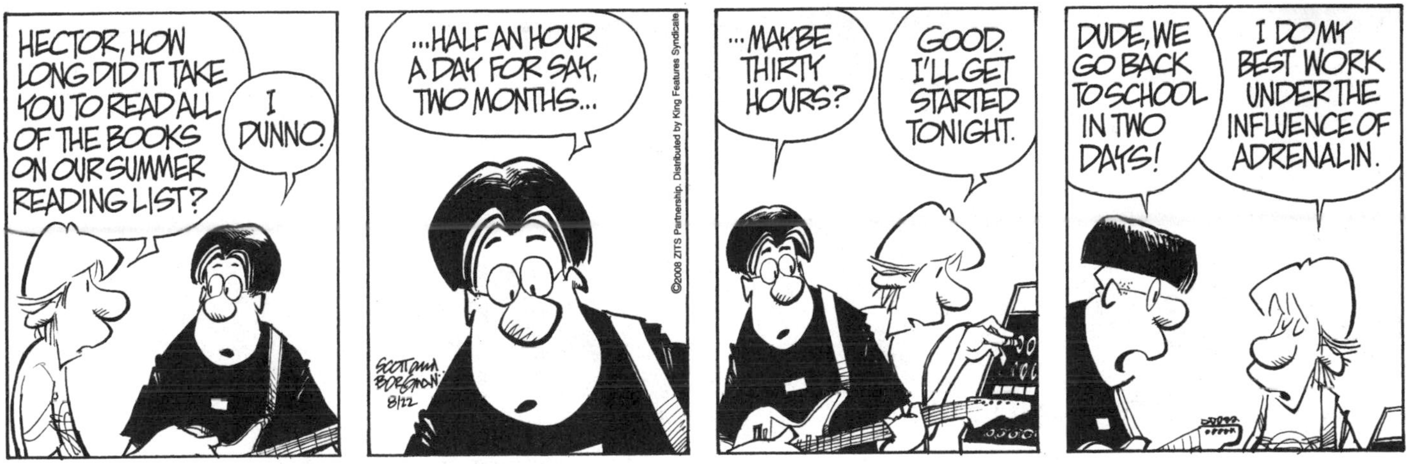
HECTOR, HOW LONG DID IT TAKE YOU TO READ ALL OF THE BOOKS ON OUR SUMMER READING LIST?
I DUNNO.
...HALF AN HOUR A DAY FOR SAY, TWO MONTHS...
©2008 ZITS Partnership. Distributed by King Features Syndicate
SCOTT AND BORGMAN
8/22
...MAYBE THIRTY HOURS?
GOOD. I'LL GET STARTED TONIGHT.
DUDE, WE GO BACK TO SCHOOL IN TWO DAYS!
I DO MY BEST WORK UNDER THE INFLUENCE OF ADRENALIN.

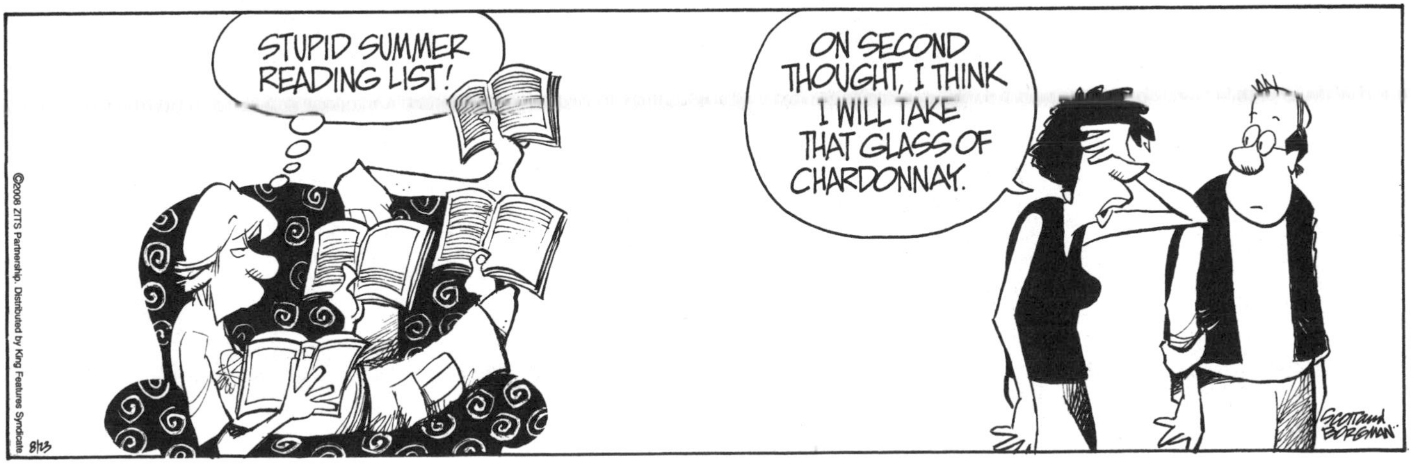
STUPID SUMMER READING LIST!
ON SECOND THOUGHT, I THINK I WILL TAKE THAT GLASS OF CHARDONNAY.
©2008 ZITS Partnership. Distributed by King Features Syndicate
8/23
SCOTT AND BORGMAN

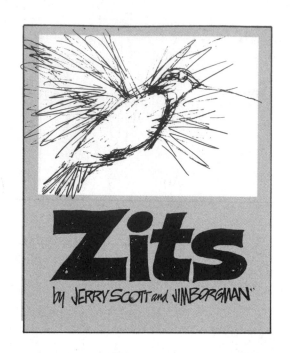

Zits
by JERRY SCOTT and JIM BORGMAN

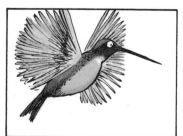

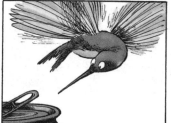

SIP!
KABOOM!
©2008 ZITS Partnership. Distributed by King Features
SCOTT and BORGMAN
I TOLD YOU THAT STUFF IS TOO SWEET.
ONE BIRD'S OPINION.
8/24

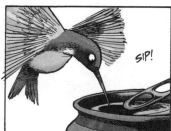

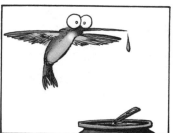

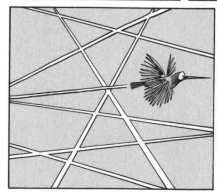

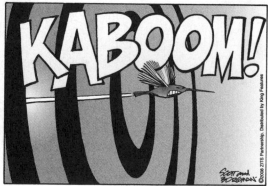

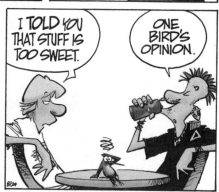

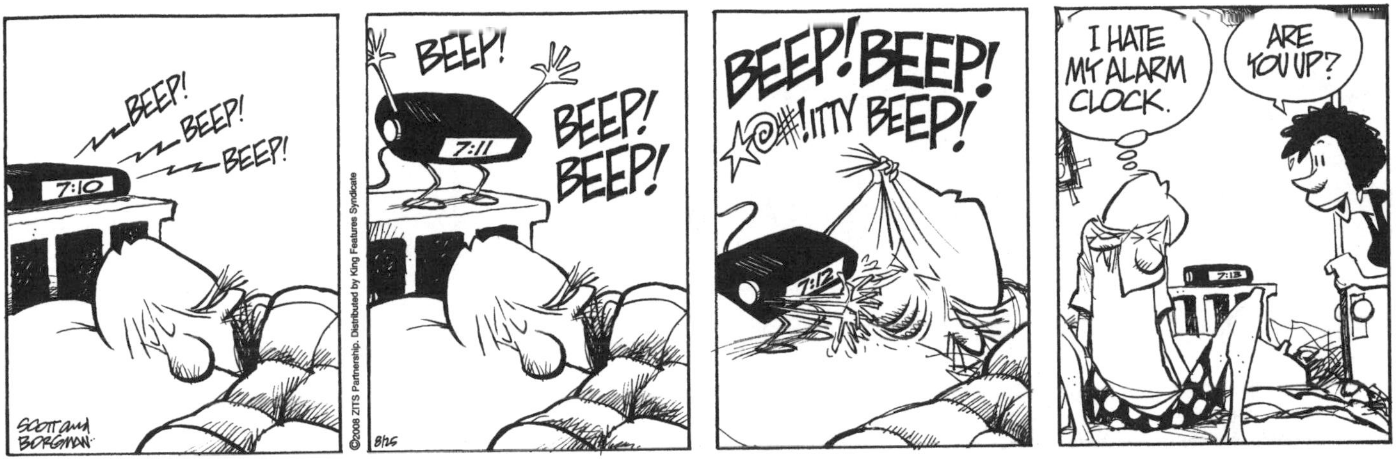
BEEP!
BEEP!
BEEP!
SCOTT and BORGMAN
©2008 ZITS Partnership. Distributed by King Features Syndicate
8/25
BEEP!
BEEP! BEEP!
BEEP! BEEP!
@#!ITTY BEEP!
I HATE MY ALARM CLOCK.
ARE YOU UP?

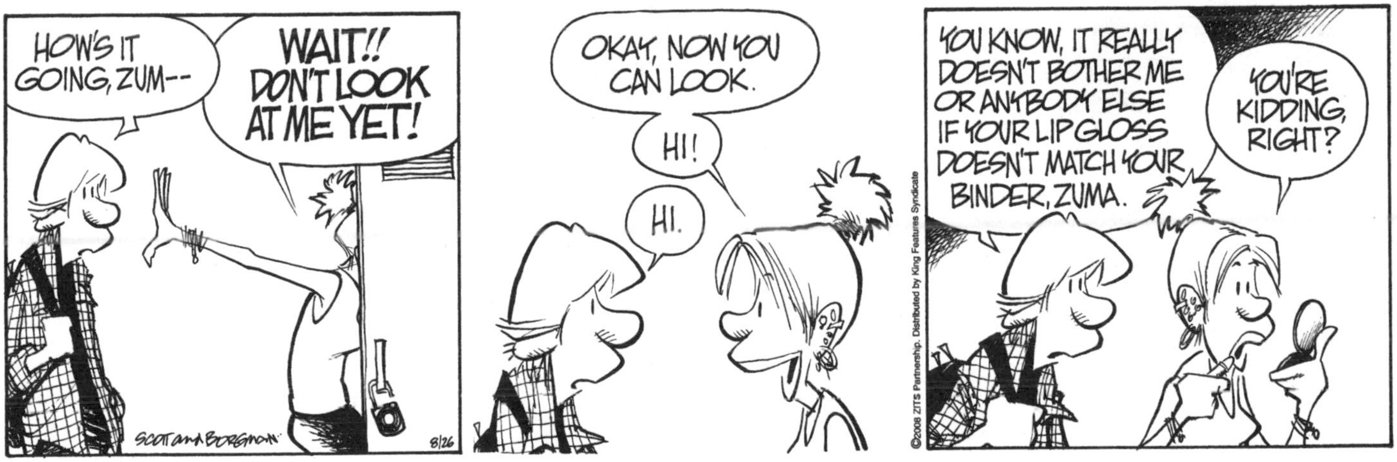
HOW'S IT GOING, ZUM--
WAIT!! DON'T LOOK AT ME YET!
SCOTT and BORGMAN
8/26
OKAY, NOW YOU CAN LOOK.
HI!
HI.
©2008 ZITS Partnership. Distributed by King Features Syndicate
YOU KNOW, IT REALLY DOESN'T BOTHER ME OR ANYBODY ELSE IF YOUR LIP GLOSS DOESN'T MATCH YOUR BINDER, ZUMA.
YOU'RE KIDDING, RIGHT?

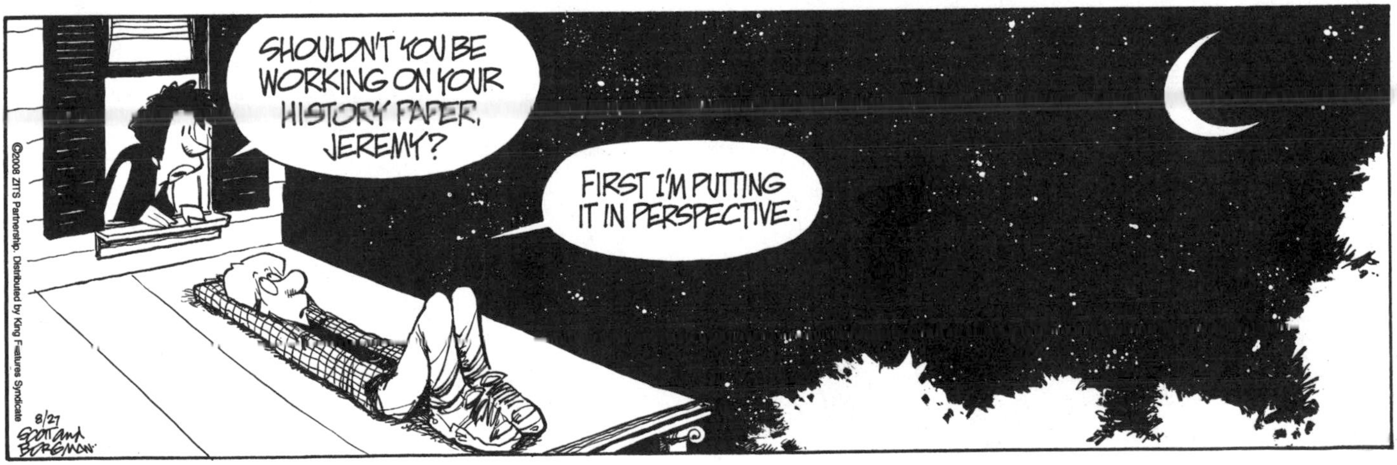
©2008 ZITS Partnership. Distributed by King Features Syndicate
SHOULDN'T YOU BE WORKING ON YOUR HISTORY PAPER, JEREMY?
FIRST I'M PUTTING IT IN PERSPECTIVE.
8/27
SCOTT and BORGMAN

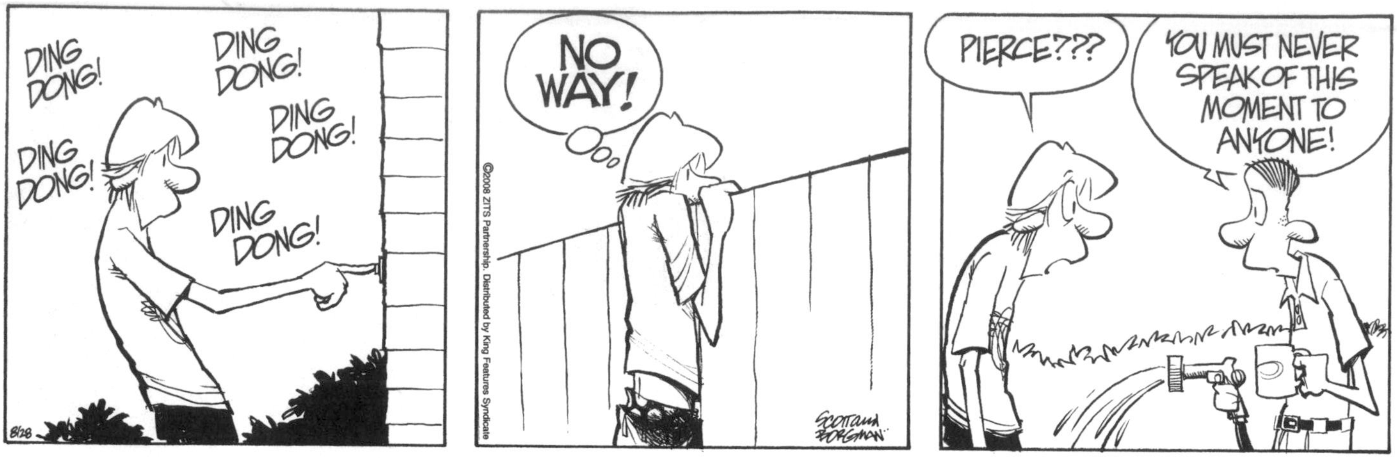
DING DONG!
DING DONG!
DING DONG!
DING DONG!
DING DONG!
NO WAY!
PIERCE???
YOU MUST NEVER SPEAK OF THIS MOMENT TO ANYONE!
©2008 ZITS Partnership. Distributed by King Features Syndicate

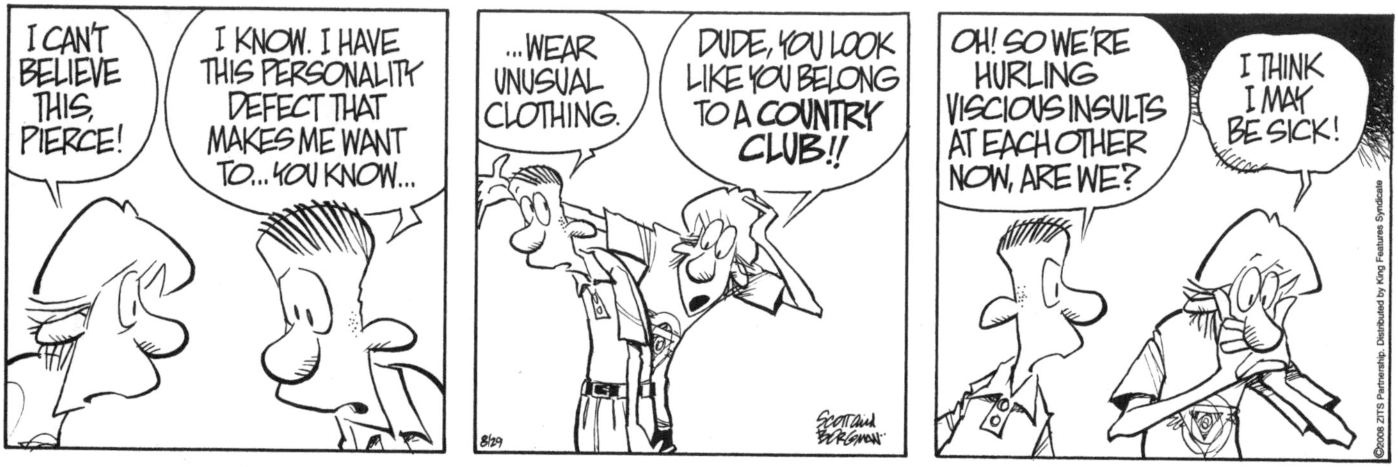
I CAN'T BELIEVE THIS, PIERCE!
I KNOW. I HAVE THIS PERSONALITY DEFECT THAT MAKES ME WANT TO... YOU KNOW...
...WEAR UNUSUAL CLOTHING.
DUDE, YOU LOOK LIKE YOU BELONG TO A COUNTRY CLUB!!
OH! SO WE'RE HURLING VISCIOUS INSULTS AT EACH OTHER NOW, ARE WE?
I THINK I MAY BE SICK!
©2008 ZITS Partnership. Distributed by King Features Syndicate

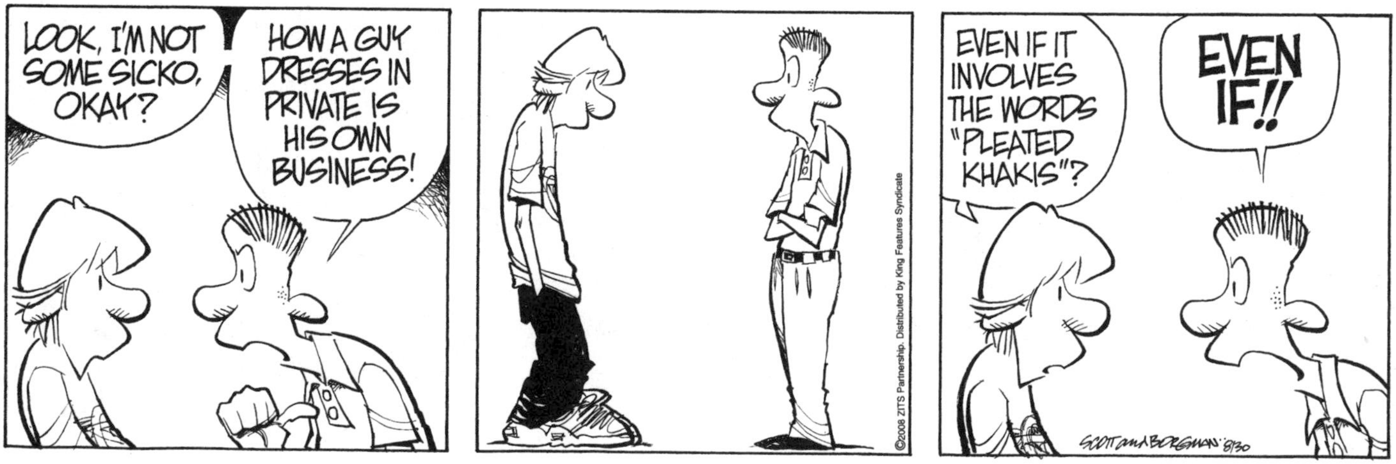
LOOK, I'M NOT SOME SICKO, OKAY?
HOW A GUY DRESSES IN PRIVATE IS HIS OWN BUSINESS!
©2008 ZITS Partnership. Distributed by King Features Syndicate
EVEN IF IT INVOLVES THE WORDS "PLEATED KHAKIS"?
EVEN IF!!

Zits
by JERRY SCOTT and JIM BORGMAN

DEEDLE! DEEDLE! TEEK!
Mom
Where r u?
Reply
Menu
Jeremy
@home
TAP! TAP! TAP! TAP!
DEEDLE! DEEDLE! TEEK!
8/31
Mom
Do me a favor and remind your dad to take his new medicine.
Jeremy
What new medicine?
Mom
It's a stool softener.
READ THE TEXT MESSAGE, THEN PLEASE BURN THE PHONE.
©2008 ZITS Partnership. Distributed by King Features Syndicate

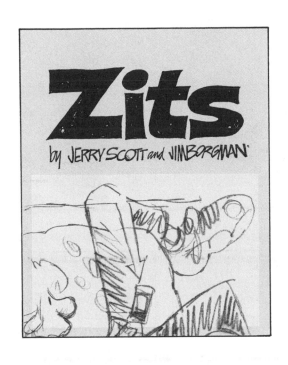

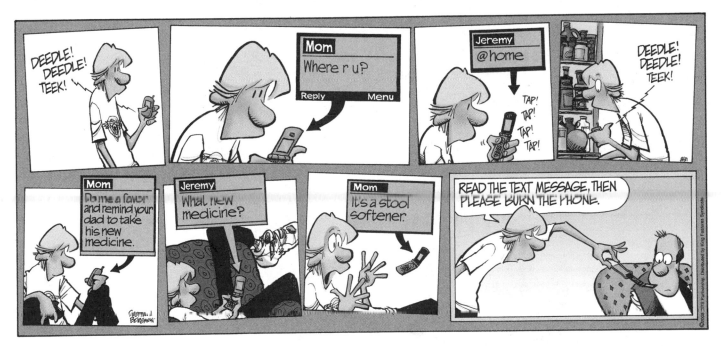

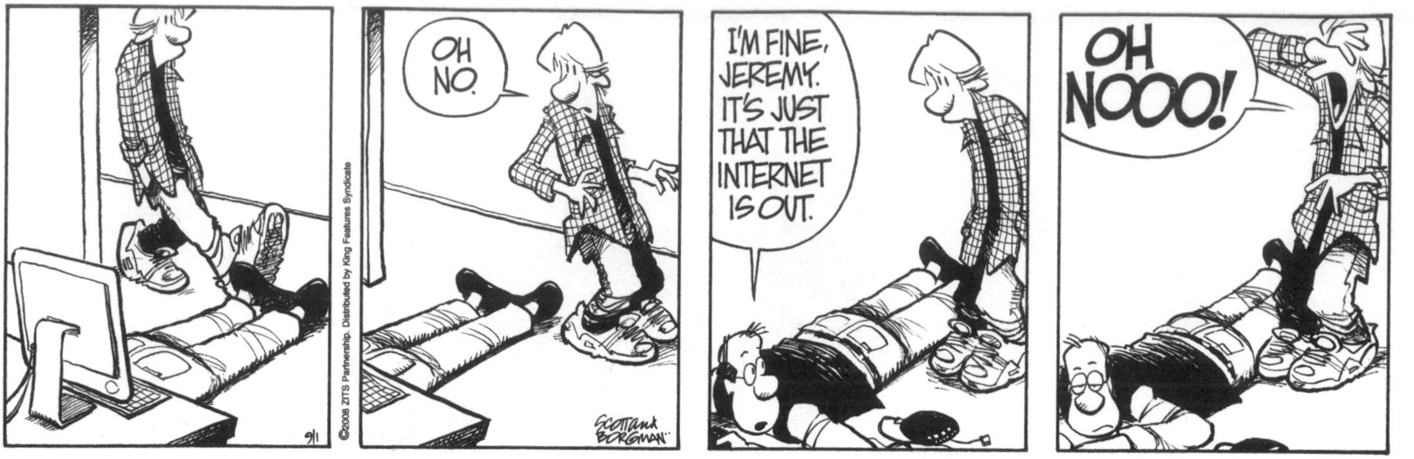
9/1
©2008 ZITS Partnership. Distributed by King Features Syndicate
OH NO.
SCOTT AND BORGMAN
I'M FINE, JEREMY. IT'S JUST THAT THE INTERNET IS OUT.
OH NOOO!

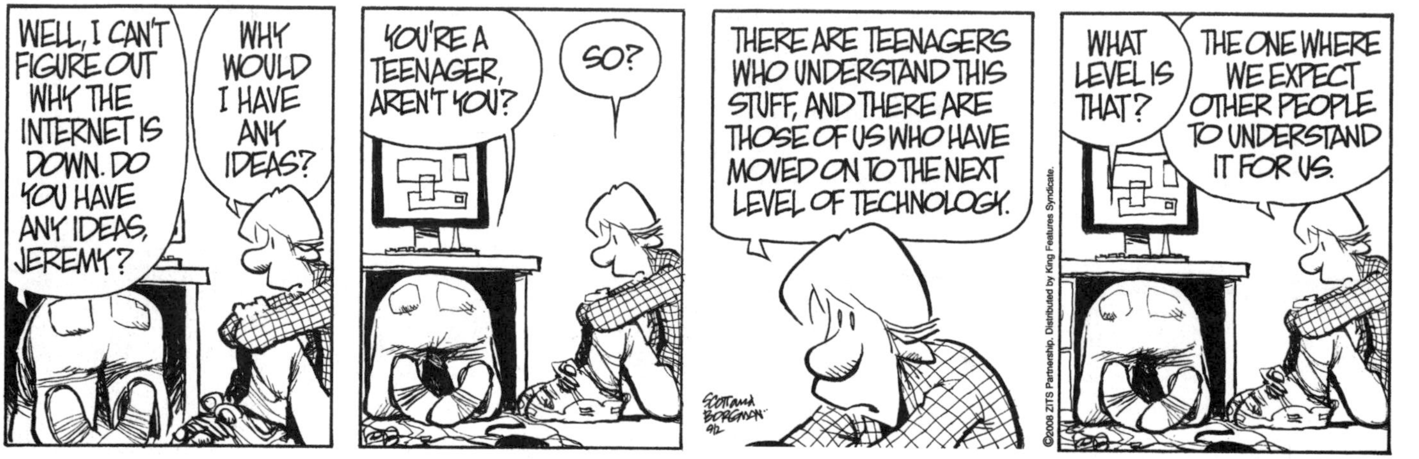
WELL, I CAN'T FIGURE OUT WHY THE INTERNET IS DOWN. DO YOU HAVE ANY IDEAS, JEREMY?
WHY WOULD I HAVE ANY IDEAS?
YOU'RE A TEENAGER, AREN'T YOU?
SO?
THERE ARE TEENAGERS WHO UNDERSTAND THIS STUFF, AND THERE ARE THOSE OF US WHO HAVE MOVED ON TO THE NEXT LEVEL OF TECHNOLOGY.
SCOTT AND BORGMAN 9/2
©2008 ZITS Partnership. Distributed by King Features Syndicate.
WHAT LEVEL IS THAT?
THE ONE WHERE WE EXPECT OTHER PEOPLE TO UNDERSTAND IT FOR US.

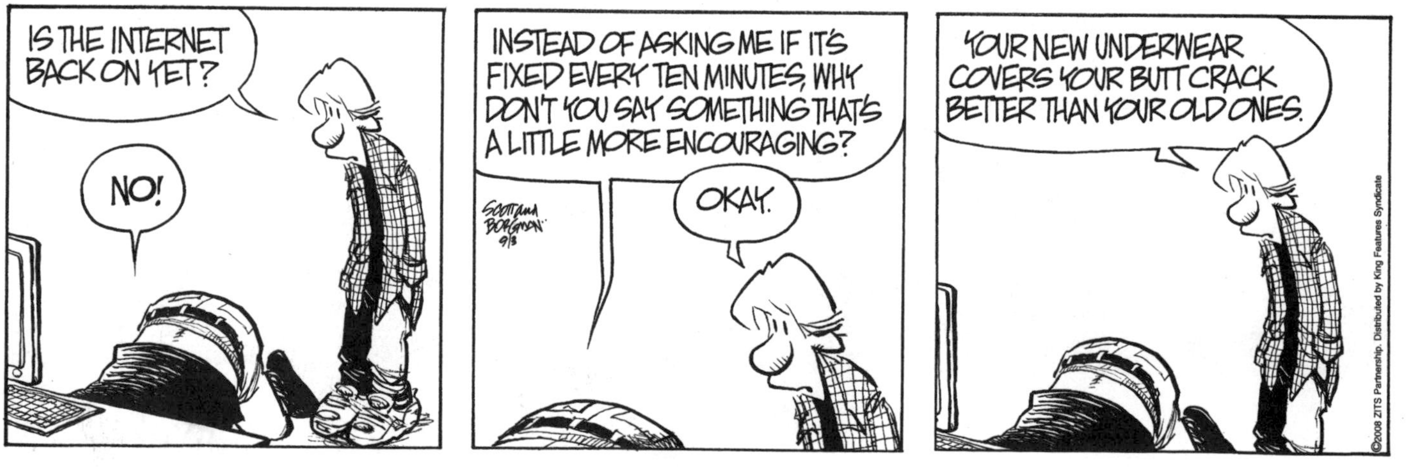
IS THE INTERNET BACK ON YET?
NO!
INSTEAD OF ASKING ME IF IT'S FIXED EVERY TEN MINUTES, WHY DON'T YOU SAY SOMETHING THAT'S A LITTLE MORE ENCOURAGING?
SCOTT AND BORGMAN 9/3
OKAY.
YOUR NEW UNDERWEAR COVERS YOUR BUTT CRACK BETTER THAN YOUR OLD ONES.
©2008 ZITS Partnership. Distributed by King Features Syndicate

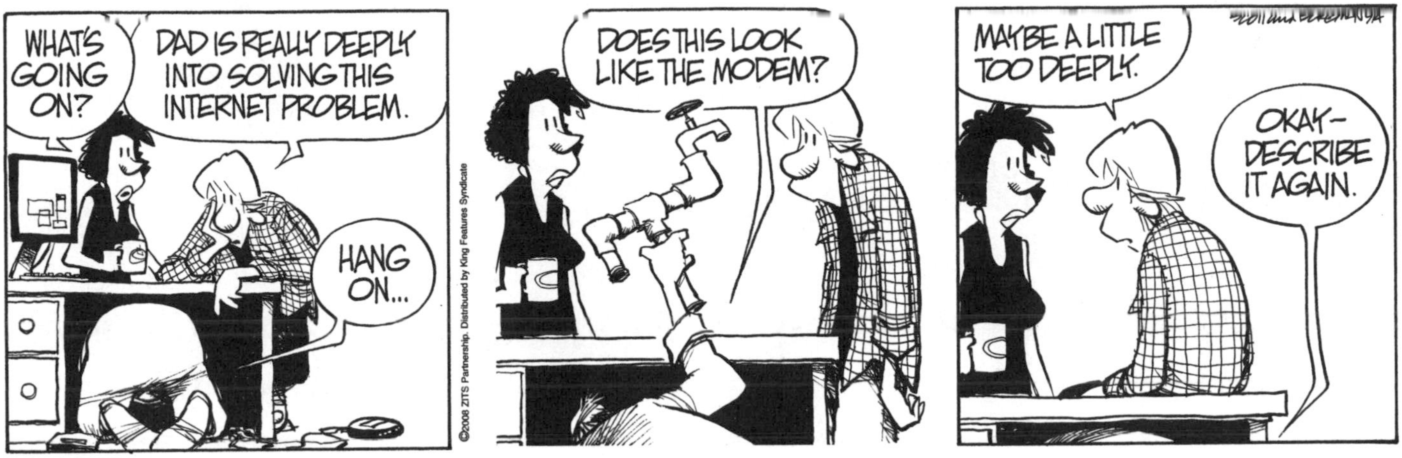
WHAT'S GOING ON?
DAD IS REALLY DEEPLY INTO SOLVING THIS INTERNET PROBLEM.
HANG ON...
DOES THIS LOOK LIKE THE MODEM?
MAYBE A LITTLE TOO DEEPLY.
OKAY- DESCRIBE IT AGAIN.

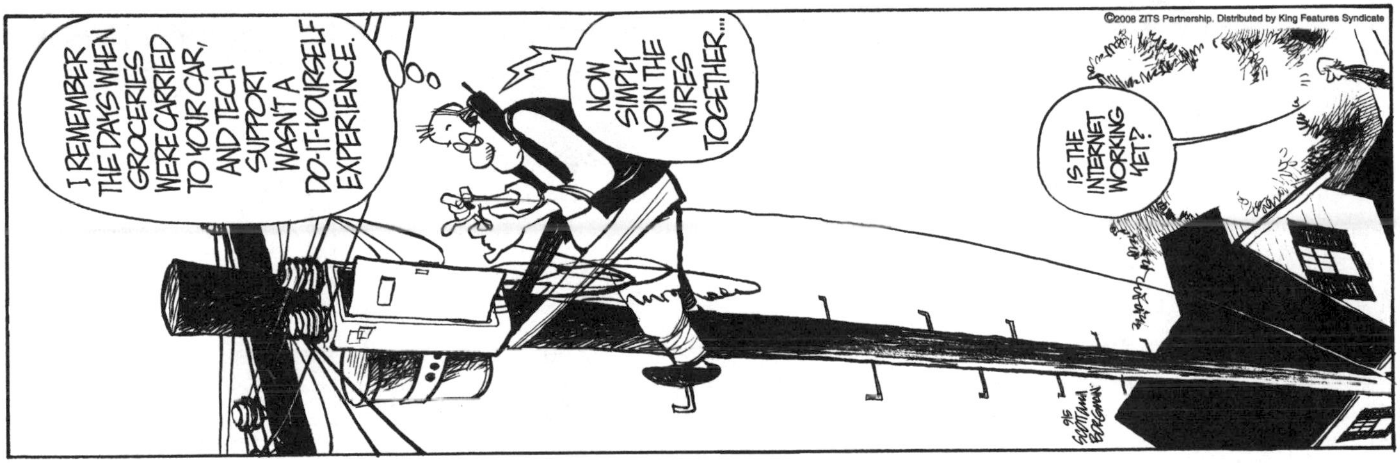
I REMEMBER THE DAYS WHEN GROCERIES WERE CARRIED TO YOUR CAR, AND TECH SUPPORT WASN'T A DO-IT-YOURSELF EXPERIENCE.
NOW SIMPLY JOIN THE WIRES TOGETHER...
IS THE INTERNET WORKING YET?

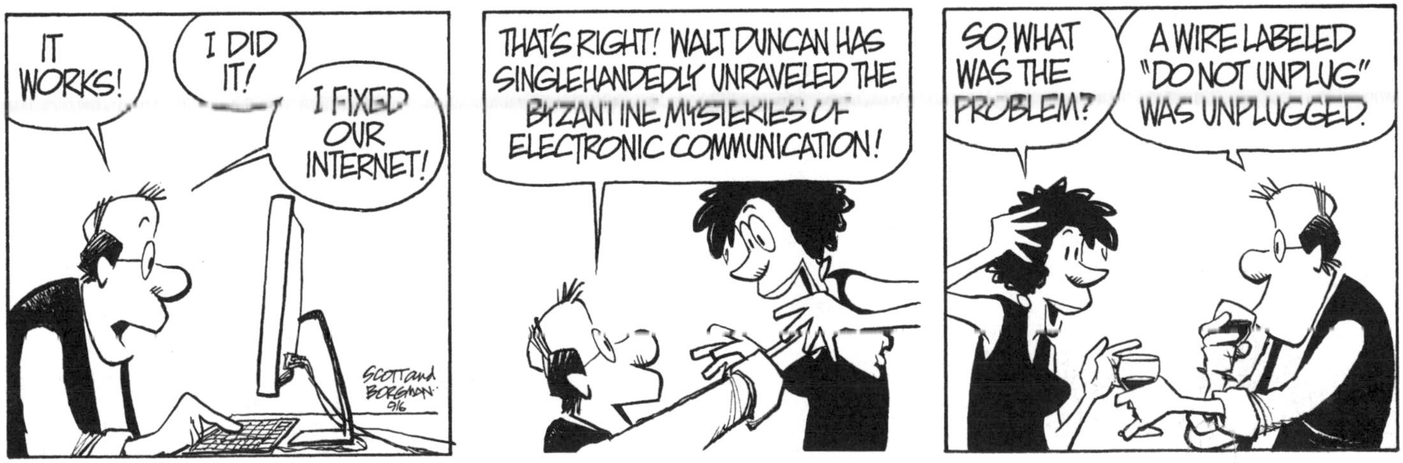
IT WORKS!
I DID IT!
I FIXED OUR INTERNET!
SCOTT and BORGMAN 9/6
THAT'S RIGHT! WALT DUNCAN HAS SINGLEHANDEDLY UNRAVELED THE BYZANTINE MYSTERIES OF ELECTRONIC COMMUNICATION!
SO, WHAT WAS THE PROBLEM?
A WIRE LABELED "DO NOT UNPLUG" WAS UNPLUGGED.

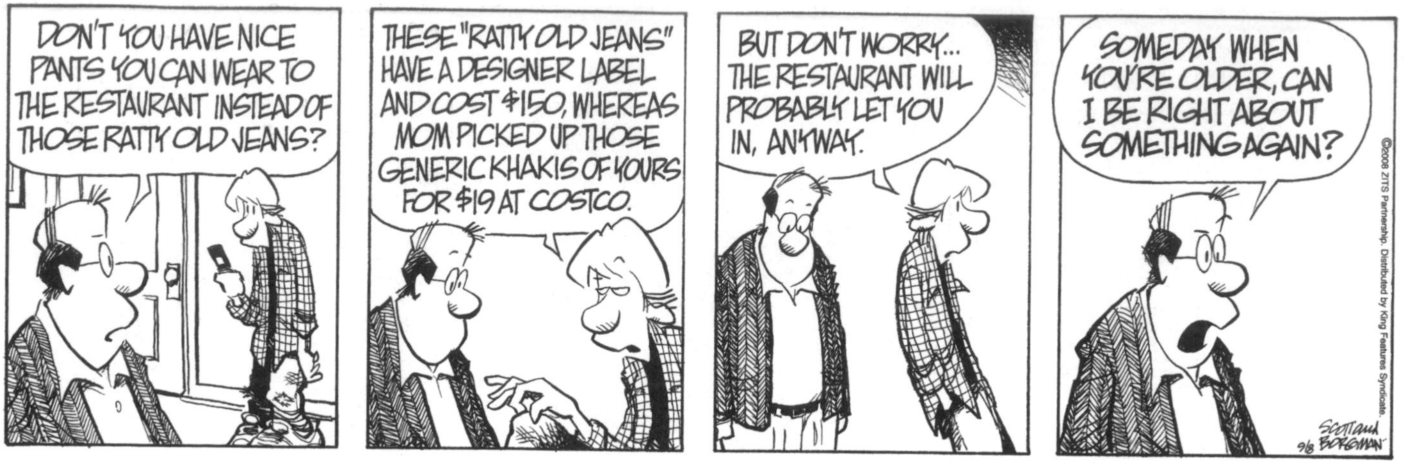
DON'T YOU HAVE NICE PANTS YOU CAN WEAR TO THE RESTAURANT INSTEAD OF THOSE RATTY OLD JEANS?
THESE "RATTY OLD JEANS" HAVE A DESIGNER LABEL AND COST $150, WHEREAS MOM PICKED UP THOSE GENERIC KHAKIS OF YOURS FOR $19 AT COSTCO.
BUT DON'T WORRY... THE RESTAURANT WILL PROBABLY LET YOU IN, ANYWAY.
SOMEDAY WHEN YOU'RE OLDER, CAN I BE RIGHT ABOUT SOMETHING AGAIN?
©2008 ZITS Partnership. Distributed by King Features Syndicate.
SCOTT and BORGMAN 9/8

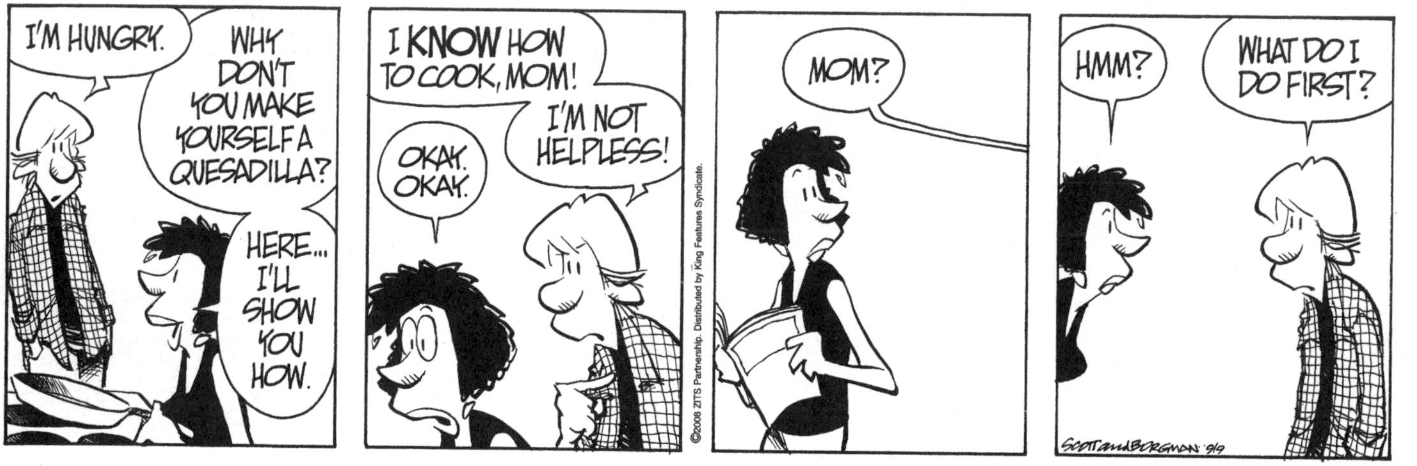
I'M HUNGRY.
WHY DON'T YOU MAKE YOURSELF A QUESADILLA?
HERE... I'LL SHOW YOU HOW.
I **KNOW** HOW TO COOK, MOM!
OKAY. OKAY.
I'M NOT HELPLESS!
MOM?
HMM?
WHAT DO I DO FIRST?
©2008 ZITS Partnership. Distributed by King Features Syndicate.
SCOTT and BORGMAN 9/9

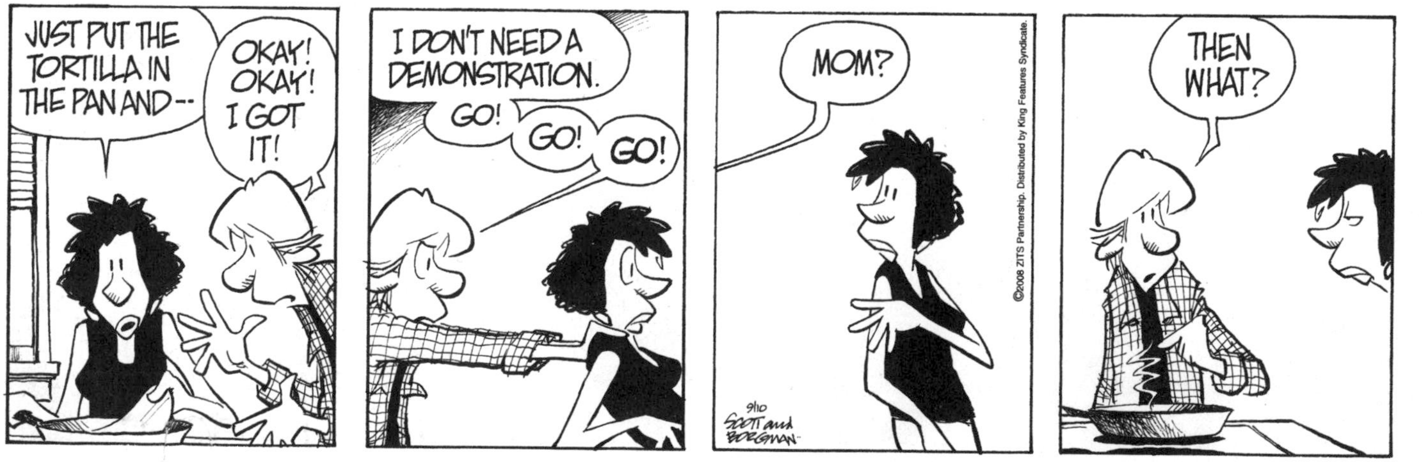
JUST PUT THE TORTILLA IN THE PAN AND--
OKAY! OKAY! I GOT IT!
I DON'T NEED A DEMONSTRATION.
GO!
GO!
GO!
MOM?
THEN WHAT?
©2008 ZITS Partnership. Distributed by King Features Syndicate.
9/10 SCOTT and BORGMAN

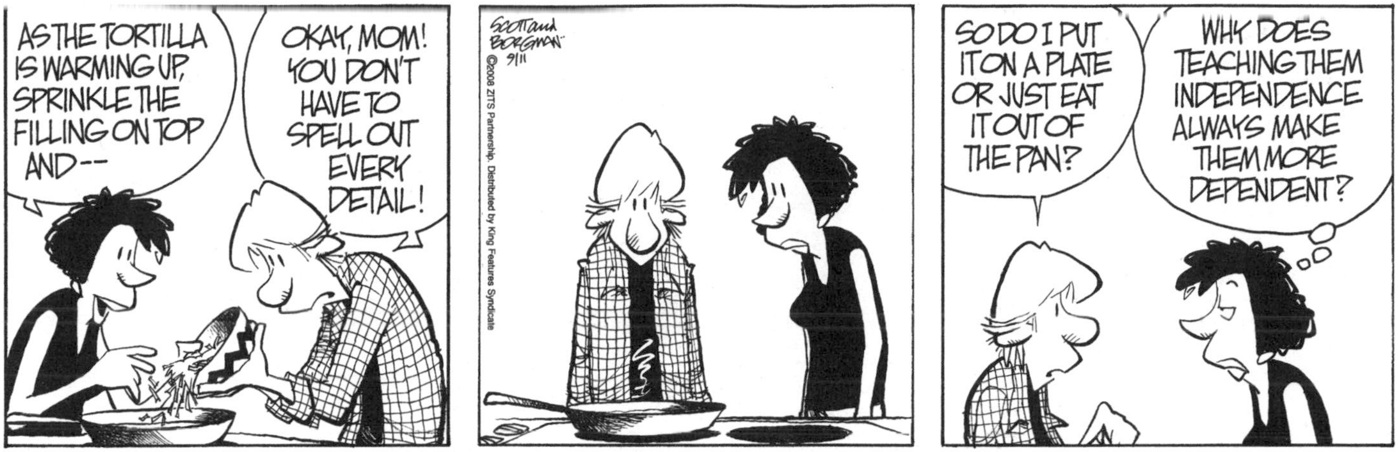
AS THE TORTILLA IS WARMING UP, SPRINKLE THE FILLING ON TOP AND--
OKAY, MOM! YOU DON'T HAVE TO SPELL OUT EVERY DETAIL!
SCOTT and BORGMAN 9/11
©2008 ZITS Partnership. Distributed by King Features Syndicate
SO DO I PUT IT ON A PLATE OR JUST EAT IT OUT OF THE PAN?
WHY DOES TEACHING THEM INDEPENDENCE ALWAYS MAKE THEM MORE DEPENDENT?

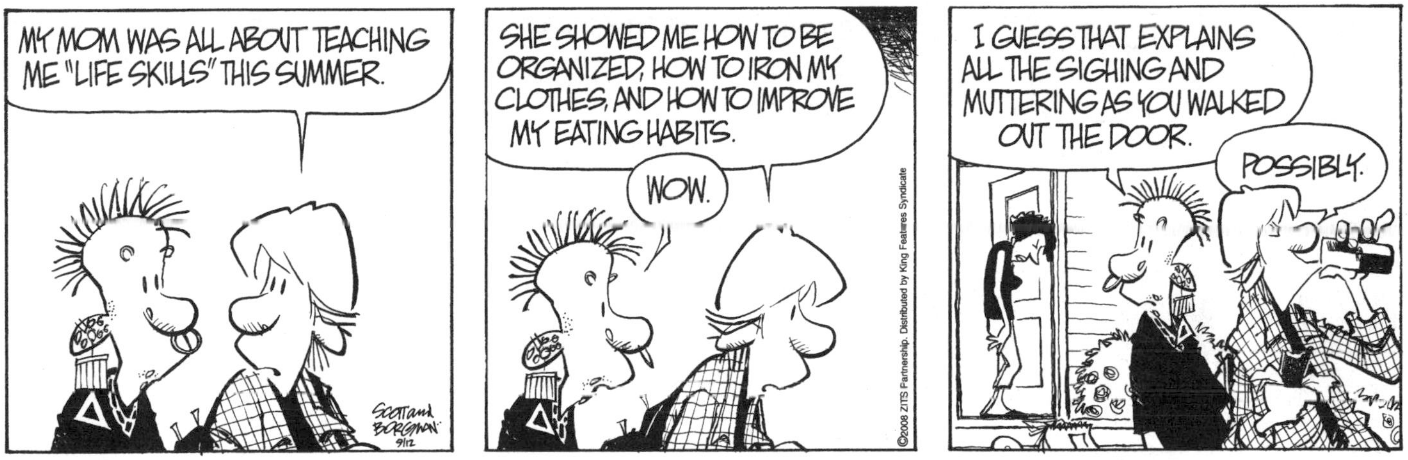
MY MOM WAS ALL ABOUT TEACHING ME "LIFE SKILLS" THIS SUMMER.
SCOTT and BORGMAN 9/12
SHE SHOWED ME HOW TO BE ORGANIZED, HOW TO IRON MY CLOTHES, AND HOW TO IMPROVE MY EATING HABITS.
WOW.
©2008 ZITS Partnership. Distributed by King Features Syndicate
I GUESS THAT EXPLAINS ALL THE SIGHING AND MUTTERING AS YOU WALKED OUT THE DOOR.
POSSIBLY.

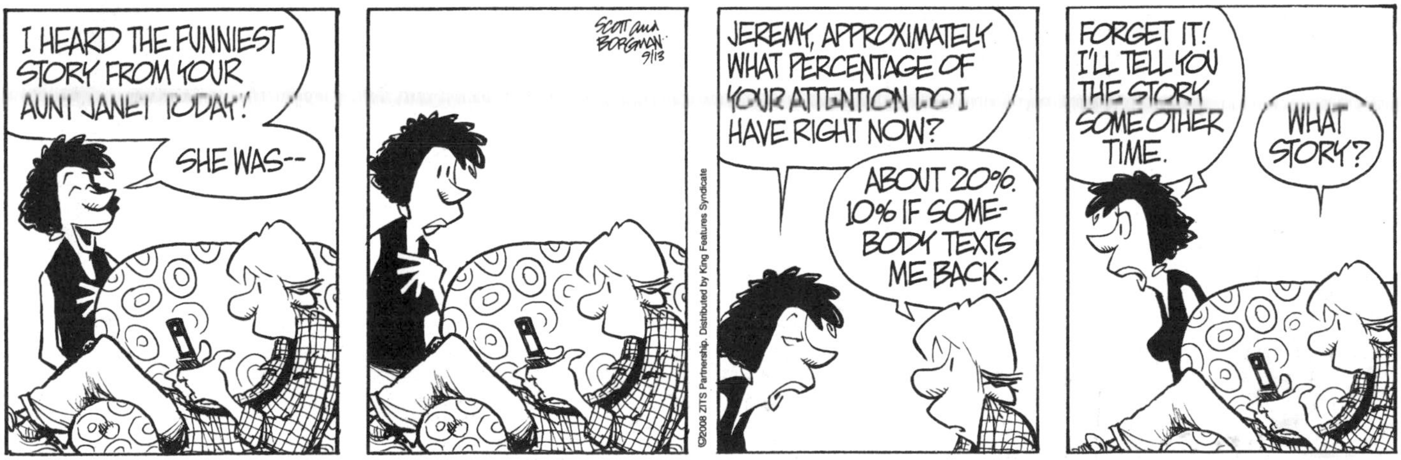
I HEARD THE FUNNIEST STORY FROM YOUR AUNT JANET TODAY!
SHE WAS--
SCOTT and BORGMAN 9/13
©2008 ZITS Partnership. Distributed by King Features Syndicate
JEREMY, APPROXIMATELY WHAT PERCENTAGE OF YOUR ATTENTION DO I HAVE RIGHT NOW?
ABOUT 20%. 10% IF SOMEBODY TEXTS ME BACK.
FORGET IT! I'LL TELL YOU THE STORY SOME OTHER TIME.
WHAT STORY?

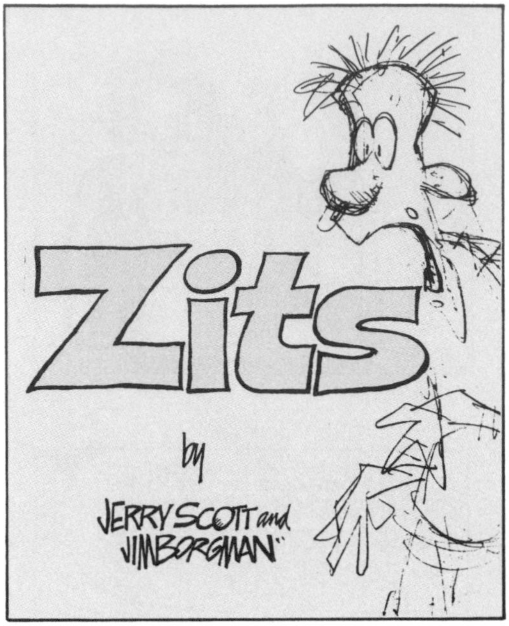
Zits
by
JERRY SCOTT and
JIM BORGMAN

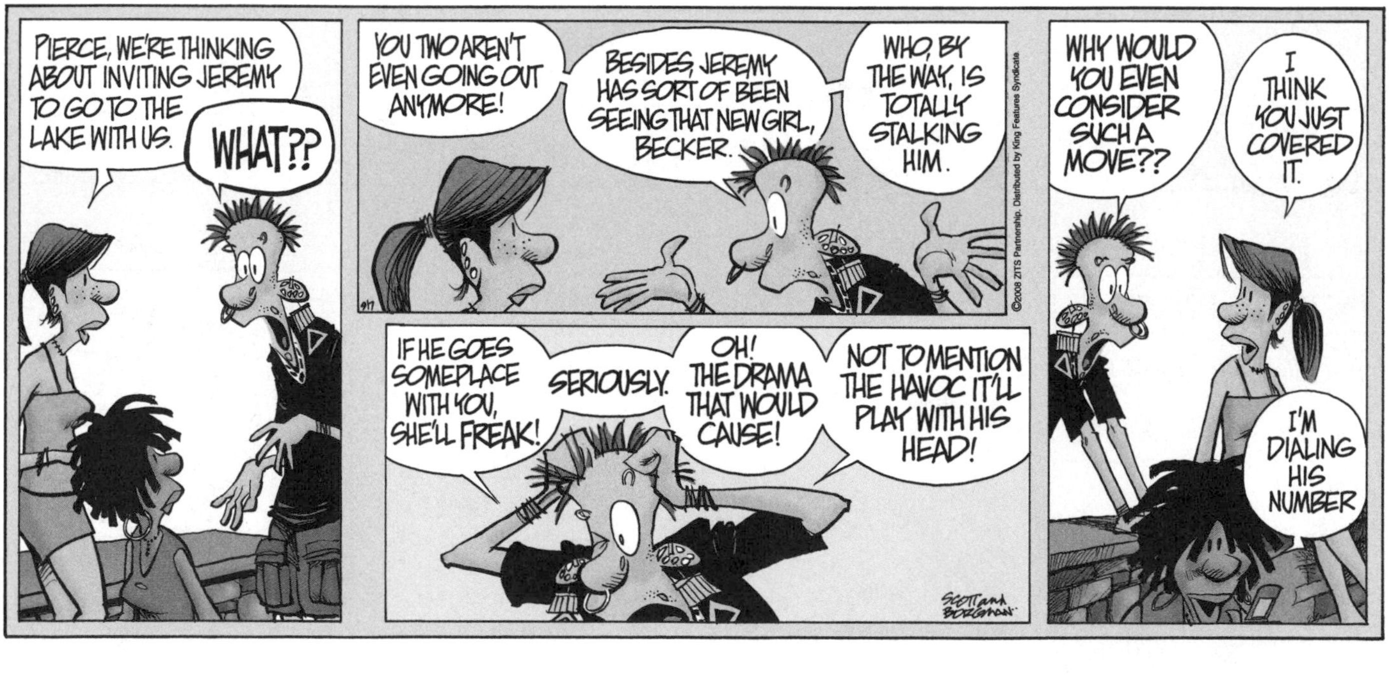
PIERCE, WE'RE THINKING ABOUT INVITING JEREMY TO GO TO THE LAKE WITH US.
WHAT??
YOU TWO AREN'T EVEN GOING OUT ANYMORE!
BESIDES, JEREMY HAS SORT OF BEEN SEEING THAT NEW GIRL, BECKER.
WHO, BY THE WAY, IS TOTALLY STALKING HIM.
©2008 ZITS Partnership. Distributed by King Features Syndicate.
IF HE GOES SOMEPLACE WITH YOU, SHE'LL FREAK!
SERIOUSLY.
OH! THE DRAMA THAT WOULD CAUSE!
NOT TO MENTION THE HAVOC IT'LL PLAY WITH HIS HEAD!
SCOTT AND BORGMAN
WHY WOULD YOU EVEN CONSIDER SUCH A MOVE??
I THINK YOU JUST COVERED IT.
I'M DIALING HIS NUMBER

Zits
by JERRY SCOTT and JIM BORGMAN

THANKS, MOM. NOBODY SAW YOU.
PICK ME UP AT 3:00.
IF YOU THINK I'M GOING TO HIDE UNDER THE DASH LIKE THIS UNTIL YOU GET YOUR LICENSE, YOU'RE CRAZY!
©2008 ZITS Partnership. Distributed by King Features Syndicate

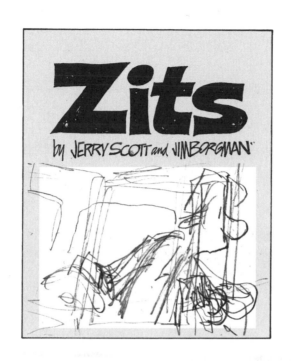

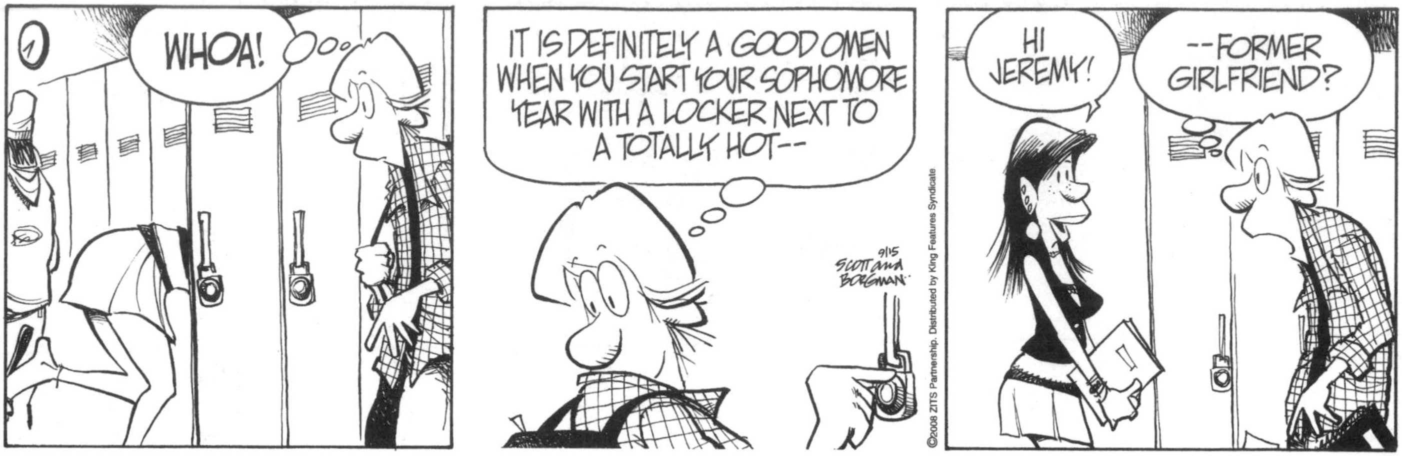
1
WHOA!
IT IS DEFINITELY A GOOD OMEN WHEN YOU START YOUR SOPHOMORE YEAR WITH A LOCKER NEXT TO A TOTALLY HOT--
9/15
SCOTT and BORGMAN
©2008 ZITS Partnership. Distributed by King Features Syndicate
HI JEREMY!
--FORMER GIRLFRIEND?

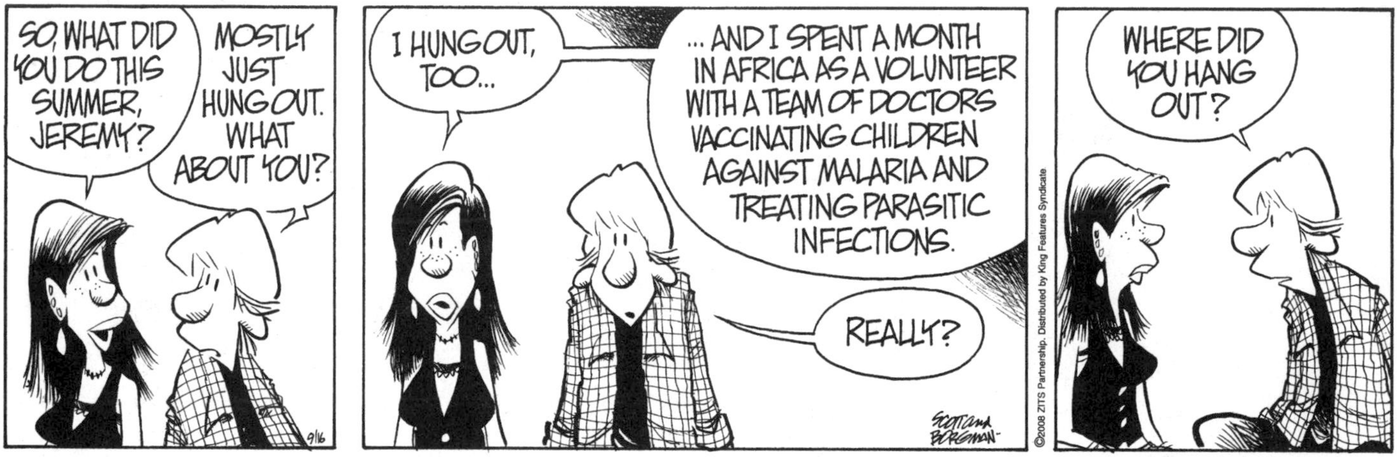
SO, WHAT DID YOU DO THIS SUMMER, JEREMY?
MOSTLY JUST HUNG OUT. WHAT ABOUT YOU?
9/16
I HUNG OUT, TOO...
... AND I SPENT A MONTH IN AFRICA AS A VOLUNTEER WITH A TEAM OF DOCTORS VACCINATING CHILDREN AGAINST MALARIA AND TREATING PARASITIC INFECTIONS.
REALLY?
SCOTT and BORGMAN
©2008 ZITS Partnership. Distributed by King Features Syndicate
WHERE DID YOU HANG OUT?

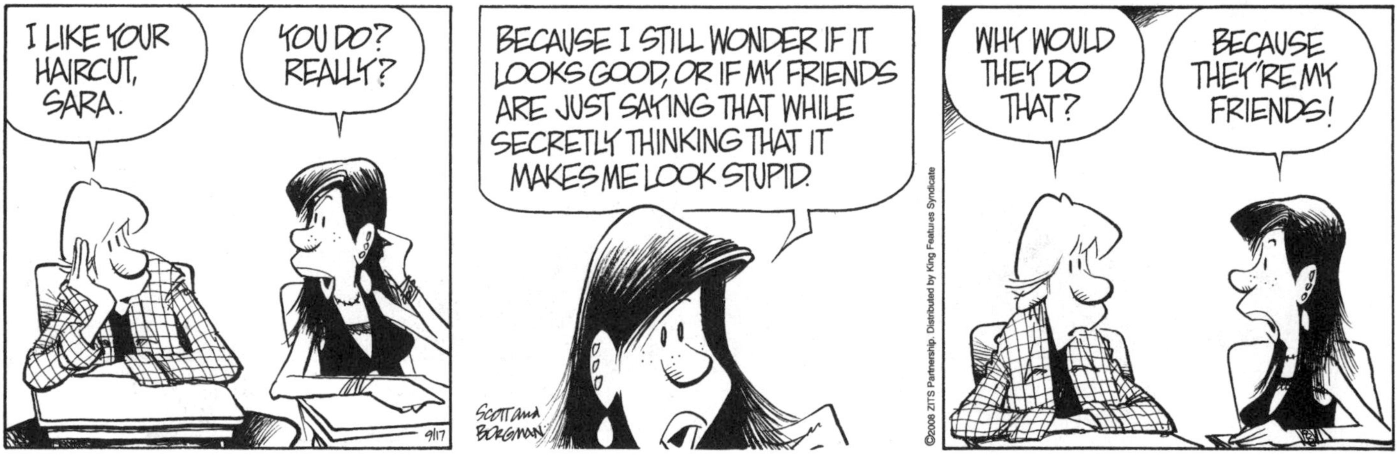
I LIKE YOUR HAIRCUT, SARA.
YOU DO? REALLY?
9/17
BECAUSE I STILL WONDER IF IT LOOKS GOOD, OR IF MY FRIENDS ARE JUST SAYING THAT WHILE SECRETLY THINKING THAT IT MAKES ME LOOK STUPID.
SCOTT and BORGMAN
©2008 ZITS Partnership. Distributed by King Features Syndicate
WHY WOULD THEY DO THAT?
BECAUSE THEY'RE MY FRIENDS!

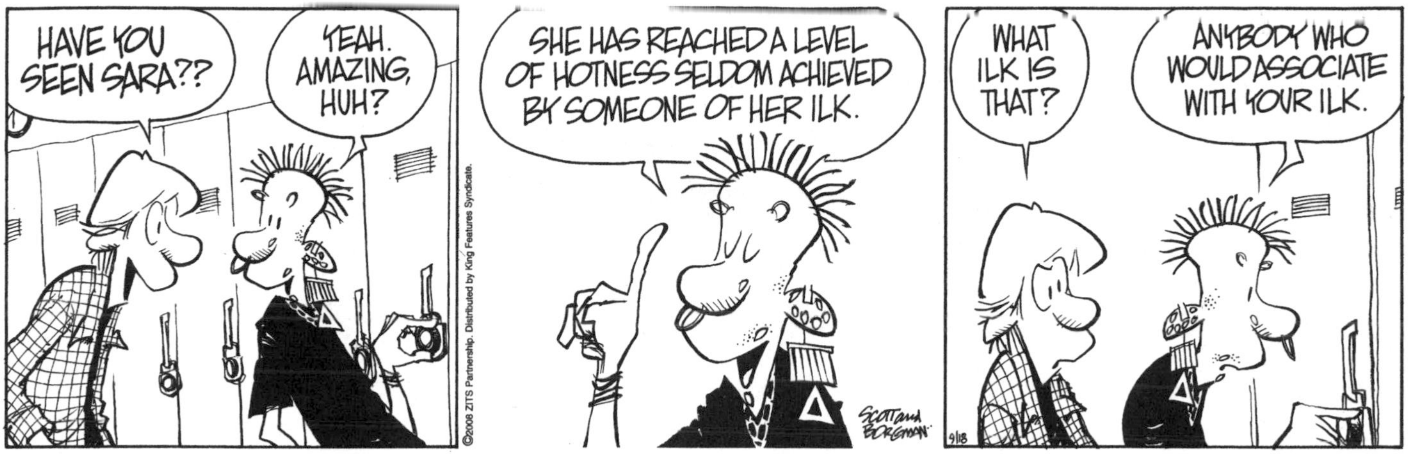

HAVE YOU SEEN SARA??
YEAH. AMAZING, HUH?
©2008 ZITS Partnership. Distributed by King Features Syndicate.
SHE HAS REACHED A LEVEL OF HOTNESS SELDOM ACHIEVED BY SOMEONE OF HER ILK.
SCOTT and BORGMAN
9/18
WHAT ILK IS THAT?
ANYBODY WHO WOULD ASSOCIATE WITH YOUR ILK.

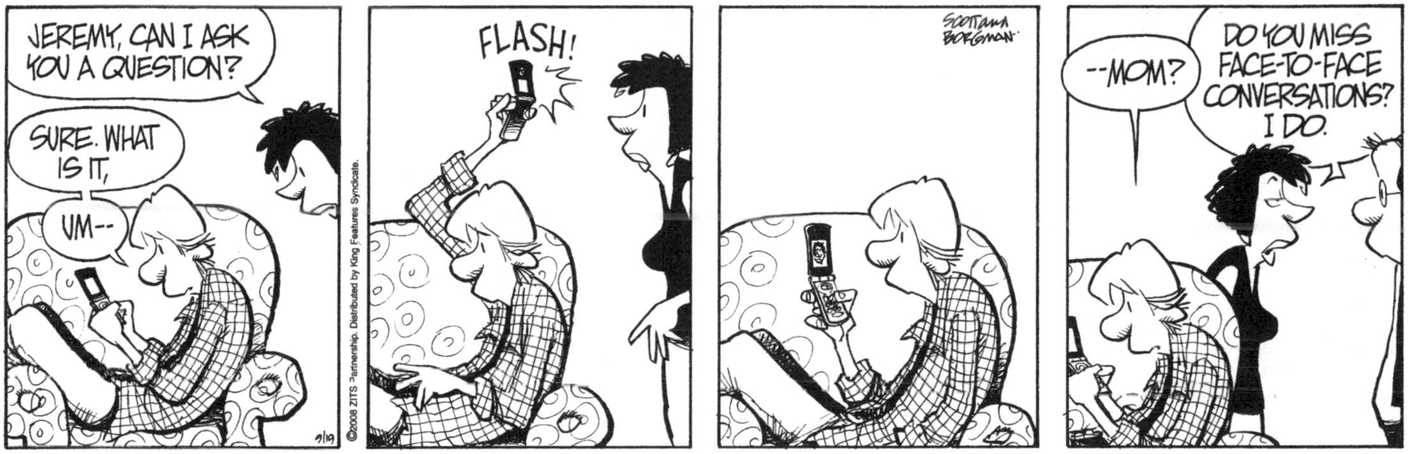

JEREMY, CAN I ASK YOU A QUESTION?
SURE. WHAT IS IT,
UM--
9/19
©2008 ZITS Partnership. Distributed by King Features Syndicate.
FLASH!
SCOTT and BORGMAN
--MOM?
DO YOU MISS FACE-TO-FACE CONVERSATIONS? I DO.

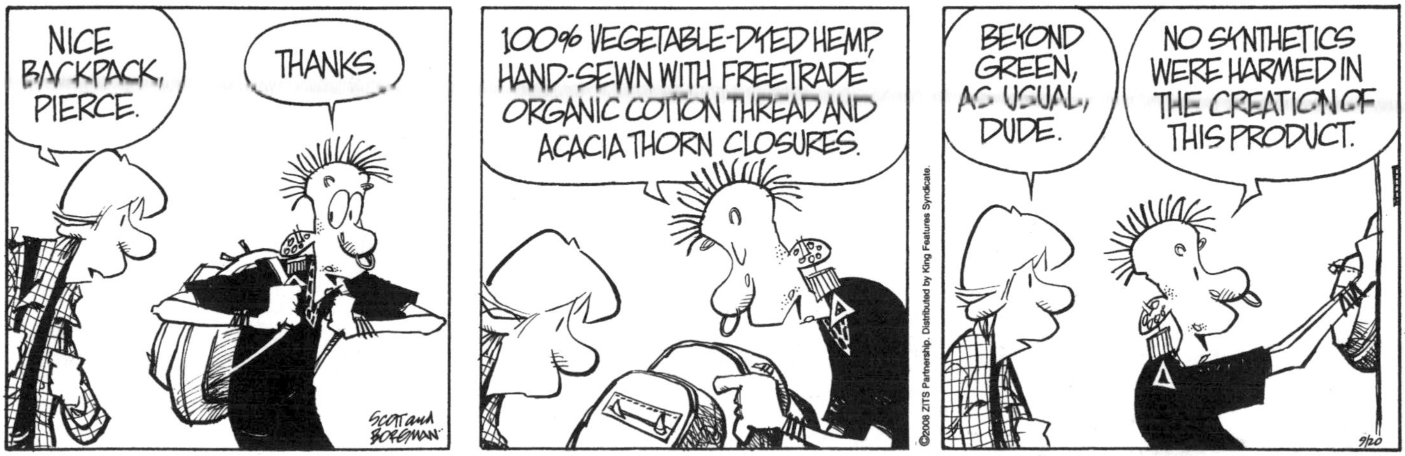

NICE BACKPACK, PIERCE.
THANKS.
SCOTT and BORGMAN
100% VEGETABLE-DYED HEMP, HAND-SEWN WITH FREETRADE ORGANIC COTTON THREAD AND ACACIA THORN CLOSURES.
©2008 ZITS Partnership. Distributed by King Features Syndicate.
BEYOND GREEN, AS USUAL, DUDE.
NO SYNTHETICS WERE HARMED IN THE CREATION OF THIS PRODUCT.
9/20

Zits
by
JERRY SCOTT and
JIM BORGMAN

THERE GOES MOWING THE YARD...
...FRONT AND BACK.
THAT'S WASHING THE DOWNSTAIRS WINDOWS.
COMING UP ON WEEDING THE FLOWERBED.
WHEN MOM BUYS MY GAS, SHE JUST HANDS ME THE CREDIT CARD AND WE WORK OUT THE PAYMENT SCHEDULE LATER!
BUT THIS IS MY FAVORITE PART!
©2008 ZITS Partnership. Distributed by King Features Syndicate
SCOTT and BORGMAN 9/24

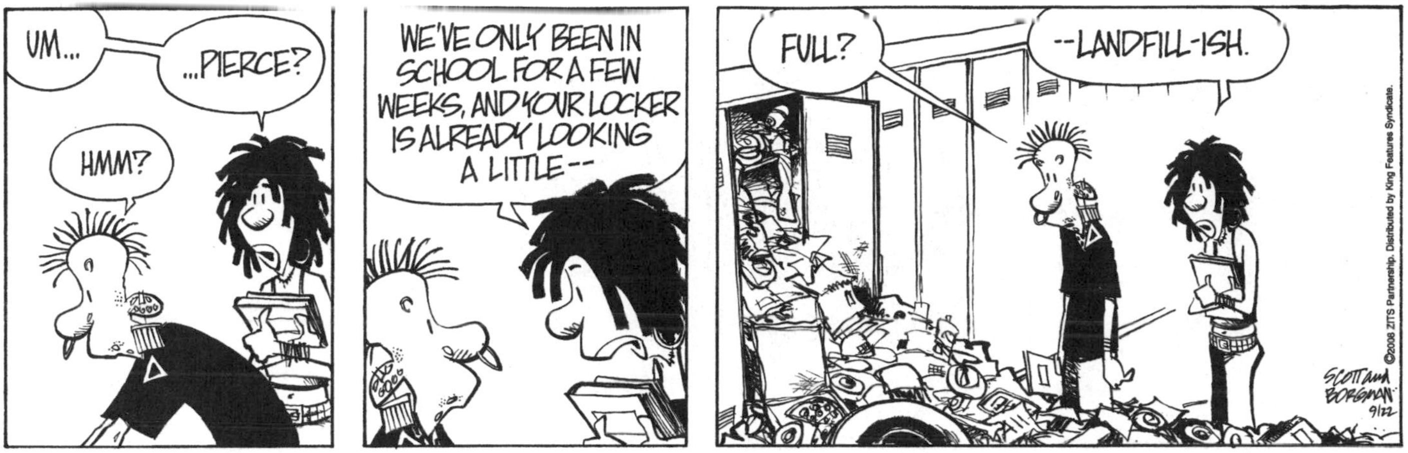
UM...
...PIERCE?
HMM?
WE'VE ONLY BEEN IN SCHOOL FOR A FEW WEEKS, AND YOUR LOCKER IS ALREADY LOOKING A LITTLE--
FULL?
--LANDFILL-ISH.
©2008 ZITS Partnership. Distributed by King Features Syndicate.
SCOTT and BORGMAN 9/22

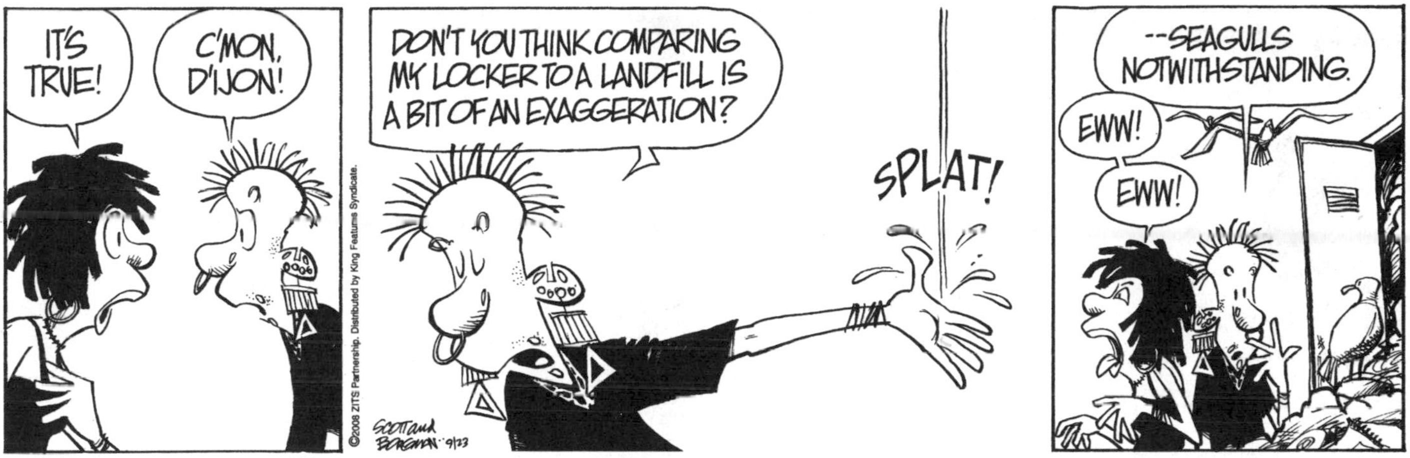
IT'S TRUE!
C'MON, D'IJON!
©2008 ZITS Partnership. Distributed by King Features Syndicate.
SCOTT and BORGMAN 9/23
DON'T YOU THINK COMPARING MY LOCKER TO A LANDFILL IS A BIT OF AN EXAGGERATION?
SPLAT!
--SEAGULLS NOTWITHSTANDING.
EWW!
EWW!

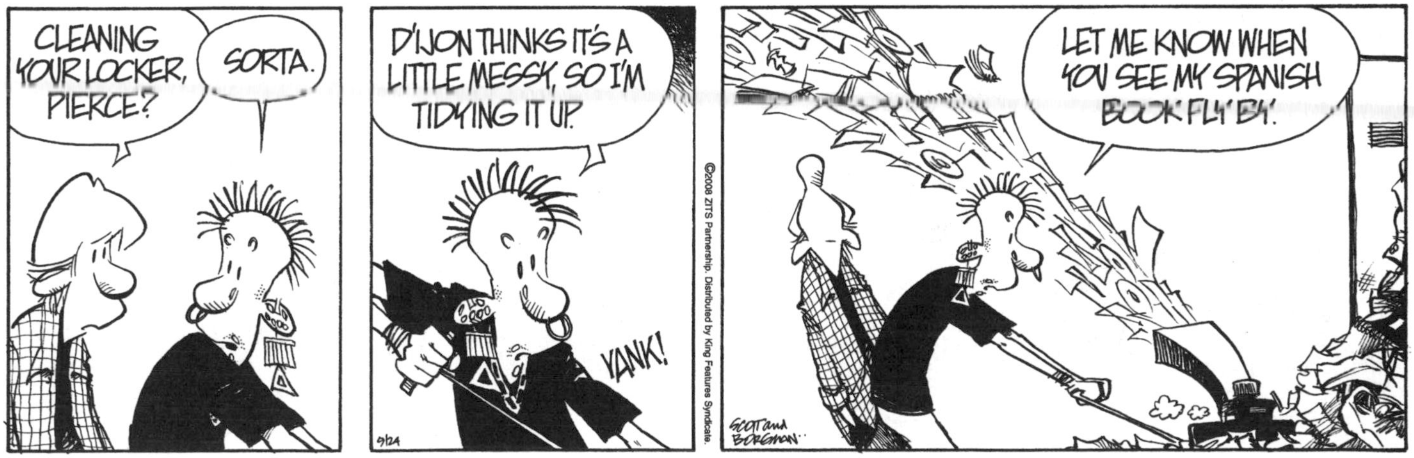
CLEANING YOUR LOCKER, PIERCE?
SORTA.
D'IJON THINKS IT'S A LITTLE MESSY, SO I'M TIDYING IT UP.
YANK!
9/24
©2008 ZITS Partnership. Distributed by King Features Syndicate.
LET ME KNOW WHEN YOU SEE MY SPANISH BOOK FLY BY.
SCOTT and BORGMAN

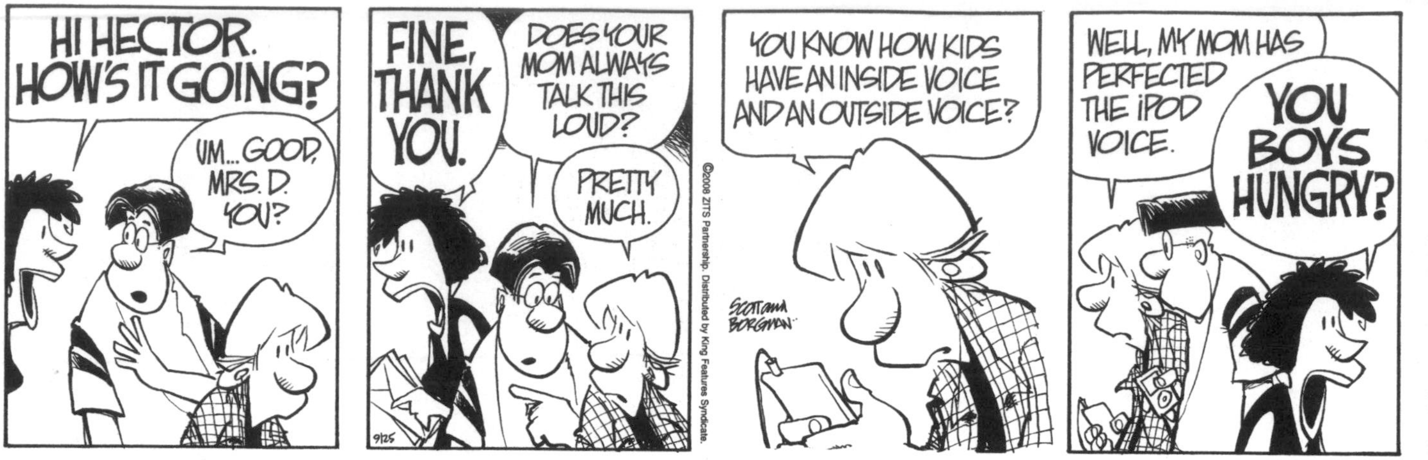
HI HECTOR. HOW'S IT GOING?
UM... GOOD, MRS. D. YOU?
FINE, THANK YOU.
DOES YOUR MOM ALWAYS TALK THIS LOUD?
PRETTY MUCH.
9/25
©2008 ZITS Partnership. Distributed by King Features Syndicate.
YOU KNOW HOW KIDS HAVE AN INSIDE VOICE AND AN OUTSIDE VOICE?
SCOTT and BORGMAN
WELL, MY MOM HAS PERFECTED THE iPOD VOICE.
YOU BOYS HUNGRY?

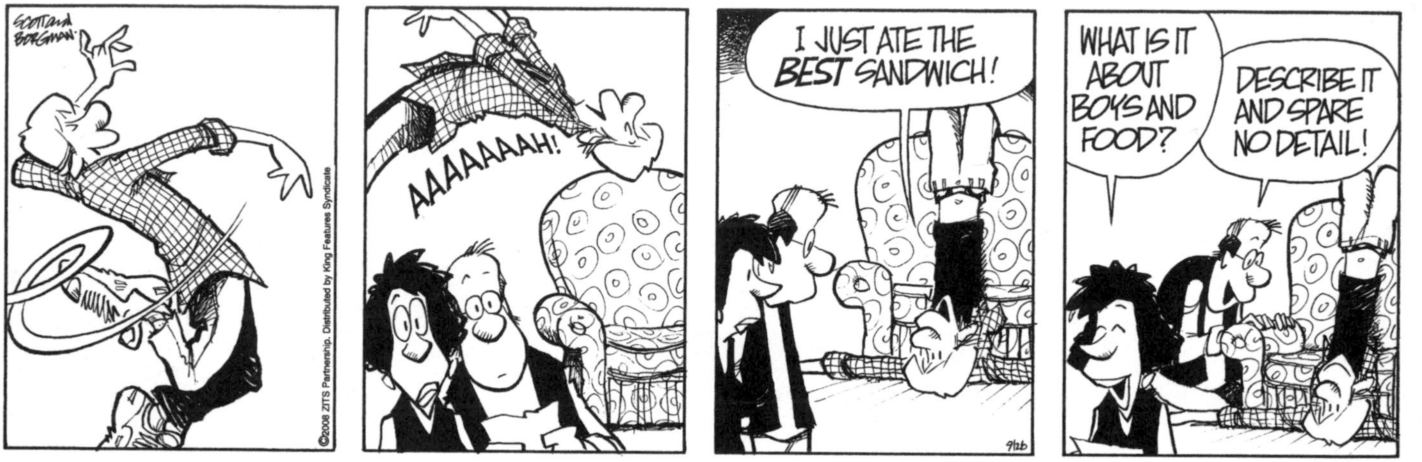
SCOTT and BORGMAN
©2008 ZITS Partnership. Distributed by King Features Syndicate
AAAAAAAH!
I JUST ATE THE BEST SANDWICH!
9/26
WHAT IS IT ABOUT BOYS AND FOOD?
DESCRIBE IT AND SPARE NO DETAIL!

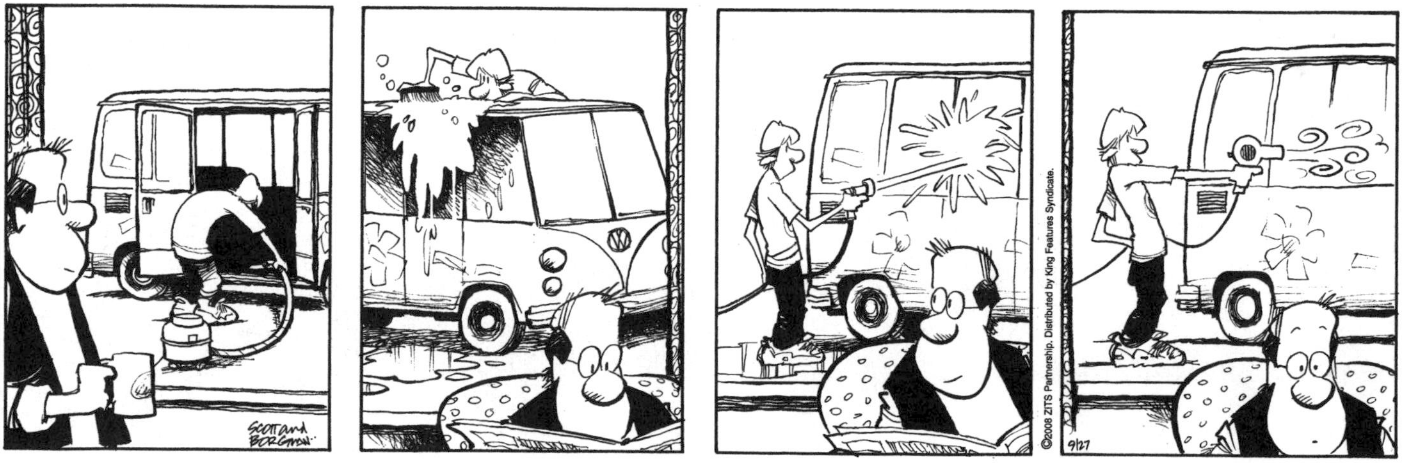
SCOTT and BORGMAN
©2008 ZITS Partnership. Distributed by King Features Syndicate.
9/27

Zits
by JERRY SCOTT and JIM BORGMAN

HI MOM. CAN YOU COME PICK ME UP?
OKAY. I'LL BE AT HECTOR'S HOUSE IN TEN MINUTES.
UM... YEAH, BUT I'M NOT AT HECTOR'S ANYMORE.
WE ALL WALKED OVER TO TIM'S.
OKAY. THEN I'LL BE AT TIM'S IN FIFTEEN MINUTES.
SCOTT and BORGMAN 9/28
AND THEN TIM'S MOM DROVE US OVER TO PIERCE'S HOUSE.
FINE. I'LL PICK YOU UP THERE.
WHAT? NO! WE GOT BORED AND WENT TO GET SOME COFFEE.
BUT WE'RE ALMOST FINISHED AND WE'RE EITHER GOING TO HANG OUT AT THE MUSIC STORE, GRAB A BURGER OR RETURN HECTOR'S LIBRARY BOOKS.
WHY DON'T YOU JUST START DRIVING TOWARD TOWN AND I'LL TEXT YOU PERIODIC LOCATION UPDATES.
BAP! BAP! BAP!
©2008 ZITS Partnership. Distributed by King Features Syndicate

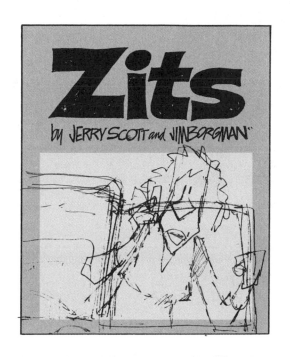

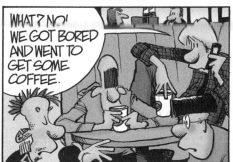

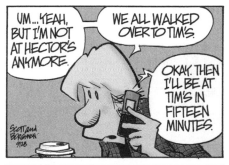

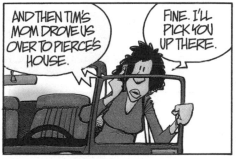

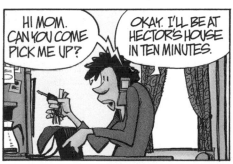

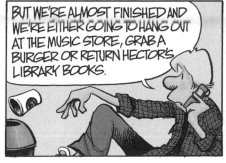

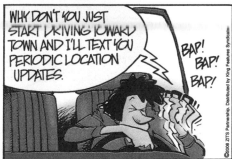

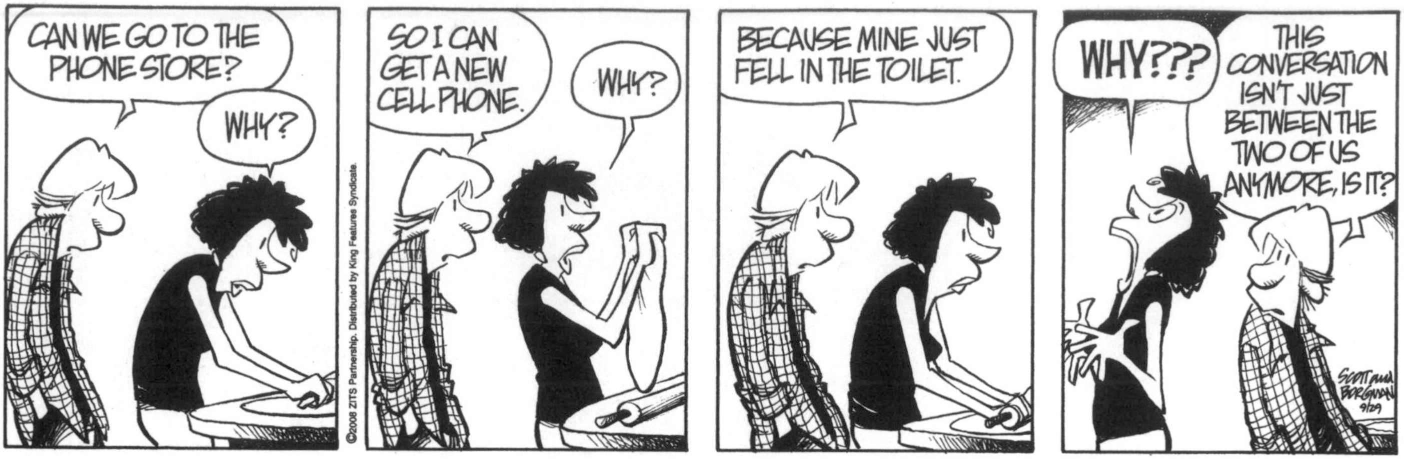
CAN WE GO TO THE PHONE STORE?
WHY?
SO I CAN GET A NEW CELL PHONE.
WHY?
BECAUSE MINE JUST FELL IN THE TOILET.
WHY???
THIS CONVERSATION ISN'T JUST BETWEEN THE TWO OF US ANYMORE, IS IT?
©2008 ZITS Partnership. Distributed by King Features Syndicate.
SCOTT AND BORGMAN 9/29

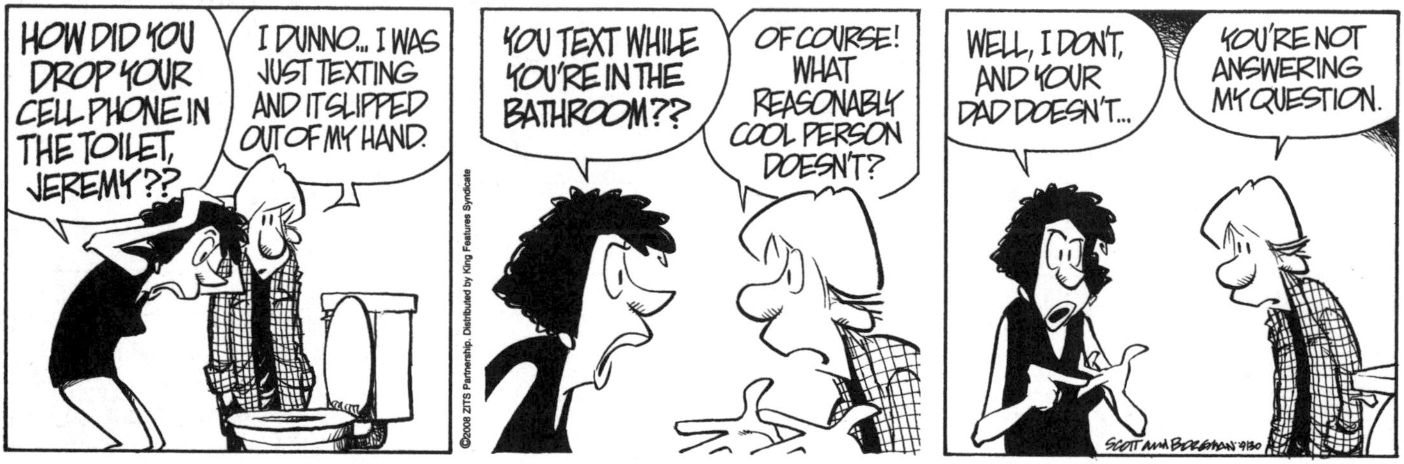
HOW DID YOU DROP YOUR CELL PHONE IN THE TOILET, JEREMY??
I DUNNO... I WAS JUST TEXTING AND IT SLIPPED OUT OF MY HAND.
YOU TEXT WHILE YOU'RE IN THE BATHROOM??
OF COURSE! WHAT REASONABLY COOL PERSON DOESN'T?
WELL, I DON'T, AND YOUR DAD DOESN'T...
YOU'RE NOT ANSWERING MY QUESTION.
©2008 ZITS Partnership. Distributed by King Features Syndicate
SCOTT AND BORGMAN 9/30

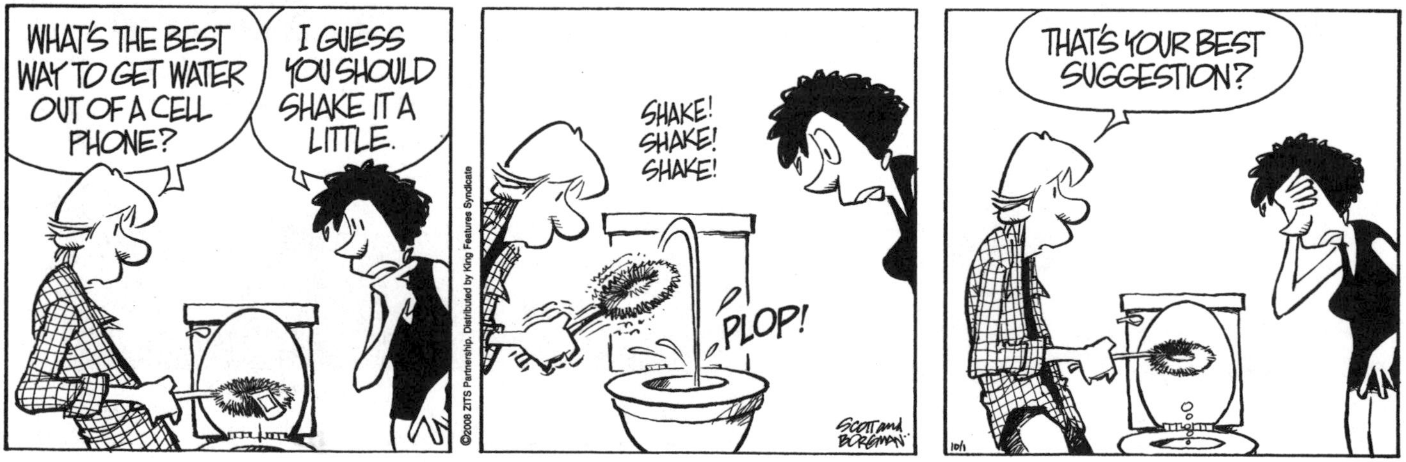
WHAT'S THE BEST WAY TO GET WATER OUT OF A CELL PHONE?
I GUESS YOU SHOULD SHAKE IT A LITTLE.
SHAKE! SHAKE! SHAKE!
PLOP!
THAT'S YOUR BEST SUGGESTION?
©2008 ZITS Partnership. Distributed by King Features Syndicate
SCOTT AND BORGMAN
10/1

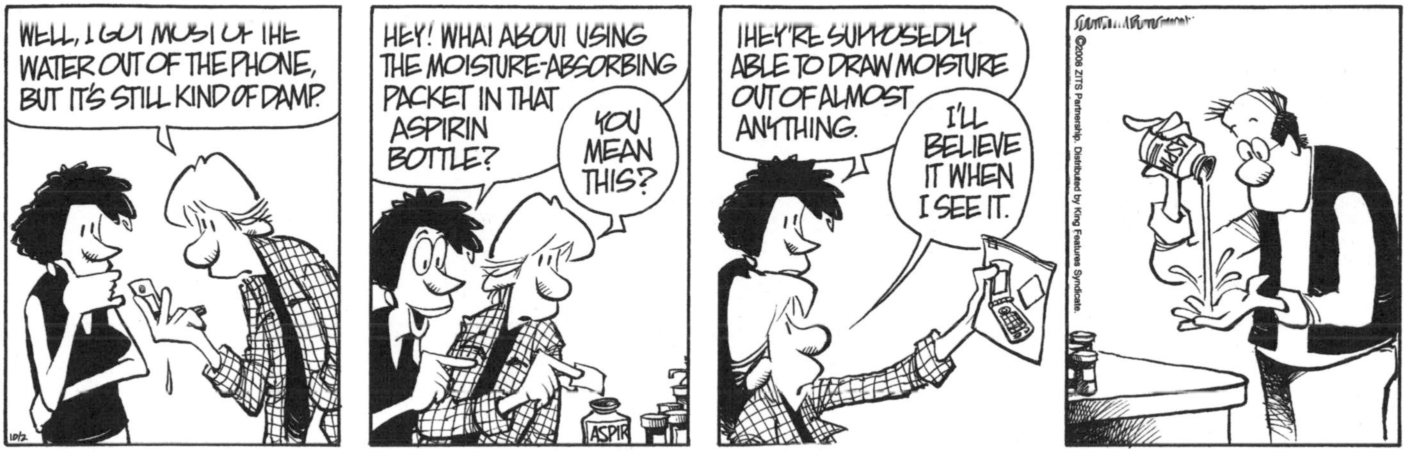
WELL, I GOT MOST OF THE WATER OUT OF THE PHONE, BUT IT'S STILL KIND OF DAMP.
HEY! WHAT ABOUT USING THE MOISTURE-ABSORBING PACKET IN THAT ASPIRIN BOTTLE?
YOU MEAN THIS?
ASPIR
THEY'RE SUPPOSEDLY ABLE TO DRAW MOISTURE OUT OF ALMOST ANYTHING.
I'LL BELIEVE IT WHEN I SEE IT.
©2008 ZITS Partnership. Distributed by King Features Syndicate.

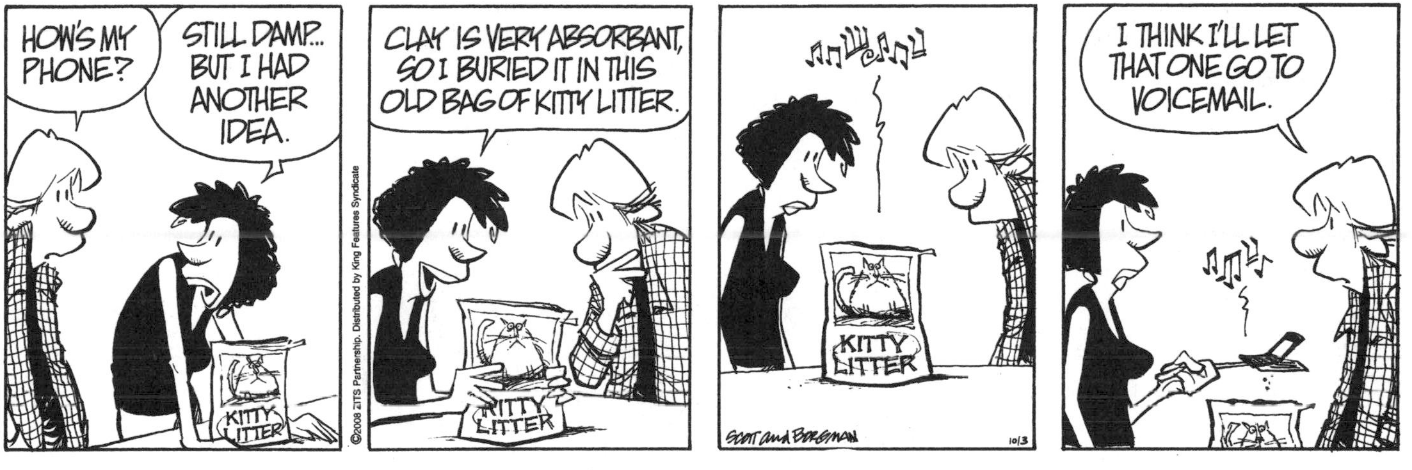
HOW'S MY PHONE?
STILL DAMP... BUT I HAD ANOTHER IDEA.
KITTY LITTER
©2008 ZITS Partnership. Distributed by King Features Syndicate
CLAY IS VERY ABSORBANT, SO I BURIED IT IN THIS OLD BAG OF KITTY LITTER.
KITTY LITTER
KITTY LITTER
SCOTT and BORGMAN
I THINK I'LL LET THAT ONE GO TO VOICEMAIL.

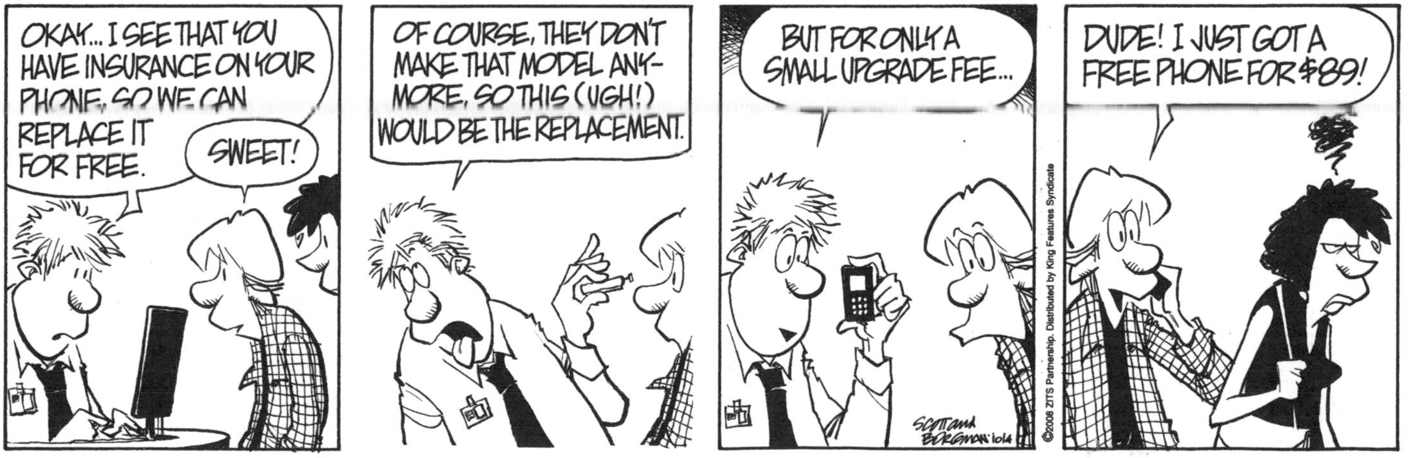
OKAY... I SEE THAT YOU HAVE INSURANCE ON YOUR PHONE, SO WE CAN REPLACE IT FOR FREE.
SWEET!
OF COURSE, THEY DON'T MAKE THAT MODEL ANY-MORE, SO THIS (UGH!) WOULD BE THE REPLACEMENT.
BUT FOR ONLY A SMALL UPGRADE FEE...
SCOTT and BORGMAN
©2008 ZITS Partnership. Distributed by King Features Syndicate
DUDE! I JUST GOT A FREE PHONE FOR $89!

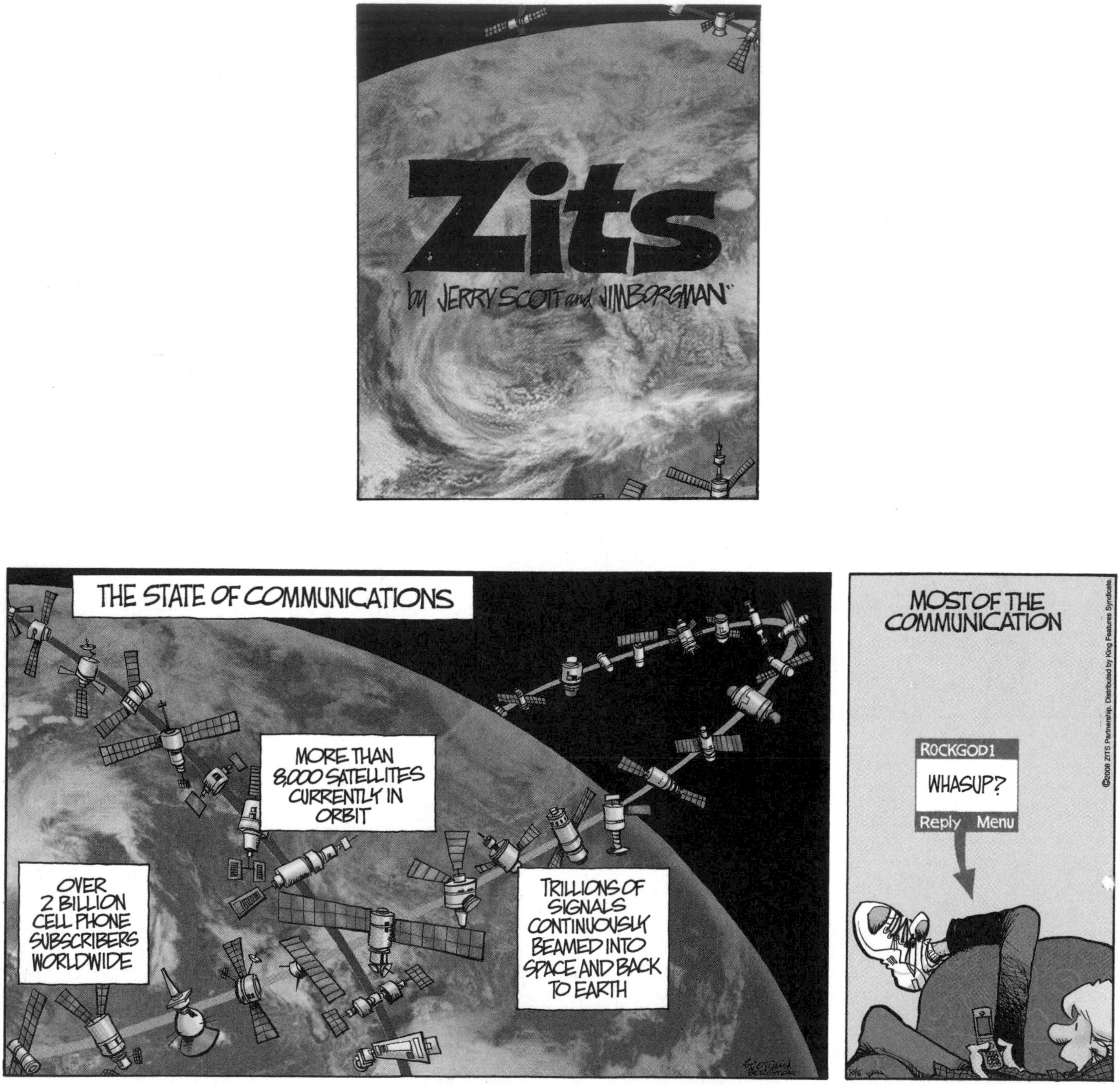
Zits
by JERRY SCOTT and JIM BORGMAN
THE STATE OF COMMUNICATIONS
OVER 2 BILLION CELL PHONE SUBSCRIBERS WORLDWIDE
MORE THAN 8,000 SATELLITES CURRENTLY IN ORBIT
TRILLIONS OF SIGNALS CONTINUOUSLY BEAMED INTO SPACE AND BACK TO EARTH
MOST OF THE COMMUNICATION
ROCKGOD1
WHASUP?
Reply Menu
©2008 ZITS Partnership. Distributed by King Features Syndicate.

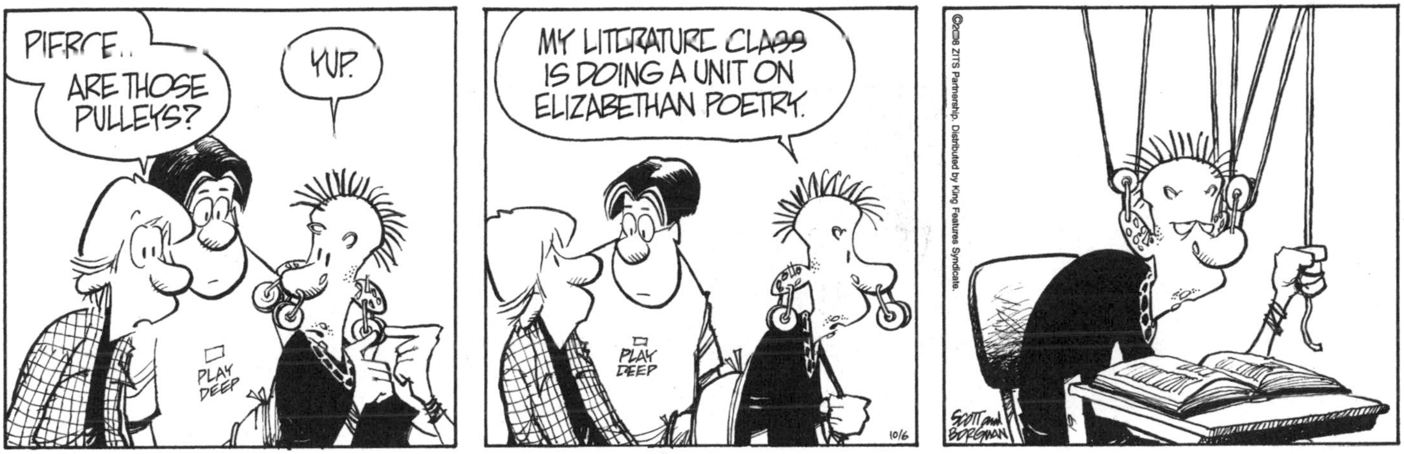
PIERCE... ARE THOSE PULLEYS?
YUP.
PLAY DEEP
MY LITERATURE CLASS IS DOING A UNIT ON ELIZABETHAN POETRY.
PLAY DEEP
10/6
©2008 ZITS Partnership. Distributed by King Features Syndicate.
SCOTT and BORGMAN

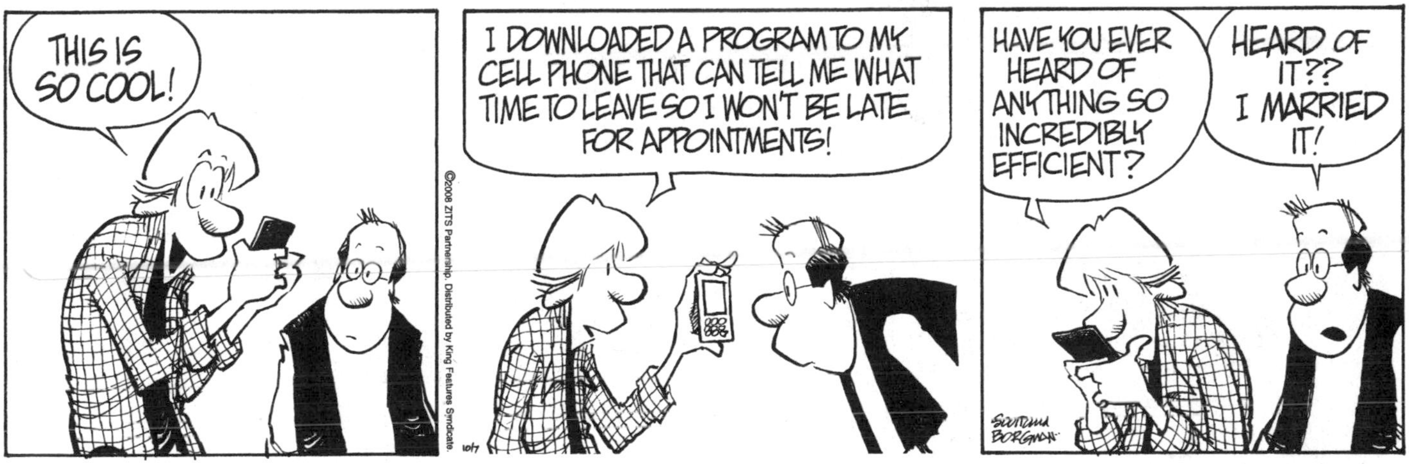
THIS IS SO COOL!
©2008 ZITS Partnership. Distributed by King Features Syndicate.
10/7
I DOWNLOADED A PROGRAM TO MY CELL PHONE THAT CAN TELL ME WHAT TIME TO LEAVE SO I WON'T BE LATE FOR APPOINTMENTS!
HAVE YOU EVER HEARD OF ANYTHING SO INCREDIBLY EFFICIENT?
HEARD OF IT?? I MARRIED IT!
SCOTT and BORGMAN

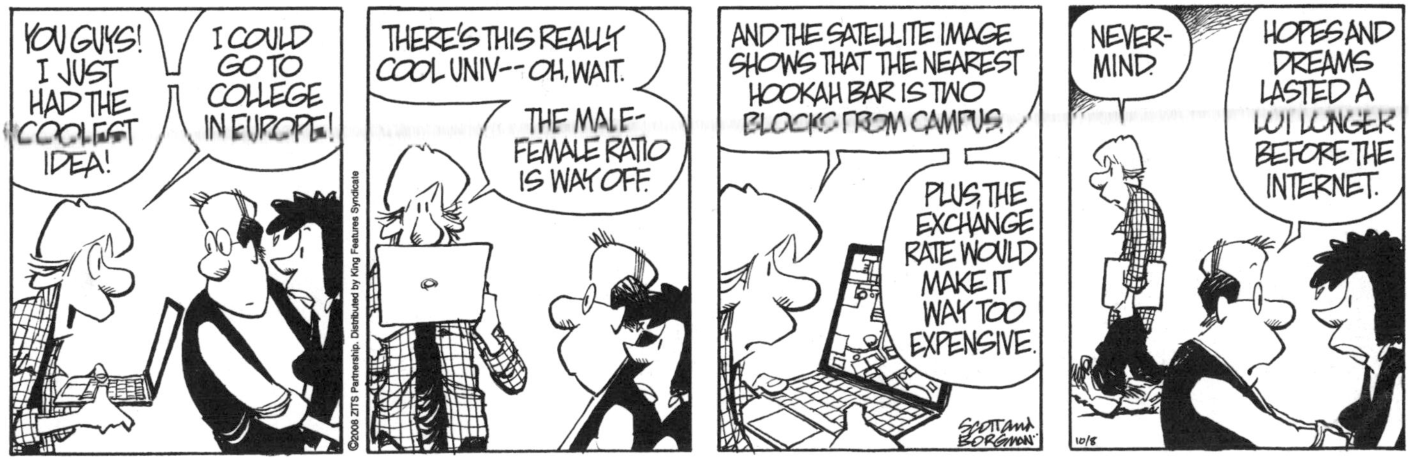
YOU GUYS! I JUST HAD THE COOLEST IDEA!
I COULD GO TO COLLEGE IN EUROPE!
©2008 ZITS Partnership. Distributed by King Features Syndicate
THERE'S THIS REALLY COOL UNIV-- OH, WAIT.
THE MALE-FEMALE RATIO IS WAY OFF.
AND THE SATELLITE IMAGE SHOWS THAT THE NEAREST HOOKAH BAR IS TWO BLOCKS FROM CAMPUS.
PLUS, THE EXCHANGE RATE WOULD MAKE IT WAY TOO EXPENSIVE.
SCOTT and BORGMAN
NEVER-MIND.
HOPES AND DREAMS LASTED A LOT LONGER BEFORE THE INTERNET.
10/8

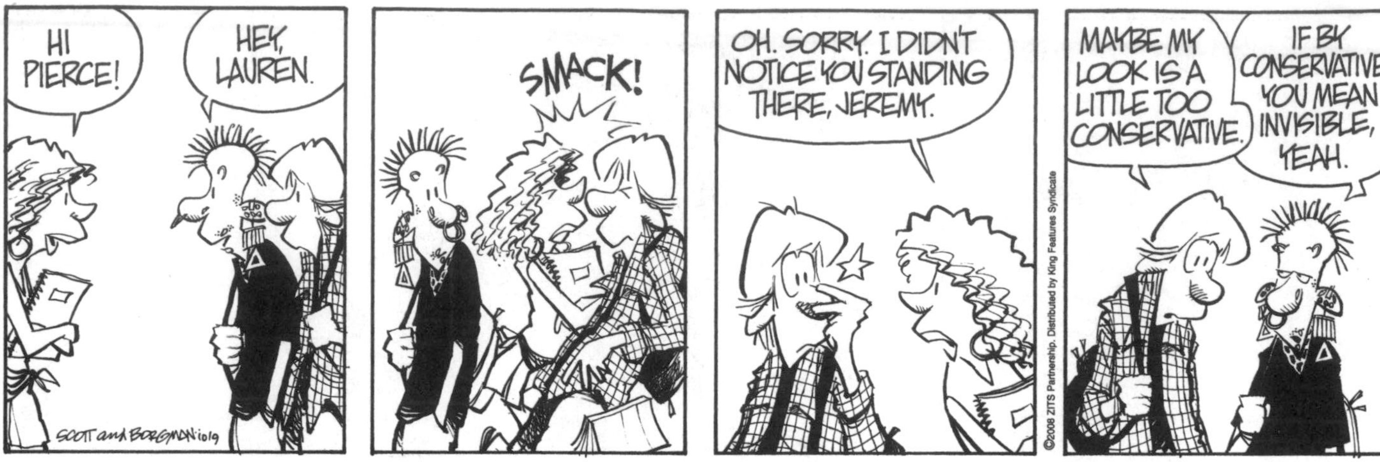
HI PIERCE!
HEY, LAUREN.
SCOTT and BORGMAN 10/9
SMACK!
OH. SORRY. I DIDN'T NOTICE YOU STANDING THERE, JEREMY.
©2008 ZITS Partnership. Distributed by King Features Syndicate
MAYBE MY LOOK IS A LITTLE TOO CONSERVATIVE.
IF BY CONSERVATIVE YOU MEAN INVISIBLE, YEAH.

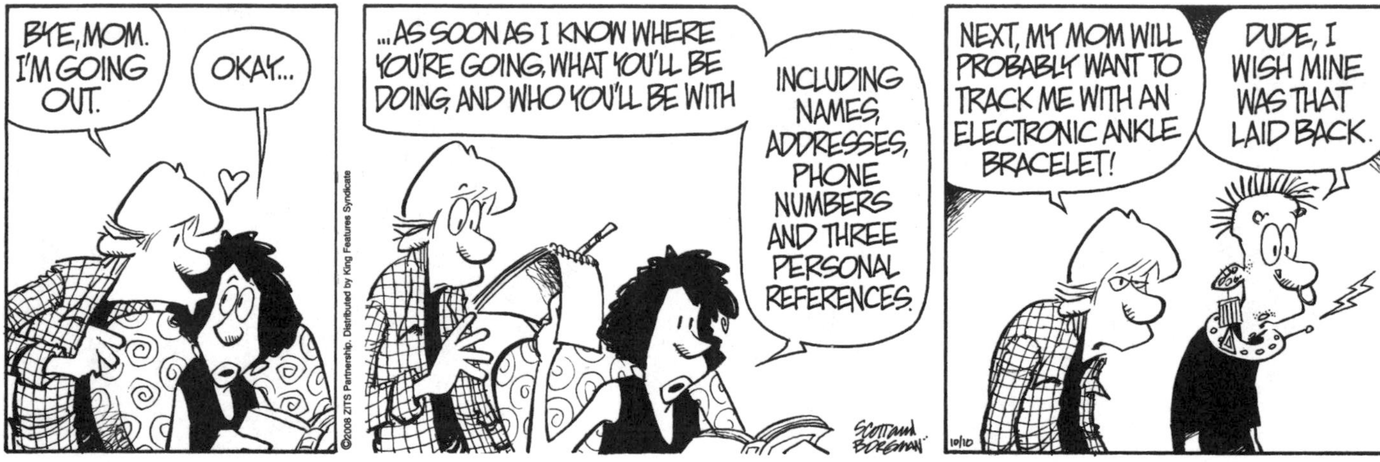
BYE, MOM. I'M GOING OUT.
OKAY...
©2008 ZITS Partnership. Distributed by King Features Syndicate
...AS SOON AS I KNOW WHERE YOU'RE GOING, WHAT YOU'LL BE DOING, AND WHO YOU'LL BE WITH
INCLUDING NAMES, ADDRESSES, PHONE NUMBERS AND THREE PERSONAL REFERENCES.
SCOTT and BORGMAN
NEXT, MY MOM WILL PROBABLY WANT TO TRACK ME WITH AN ELECTRONIC ANKLE BRACELET!
DUDE, I WISH MINE WAS THAT LAID BACK.
10/10

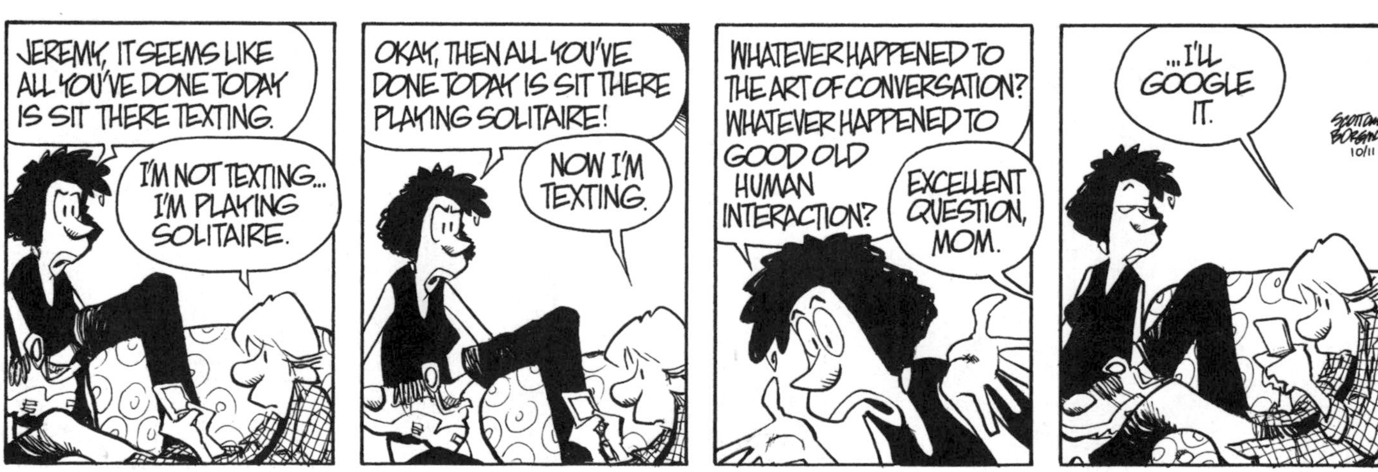
JEREMY, IT SEEMS LIKE ALL YOU'VE DONE TODAY IS SIT THERE TEXTING.
I'M NOT TEXTING... I'M PLAYING SOLITAIRE.
OKAY, THEN ALL YOU'VE DONE TODAY IS SIT THERE PLAYING SOLITAIRE!
NOW I'M TEXTING.
WHATEVER HAPPENED TO THE ART OF CONVERSATION? WHATEVER HAPPENED TO GOOD OLD HUMAN INTERACTION?
EXCELLENT QUESTION, MOM.
...I'LL GOOGLE IT.
SCOTT and BORGMAN 10/11

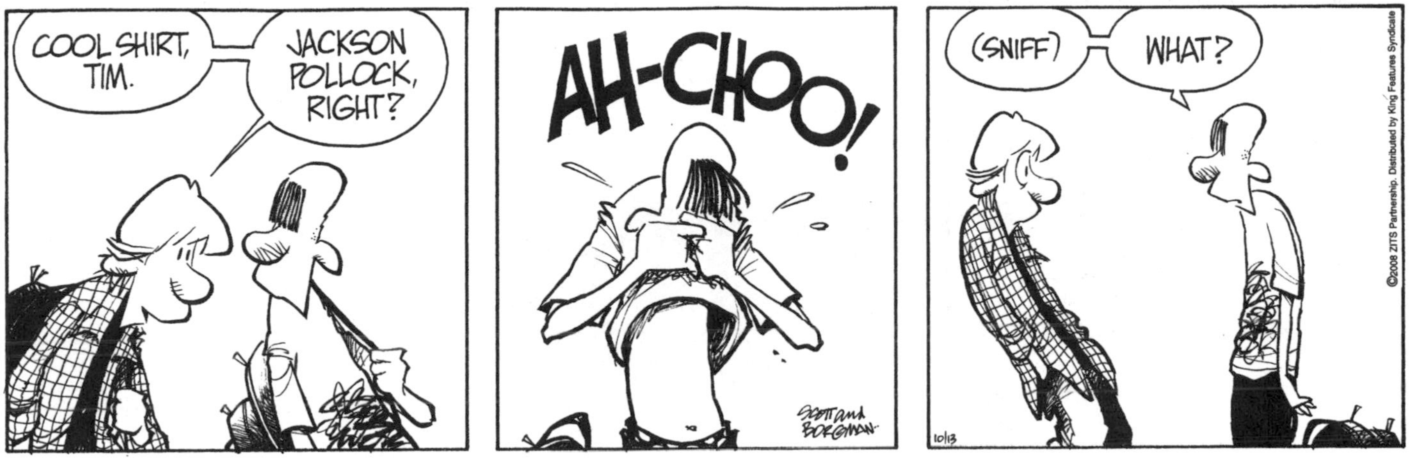
COOL SHIRT, TIM.
JACKSON POLLOCK, RIGHT?
AH-CHOO!
(SNIFF)
WHAT?
SCOTT and BORGMAN
10/13
©2008 ZITS Partnership. Distributed by King Features Syndicate

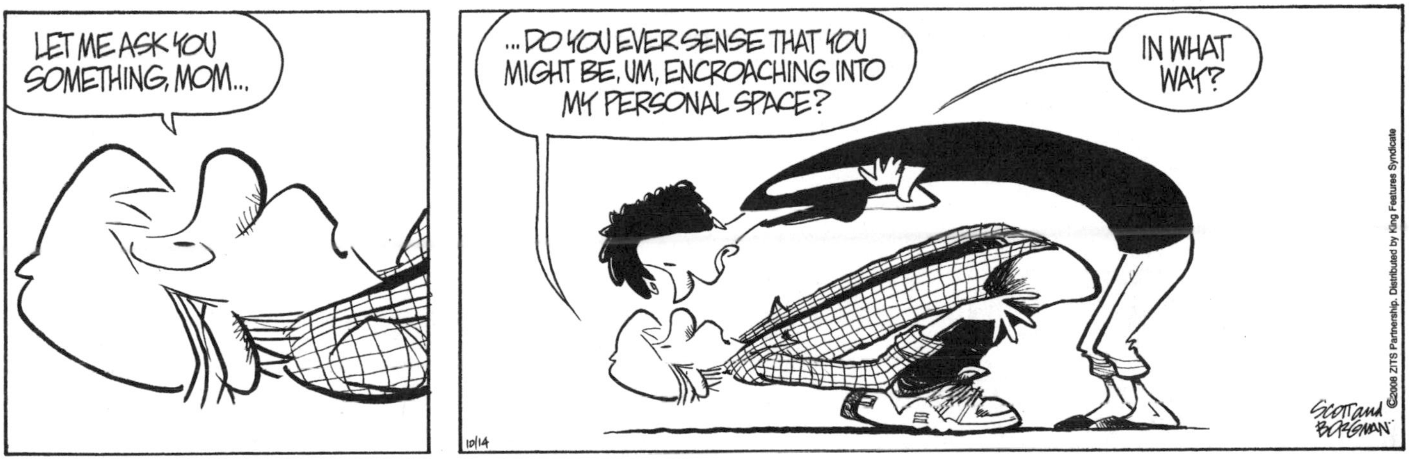
LET ME ASK YOU SOMETHING, MOM...
...DO YOU EVER SENSE THAT YOU MIGHT BE, UM, ENCROACHING INTO MY PERSONAL SPACE?
IN WHAT WAY?
10/14
SCOTT and BORGMAN
©2008 ZITS Partnership. Distributed by King Features Syndicate

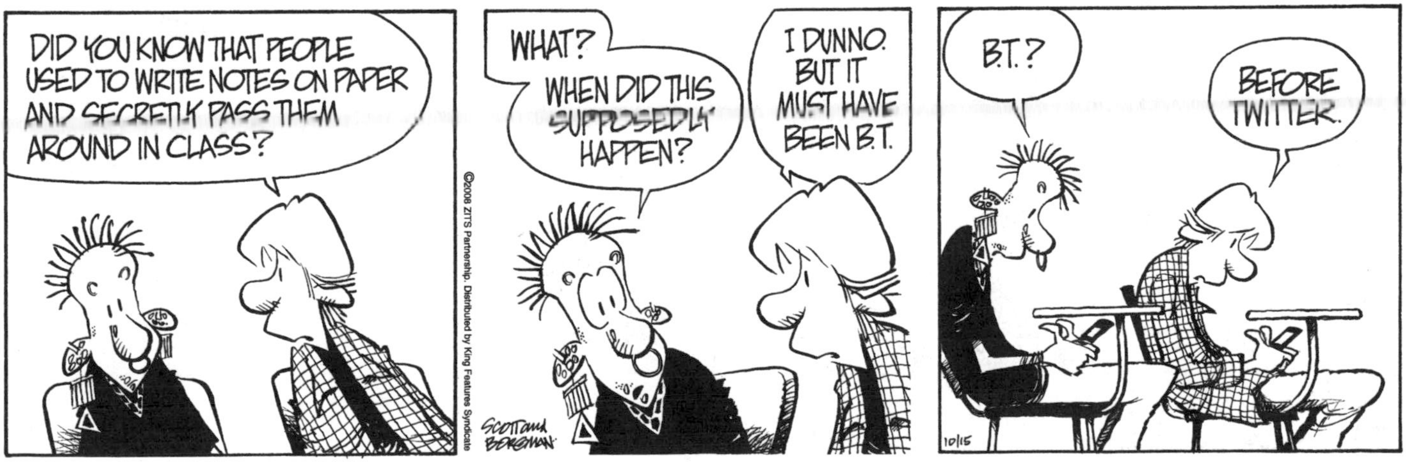
DID YOU KNOW THAT PEOPLE USED TO WRITE NOTES ON PAPER AND SECRETLY PASS THEM AROUND IN CLASS?
©2008 ZITS Partnership. Distributed by King Features Syndicate
WHAT?
WHEN DID THIS SUPPOSEDLY HAPPEN?
I DUNNO. BUT IT MUST HAVE BEEN B.T.
SCOTT and BORGMAN
B.T.?
BEFORE TWITTER.
10/15

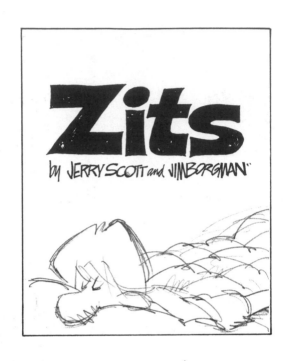

Zits
by JERRY SCOTT and JIM BORGMAN

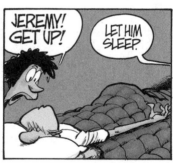

JEREMY! GET UP!
LET HIM SLEEP.
WHAT??
THE POOR KID WAS UP PAST MIDNIGHT STUDYING!
BUT--
THE SCHOOLS EXPECT THEM TO BE IN CLASS ALL DAY, DO HOMEWORK ALL NIGHT, AND THEN BE BACK AT IT BRIGHT AND EARLY THE NEXT MORNING!
STUDIES SHOW THAT TEENAGERS NEED (NEED!) 10-12 HOURS OF SLEEP EVERY NIGHT TO BE HEALTHY.
I'VE READ THAT!
WELL, THEN CUT HIM SOME SLACK!
THE WORLD WON'T END IF HE MISSES A CLASS TODAY.
GOOD POINT
ONE HOUR LATER
HUH?
I'M LATE!!
I KNOW YOU WERE EXHAUSTED.
©2008 ZITS Partnership. Distributed by King Features Syndicate
SO YOU JUST LET ME SLEEP??
IF YOU WON'T LISTEN TO YOUR BODY, I WILL.
SCOTT and BORGMAN 10/12

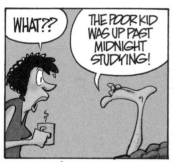

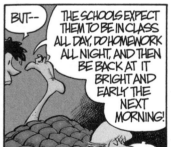

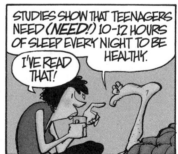

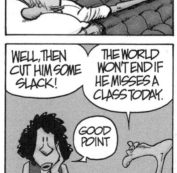

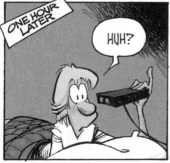

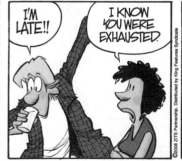

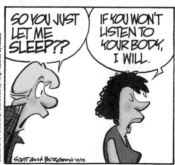

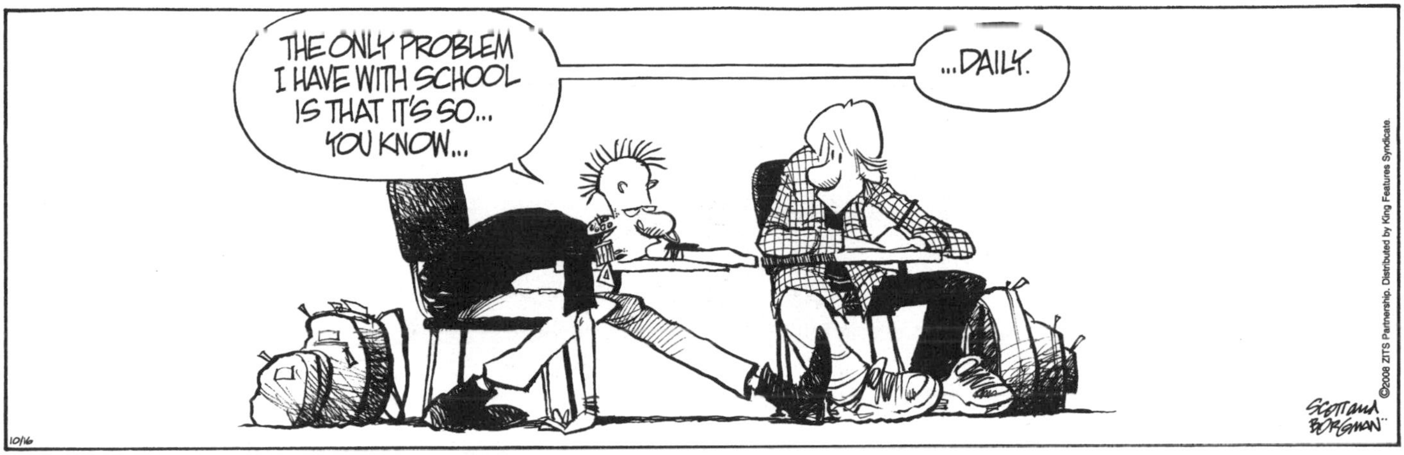
THE ONLY PROBLEM I HAVE WITH SCHOOL IS THAT IT'S SO... YOU KNOW...
...DAILY.
©2008 ZITS Partnership. Distributed by King Features Syndicate.
SCOTT and BORGMAN
10/16

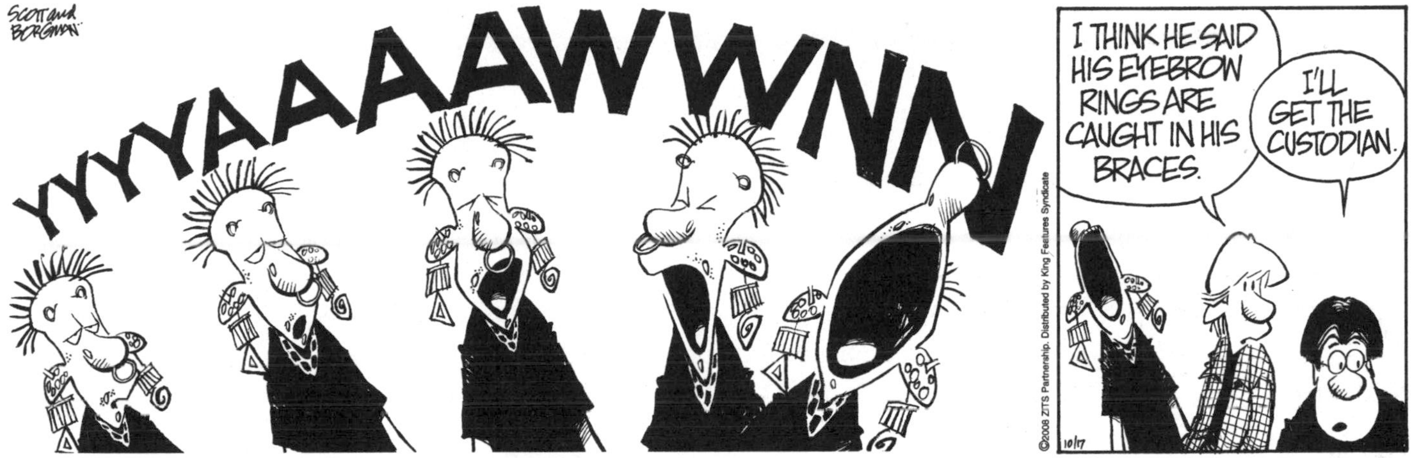
SCOTT and BORGMAN
YYYYAAAAAWWNN
I THINK HE SAID HIS EYEBROW RINGS ARE CAUGHT IN HIS BRACES.
I'LL GET THE CUSTODIAN.
©2008 ZITS Partnership. Distributed by King Features Syndicate
10/17

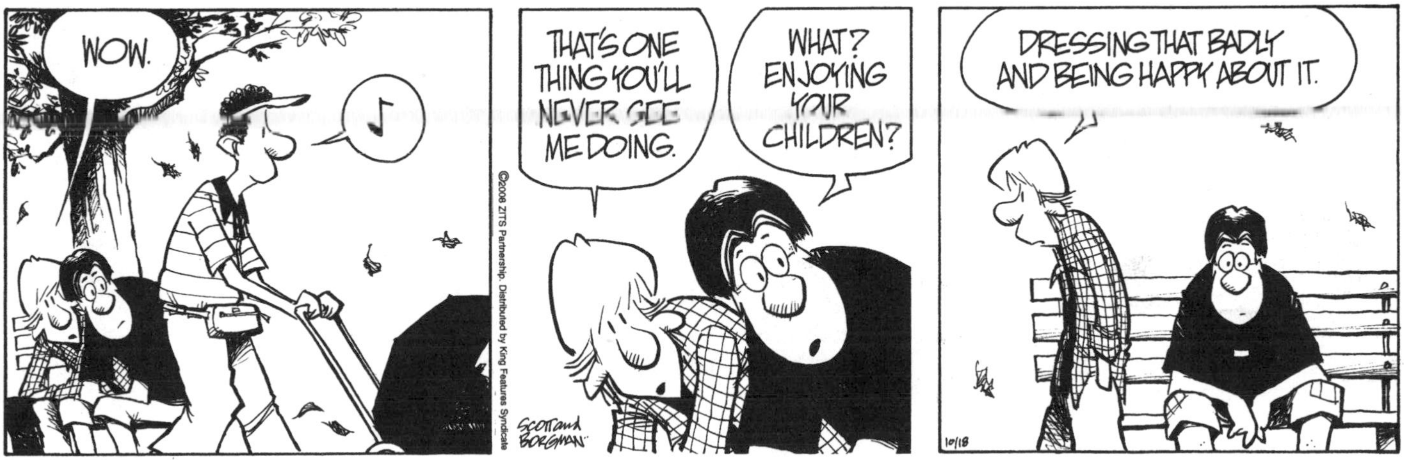
WOW.
THAT'S ONE THING YOU'LL NEVER SEE ME DOING.
WHAT? ENJOYING YOUR CHILDREN?
DRESSING THAT BADLY AND BEING HAPPY ABOUT IT.
©2008 ZITS Partnership. Distributed by King Features Syndicate
SCOTT and BORGMAN
10/18

Zits
by JERRY SCOTT and JIM BORGMAN

THERE MUST BE A NAME FOR THAT.
MAYBE...
NO.
WAIT!
I GOT IT!
TEXT-A-POST-I-CHAT-A-MMUNICATION!
NICE!
MENTAL NOTE: ADD BEDROOM DOOR DEADBOLT TO CHRISTMAS LIST.
SCOTT and BORGMAN
©2008 ZITS Partnership. Distributed by King Features Syndicate

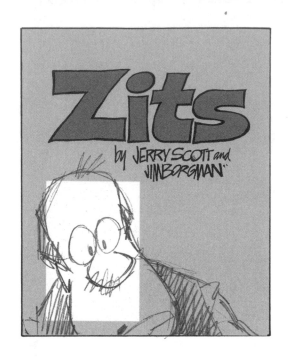

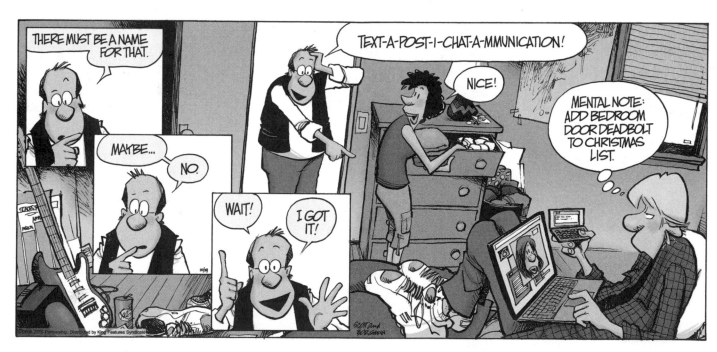

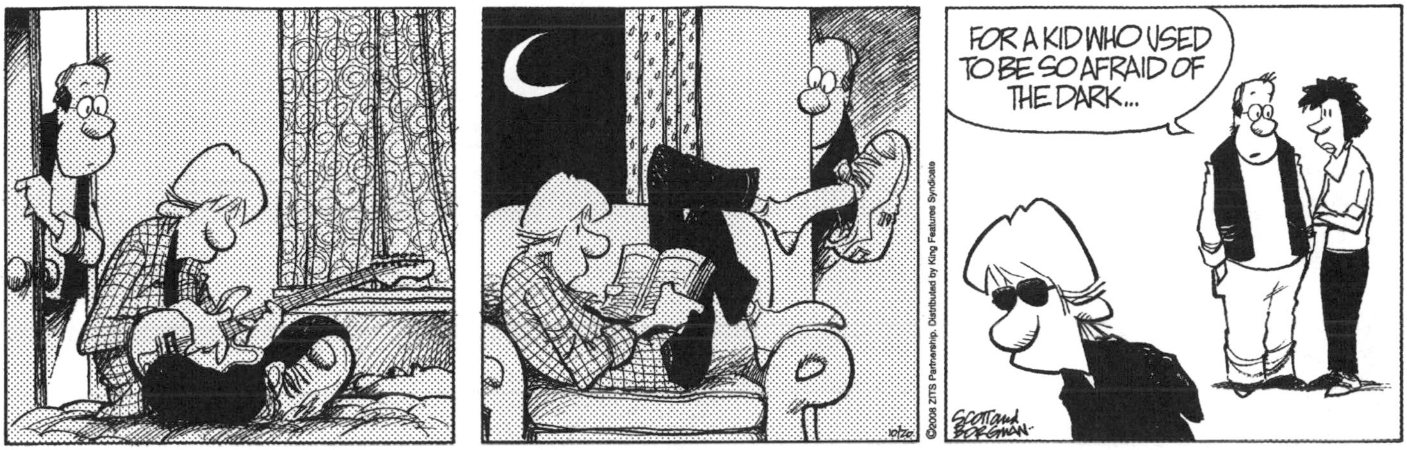
FOR A KID WHO USED TO BE SO AFRAID OF THE DARK...
©2008 ZITS Partnership. Distributed by King Features Syndicate
SCOTT and BORGMAN

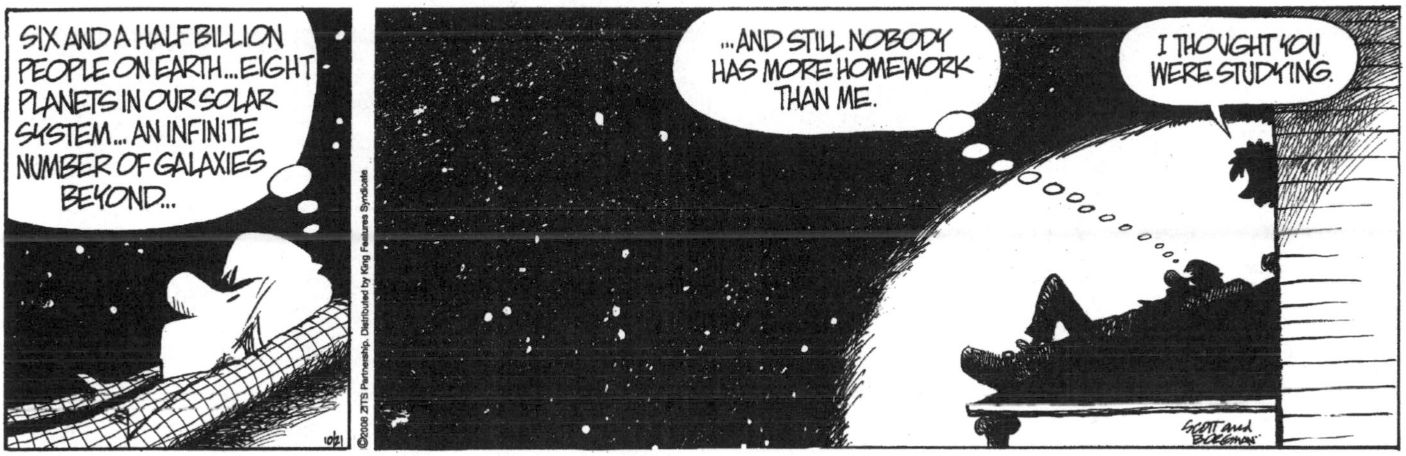
SIX AND A HALF BILLION PEOPLE ON EARTH...EIGHT PLANETS IN OUR SOLAR SYSTEM... AN INFINITE NUMBER OF GALAXIES BEYOND...
©2008 ZITS Partnership. Distributed by King Features Syndicate
...AND STILL NOBODY HAS MORE HOMEWORK THAN ME.
I THOUGHT YOU WERE STUDYING.
SCOTT and BORGMAN

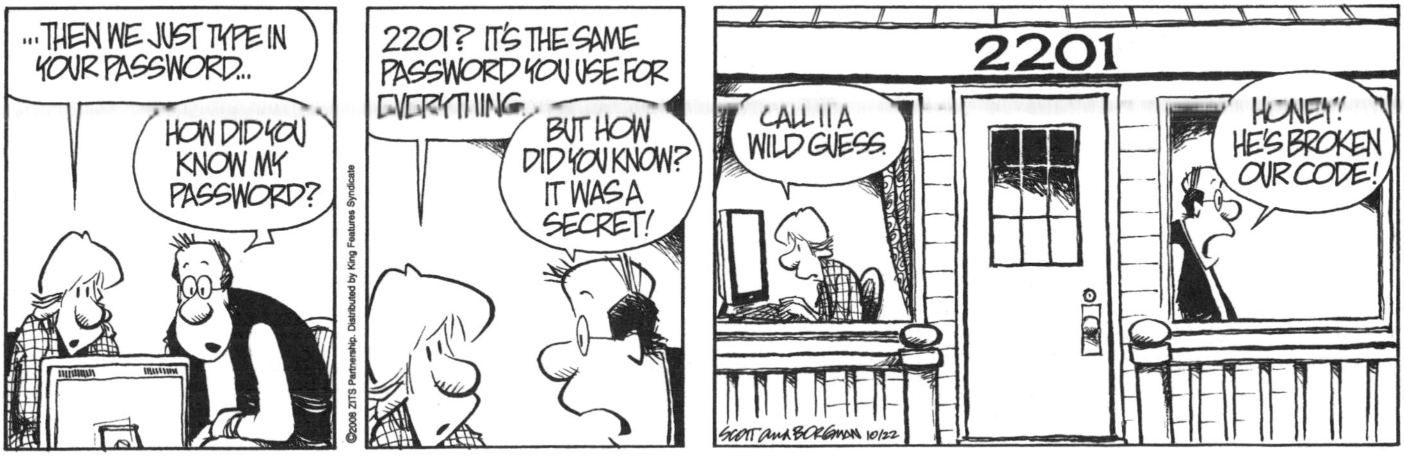
...THEN WE JUST TYPE IN YOUR PASSWORD...
HOW DID YOU KNOW MY PASSWORD?
©2008 ZITS Partnership. Distributed by King Features Syndicate
2201? IT'S THE SAME PASSWORD YOU USE FOR EVERYTHING.
BUT HOW DID YOU KNOW? IT WAS A SECRET!
2201
CALL IT A WILD GUESS.
HONEY! HE'S BROKEN OUR CODE!
SCOTT and BORGMAN 10/22

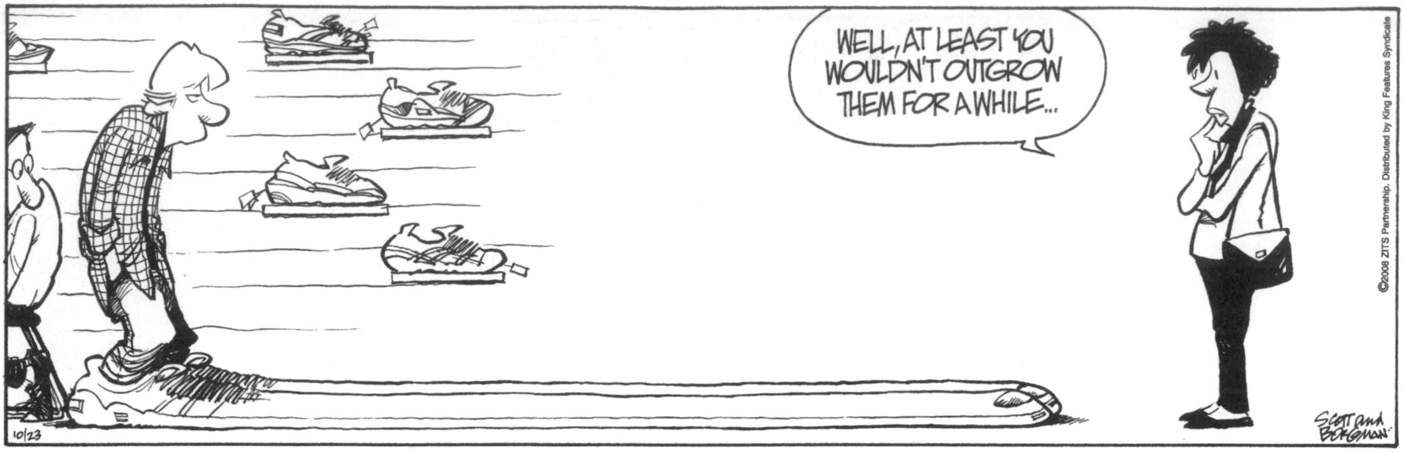
WELL, AT LEAST YOU WOULDN'T OUTGROW THEM FOR A WHILE...
©2008 ZITS Partnership. Distributed by King Features Syndicate
10/23
SCOTT AND BORGMAN

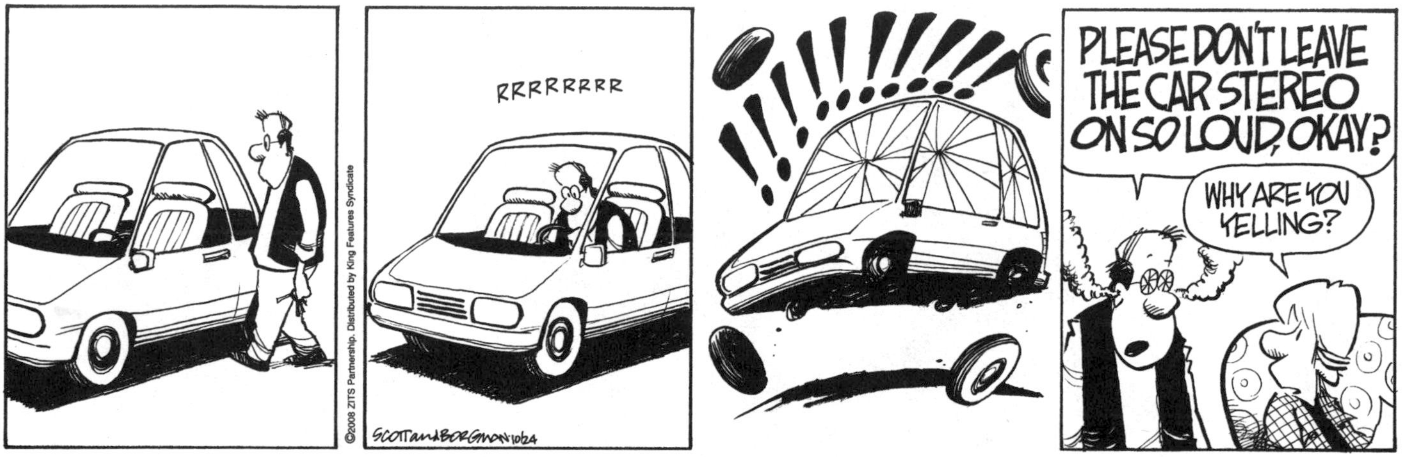
©2008 ZITS Partnership. Distributed by King Features Syndicate
RRRRRRRR
SCOTT AND BORGMAN 10/24
PLEASE DON'T LEAVE THE CAR STEREO ON SO LOUD, OKAY?
WHY ARE YOU YELLING?

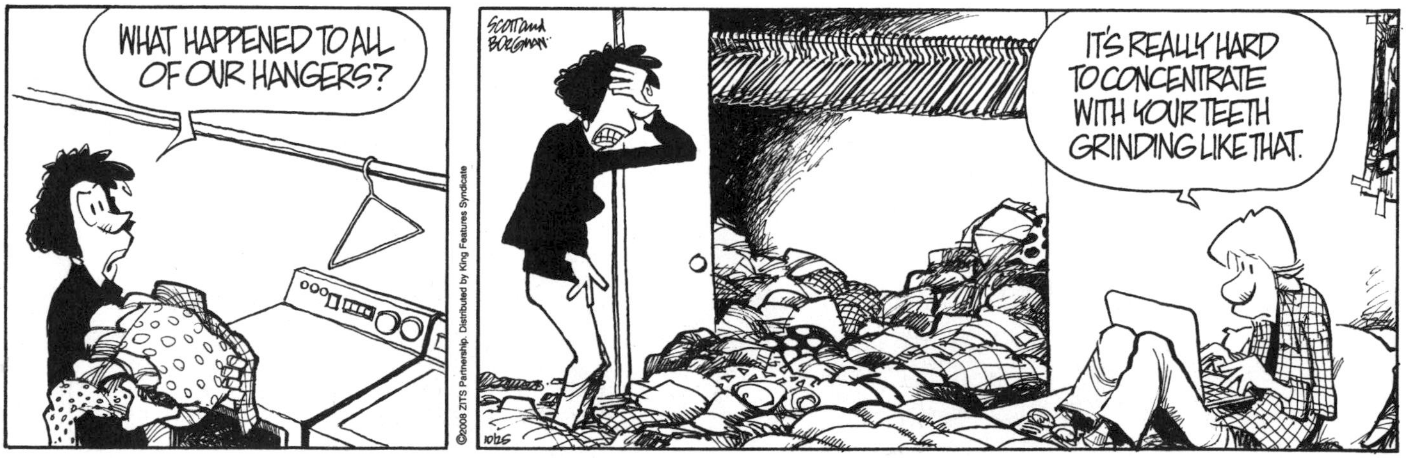
WHAT HAPPENED TO ALL OF OUR HANGERS?
©2008 ZITS Partnership. Distributed by King Features Syndicate
SCOTT AND BORGMAN
10/25
IT'S REALLY HARD TO CONCENTRATE WITH YOUR TEETH GRINDING LIKE THAT.

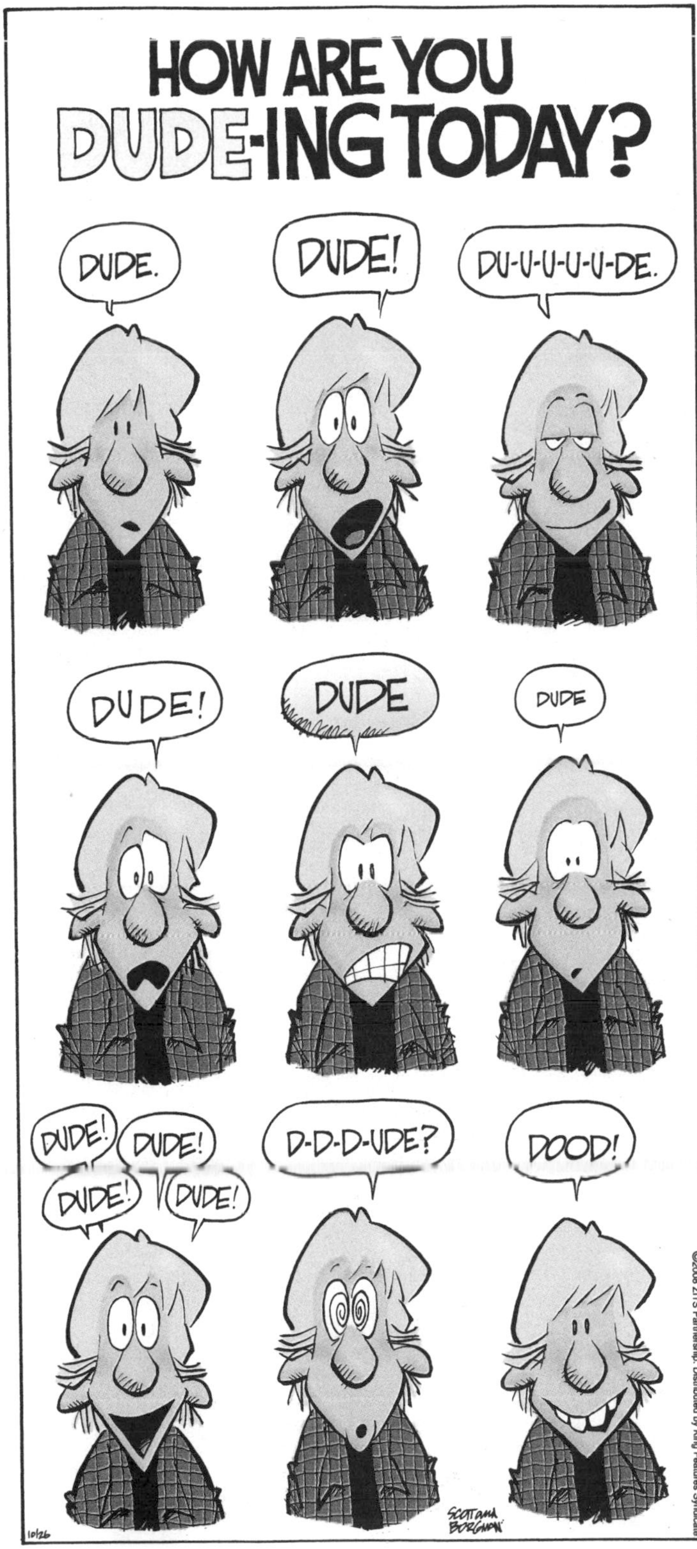
HOW ARE YOU DUDE-ING TODAY?
DUDE.
DUDE!
DU-U-U-U-U-DE.
DUDE!
DUDE
DUDE
DUDE!
DUDE!
DUDE!
DUDE!
D-D-D-UDE?
DOOD!

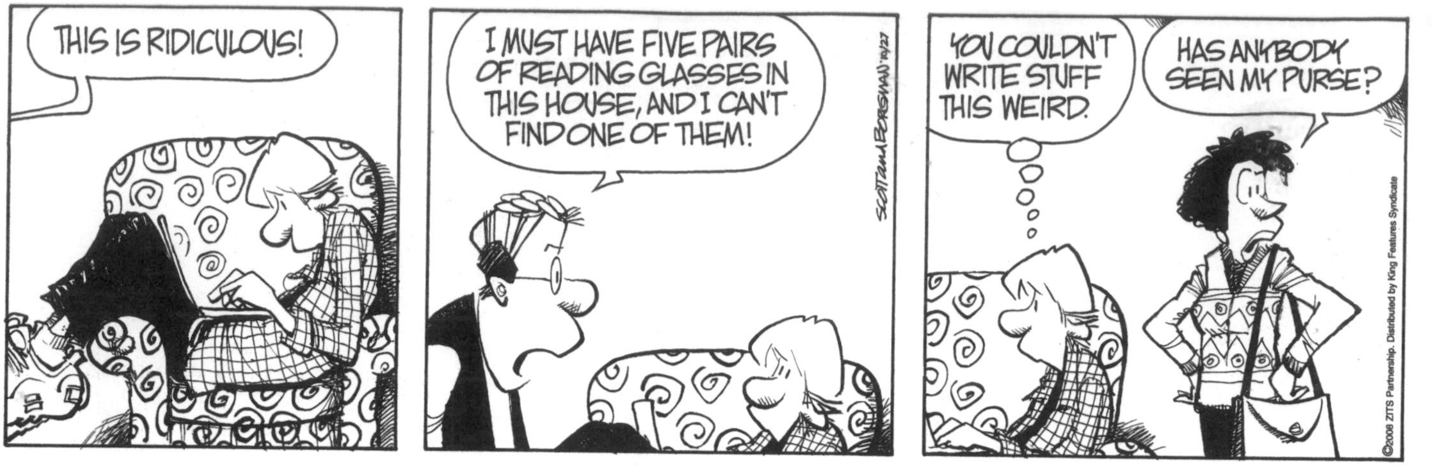
THIS IS RIDICULOUS!
I MUST HAVE FIVE PAIRS OF READING GLASSES IN THIS HOUSE, AND I CAN'T FIND ONE OF THEM!
SCOTT and BORGMAN 10/27
YOU COULDN'T WRITE STUFF THIS WEIRD.
HAS ANYBODY SEEN MY PURSE?
©2008 ZITS Partnership. Distributed by King Features Syndicate

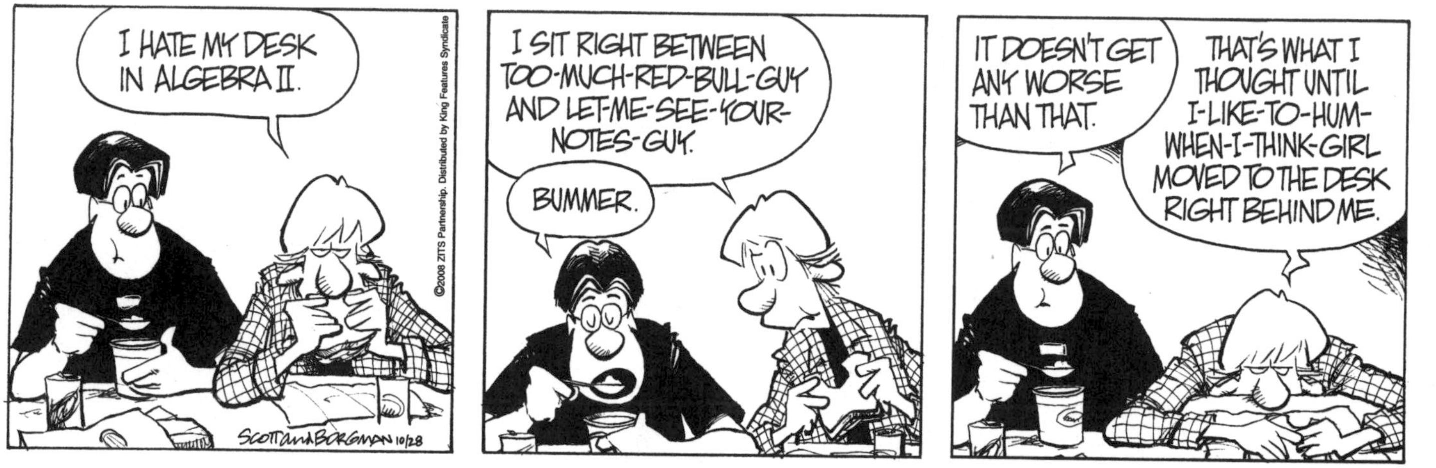
I HATE MY DESK IN ALGEBRA II.
©2008 ZITS Partnership. Distributed by King Features Syndicate
SCOTT and BORGMAN 10/28
I SIT RIGHT BETWEEN TOO-MUCH-RED-BULL-GUY AND LET-ME-SEE-YOUR-NOTES-GUY.
BUMMER.
IT DOESN'T GET ANY WORSE THAN THAT.
THAT'S WHAT I THOUGHT UNTIL I-LIKE-TO-HUM-WHEN-I-THINK-GIRL MOVED TO THE DESK RIGHT BEHIND ME.

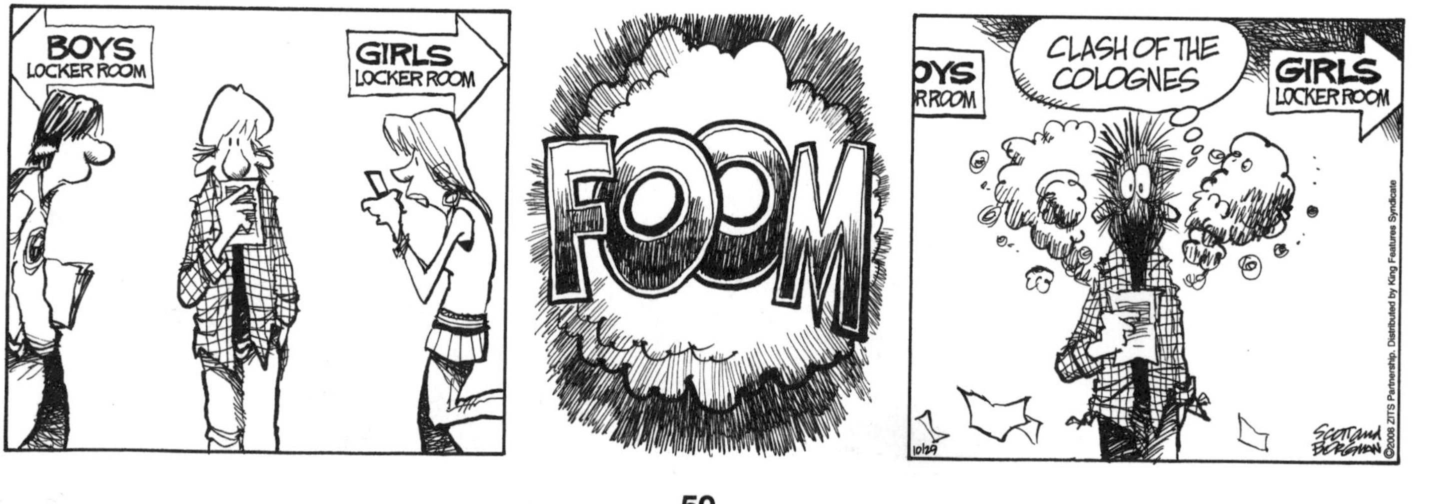
BOYS LOCKER ROOM
GIRLS LOCKER ROOM
FOOM
CLASH OF THE COLOGNES
OYS
R ROOM
GIRLS LOCKER ROOM
10/29
SCOTT and BORGMAN
©2008 ZITS Partnership. Distributed by King Features Syndicate

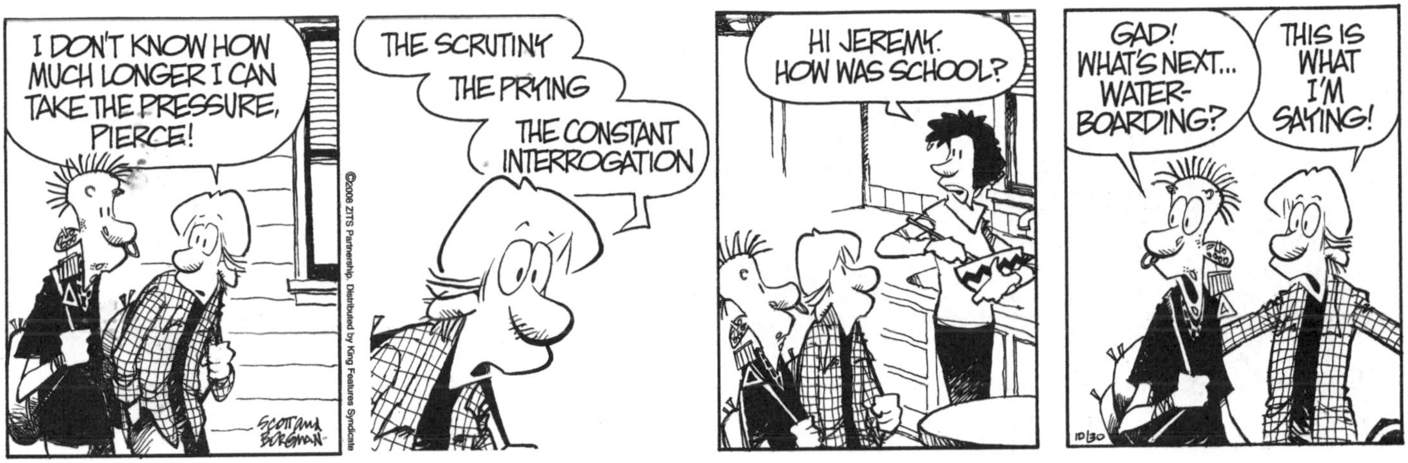
I DON'T KNOW HOW MUCH LONGER I CAN TAKE THE PRESSURE, PIERCE!
SCOTT AND BORGMAN
©2008 ZITS Partnership. Distributed by King Features Syndicate
THE SCRUTINY
THE PRYING
THE CONSTANT INTERROGATION
HI JEREMY. HOW WAS SCHOOL?
GAD! WHAT'S NEXT... WATER-BOARDING?
THIS IS WHAT I'M SAYING!
10/30

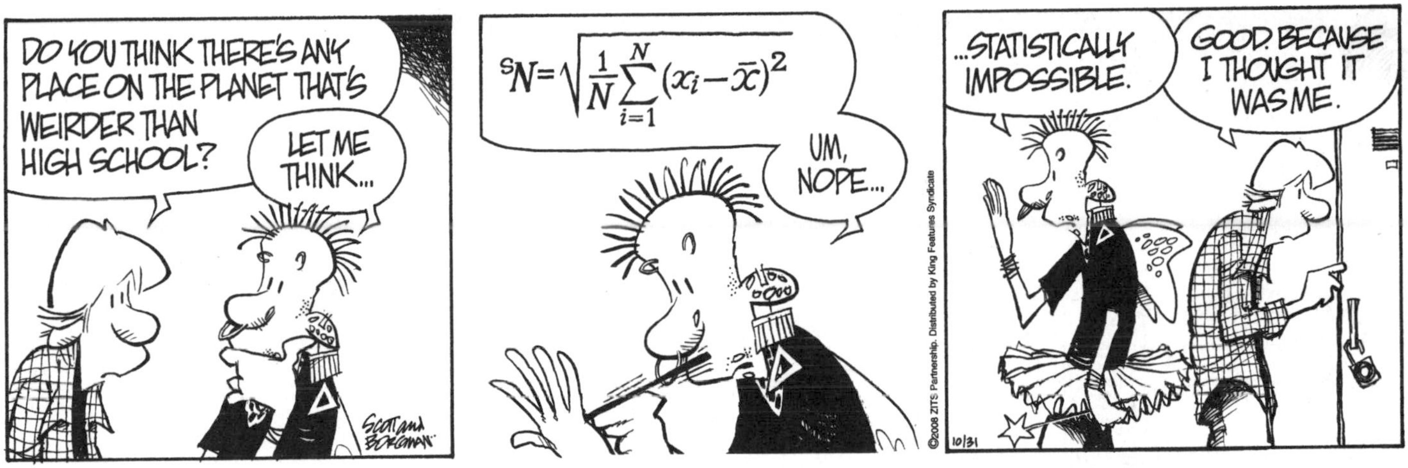
DO YOU THINK THERE'S ANY PLACE ON THE PLANET THAT'S WEIRDER THAN HIGH SCHOOL?
LET ME THINK...
SCOTT AND BORGMAN
$^{s}N=\sqrt{\frac{1}{N}\sum_{i=1}^{N}(x_i-\bar{x})^2}$
UM, NOPE...
©2008 ZITS Partnership. Distributed by King Features Syndicate
10/31
...STATISTICALLY IMPOSSIBLE.
GOOD. BECAUSE I THOUGHT IT WAS ME.

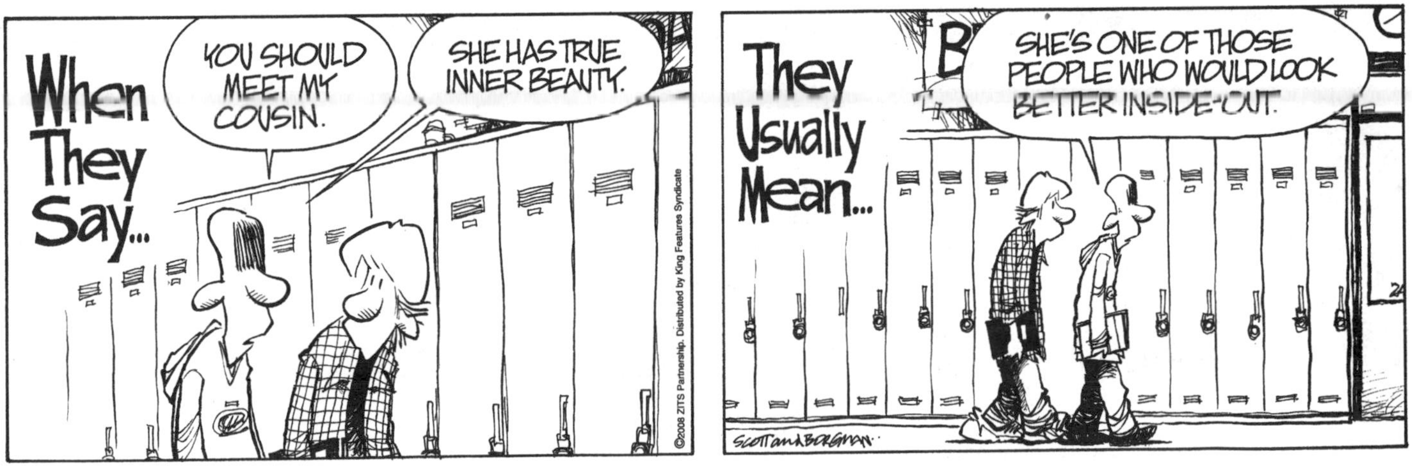
When They Say...
YOU SHOULD MEET MY COUSIN.
SHE HAS TRUE INNER BEAUTY.
©2008 ZITS Partnership. Distributed by King Features Syndicate
They Usually Mean...
SHE'S ONE OF THOSE PEOPLE WHO WOULD LOOK BETTER INSIDE-OUT.
SCOTT AND BORGMAN

Zits
by JERRY SCOTT and JIM BORGMAN

DID YOU BRUSH YOUR TEETH, JEREMY?
YES.
USE DEODORANT?
YES.
DO YOU HAVE ALL OF YOUR HOMEWORK?
YES.
BACKPACK? LUNCH? iPOD?
YES. YES. YES.
CELL PHONE?
YES!!
HEY... WHERE ARE MY SHOES?
ZOOM
SCOTT and BORGMAN 11/2
©2008 ZITS Partnership. Distributed by King Features Syndicate
MY MOM IS SO FORGETFUL.
THEY ALL ARE.

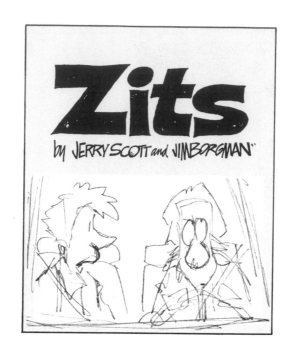

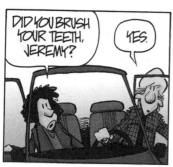

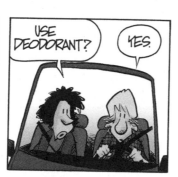

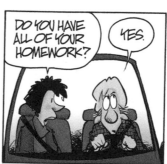

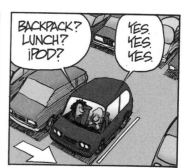

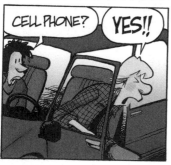

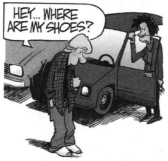

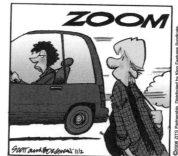

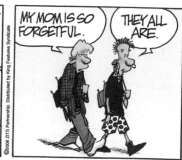

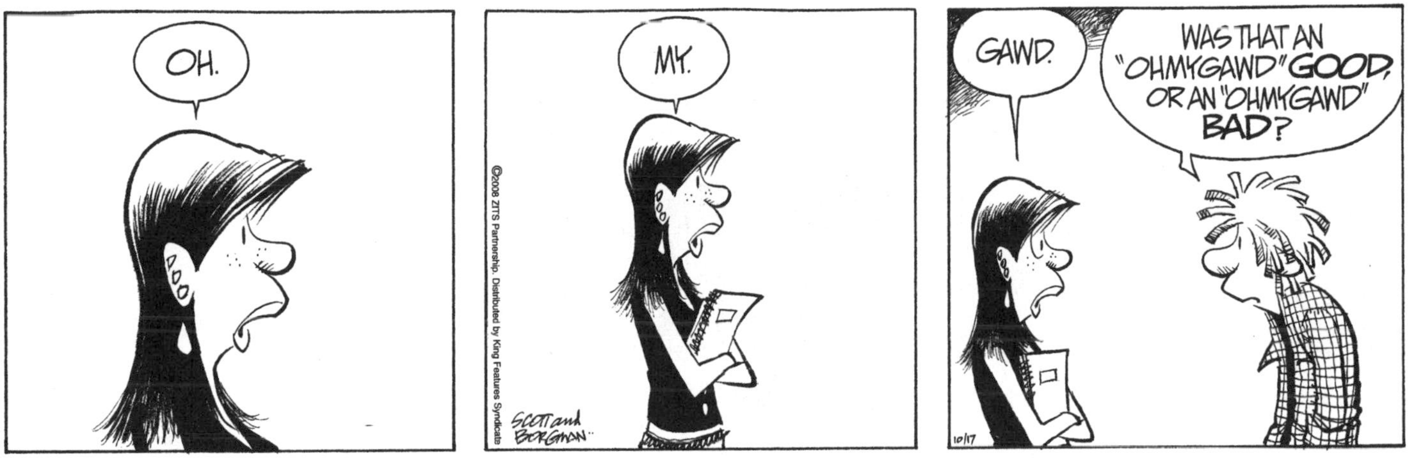
OH.
MY.
©2008 ZITS Partnership. Distributed by King Features Syndicate
SCOTT and BORGMAN
GAWD.
WAS THAT AN "OHMYGAWD" GOOD, OR AN "OHMYGAWD" BAD?
10/17

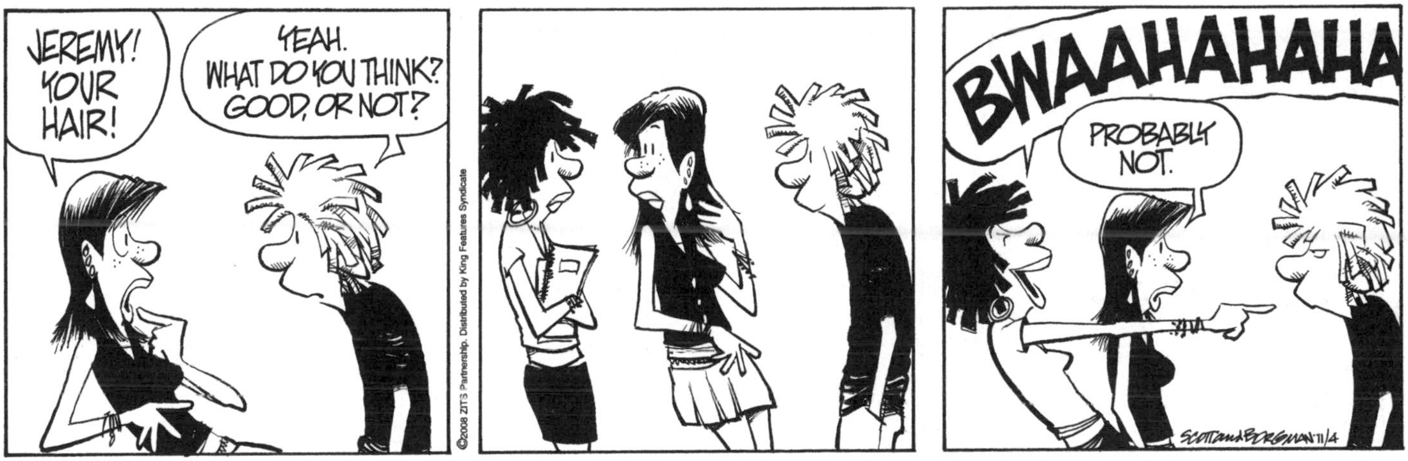
JEREMY! YOUR HAIR!
YEAH. WHAT DO YOU THINK? GOOD, OR NOT?
©2008 ZITS Partnership. Distributed by King Features Syndicate
BWAAHAHAHA
PROBABLY NOT.
SCOTT and BORGMAN 11/4

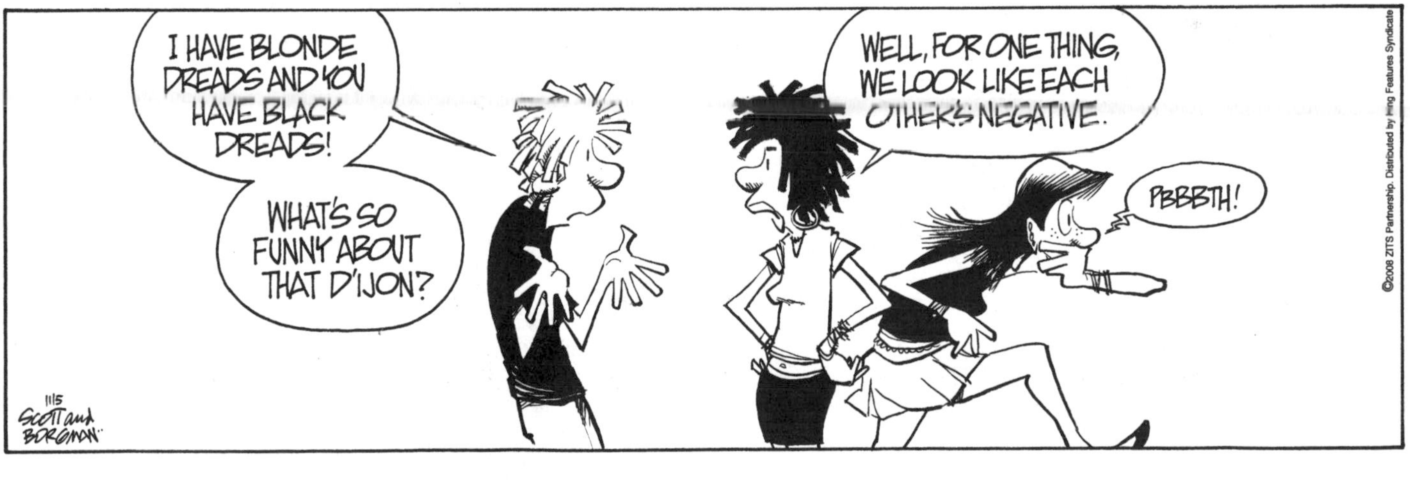
I HAVE BLONDE DREADS AND YOU HAVE BLACK DREADS!
WHAT'S SO FUNNY ABOUT THAT D'IJON?
WELL, FOR ONE THING, WE LOOK LIKE EACH OTHER'S NEGATIVE.
PBBBTH!
11/5 SCOTT and BORGMAN
©2008 ZITS Partnership. Distributed by King Features Syndicate

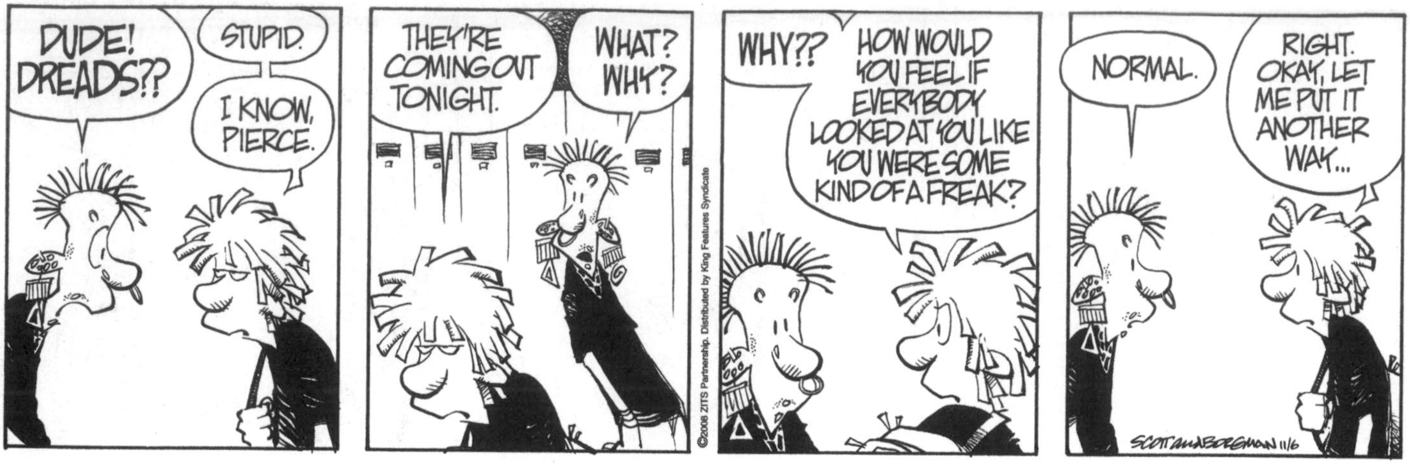
DUDE! DREADS??
STUPID.
I KNOW, PIERCE.
THEY'RE COMING OUT TONIGHT.
WHAT? WHY?
©2008 ZITS Partnership. Distributed by King Features Syndicate
WHY??
HOW WOULD YOU FEEL IF EVERYBODY LOOKED AT YOU LIKE YOU WERE SOME KIND OF A FREAK?
NORMAL.
RIGHT. OKAY, LET ME PUT IT ANOTHER WAY...
SCOTT and BORGMAN 11/6

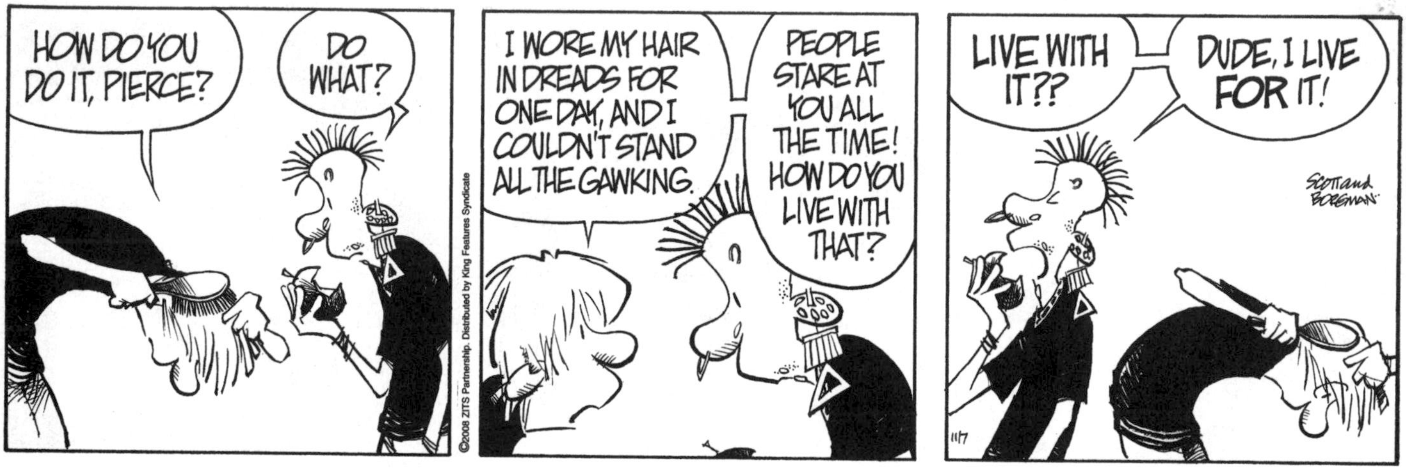
HOW DO YOU DO IT, PIERCE?
DO WHAT?
©2008 ZITS Partnership. Distributed by King Features Syndicate
I WORE MY HAIR IN DREADS FOR ONE DAY, AND I COULDN'T STAND ALL THE GAWKING.
PEOPLE STARE AT YOU ALL THE TIME! HOW DO YOU LIVE WITH THAT?
11/7
LIVE WITH IT??
DUDE, I LIVE **FOR** IT!
SCOTT and BORGMAN

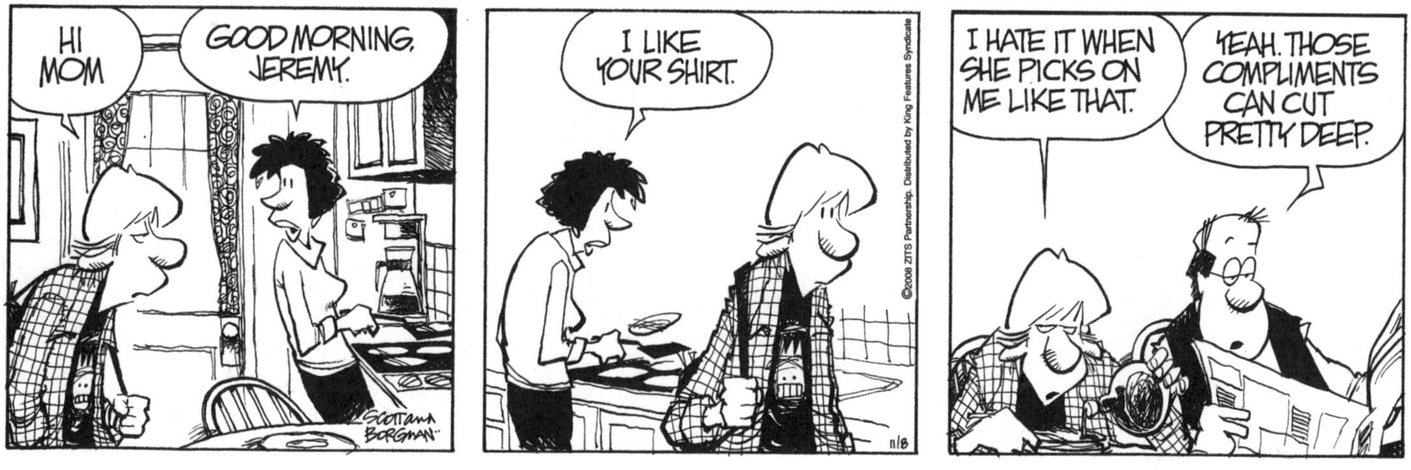
HI MOM
GOOD MORNING, JEREMY.
SCOTT and BORGMAN
I LIKE YOUR SHIRT.
©2008 ZITS Partnership. Distributed by King Features Syndicate
11/8
I HATE IT WHEN SHE PICKS ON ME LIKE THAT.
YEAH. THOSE COMPLIMENTS CAN CUT PRETTY DEEP.

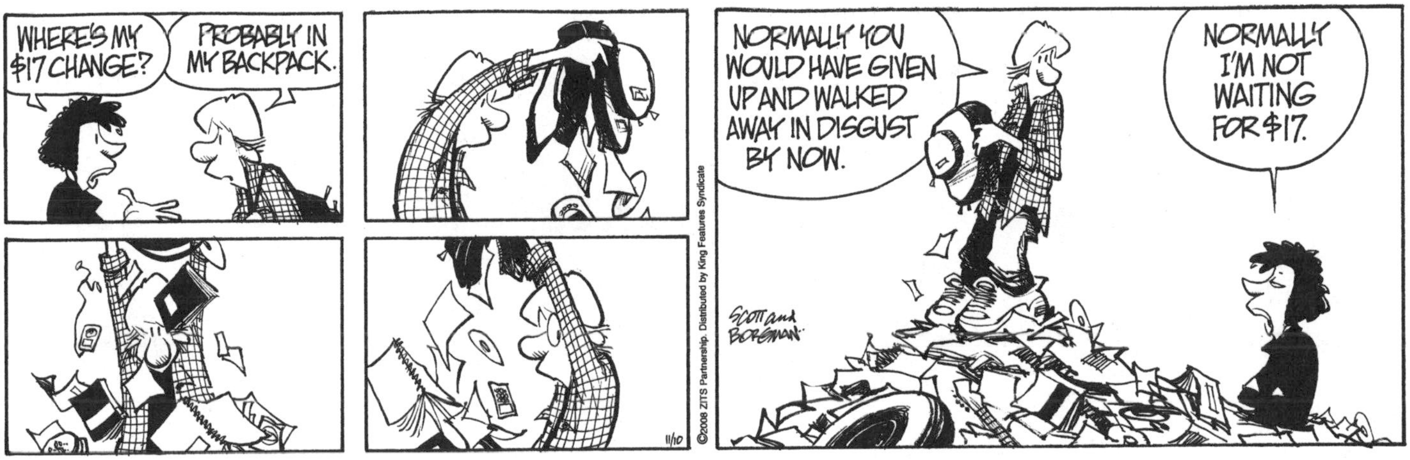
WHERE'S MY $17 CHANGE?
PROBABLY IN MY BACKPACK.
NORMALLY YOU WOULD HAVE GIVEN UP AND WALKED AWAY IN DISGUST BY NOW.
NORMALLY I'M NOT WAITING FOR $17.
SCOTT AND BORGMAN
©2008 ZITS Partnership. Distributed by King Features Syndicate
11/10

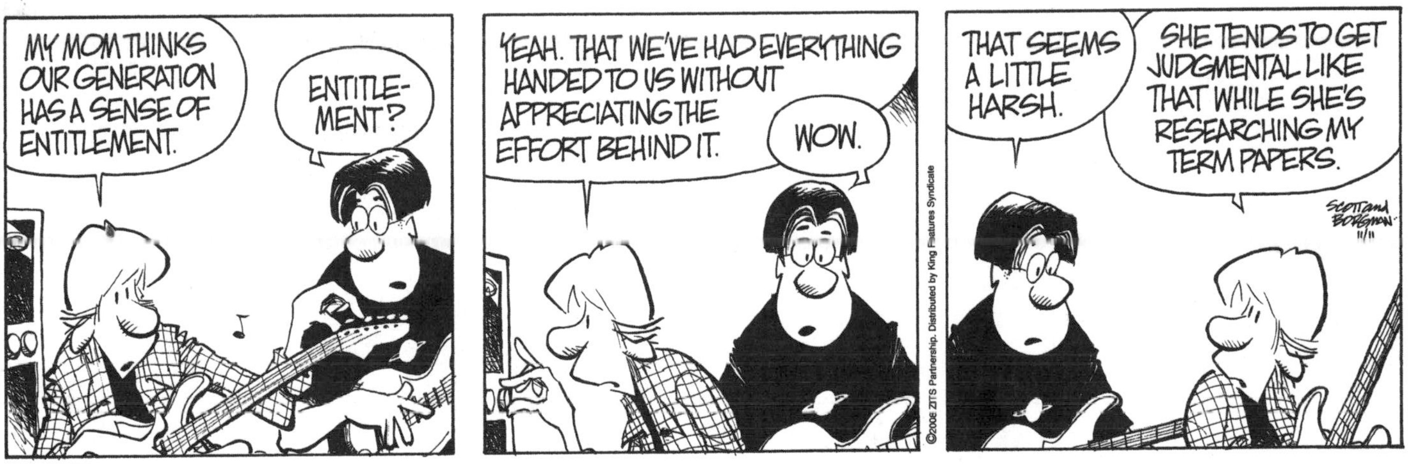
MY MOM THINKS OUR GENERATION HAS A SENSE OF ENTITLEMENT.
ENTITLE-MENT?
YEAH. THAT WE'VE HAD EVERYTHING HANDED TO US WITHOUT APPRECIATING THE EFFORT BEHIND IT.
WOW.
THAT SEEMS A LITTLE HARSH.
SHE TENDS TO GET JUDGMENTAL LIKE THAT WHILE SHE'S RESEARCHING MY TERM PAPERS.
SCOTT AND BORGMAN 11/11
©2008 ZITS Partnership. Distributed by King Features Syndicate

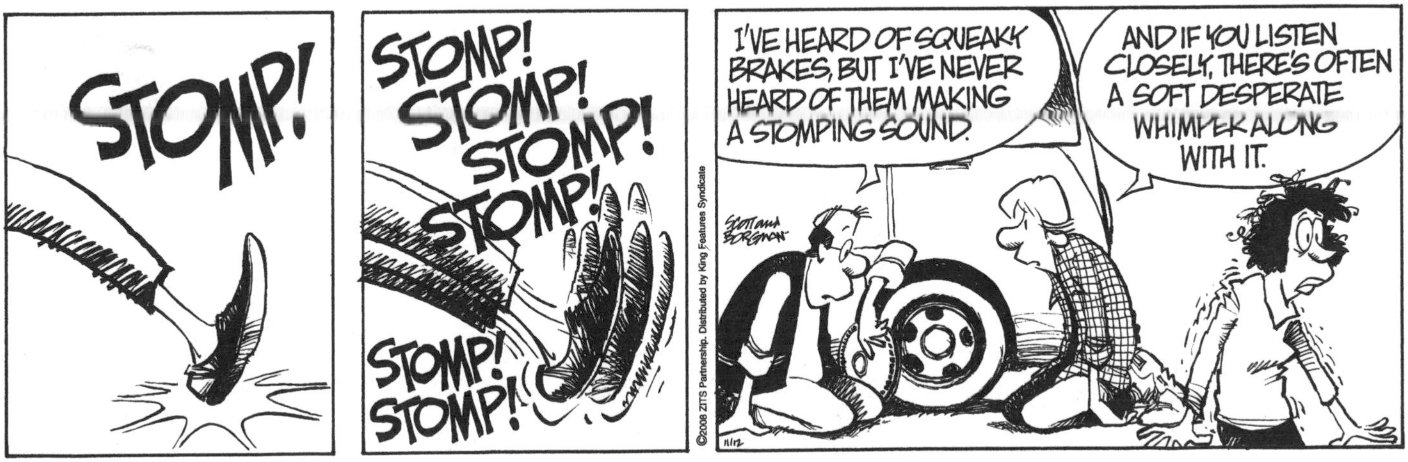
STOMP!
STOMP! STOMP! STOMP! STOMP!
STOMP! STOMP!
I'VE HEARD OF SQUEAKY BRAKES, BUT I'VE NEVER HEARD OF THEM MAKING A STOMPING SOUND.
AND IF YOU LISTEN CLOSELY, THERE'S OFTEN A SOFT DESPERATE WHIMPER ALONG WITH IT.
SCOTT AND BORGMAN
©2008 ZITS Partnership. Distributed by King Features Syndicate
11/12

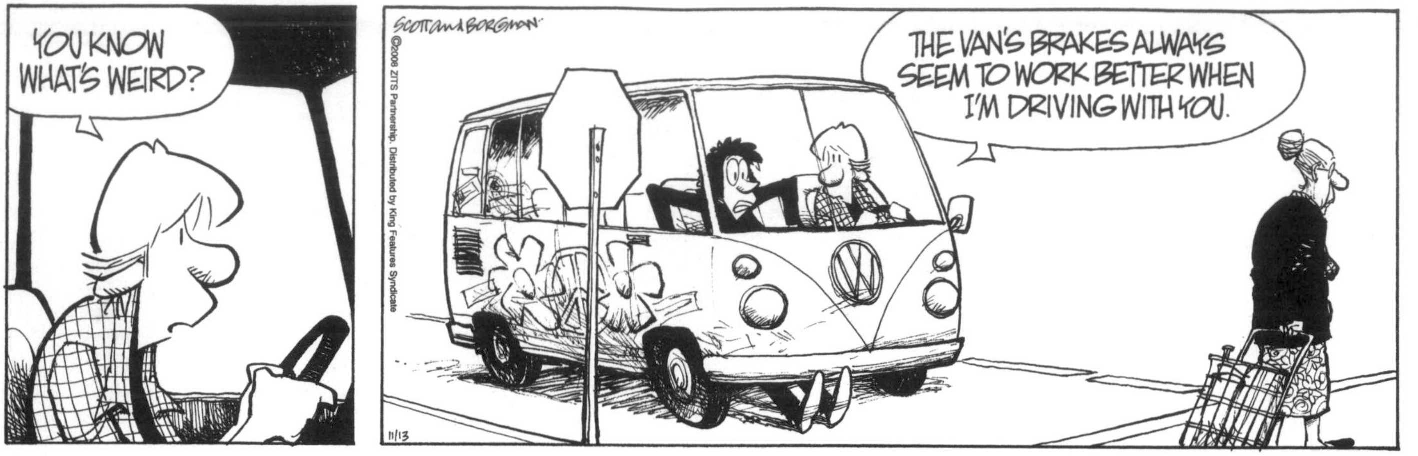
YOU KNOW WHAT'S WEIRD?
SCOTT and BORGMAN
©2008 ZITS Partnership. Distributed by King Features Syndicate
THE VAN'S BRAKES ALWAYS SEEM TO WORK BETTER WHEN I'M DRIVING WITH YOU.
11/13

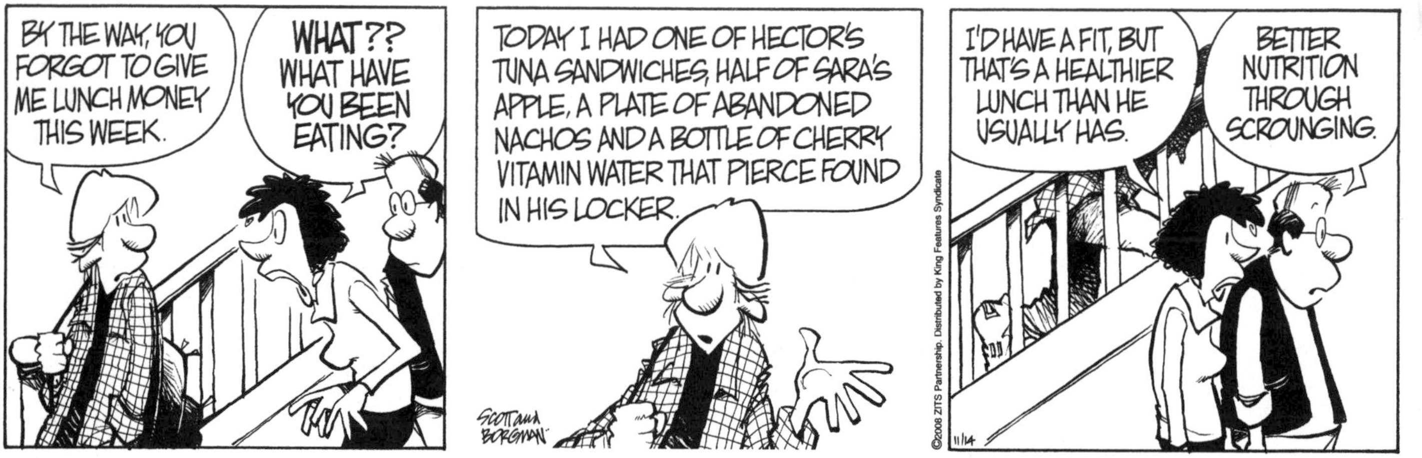
BY THE WAY, YOU FORGOT TO GIVE ME LUNCH MONEY THIS WEEK.
WHAT?? WHAT HAVE YOU BEEN EATING?
TODAY I HAD ONE OF HECTOR'S TUNA SANDWICHES, HALF OF SARA'S APPLE, A PLATE OF ABANDONED NACHOS AND A BOTTLE OF CHERRY VITAMIN WATER THAT PIERCE FOUND IN HIS LOCKER.
SCOTT and BORGMAN
I'D HAVE A FIT, BUT THAT'S A HEALTHIER LUNCH THAN HE USUALLY HAS.
BETTER NUTRITION THROUGH SCROUNGING.
©2008 ZITS Partnership. Distributed by King Features Syndicate
11/14

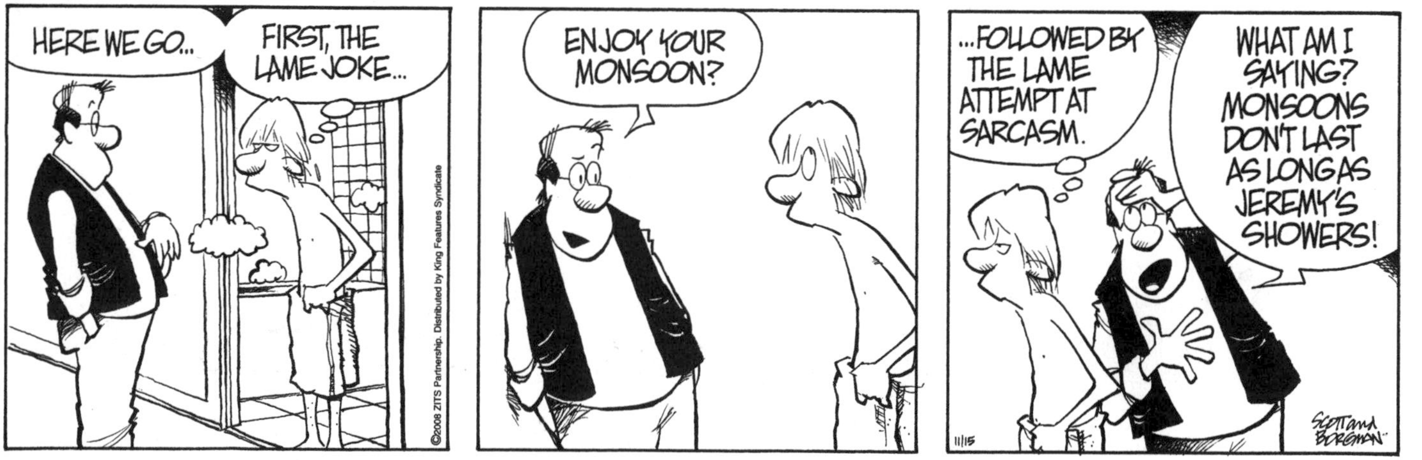
HERE WE GO...
FIRST, THE LAME JOKE...
©2008 ZITS Partnership. Distributed by King Features Syndicate
ENJOY YOUR MONSOON?
...FOLLOWED BY THE LAME ATTEMPT AT SARCASM.
WHAT AM I SAYING? MONSOONS DON'T LAST AS LONG AS JEREMY'S SHOWERS!
11/15
SCOTT and BORGMAN

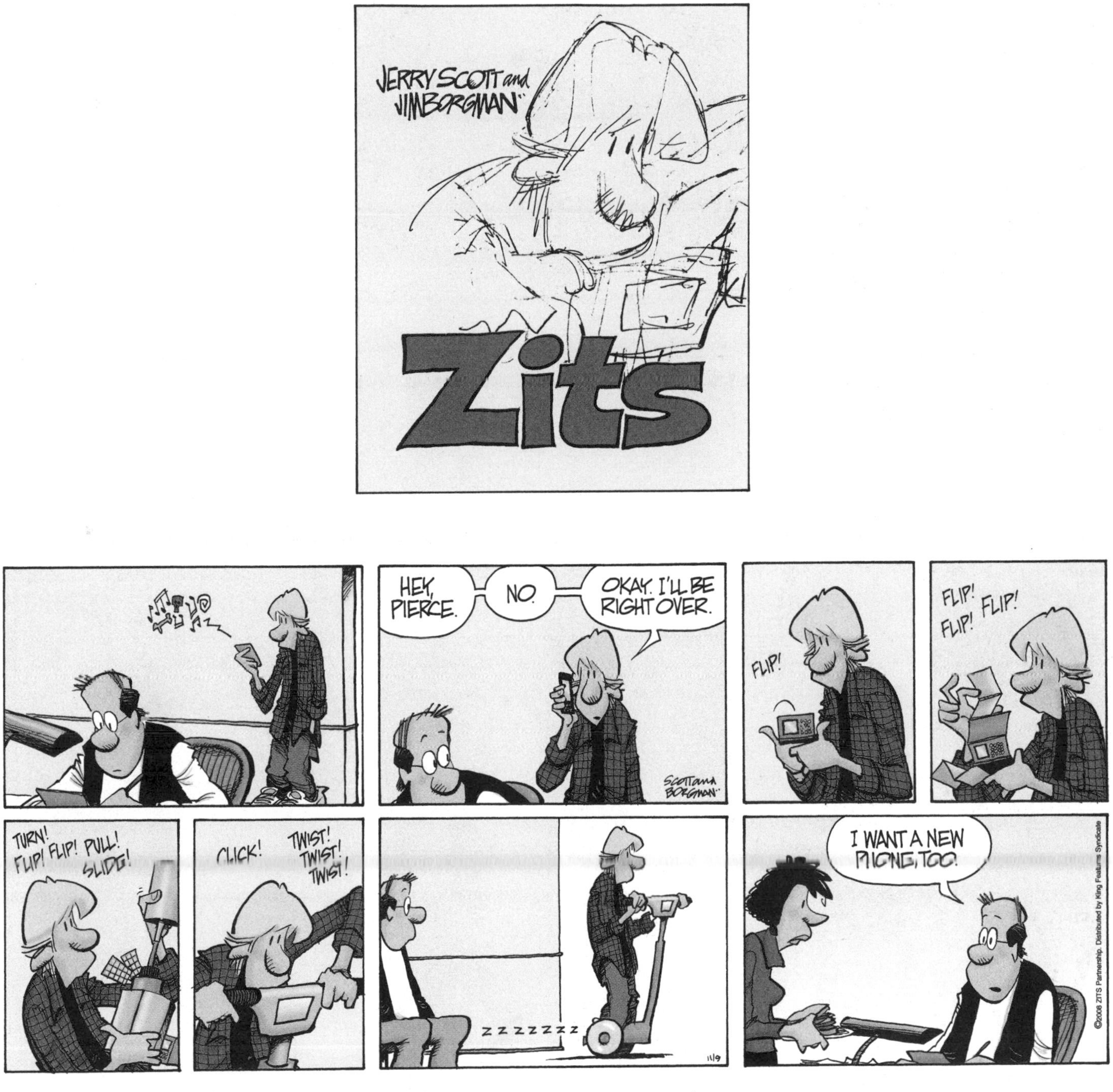
JERRY SCOTT and JIM BORGMAN
ZITS
HEY, PIERCE.
NO.
OKAY. I'LL BE RIGHT OVER.
SCOTT and BORGMAN
FLIP!
FLIP! FLIP! FLIP!
TURN! FLIP! FLIP! PULL! SLIDE!
CLICK! TWIST! TWIST! TWIST!
ZZZZZZZ
11/9
I WANT A NEW PHONE, TOO!
©2008 ZITS Partnership. Distributed by King Features Syndicate

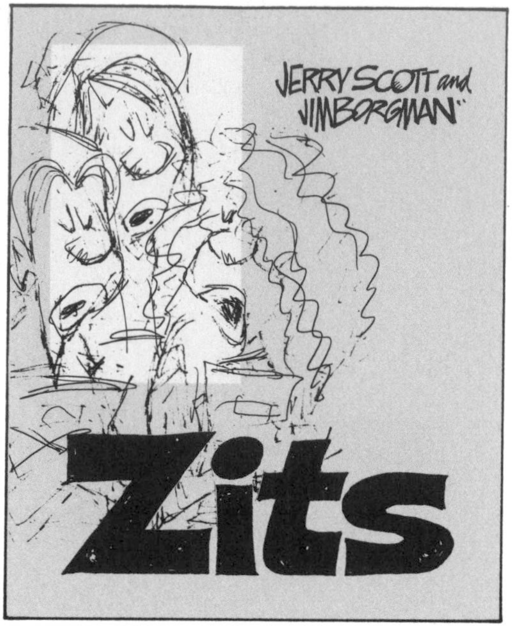

JERRY SCOTT and JIM BORGMAN
Zits

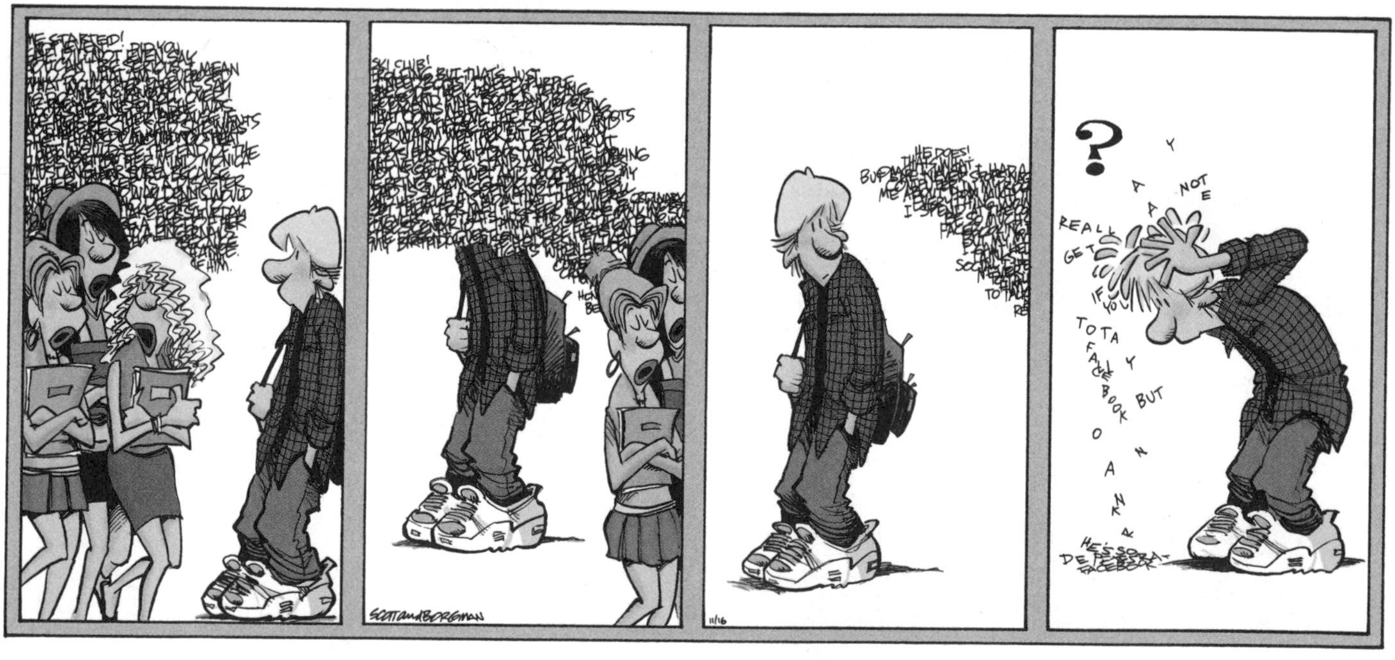

SCOTT and BORGMAN
11/16
?

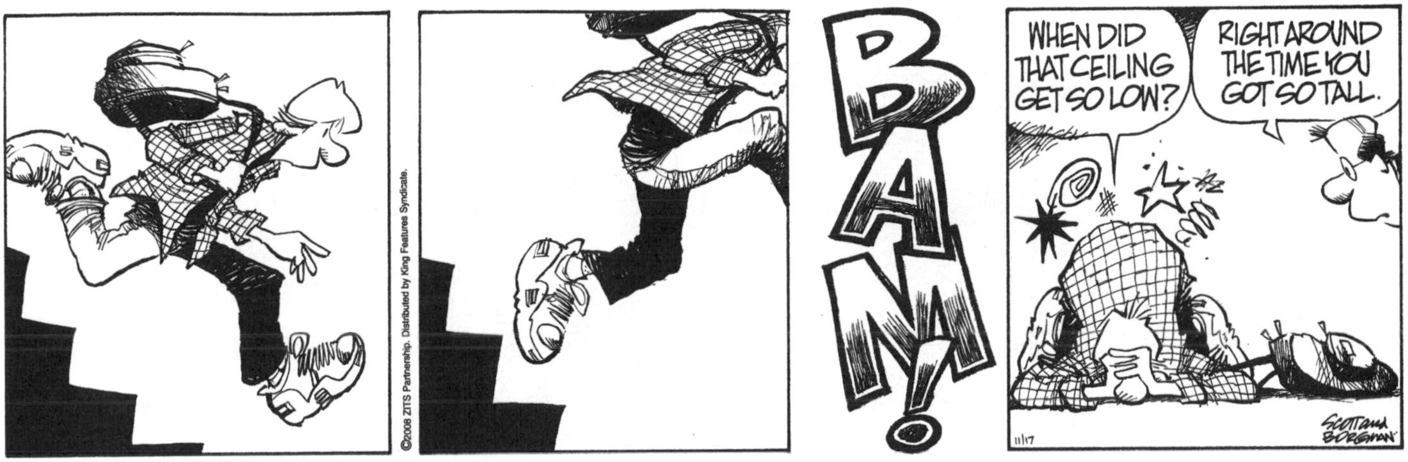
©2008 ZITS Partnership. Distributed by King Features Syndicate.
BAM!
WHEN DID THAT CEILING GET SO LOW?
RIGHT AROUND THE TIME YOU GOT SO TALL.
11/17
SCOTT AND BORGMAN

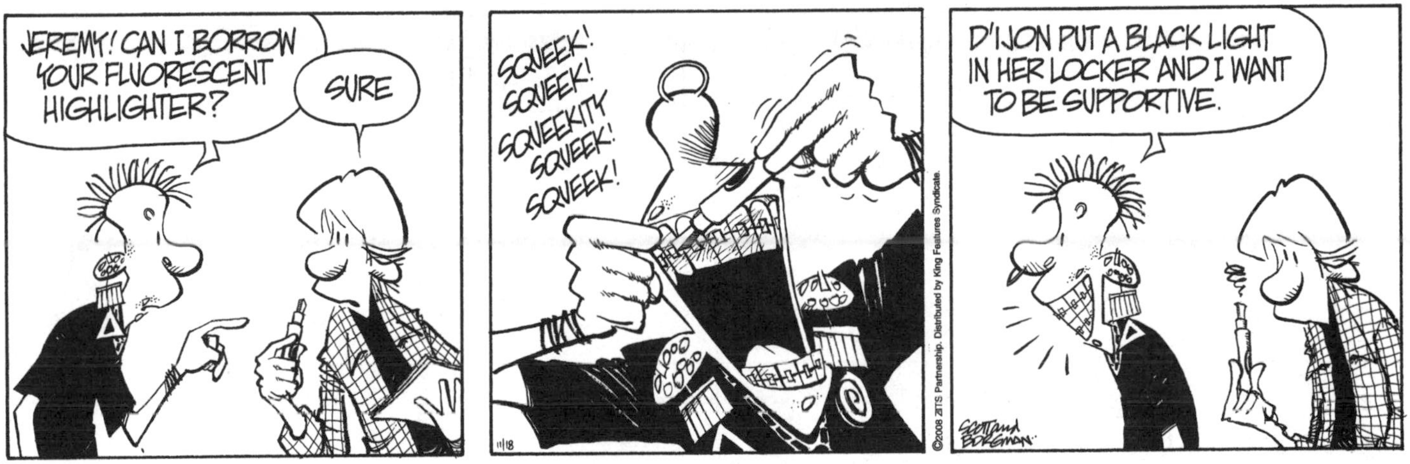
JEREMY! CAN I BORROW YOUR FLUORESCENT HIGHLIGHTER?
SURE
SQUEEK! SQUEEK! SQUEEKITY SQUEEK! SQUEEK!
11/18
©2008 ZITS Partnership. Distributed by King Features Syndicate.
D'IJON PUT A BLACK LIGHT IN HER LOCKER AND I WANT TO BE SUPPORTIVE.
SCOTT AND BORGMAN

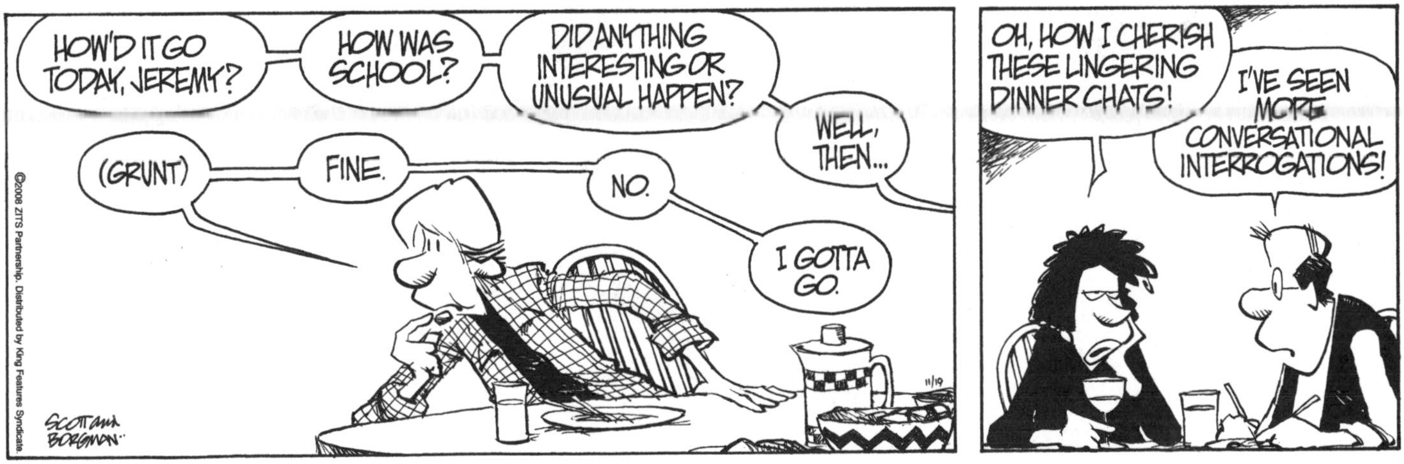
HOW'D IT GO TODAY, JEREMY?
(GRUNT)
HOW WAS SCHOOL?
FINE.
DID ANYTHING INTERESTING OR UNUSUAL HAPPEN?
NO.
WELL, THEN...
I GOTTA GO.
©2008 ZITS Partnership. Distributed by King Features Syndicate.
SCOTT AND BORGMAN
11/19
OH, HOW I CHERISH THESE LINGERING DINNER CHATS!
I'VE SEEN MORE CONVERSATIONAL INTERROGATIONS!

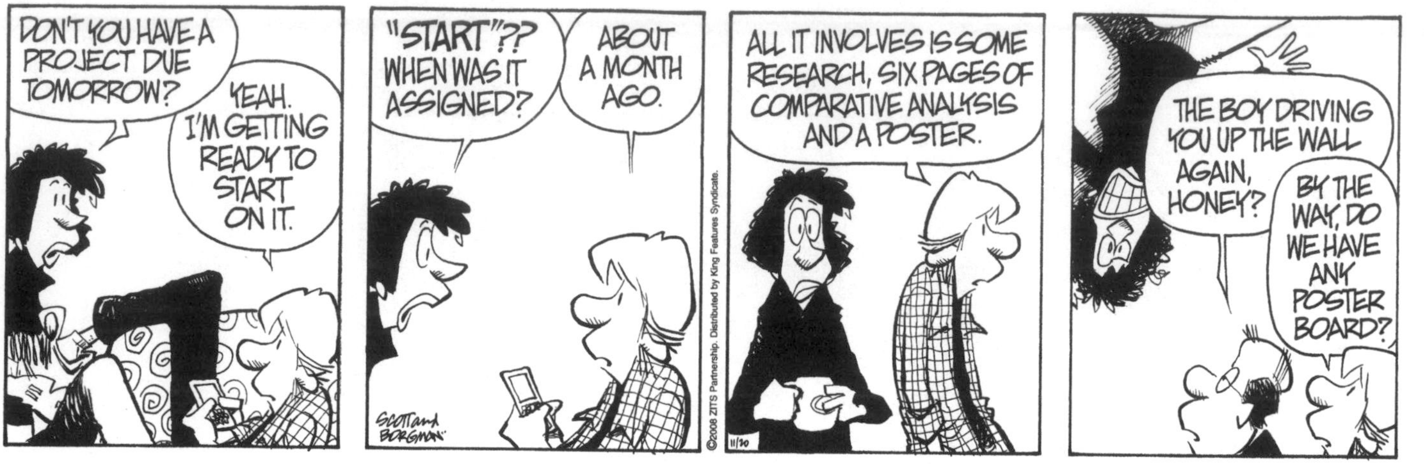
DON'T YOU HAVE A PROJECT DUE TOMORROW?
YEAH. I'M GETTING READY TO START ON IT.
"START"?? WHEN WAS IT ASSIGNED?
ABOUT A MONTH AGO.
ALL IT INVOLVES IS SOME RESEARCH, SIX PAGES OF COMPARATIVE ANALYSIS AND A POSTER.
THE BOY DRIVING YOU UP THE WALL AGAIN, HONEY?
BY THE WAY, DO WE HAVE ANY POSTER BOARD?
©2008 ZITS Partnership. Distributed by King Features Syndicate.

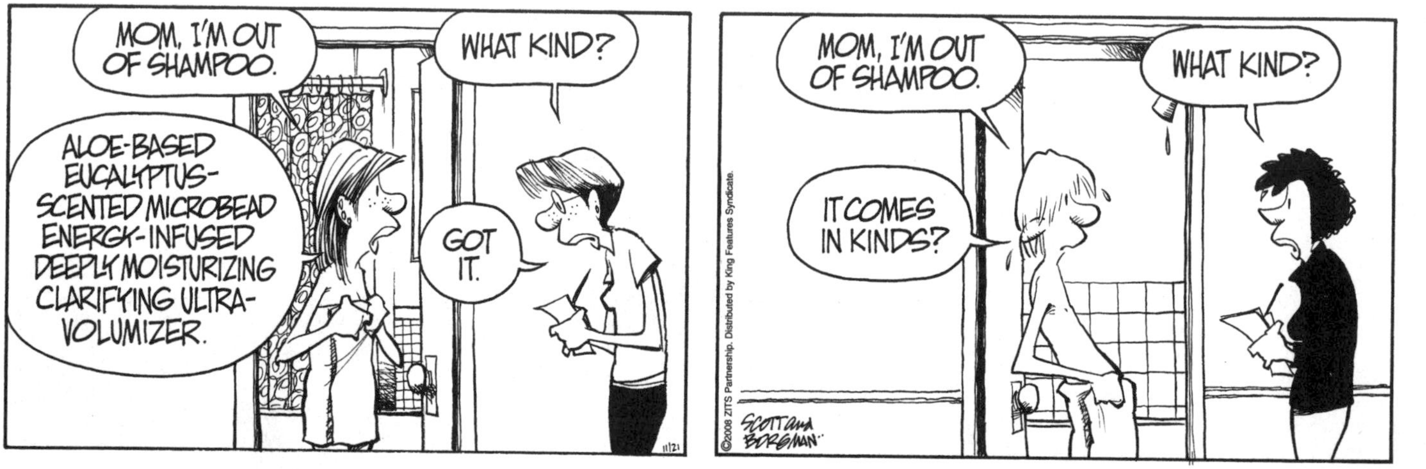
MOM, I'M OUT OF SHAMPOO.
WHAT KIND?
ALOE-BASED EUCALYPTUS-SCENTED MICROBEAD ENERGY-INFUSED DEEPLY MOISTURIZING CLARIFYING ULTRA-VOLUMIZER.
GOT IT.
MOM, I'M OUT OF SHAMPOO.
WHAT KIND?
IT COMES IN KINDS?
©2008 ZITS Partnership. Distributed by King Features Syndicate.

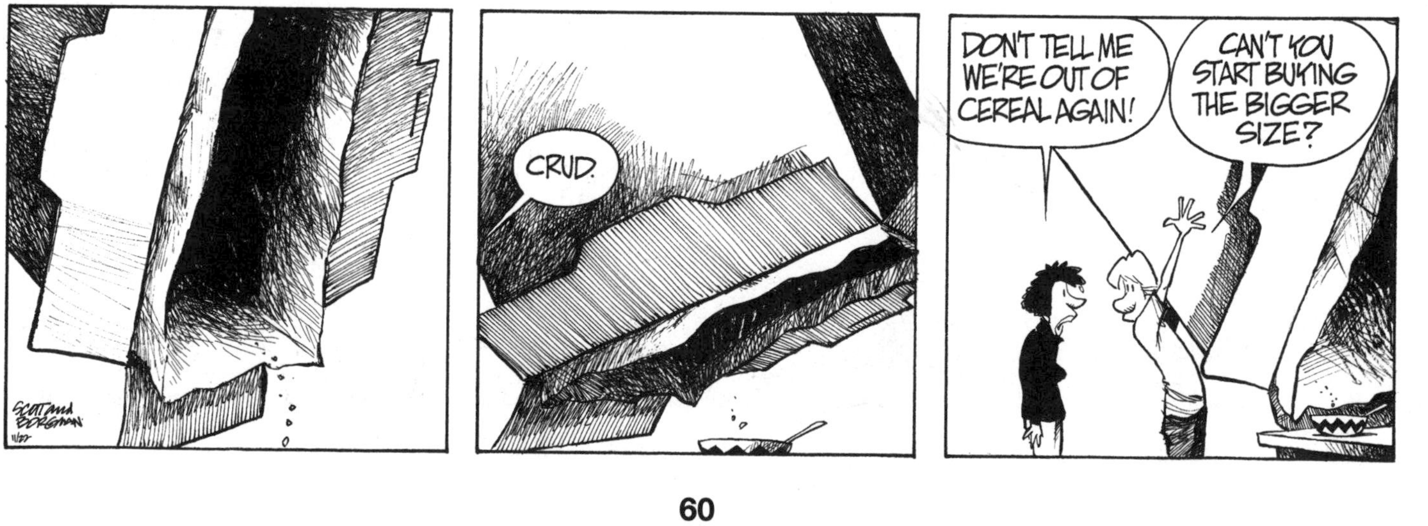
CRUD.
DON'T TELL ME WE'RE OUT OF CEREAL AGAIN!
CAN'T YOU START BUYING THE BIGGER SIZE?

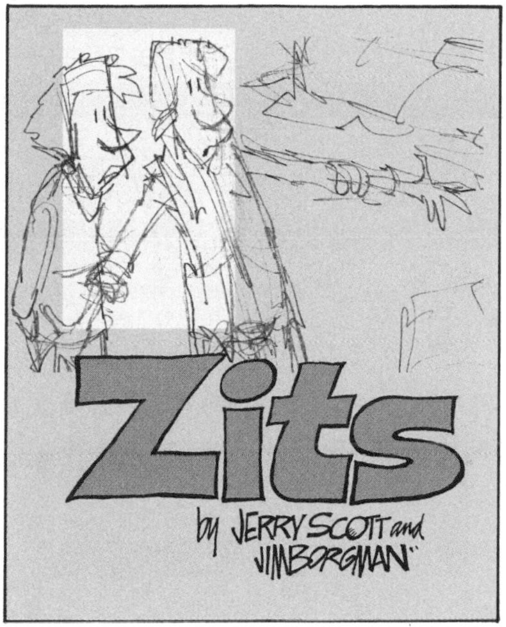
Zits
by JERRY SCOTT and JIM BORGMAN

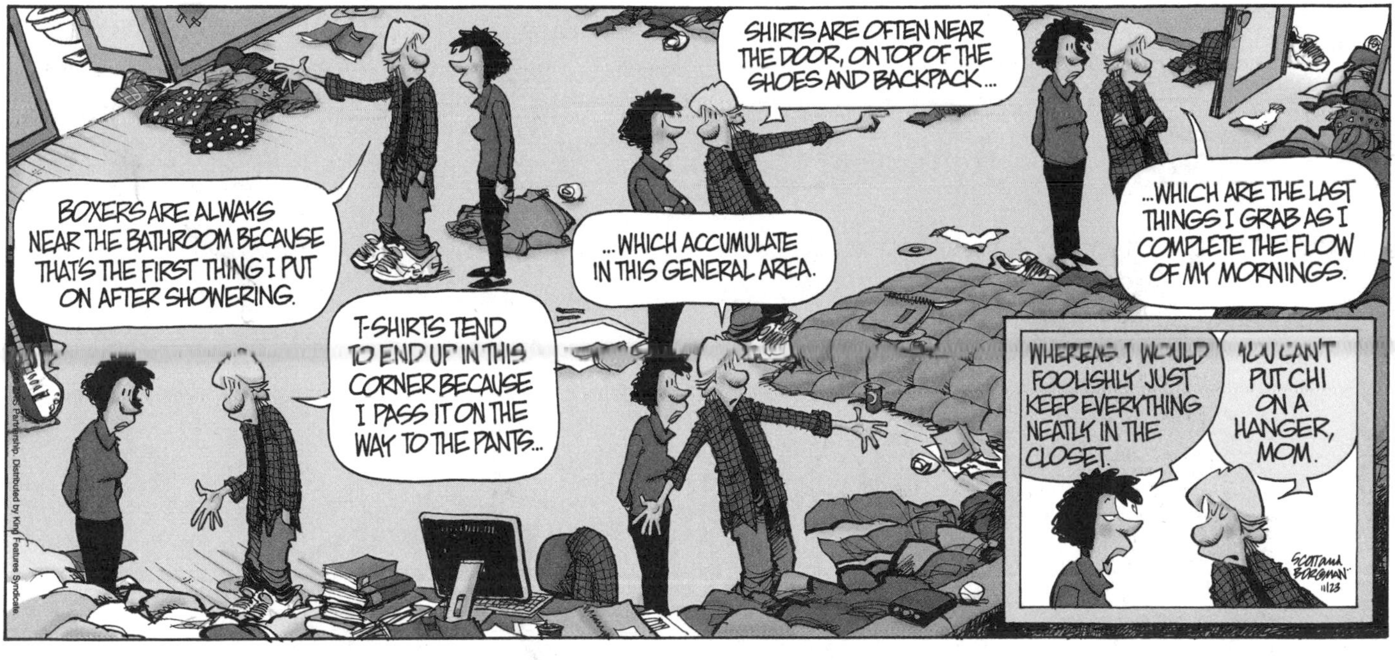
BOXERS ARE ALWAYS NEAR THE BATHROOM BECAUSE THAT'S THE FIRST THING I PUT ON AFTER SHOWERING.
T-SHIRTS TEND TO END UP IN THIS CORNER BECAUSE I PASS IT ON THE WAY TO THE PANTS...
...WHICH ACCUMULATE IN THIS GENERAL AREA.
SHIRTS ARE OFTEN NEAR THE DOOR, ON TOP OF THE SHOES AND BACKPACK...
...WHICH ARE THE LAST THINGS I GRAB AS I COMPLETE THE FLOW OF MY MORNINGS.
WHEREAS I WOULD FOOLISHLY JUST KEEP EVERYTHING NEATLY IN THE CLOSET.
YOU CAN'T PUT CHI ON A HANGER, MOM.
SCOTT and BORGMAN 11/23
Partnership. Distributed by King Features Syndicate.

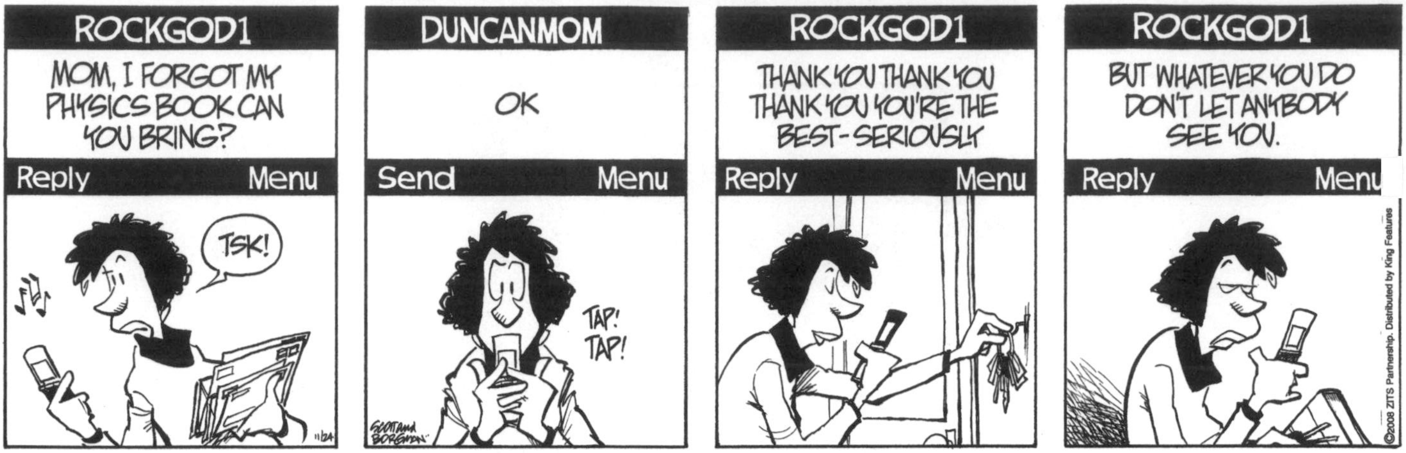
ROCKGOD1
MOM, I FORGOT MY PHYSICS BOOK CAN YOU BRING?
Reply
Menu
TSK!
11/24
DUNCANMOM
OK
Send
Menu
TAP! TAP!
ROCKGOD1
THANK YOU THANK YOU THANK YOU YOU'RE THE BEST - SERIOUSLY
Reply
Menu
ROCKGOD1
BUT WHATEVER YOU DO DON'T LET ANYBODY SEE YOU.
Reply
Menu
©2008 ZITS Partnership. Distributed by King Features

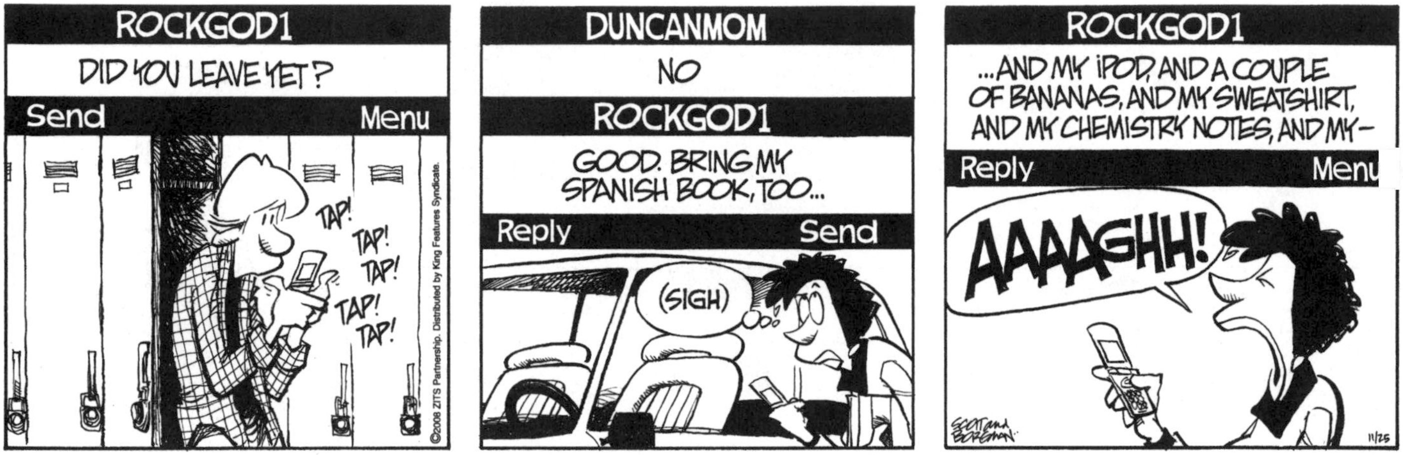
ROCKGOD1
DID YOU LEAVE YET?
Send
Menu
TAP! TAP! TAP! TAP! TAP!
©2008 ZITS Partnership. Distributed by King Features Syndicate.
DUNCANMOM
NO
ROCKGOD1
GOOD. BRING MY SPANISH BOOK, TOO...
Reply
Send
(SIGH)
ROCKGOD1
...AND MY iPOD, AND A COUPLE OF BANANAS, AND MY SWEATSHIRT, AND MY CHEMISTRY NOTES, AND MY–
Reply
Menu
AAAAGHH!
11/25

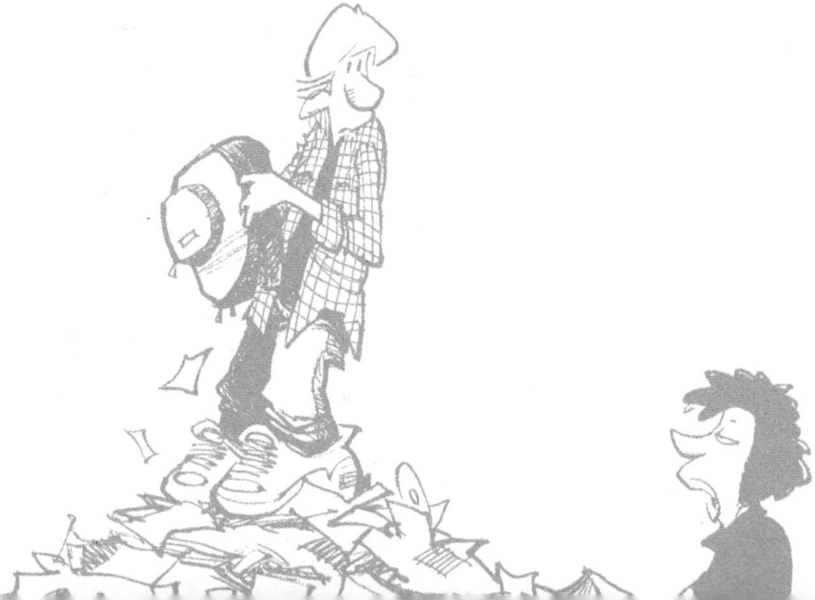

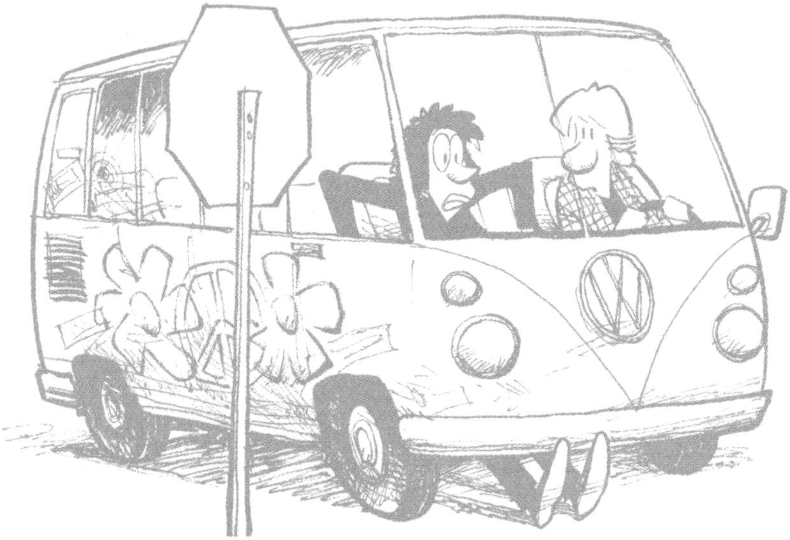

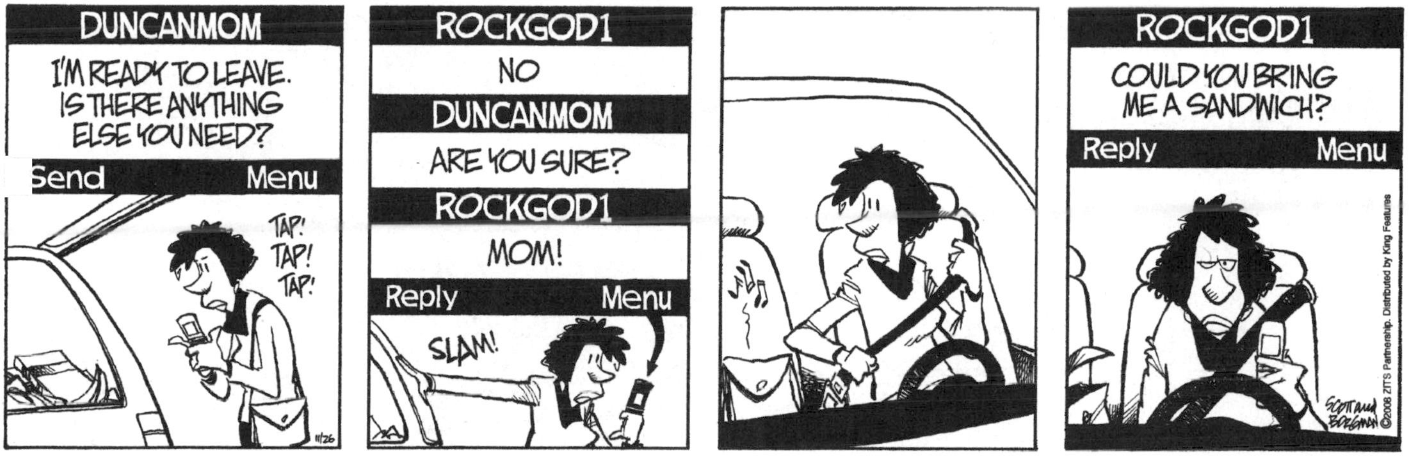
DUNCANMOM
I'M READY TO LEAVE. IS THERE ANYTHING ELSE YOU NEED?
Send
Menu
TAP! TAP! TAP!
11/26
ROCKGOD1
NO
DUNCANMOM
ARE YOU SURE?
ROCKGOD1
MOM!
Reply
Menu
SLAM!
ROCKGOD1
COULD YOU BRING ME A SANDWICH?
Reply
Menu
©2008 ZITS Partnership. Distributed by King Features
SCOTT and BORGMAN

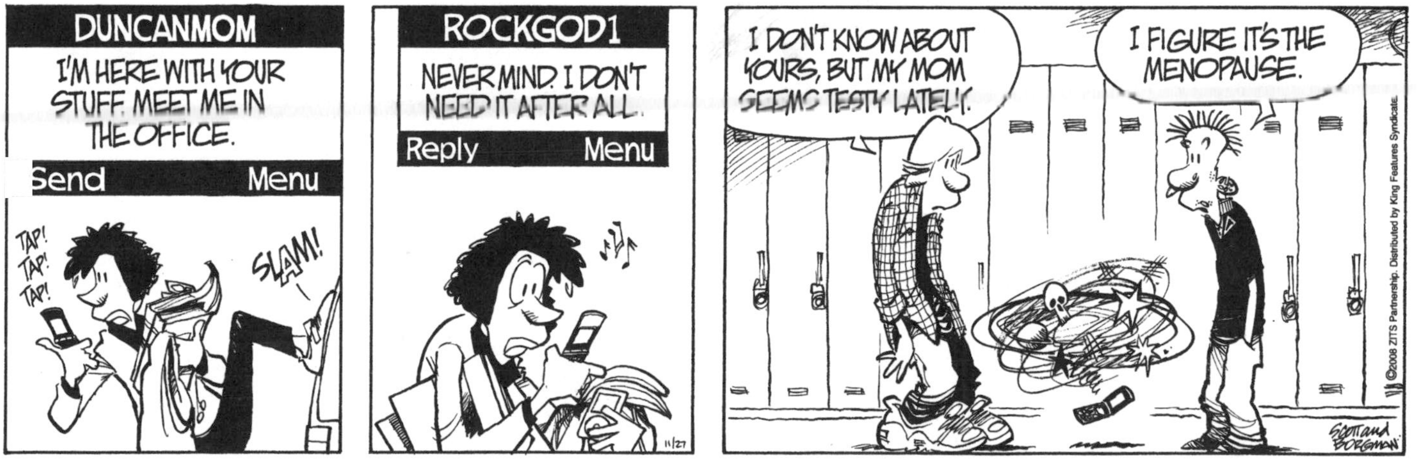
DUNCANMOM
I'M HERE WITH YOUR STUFF. MEET ME IN THE OFFICE.
Send
Menu
TAP! TAP! TAP!
SLAM!
ROCKGOD1
NEVER MIND. I DON'T NEED IT AFTER ALL.
Reply
Menu
11/27
I DON'T KNOW ABOUT YOURS, BUT MY MOM SEEMS TESTY LATELY.
I FIGURE IT'S THE MENOPAUSE.
©2008 ZITS Partnership. Distributed by King Features Syndicate.
SCOTT and BORGMAN

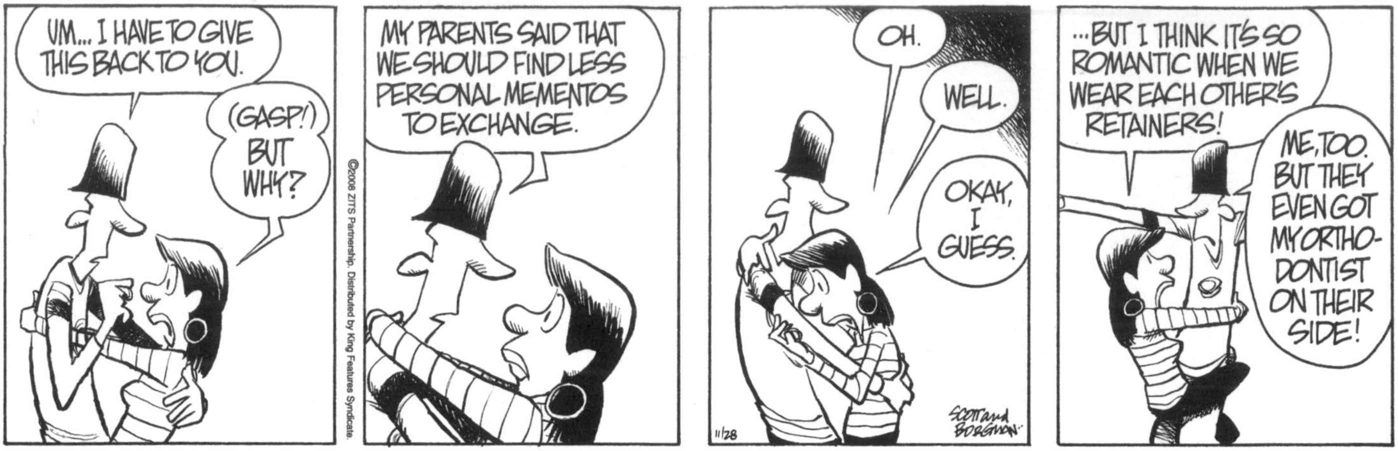
UM... I HAVE TO GIVE THIS BACK TO YOU.
(GASP!) BUT WHY?
MY PARENTS SAID THAT WE SHOULD FIND LESS PERSONAL MEMENTOS TO EXCHANGE.
©2006 ZITS Partnership. Distributed by King Features Syndicate.
OH.
WELL.
OKAY, I GUESS.
11/28
SCOTT and BORGMAN
...BUT I THINK IT'S SO ROMANTIC WHEN WE WEAR EACH OTHER'S RETAINERS!
ME, TOO. BUT THEY EVEN GOT MY ORTHODONTIST ON THEIR SIDE!

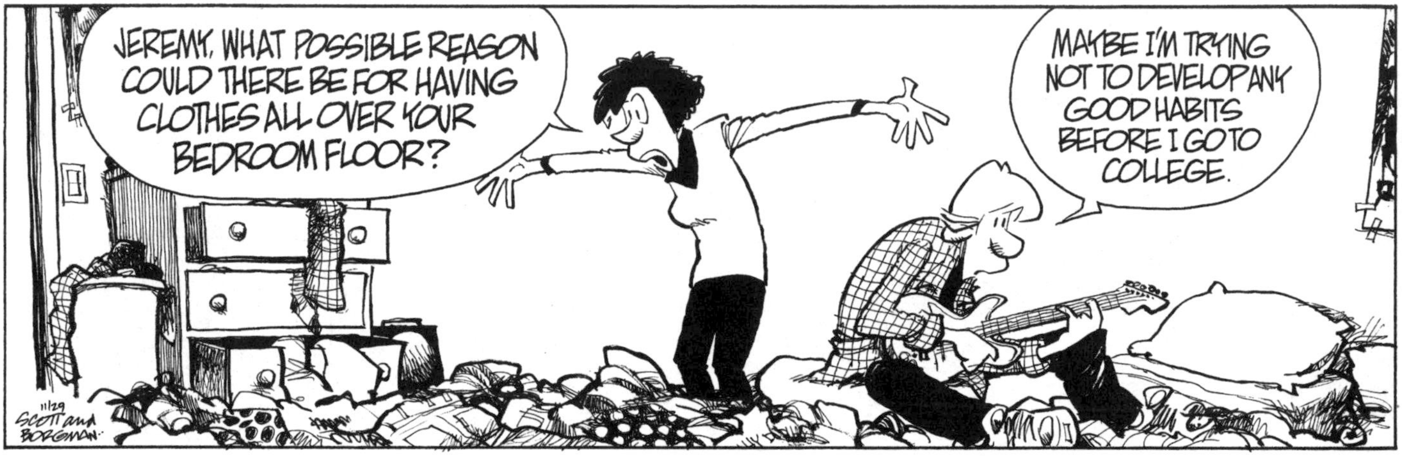
JEREMY, WHAT POSSIBLE REASON COULD THERE BE FOR HAVING CLOTHES ALL OVER YOUR BEDROOM FLOOR?
MAYBE I'M TRYING NOT TO DEVELOP ANY GOOD HABITS BEFORE I GO TO COLLEGE.
11/29
SCOTT and BORGMAN

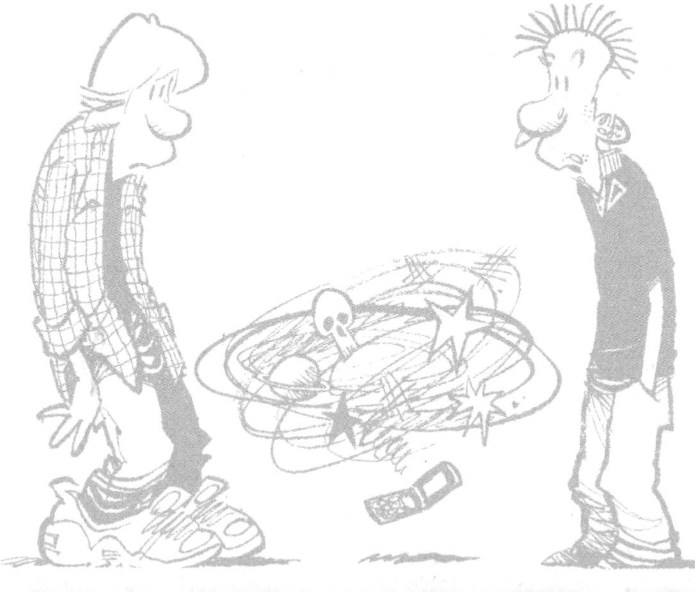

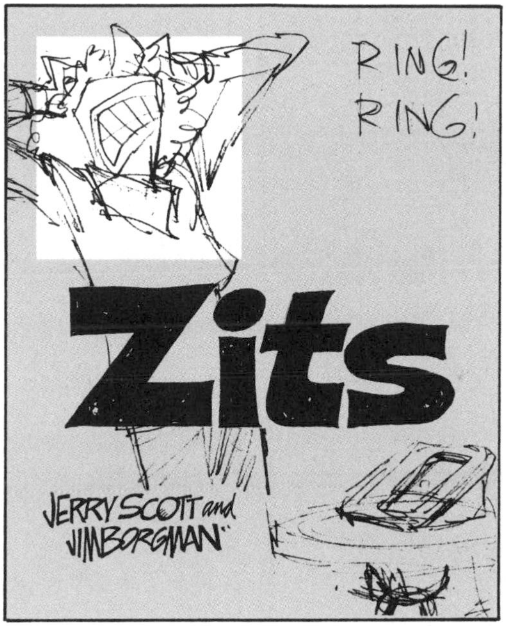
RING!
RING!
Zits
JERRY SCOTT and
JIM BORGMAN

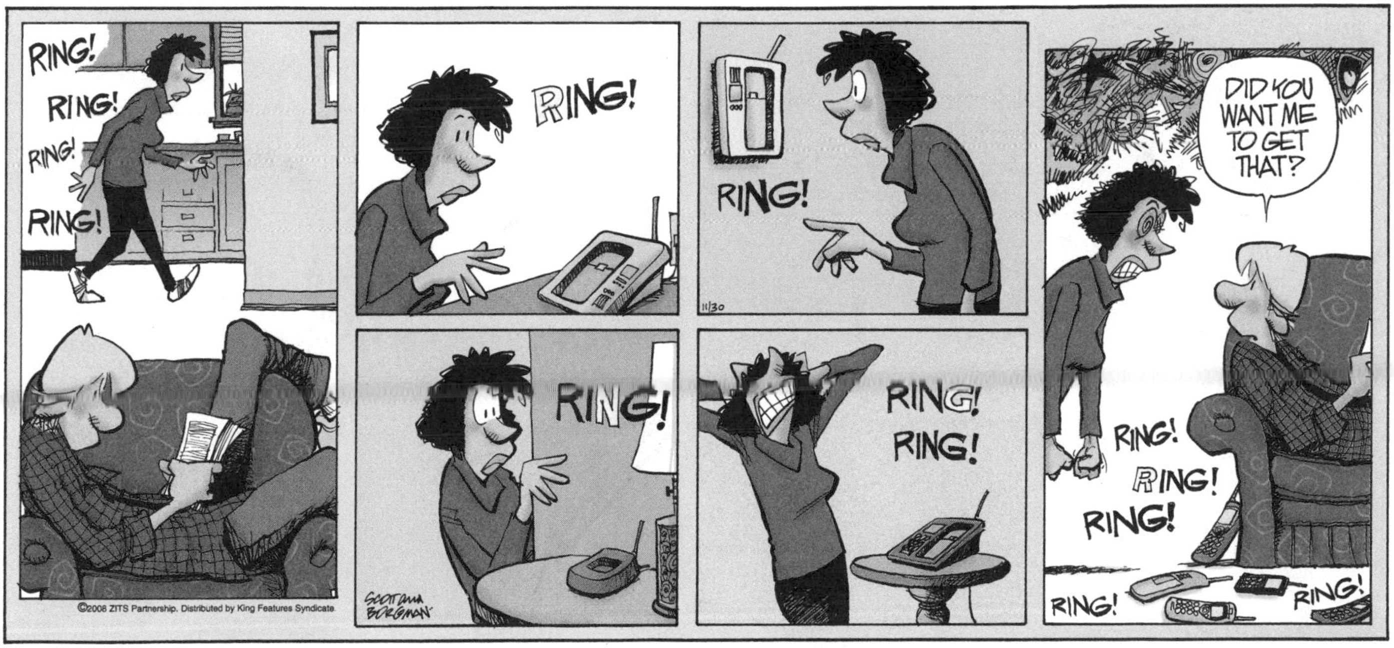
RING!
RING!
RING!
RING!
RING!
RING!
RING!
RING!
RING!
DID YOU WANT ME TO GET THAT?
RING!
RING!
RING!
RING!
RING!
©2008 ZITS Partnership. Distributed by King Features Syndicate.

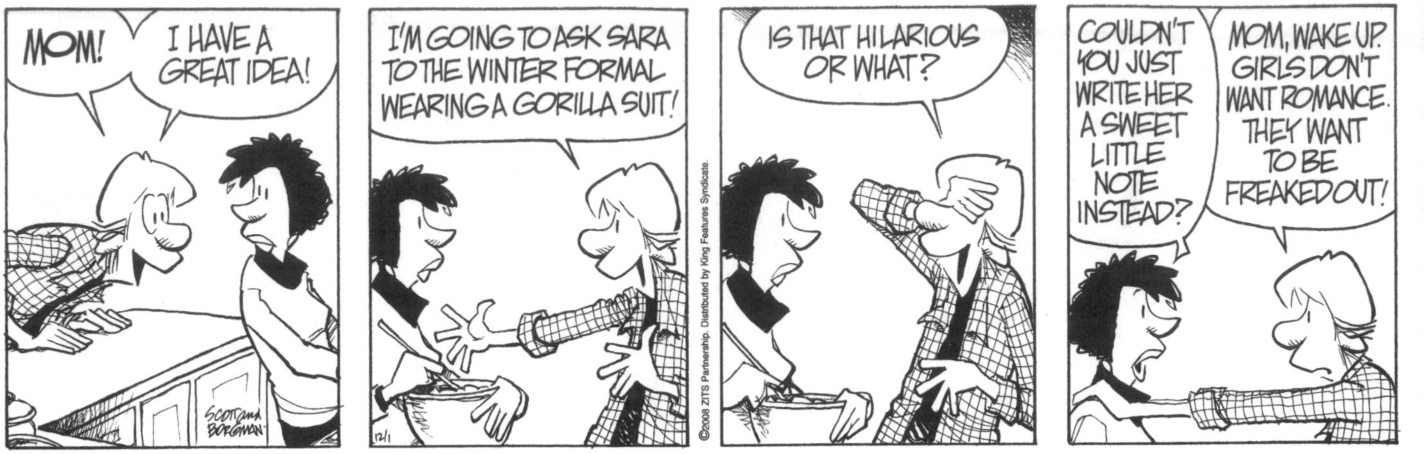

MOM!
I HAVE A GREAT IDEA!
SCOTT and BORGMAN
I'M GOING TO ASK SARA TO THE WINTER FORMAL WEARING A GORILLA SUIT!
12/1
©2008 ZITS Partnership. Distributed by King Features Syndicate.
IS THAT HILARIOUS OR WHAT?
COULDN'T YOU JUST WRITE HER A SWEET LITTLE NOTE INSTEAD?
MOM, WAKE UP. GIRLS DON'T WANT ROMANCE. THEY WANT TO BE FREAKED OUT!

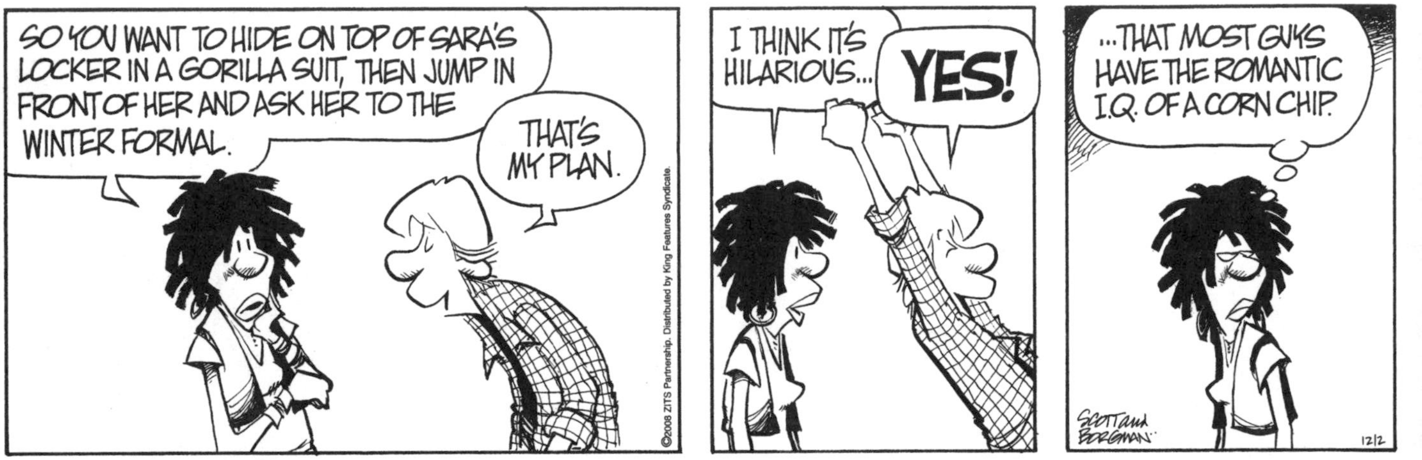

SO YOU WANT TO HIDE ON TOP OF SARA'S LOCKER IN A GORILLA SUIT, THEN JUMP IN FRONT OF HER AND ASK HER TO THE WINTER FORMAL.
THAT'S MY PLAN.
©2008 ZITS Partnership. Distributed by King Features Syndicate.
I THINK IT'S HILARIOUS...
YES!
...THAT MOST GUYS HAVE THE ROMANTIC I.Q. OF A CORN CHIP.
SCOTT and BORGMAN
12/2

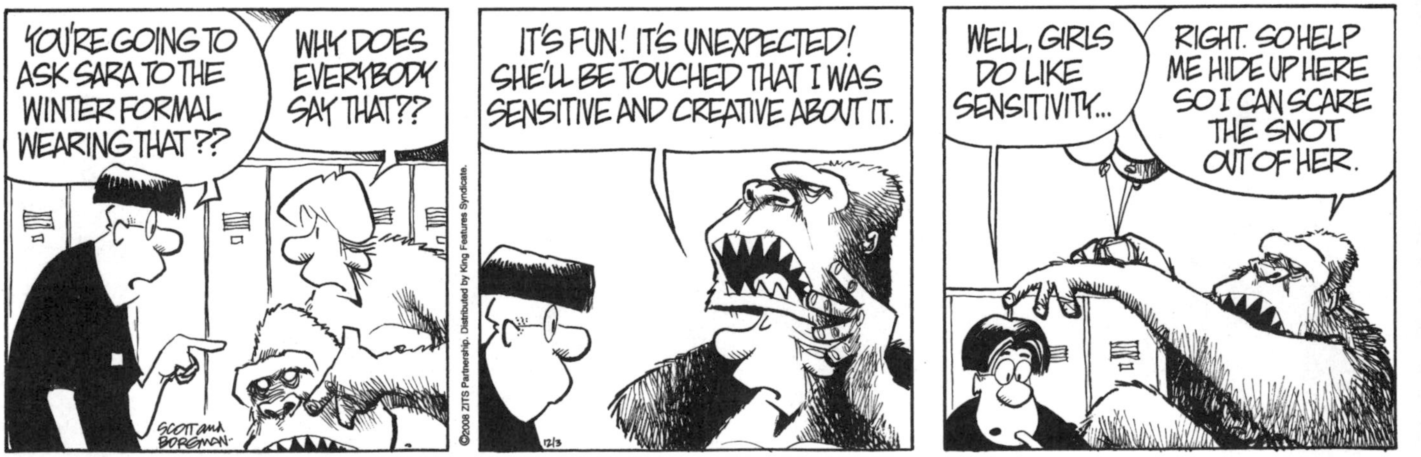

YOU'RE GOING TO ASK SARA TO THE WINTER FORMAL WEARING THAT??
WHY DOES EVERYBODY SAY THAT??
SCOTT and BORGMAN
©2008 ZITS Partnership. Distributed by King Features Syndicate.
IT'S FUN! IT'S UNEXPECTED! SHE'LL BE TOUCHED THAT I WAS SENSITIVE AND CREATIVE ABOUT IT.
12/3
WELL, GIRLS DO LIKE SENSITIVITY...
RIGHT. SO HELP ME HIDE UP HERE SO I CAN SCARE THE SNOT OUT OF HER.

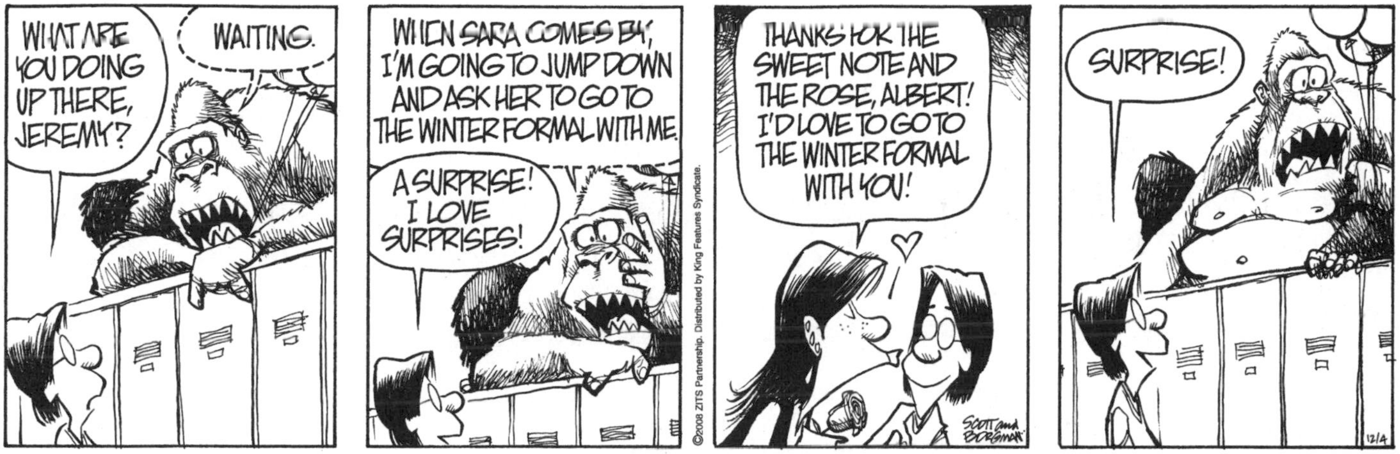
WHAT ARE YOU DOING UP THERE, JEREMY??
WAITING.
WHEN SARA COMES BY, I'M GOING TO JUMP DOWN AND ASK HER TO GO TO THE WINTER FORMAL WITH ME.
A SURPRISE! I LOVE SURPRISES!
©2008 ZITS Partnership. Distributed by King Features Syndicate.
THANKS FOR THE SWEET NOTE AND THE ROSE, ALBERT! I'D LOVE TO GO TO THE WINTER FORMAL WITH YOU!
SCOTT and BORGMAN
SURPRISE!
12/4

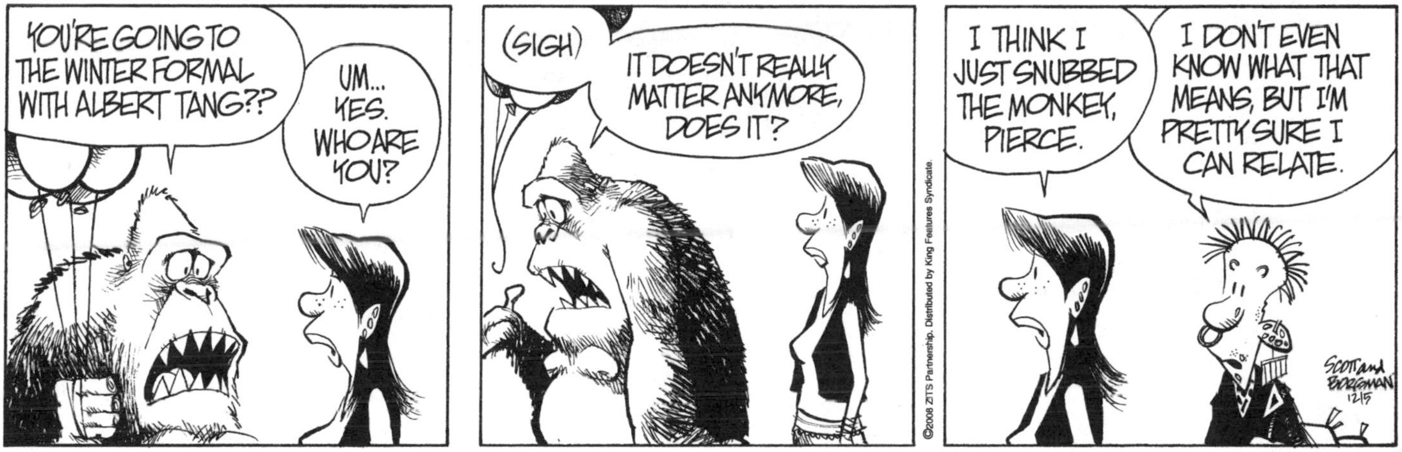
YOU'RE GOING TO THE WINTER FORMAL WITH ALBERT TANG??
UM... YES. WHO ARE YOU?
(SIGH)
IT DOESN'T REALLY MATTER ANYMORE, DOES IT?
©2008 ZITS Partnership. Distributed by King Features Syndicate.
I THINK I JUST SNUBBED THE MONKEY, PIERCE.
I DON'T EVEN KNOW WHAT THAT MEANS, BUT I'M PRETTY SURE I CAN RELATE.
SCOTT and BORGMAN
12/5

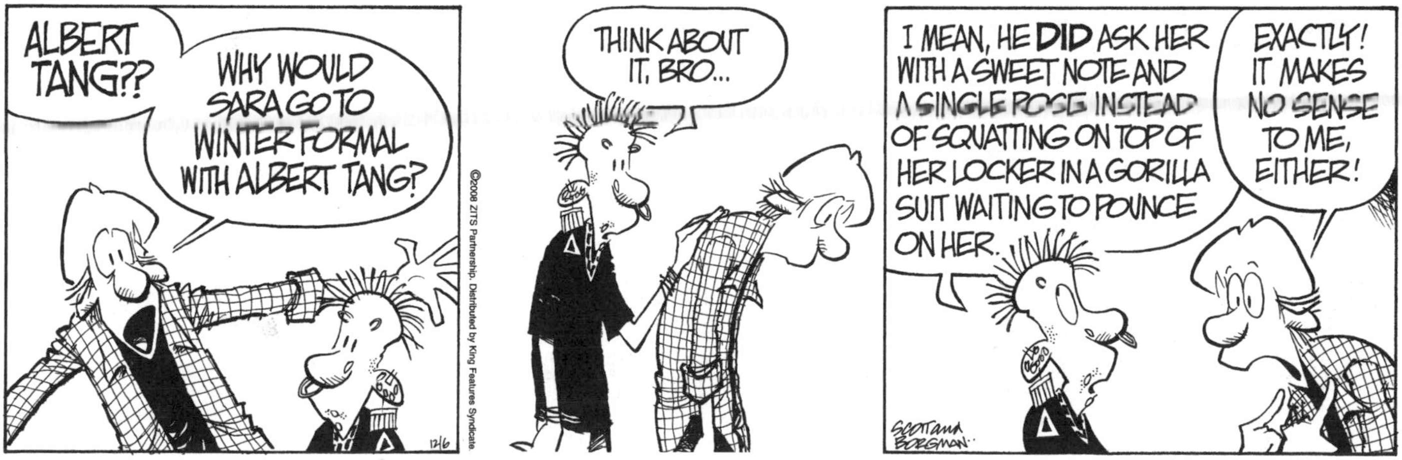
ALBERT TANG??
WHY WOULD SARA GO TO WINTER FORMAL WITH ALBERT TANG?
12/6
©2008 ZITS Partnership. Distributed by King Features Syndicate.
THINK ABOUT IT, BRO...
I MEAN, HE DID ASK HER WITH A SWEET NOTE AND A SINGLE ROSE INSTEAD OF SQUATTING ON TOP OF HER LOCKER IN A GORILLA SUIT WAITING TO POUNCE ON HER.
EXACTLY! IT MAKES NO SENSE TO ME, EITHER!
SCOTT and BORGMAN

BZZRRRRRRR!
6:45
by
JERRY SCOTT and
JIM BORGMAN
Zits

BZZRRRRRRR!
6:45
SLAP!
SLAP!
12/7
SLAP!
DRAG!
SLAP!
DRAG!
BUMP!
BUMP!
BUMP!
SLAP!
DRAG!
SLAP!
DRAG!
SLURP!
MUNCH!
MUNCH!
MUNCH!
WOULDN'T IT BE SIMPLER TO JUST EAT BREAKFAST AFTER YOU'RE DRESSED?
I'M NOT ABOUT EFFICIENCY, MOM. I'M ABOUT MAXIMIZING MATTRESS TIME.
SCOTT and BORGMAN

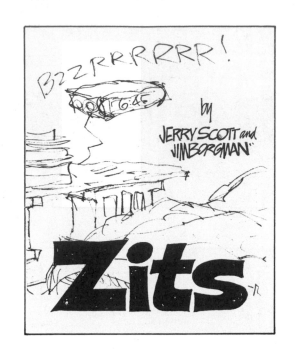

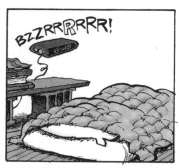

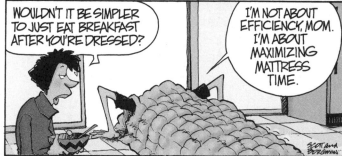

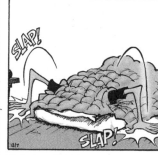

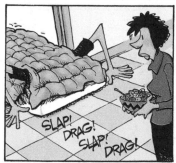

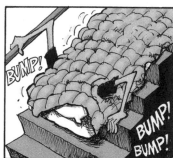

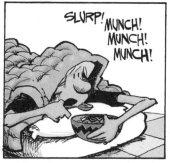

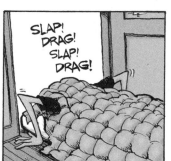

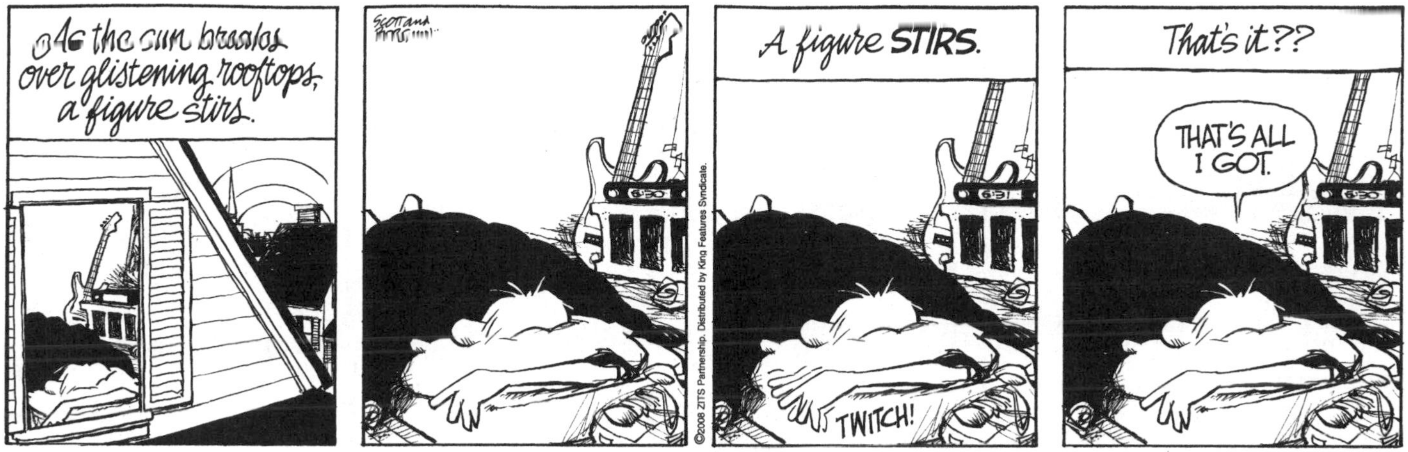
As the sun breaks over glistening rooftops, a figure stirs.
6:30
©2008 ZITS Partnership. Distributed by King Features Syndicate.
A figure STIRS.
6:31
TWITCH!
That's it??
THAT'S ALL I GOT.
6:30

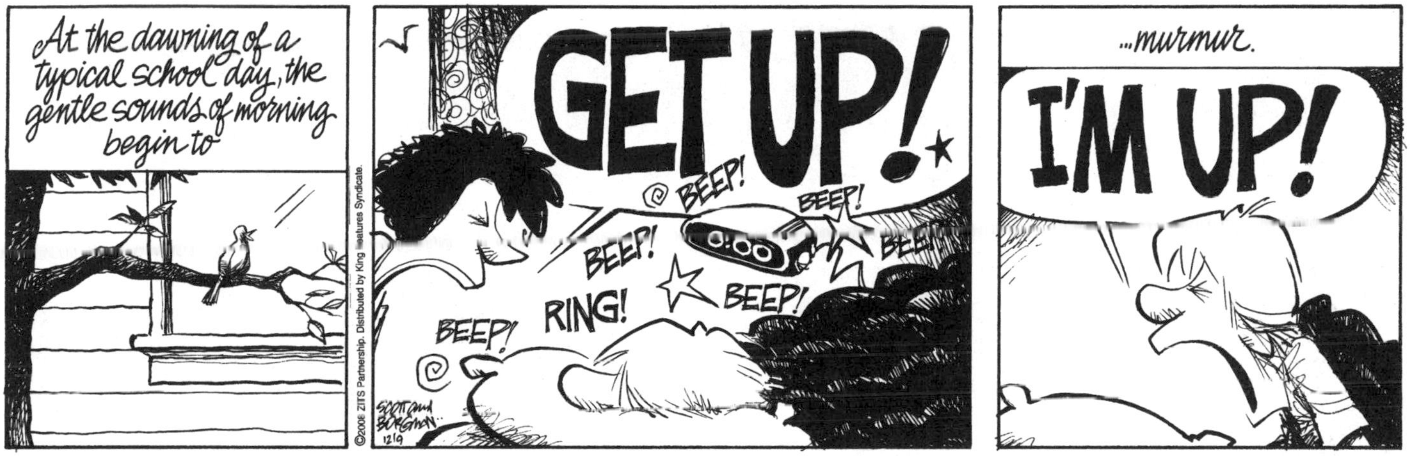
At the dawning of a typical school day, the gentle sounds of morning begin to
©2008 ZITS Partnership. Distributed by King Features Syndicate.
GET UP!
BEEP!
BEEP!
BEEP!
BEEP!
RING!
BEEP!
BEEP!
...murmur.
I'M UP!

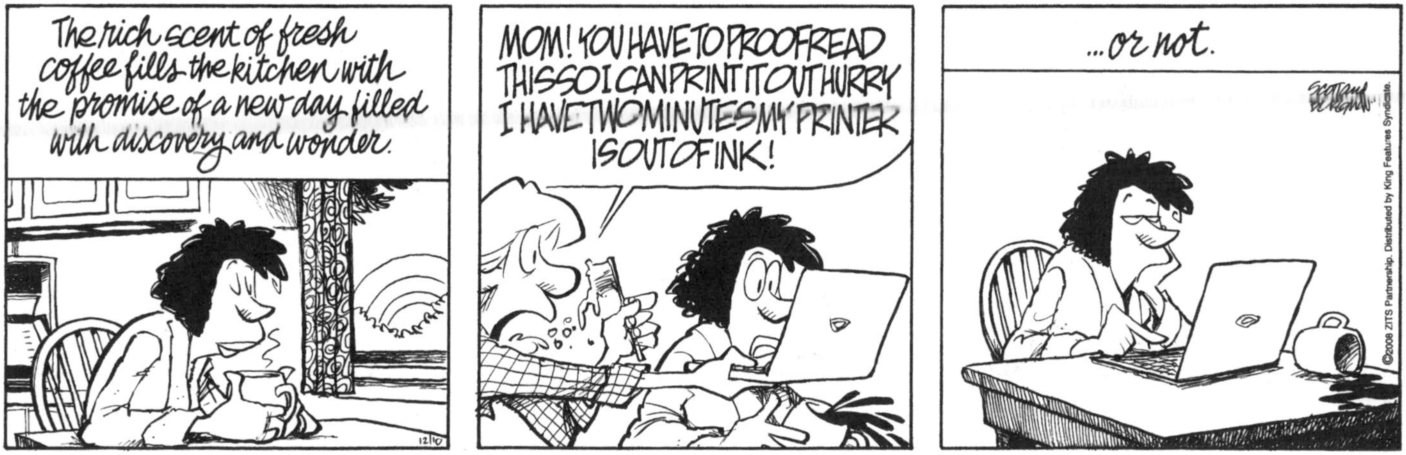
The rich scent of fresh coffee fills the kitchen with the promise of a new day filled with discovery and wonder.
MOM! YOU HAVE TO PROOFREAD THIS SO I CAN PRINT IT OUT HURRY I HAVE TWO MINUTES MY PRINTER IS OUT OF INK!
...or not.
©2008 ZITS Partnership. Distributed by King Features Syndicate.

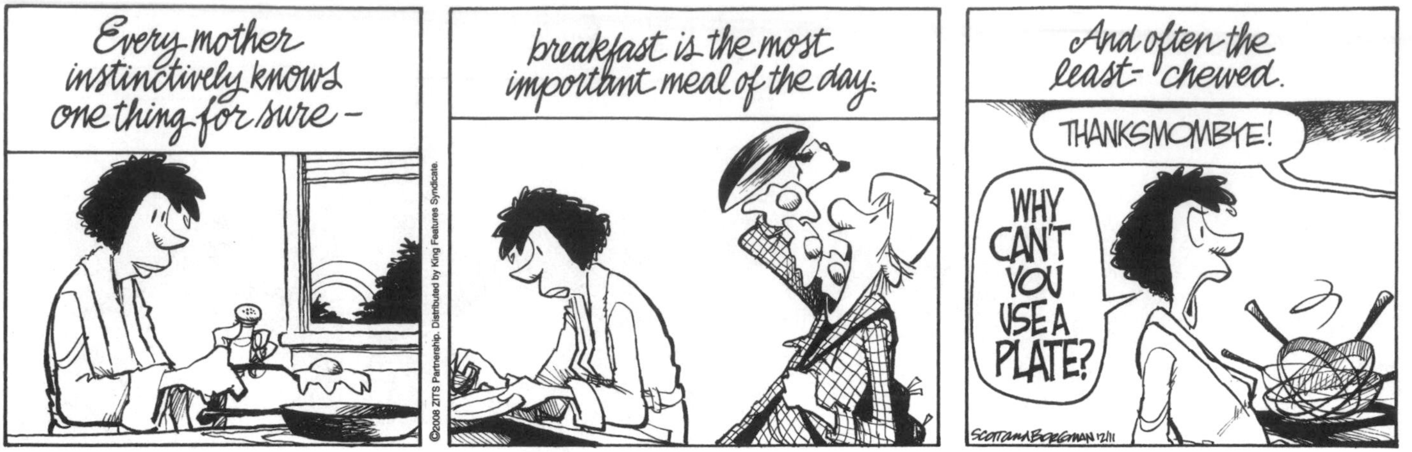
Every mother instinctively knows one thing for sure -
breakfast is the most important meal of the day.
And often the least-chewed.
THANKSMOMBYE!
WHY CAN'T YOU USE A PLATE?
SCOTT and BORGMAN 12/11
©2008 ZITS Partnership. Distributed by King Features Syndicate.

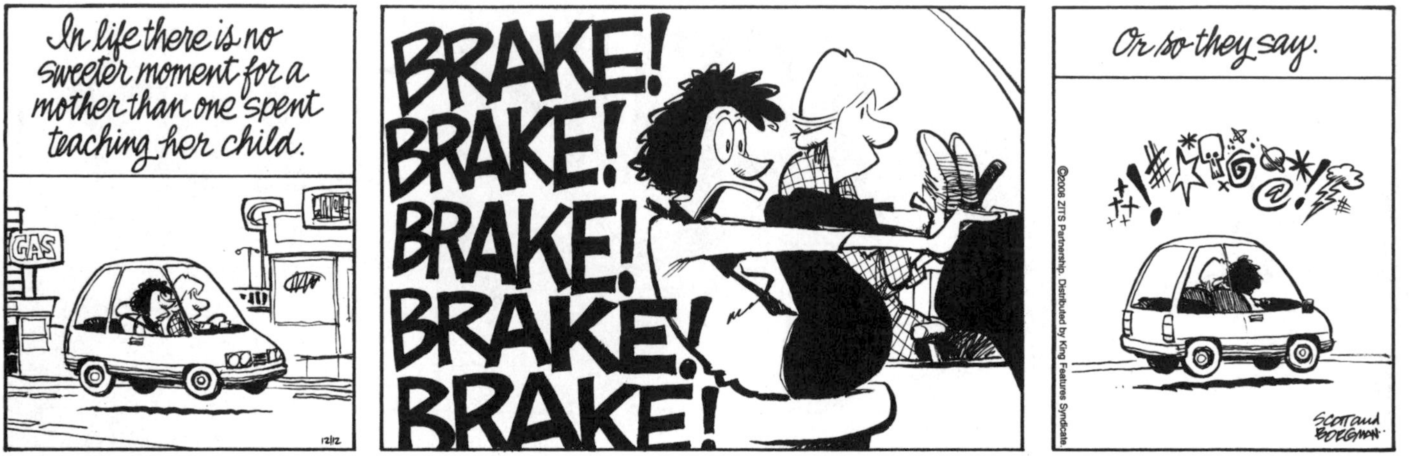
In life there is no sweeter moment for a mother than one spent teaching her child.
GAS
12/12
BRAKE! BRAKE! BRAKE! BRAKE! BRAKE!
Or so they say.
SCOTT and BORGMAN
©2008 ZITS Partnership. Distributed by King Features Syndicate.

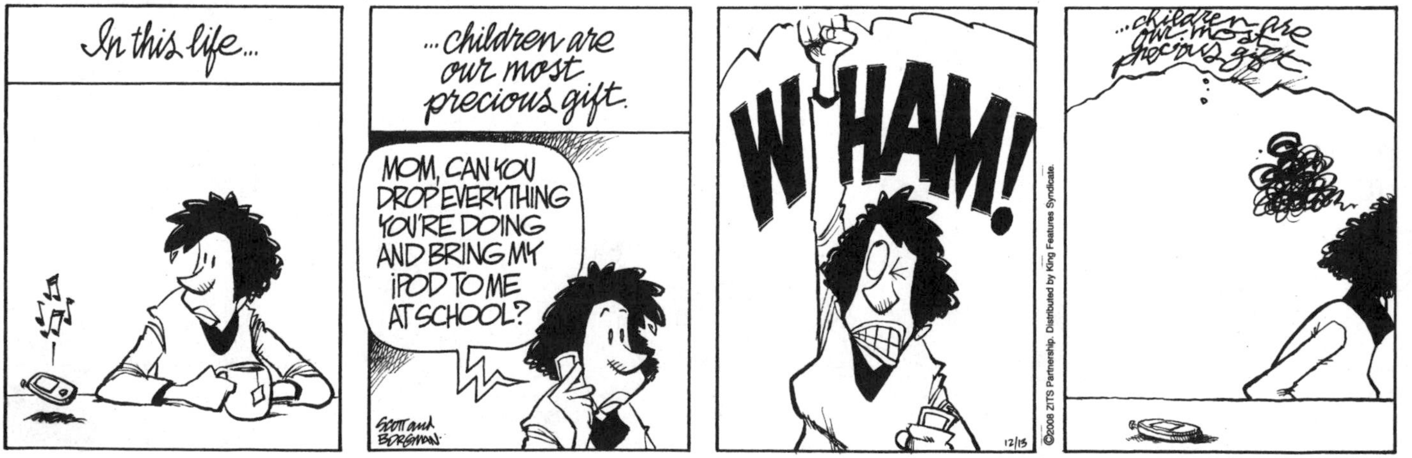
In this life...
...children are our most precious gift.
MOM, CAN YOU DROP EVERYTHING YOU'RE DOING AND BRING MY iPOD TO ME AT SCHOOL?
SCOTT and BORGMAN
WHAM!
12/13
©2008 ZITS Partnership. Distributed by King Features Syndicate.
...children are our most precious gift

Zits
by
JERRY SCOTT and
JIM BORGMAN

VRRRRMMMMMMM!
©2008 ZITS Partnership. Distributed by King Features Syndicate
CLICK
SCOTT and BORGMAN
12/14
REMEMBER BACK BEFORE I GOT MY PERMIT WHEN YOU HAD TO WALK TO OUR MAILBOX?
YEAH. THIS MAKES MY UNGODLY CAR INSURANCE PREMIUMS SO TOTALLY WORTH IT!

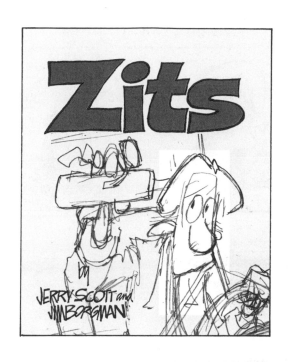

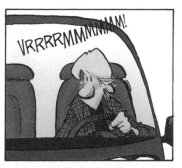

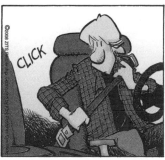

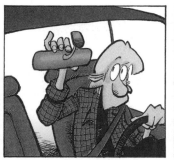

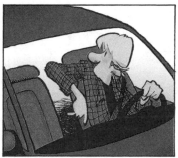

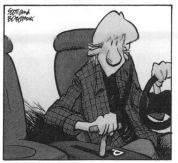

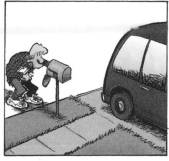

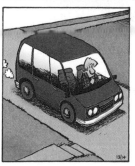

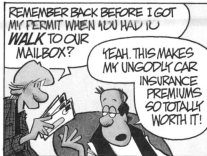

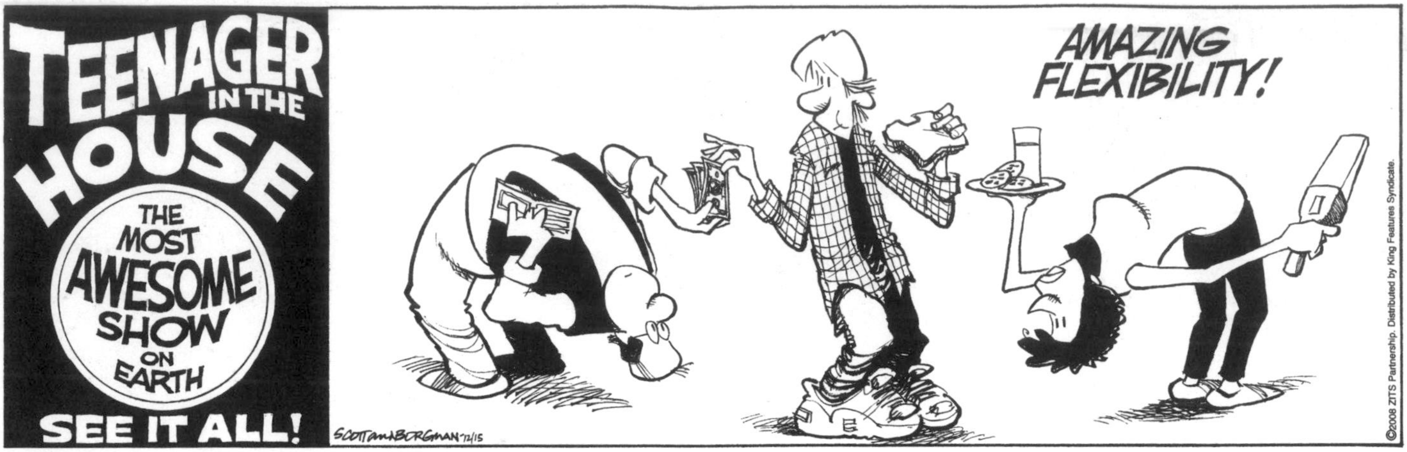
TEENAGER IN THE HOUSE
THE MOST AWESOME SHOW ON EARTH
SEE IT ALL!
AMAZING FLEXIBILITY!
SCOTT AND BORGMAN 12/15
©2008 ZITS Partnership. Distributed by King Features Syndicate.

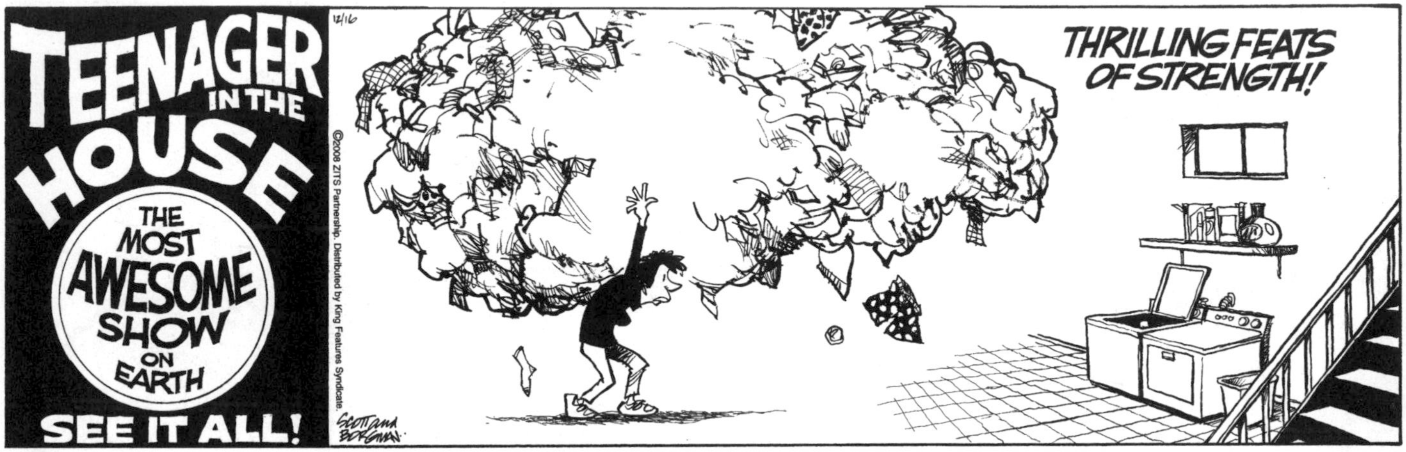
TEENAGER IN THE HOUSE
THE MOST AWESOME SHOW ON EARTH
SEE IT ALL!
12/16
THRILLING FEATS OF STRENGTH!
©2008 ZITS Partnership. Distributed by King Features Syndicate.
SCOTT AND BORGMAN

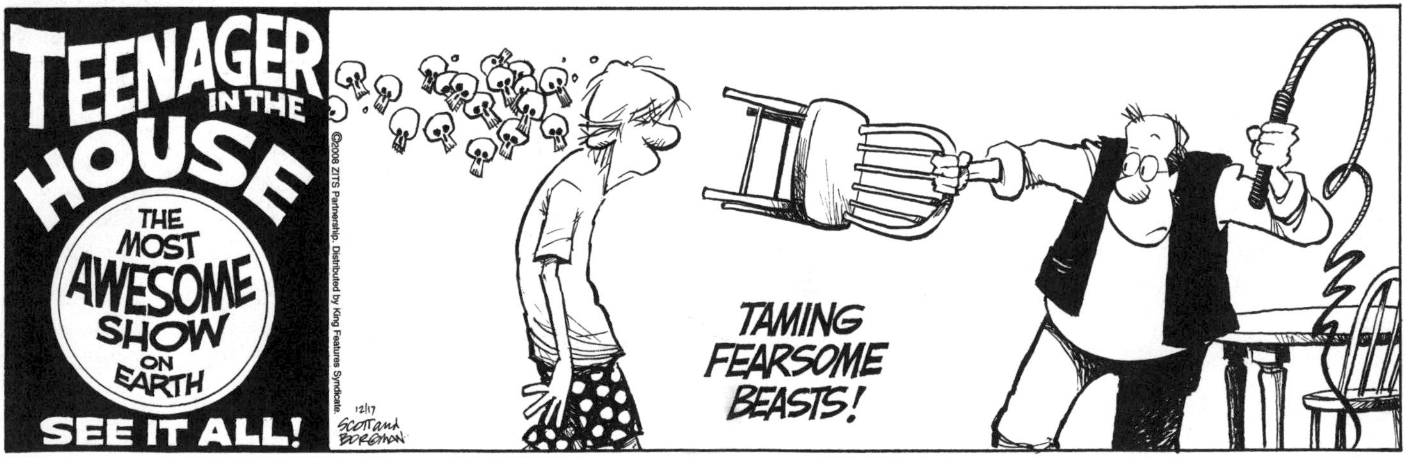
TEENAGER IN THE HOUSE
THE MOST AWESOME SHOW ON EARTH
SEE IT ALL!
©2008 ZITS Partnership. Distributed by King Features Syndicate.
TAMING FEARSOME BEASTS!
12/17
SCOTT AND BORGMAN

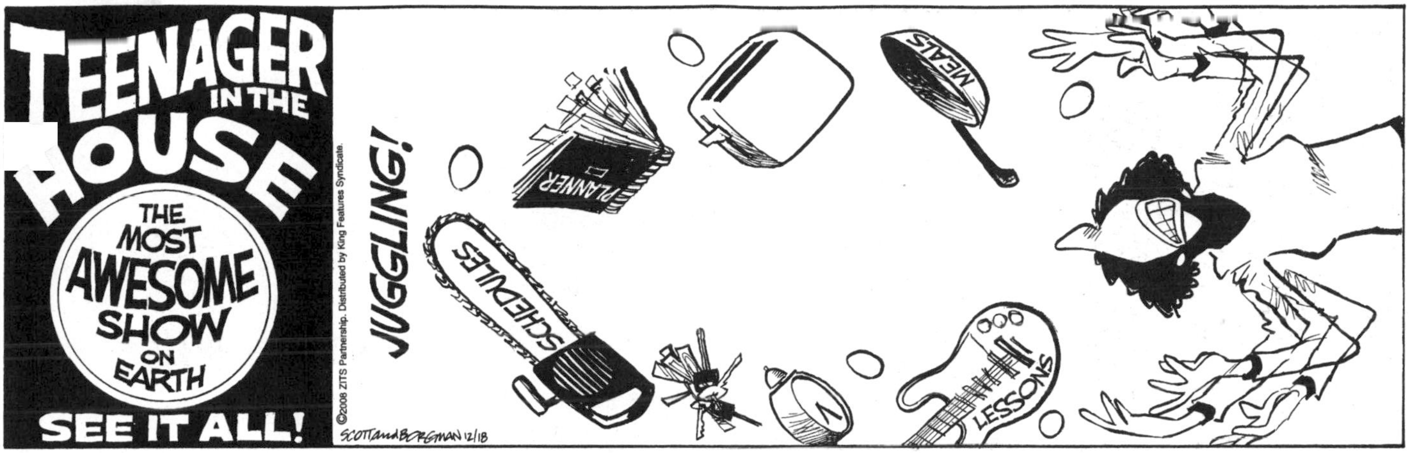
TEENAGER IN THE HOUSE
THE MOST AWESOME SHOW ON EARTH
SEE IT ALL!
©2008 ZITS Partnership. Distributed by King Features Syndicate.
JUGGLING!
PLANNER
MEALS
SCHEDULES
LESSONS
SCOTT and BORGMAN 12/18

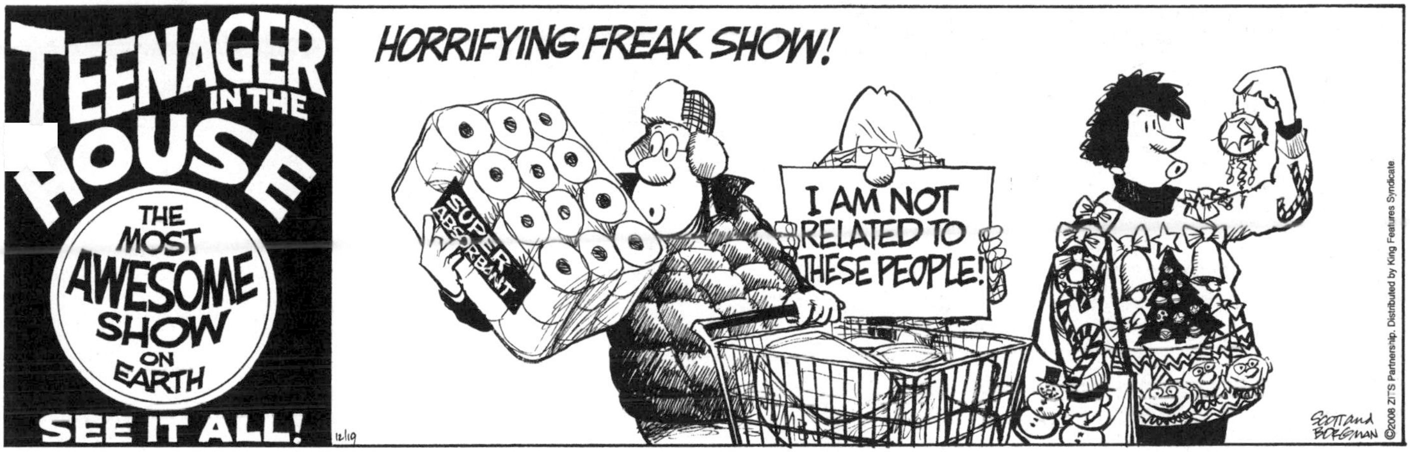
TEENAGER IN THE HOUSE
THE MOST AWESOME SHOW ON EARTH
SEE IT ALL!
12/19
HORRIFYING FREAK SHOW!
SUPER ABSORBANT
I AM NOT RELATED TO THESE PEOPLE!
SCOTT and BORGMAN
©2008 ZITS Partnership. Distributed by King Features Syndicate

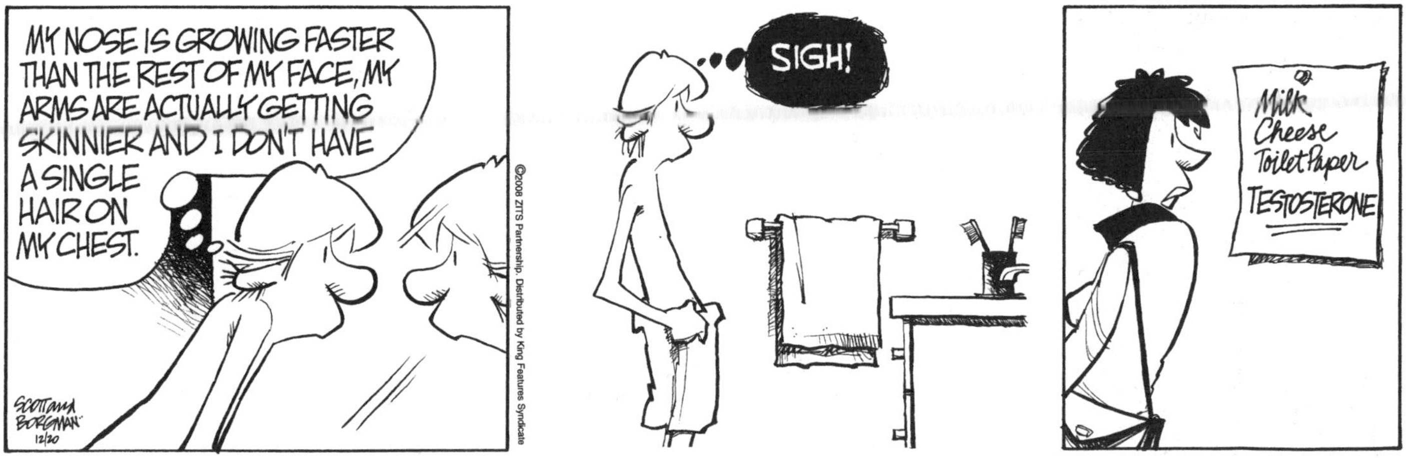
MY NOSE IS GROWING FASTER THAN THE REST OF MY FACE, MY ARMS ARE ACTUALLY GETTING SKINNIER AND I DON'T HAVE A SINGLE HAIR ON MY CHEST.
SCOTT and BORGMAN 12/20
©2008 ZITS Partnership. Distributed by King Features Syndicate
SIGH!
Milk
Cheese
Toilet Paper
TESTOSTERONE

Zits
by JERRY SCOTT and JIM BORGMAN

HERE YOU GO.
HUH?
OH.
SCOTT and BORGMAN
©2008 ZITS Partnership. Distributed by King Features Syndicate.
OKAY.
FESTIVE.
MERRY CHRISTMAS, DUDE!
12/21

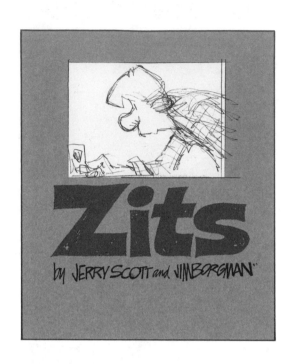

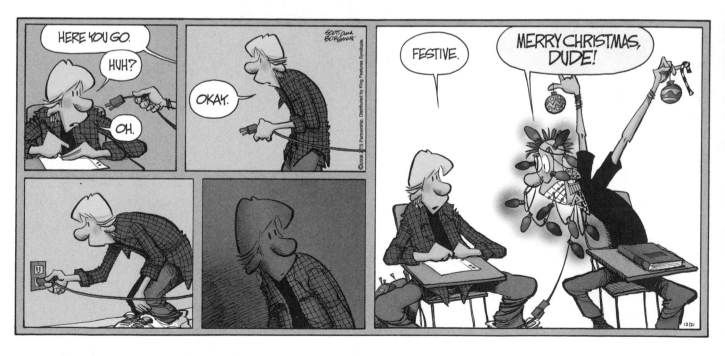

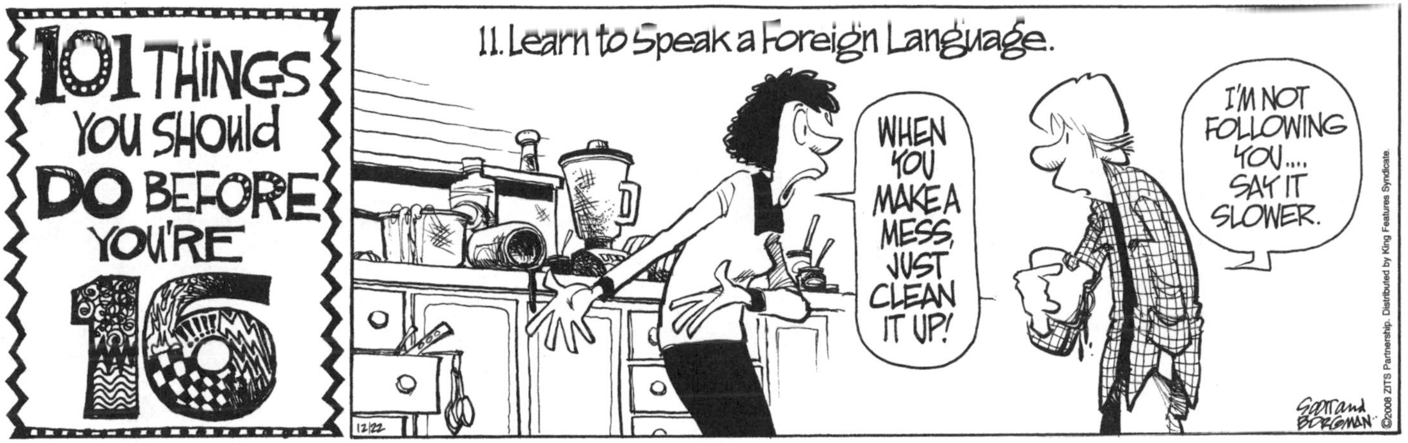
101 THINGS YOU SHOULD DO BEFORE YOU'RE 16
11. Learn to Speak a Foreign Language.
WHEN YOU MAKE A MESS, JUST CLEAN IT UP!
I'M NOT FOLLOWING YOU.... SAY IT SLOWER.
12/22
SCOTT AND BORGMAN
©2008 ZITS Partnership. Distributed by King Features Syndicate.

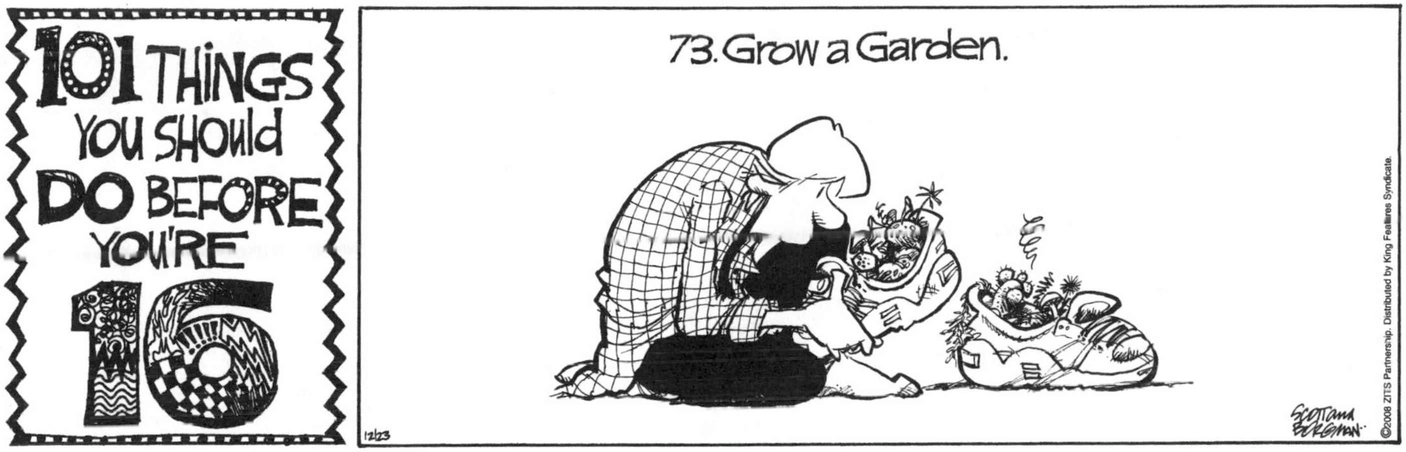
101 THINGS YOU SHOULD DO BEFORE YOU'RE 16
73. Grow a Garden.
12/23
SCOTT AND BORGMAN
©2008 ZITS Partnership. Distributed by King Features Syndicate.

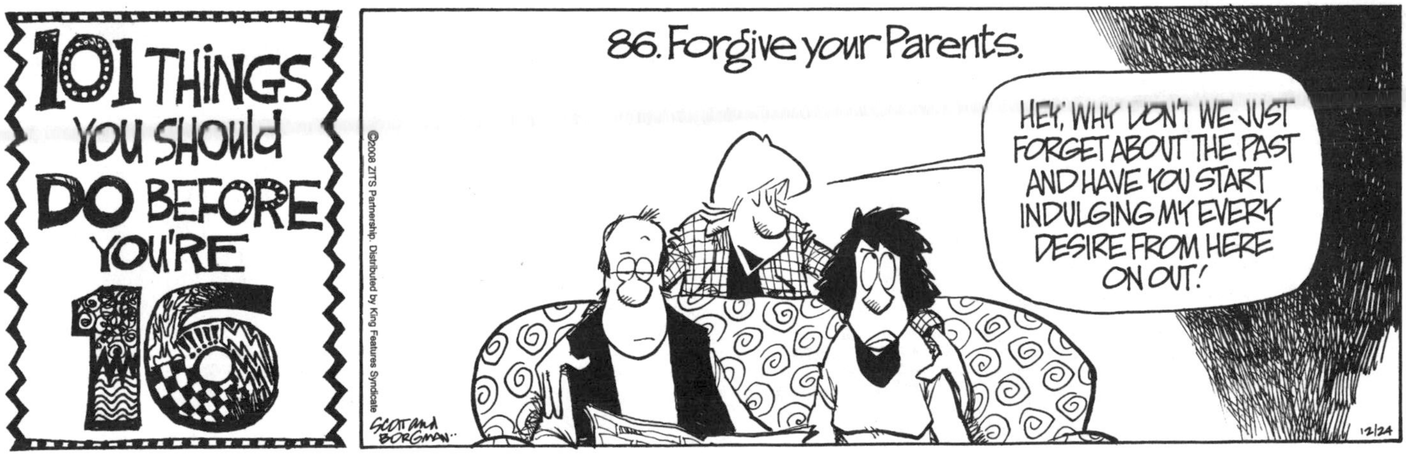
101 THINGS YOU SHOULD DO BEFORE YOU'RE 16
86. Forgive your Parents.
HEY, WHY DON'T WE JUST FORGET ABOUT THE PAST AND HAVE YOU START INDULGING MY EVERY DESIRE FROM HERE ON OUT!
©2008 ZITS Partnership. Distributed by King Features Syndicate
SCOTT AND BORGMAN
12/24

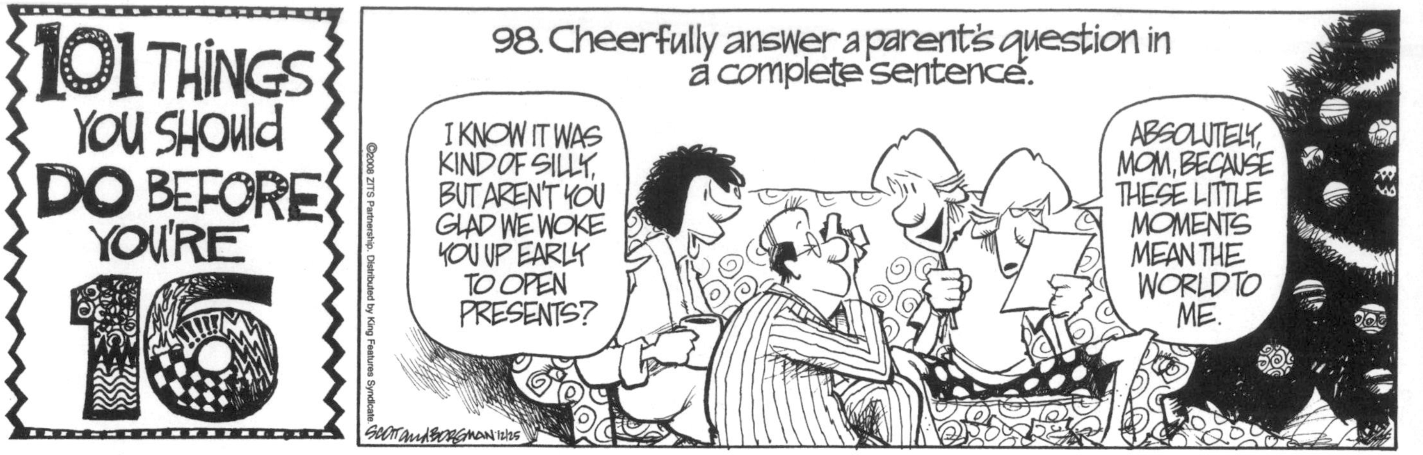
101 THINGS YOU SHOULD DO BEFORE YOU'RE 16
98. Cheerfully answer a parent's question in a complete sentence.
I KNOW IT WAS KIND OF SILLY, BUT AREN'T YOU GLAD WE WOKE YOU UP EARLY TO OPEN PRESENTS?
ABSOLUTELY, MOM, BECAUSE THESE LITTLE MOMENTS MEAN THE WORLD TO ME.
©2008 ZITS Partnership. Distributed by King Features Syndicate
SCOTT and BORGMAN 12/25

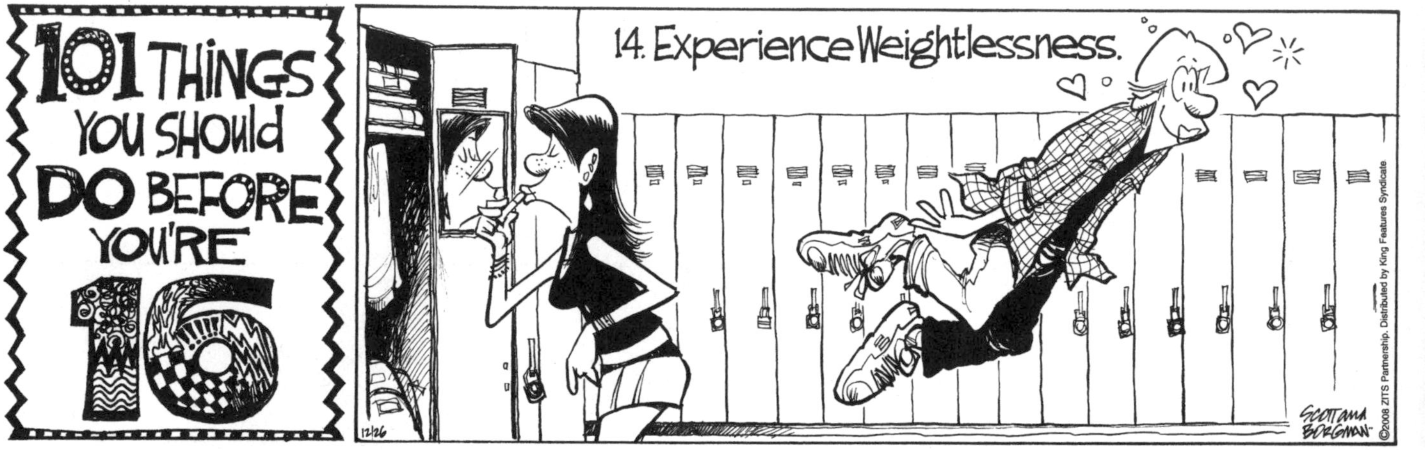
101 THINGS YOU SHOULD DO BEFORE YOU'RE 16
14. Experience Weightlessness.
12/26
SCOTT and BORGMAN
©2008 ZITS Partnership. Distributed by King Features Syndicate

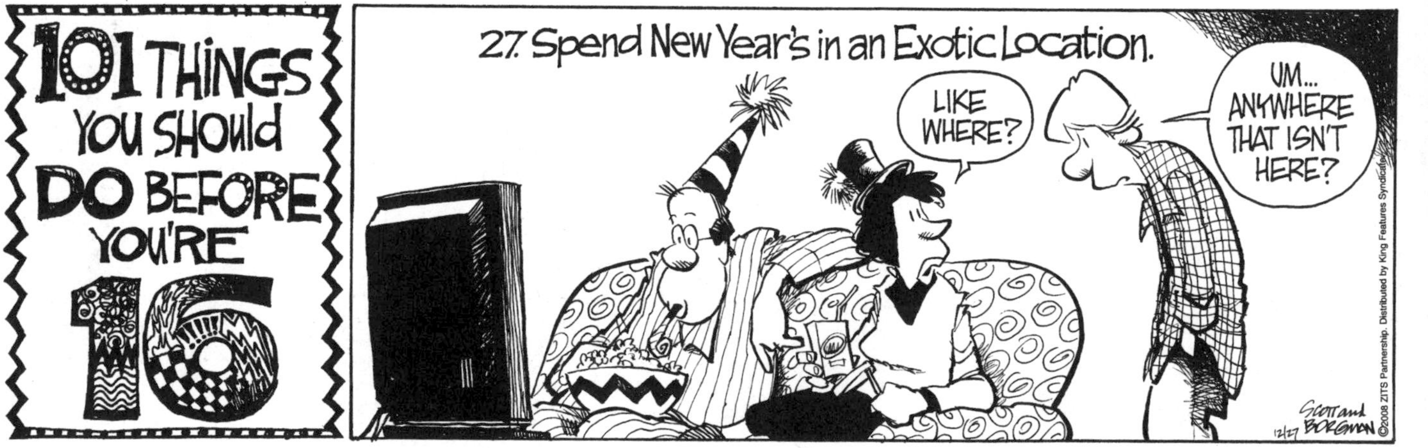
101 THINGS YOU SHOULD DO BEFORE YOU'RE 16
27. Spend New Year's in an Exotic Location.
LIKE WHERE?
UM... ANYWHERE THAT ISN'T HERE?
©2008 ZITS Partnership. Distributed by King Features Syndicate
SCOTT and BORGMAN 12/27

Zits
by JERRY SCOTT and JIM BORGMAN

JEREMY, IF YOU HAVE ANY DIRTY CLOTHES YOU WANT WASHED, YOU'D BETTER BRING THEM TO ME NOW.
SCOTT and BORGMAN
©2008 ZITS Partnership. Distributed by King Features Syndicate.
12/28

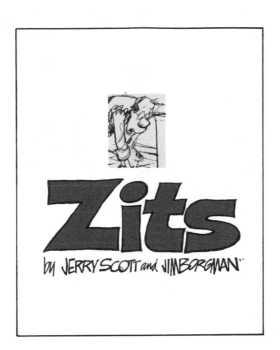

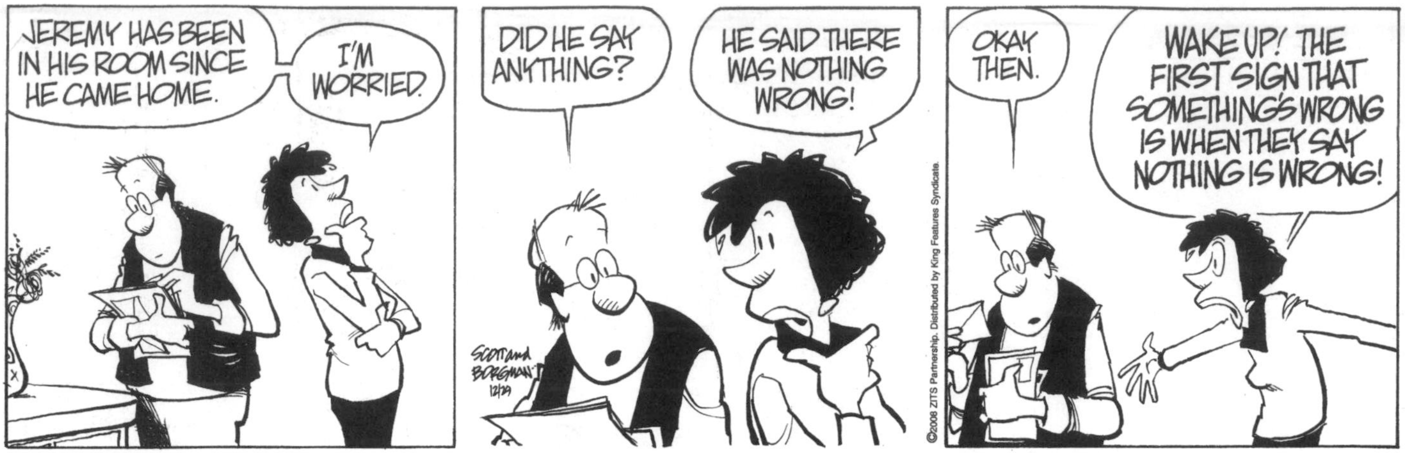
JEREMY HAS BEEN IN HIS ROOM SINCE HE CAME HOME.
I'M WORRIED.
DID HE SAY ANYTHING?
HE SAID THERE WAS NOTHING WRONG!
OKAY THEN.
WAKE UP! THE FIRST SIGN THAT SOMETHING'S WRONG IS WHEN THEY SAY NOTHING IS WRONG!

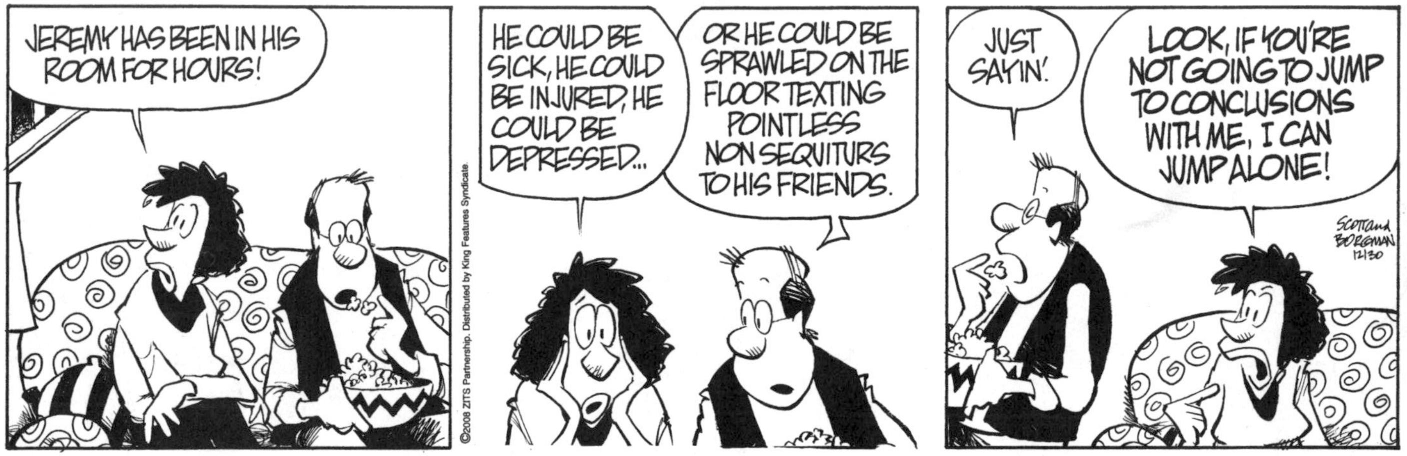
JEREMY HAS BEEN IN HIS ROOM FOR HOURS!
HE COULD BE SICK, HE COULD BE INJURED, HE COULD BE DEPRESSED...
OR HE COULD BE SPRAWLED ON THE FLOOR TEXTING POINTLESS NON SEQUITURS TO HIS FRIENDS.
JUST SAYIN'.
LOOK, IF YOU'RE NOT GOING TO JUMP TO CONCLUSIONS WITH ME, I CAN JUMP ALONE!

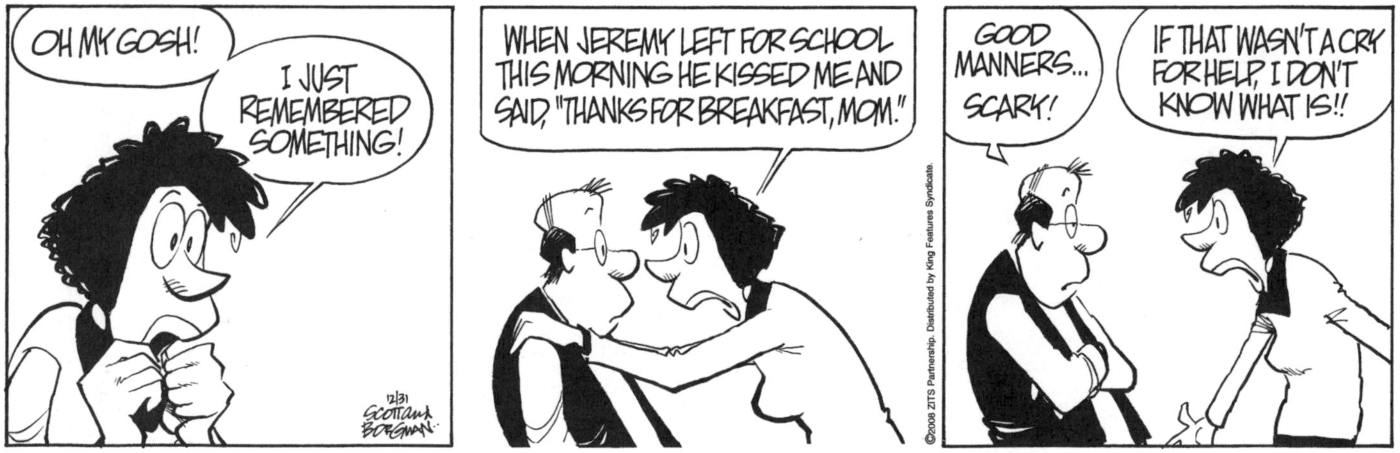
OH MY GOSH!
I JUST REMEMBERED SOMETHING!
WHEN JEREMY LEFT FOR SCHOOL THIS MORNING HE KISSED ME AND SAID, "THANKS FOR BREAKFAST, MOM."
GOOD MANNERS... SCARY!
IF THAT WASN'T A CRY FOR HELP, I DON'T KNOW WHAT IS!!

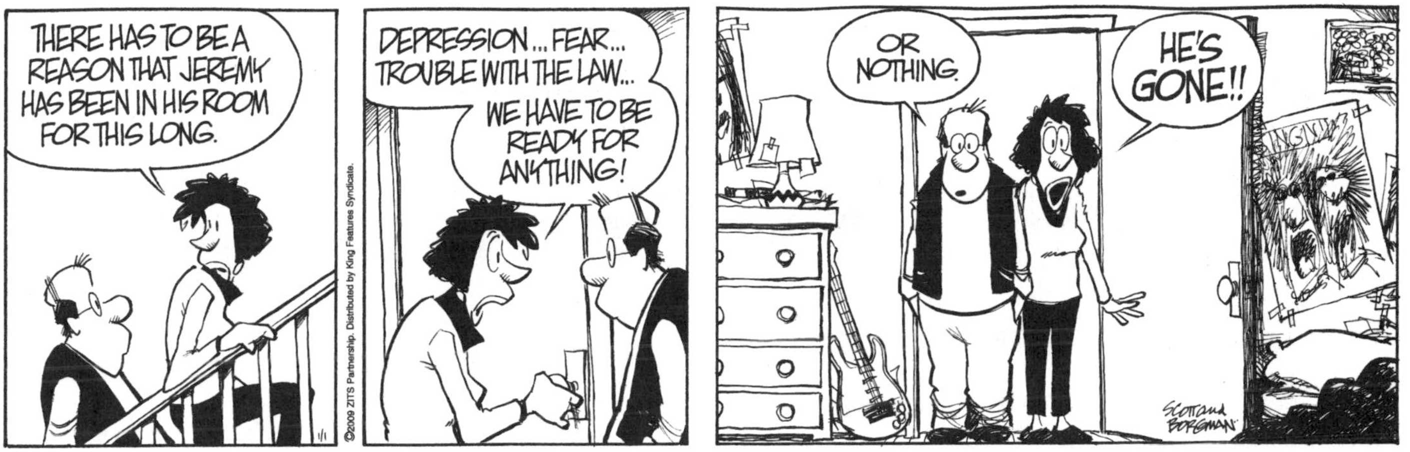
THERE HAS TO BE A REASON THAT JEREMY HAS BEEN IN HIS ROOM FOR THIS LONG.
1/1
©2009 ZITS Partnership. Distributed by King Features Syndicate.
DEPRESSION... FEAR... TROUBLE WITH THE LAW...
WE HAVE TO BE READY FOR ANYTHING!
OR NOTHING.
HE'S GONE!!
SCOTT and BORGMAN

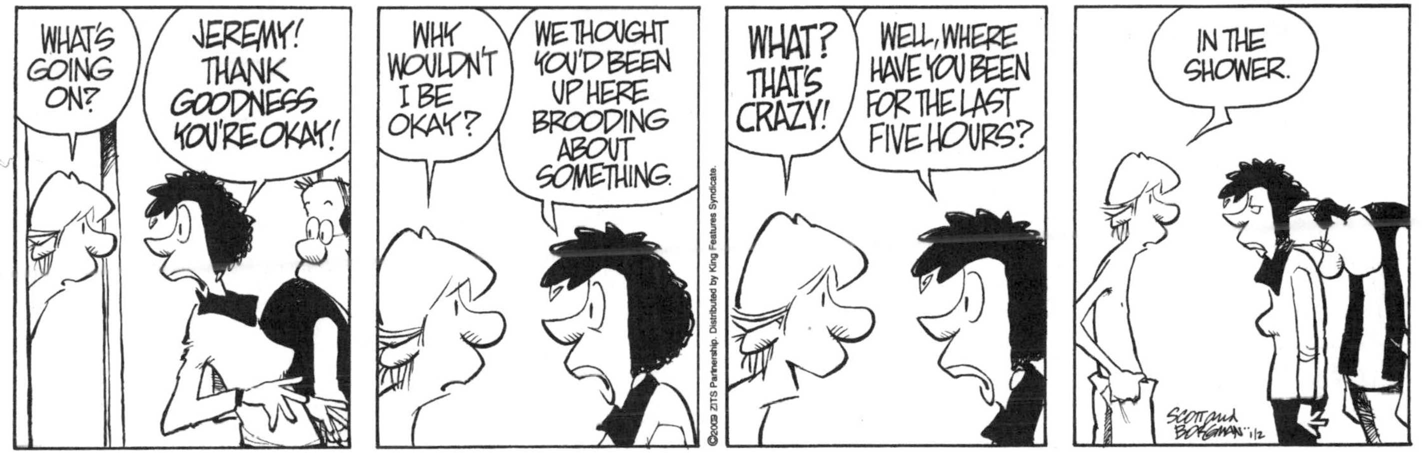
WHAT'S GOING ON?
JEREMY! THANK GOODNESS YOU'RE OKAY!
WHY WOULDN'T I BE OKAY?
WE THOUGHT YOU'D BEEN UP HERE BROODING ABOUT SOMETHING.
©2009 ZITS Partnership. Distributed by King Features Syndicate.
WHAT? THAT'S CRAZY!
WELL, WHERE HAVE YOU BEEN FOR THE LAST FIVE HOURS?
IN THE SHOWER.
SCOTT and BORGMAN 1/2

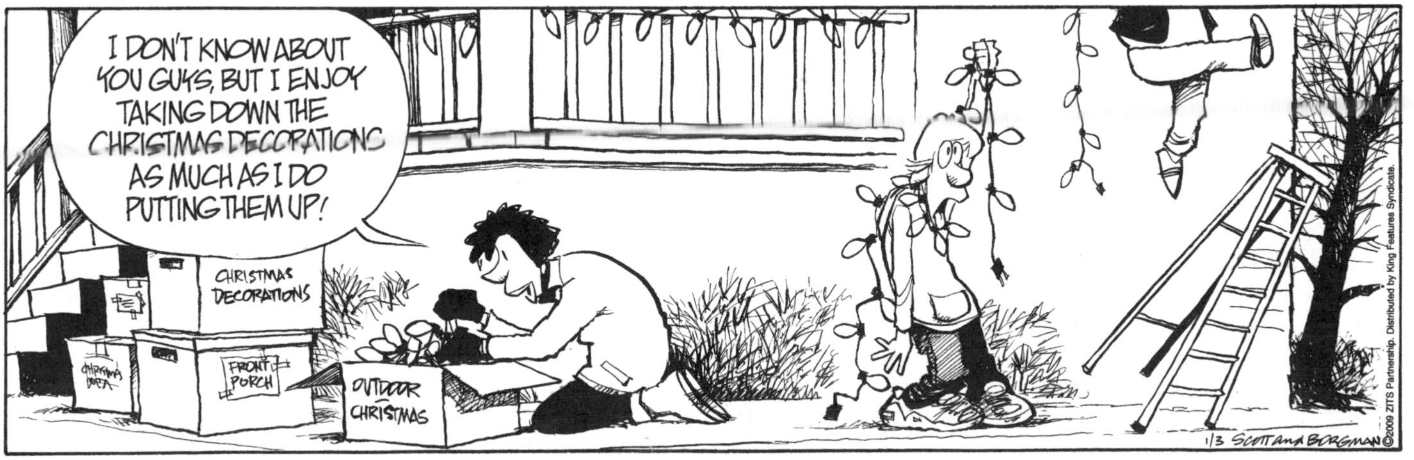
I DON'T KNOW ABOUT YOU GUYS, BUT I ENJOY TAKING DOWN THE CHRISTMAS DECORATIONS AS MUCH AS I DO PUTTING THEM UP!
CHRISTMAS DECORATIONS
FRONT PORCH
OUTDOOR CHRISTMAS
1/3 SCOTT and BORGMAN
©2009 ZITS Partnership. Distributed by King Features Syndicate.

HI MOM

HELLO, JEREMY.

WHAT'S WRONG?

NOTHING'S WRONG. WHAT COULD BE WRONG?

JUST BECAUSE MY OWN SON FORGOT MY BIRTHDAY DOESN'T MEAN THAT ANYTHING IS WRONG!!

SCOTTANDBORGMAN 1·15

WAIT-- ARE YOU TRYING TO TELL ME SOMETHING?

TODAY IS MY BIRTHDAY, JEREMY.

YOU FORGOT YOUR OWN MOTHER'S BIRTHDAY!

TAP TAP

SCOTTand BORGMAN

1/6

ROCKGOD1

happy b-day mom.

Reply   Menu

©2009 ZITS Partnership. Distributed by King Features Syndicate.

A TEXT MESSAGE AFTER THE FACT DOES NOT FIX THIS!

BUT YOU ALWAYS SAID IT'S THE THOUGHT THAT COUNTS!

OKAY, I FORGOT YOUR BIRTHDAY. WHAT'S THE BIG DEAL?

I'M YOUR MOTHER, JEREMY! SHOW ME A LITTLE RESPECT!

OKAY.

SCOTTand BORGMAN 1·7

WELCOME TO THE TOP 100 ON MY SPEED DIAL LIST.

SHOW ME A LITTLE MORE.

©2009 ZITS Partnership. Distributed by King Features Syndicate.

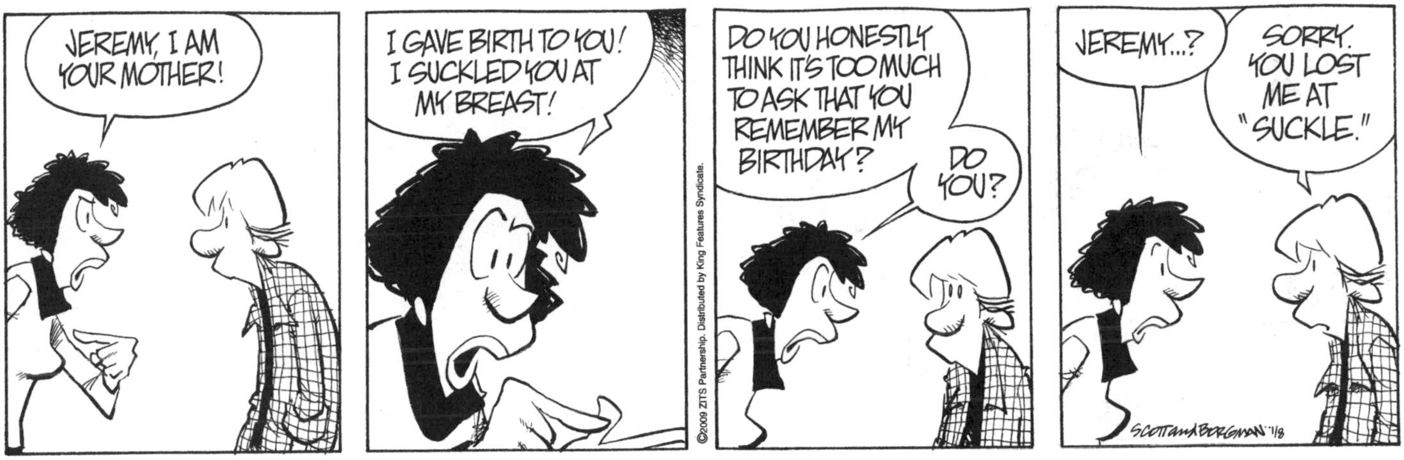
JEREMY, I AM YOUR MOTHER!
I GAVE BIRTH TO YOU! I SUCKLED YOU AT MY BREAST!
DO YOU HONESTLY THINK IT'S TOO MUCH TO ASK THAT YOU REMEMBER MY BIRTHDAY?
DO YOU?
JEREMY...?
SORRY. YOU LOST ME AT "SUCKLE."
SCOTT and BORGMAN 1/8

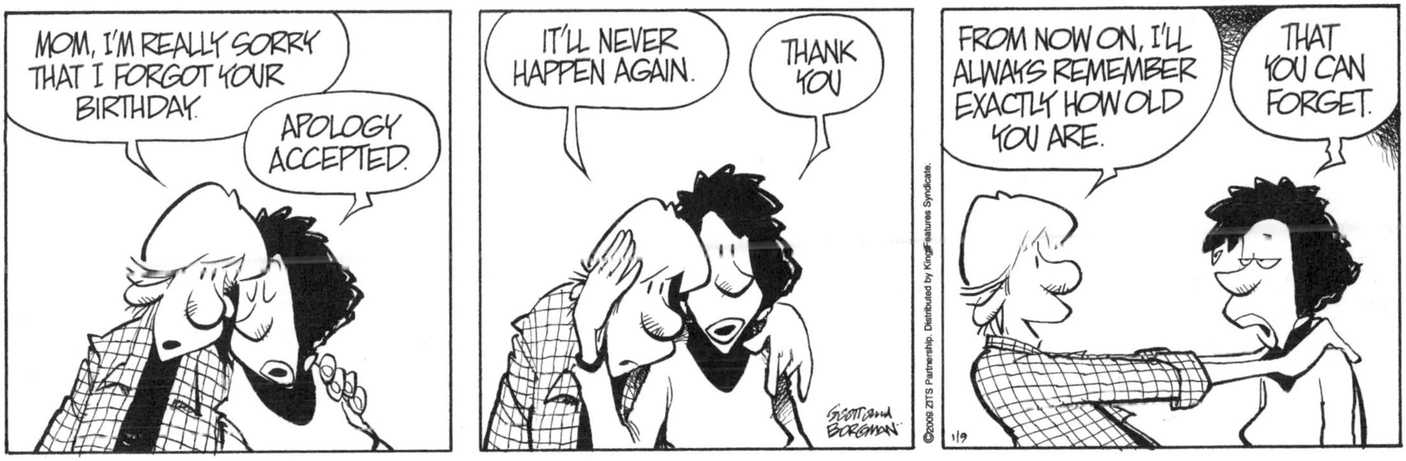
MOM, I'M REALLY SORRY THAT I FORGOT YOUR BIRTHDAY.
APOLOGY ACCEPTED.
IT'LL NEVER HAPPEN AGAIN.
THANK YOU
SCOTT and BORGMAN
FROM NOW ON, I'LL ALWAYS REMEMBER EXACTLY HOW OLD YOU ARE.
THAT YOU CAN FORGET.
1/9

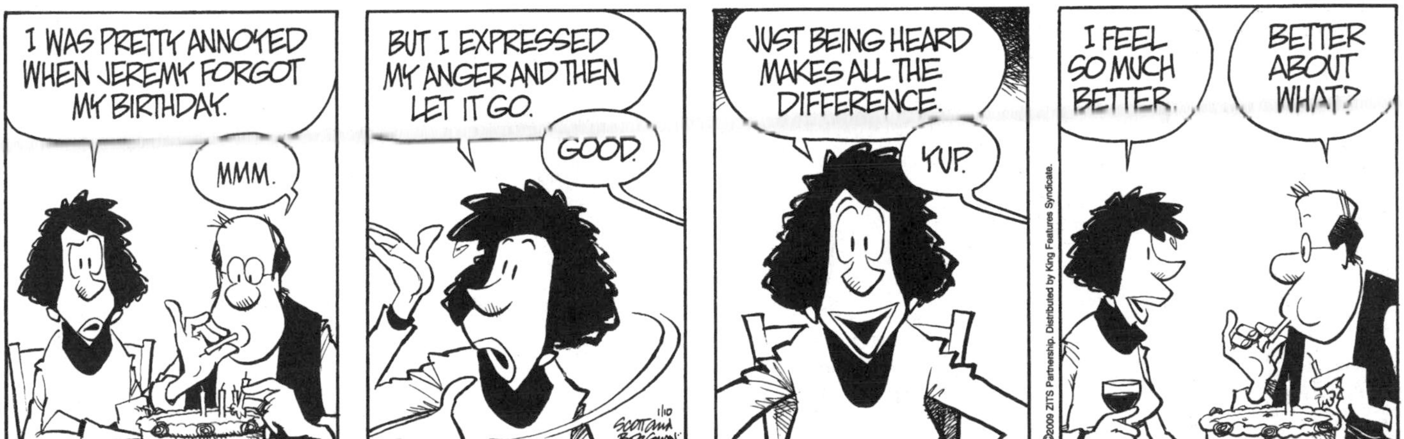
I WAS PRETTY ANNOYED WHEN JEREMY FORGOT MY BIRTHDAY.
MMM.
BUT I EXPRESSED MY ANGER AND THEN LET IT GO.
GOOD.
1/10 SCOTT and BORGMAN
JUST BEING HEARD MAKES ALL THE DIFFERENCE.
YUP.
I FEEL SO MUCH BETTER.
BETTER ABOUT WHAT?

Zits
by JERRY SCOTT and JIM BORGMAN

I'M HOME.
SCOTT and BORGMAN
©2009 ZITS Partnership. Distributed by King Features Syndicate.
1/4
I'M GOING OUT AGAIN.
ALONG ABOUT THE SIXTEENTH YEAR, THE PITTER-PATTER OF LITTLE FEET GIVES WAY TO THE RANSACKING OF THE REFRIGERATOR.
I'D BETTER NOT FIND ANY CHICKEN BONES IN THE SHRUBBERY AGAIN!

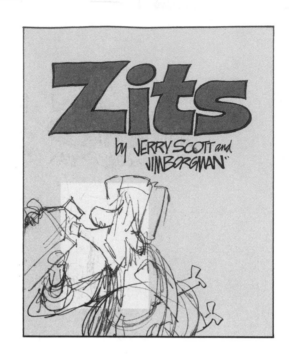

Zits
by JERRY SCOTT and JIM BORGMAN

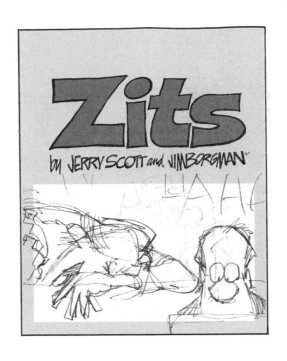

DAD!
CHECK OUT THIS VIDEO ON YOUTUBE!
(SNICKER!)
BWAAHAHA HAHA!
HA! HA! HA! HA! HA! HA!
SNORT!
HA HA HAHA!
HAHA! HAHA HA!
HOO!
HEE!
THAT HAS TO BE THE MOST HILARIOUS THING I'VE EVER SEEN!
THE HUMOR GENE HAS APPARENTLY SKIPPED A GENERATION.
SCOTT and BORGMAN 1/11
©2009 ZITS Partnership. Distributed by King Features Syndicate.

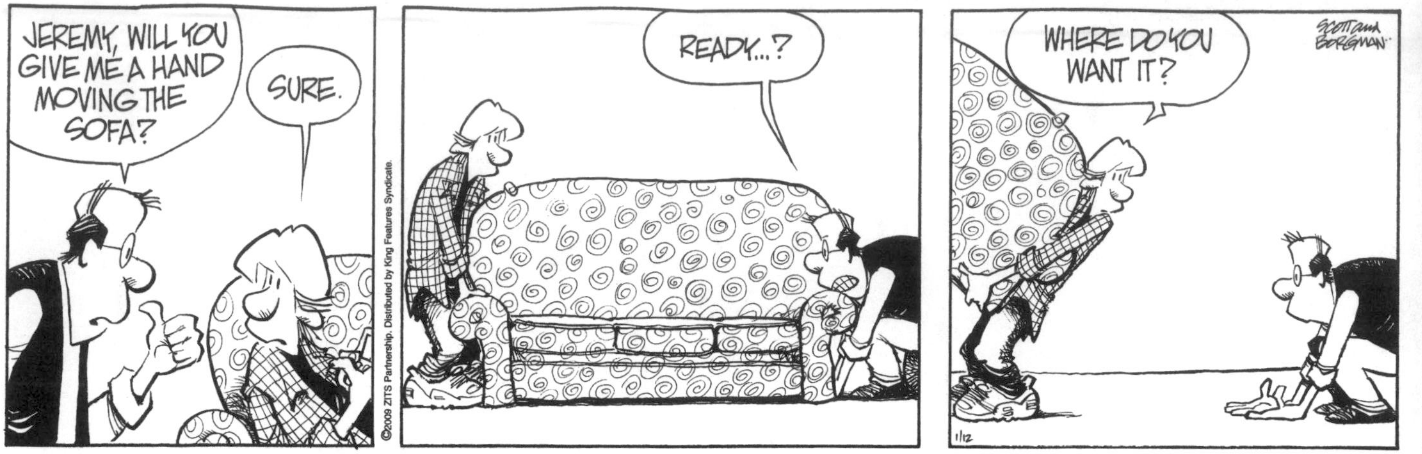
JEREMY, WILL YOU GIVE ME A HAND MOVING THE SOFA?
SURE.
©2009 ZITS Partnership. Distributed by King Features Syndicate.
READY...?
WHERE DO YOU WANT IT?
SCOTT and BORGMAN
1/12

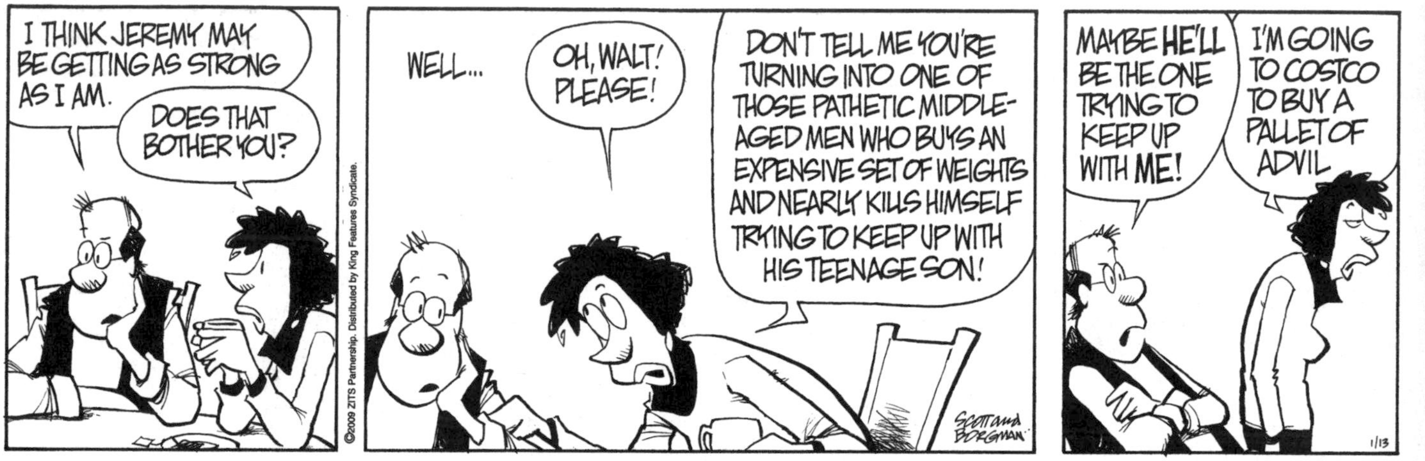
I THINK JEREMY MAY BE GETTING AS STRONG AS I AM.
DOES THAT BOTHER YOU?
©2009 ZITS Partnership. Distributed by King Features Syndicate.
WELL...
OH, WALT! PLEASE!
DON'T TELL ME YOU'RE TURNING INTO ONE OF THOSE PATHETIC MIDDLE-AGED MEN WHO BUYS AN EXPENSIVE SET OF WEIGHTS AND NEARLY KILLS HIMSELF TRYING TO KEEP UP WITH HIS TEENAGE SON!
SCOTT and BORGMAN
MAYBE **HE'LL** BE THE ONE TRYING TO KEEP UP WITH **ME**!
I'M GOING TO COSTCO TO BUY A PALLET OF ADVIL
1/13

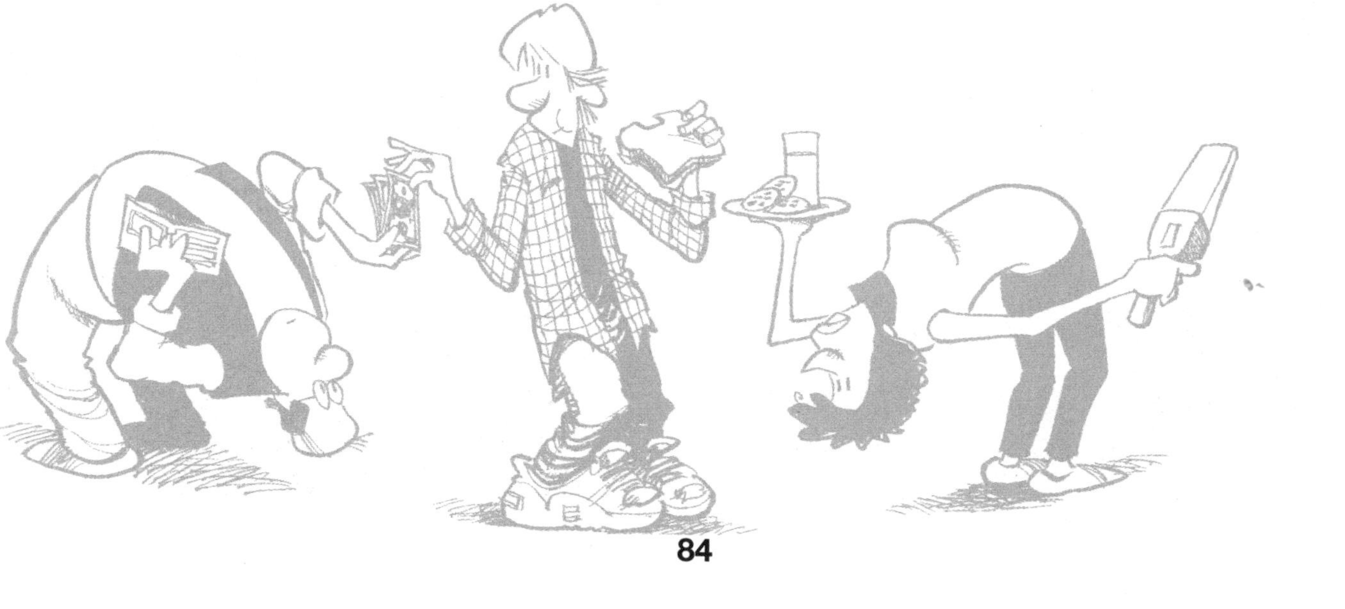

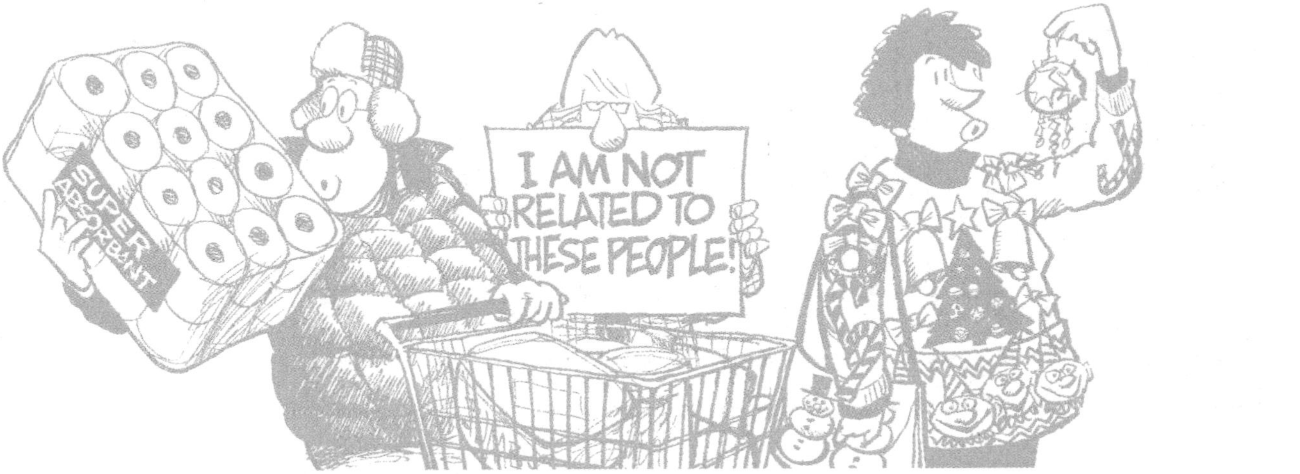
SUPER ABSORBANT
I AM NOT RELATED TO THESE PEOPLE!

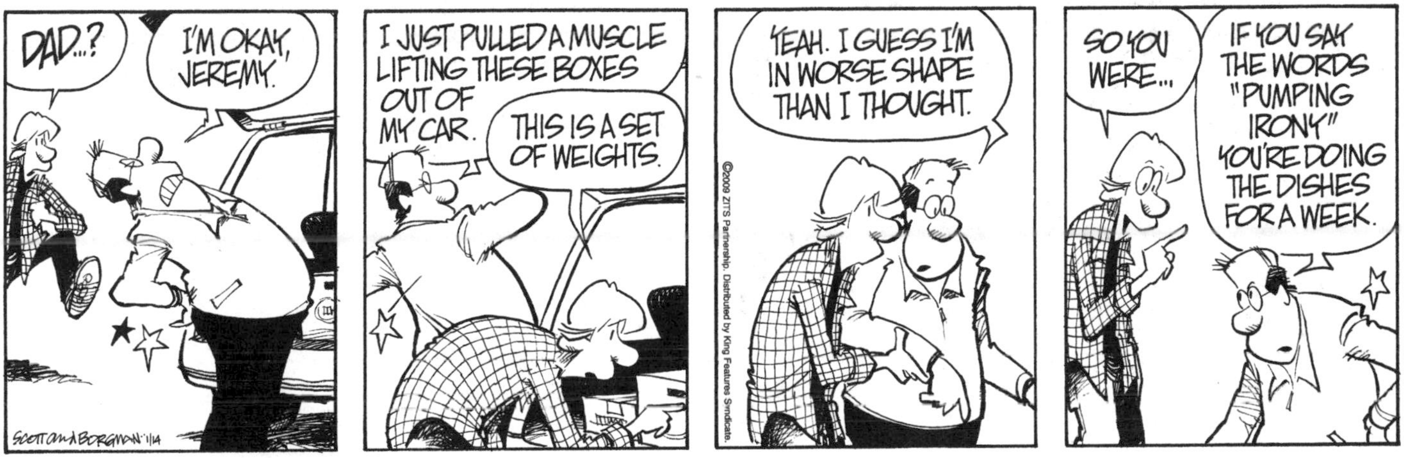
DAD...?
I'M OKAY, JEREMY.
I JUST PULLED A MUSCLE LIFTING THESE BOXES OUT OF MY CAR.
THIS IS A SET OF WEIGHTS.
YEAH. I GUESS I'M IN WORSE SHAPE THAN I THOUGHT.
SO YOU WERE...
IF YOU SAY THE WORDS "PUMPING IRONY" YOU'RE DOING THE DISHES FOR A WEEK.
SCOTT AND BORGMAN 1/14
©2009 ZITS Partnership. Distributed by King Features Syndicate.

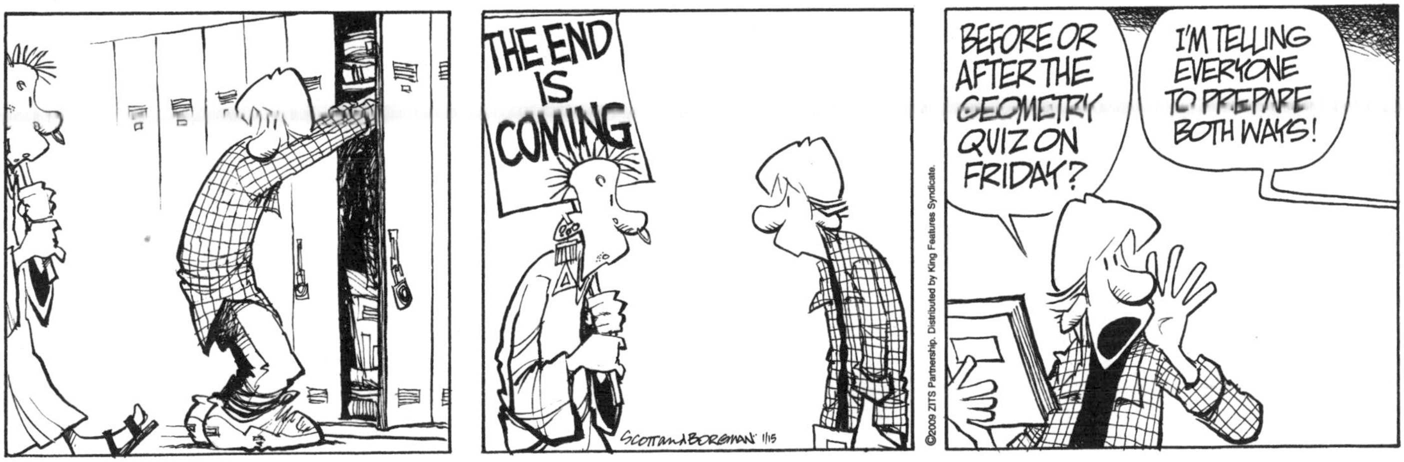
THE END IS COMING
SCOTT AND BORGMAN 1/15
BEFORE OR AFTER THE GEOMETRY QUIZ ON FRIDAY?
I'M TELLING EVERYONE TO PREPARE BOTH WAYS!
©2009 ZITS Partnership. Distributed by King Features Syndicate.

IN LESS THAN TWO YEARS THE ANCIENT MAYAN CALENDAR REACHES THE END OF A 5,126 YEAR ERA AND RESETS ITSELF TO ZERO!

DO YOU HAVE ANY IDEA WHAT THIS COULD MEAN??

THAT A BUNCH OF ANCIENT MAYANS WILL BE DATING THEIR CHECKS "5,127" BY MISTAKE?

WHY CAN'T YOU EVER TAKE UNFOUNDED SCIENCE SERIOUSLY?

THE END IS COMING

LOOK, JEREMY, THE ANCIENT MAYAN CALENDAR IS ABOUT TO RESET ITSELF TO ZERO!

AT THAT MOMENT, THE SUN WILL BE ALIGNED WITH THE CENTER OF THE MILKY WAY FOR THE FIRST TIME IN 26,000 YEARS!!

AND THAT WILL MEAN...?

CHAOS! DESTRUCTION! MAYBE THE END OF CIVILIZATION AS WE KNOW IT!

OR MAYBE NOT.

WHY DO YOU ALWAYS HAVE TO BE SO NEGATIVE?

THE END IS COMING

Zits
by
JERRY SCOTT and
JIM BORGMAN

Classic Literature
AS WRITTEN
Beowulf was king in that Danish castle,
Shild's son ruling as long as his father
And as loved, a famous lord of men.
AS READ
ROCKGOD
still studying?
Send
BASSPLYR
Dude.
u 2?
Reply
Menu
ROCKGOD
Dude.
Reply
Menu
Playlists
▸Chill
▸Study Mix
▸Band Mix
▸Guitar Mix
1/18
SCOTT and BORGMAN
©2009 ZITS Partnership. Distributed by King Features Syndicate

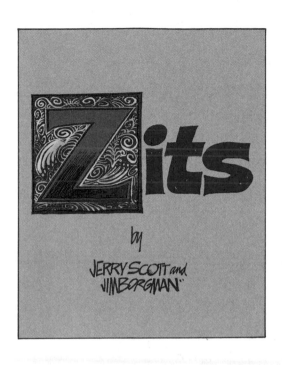

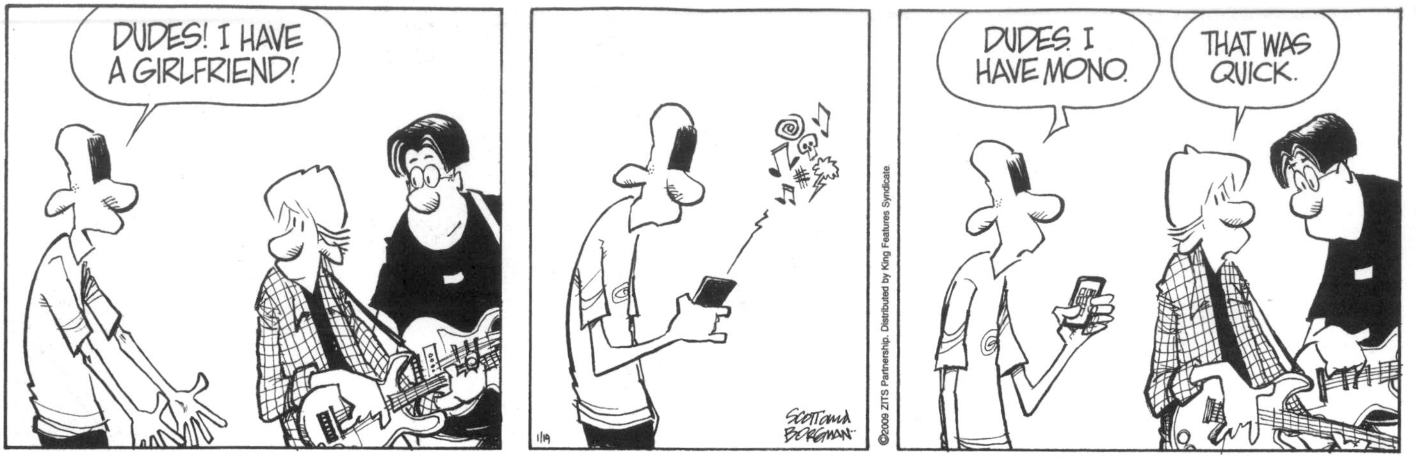
DUDES! I HAVE A GIRLFRIEND!
DUDES. I HAVE MONO.
THAT WAS QUICK.
1/19
SCOTT and BORGMAN
©2009 ZITS Partnership. Distributed by King Features Syndicate

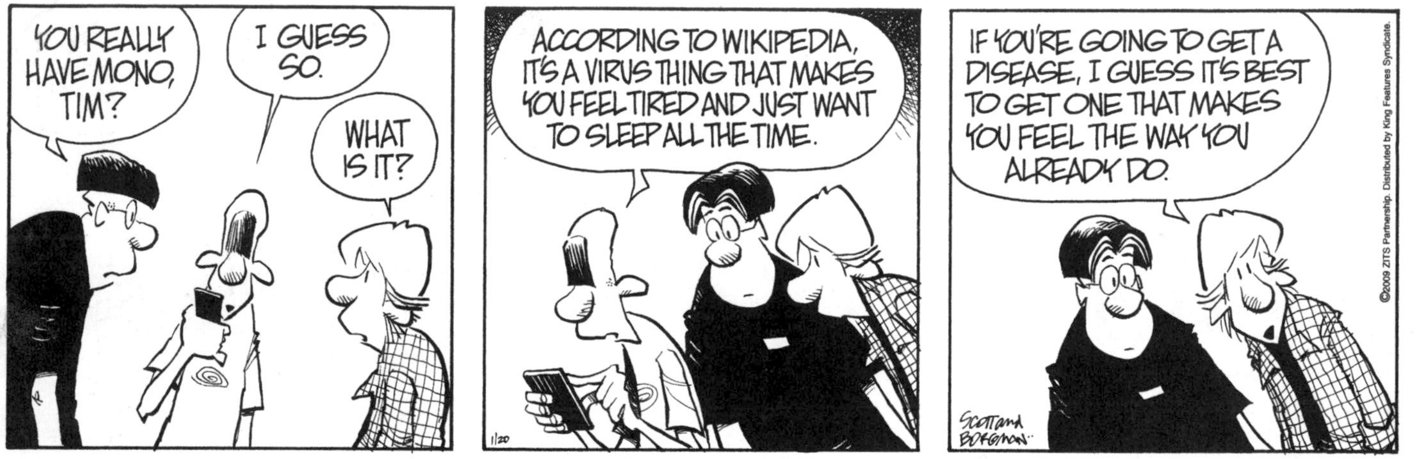
YOU REALLY HAVE MONO, TIM?
I GUESS SO.
WHAT IS IT?
ACCORDING TO WIKIPEDIA, IT'S A VIRUS THING THAT MAKES YOU FEEL TIRED AND JUST WANT TO SLEEP ALL THE TIME.
IF YOU'RE GOING TO GET A DISEASE, I GUESS IT'S BEST TO GET ONE THAT MAKES YOU FEEL THE WAY YOU ALREADY DO.
1/20
SCOTT and BORGMAN
©2009 ZITS Partnership. Distributed by King Features Syndicate.

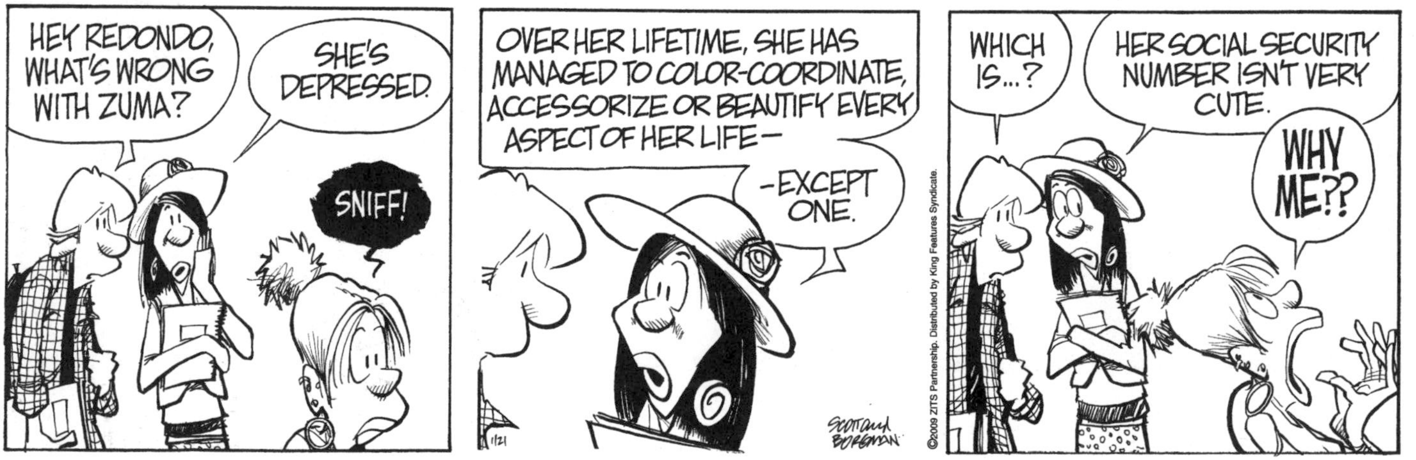
HEY REDONDO, WHAT'S WRONG WITH ZUMA?
SHE'S DEPRESSED.
SNIFF!
OVER HER LIFETIME, SHE HAS MANAGED TO COLOR-COORDINATE, ACCESSORIZE OR BEAUTIFY EVERY ASPECT OF HER LIFE—
—EXCEPT ONE.
WHICH IS...?
HER SOCIAL SECURITY NUMBER ISN'T VERY CUTE.
WHY ME??
1/21
SCOTT and BORGMAN
©2009 ZITS Partnership. Distributed by King Features Syndicate.

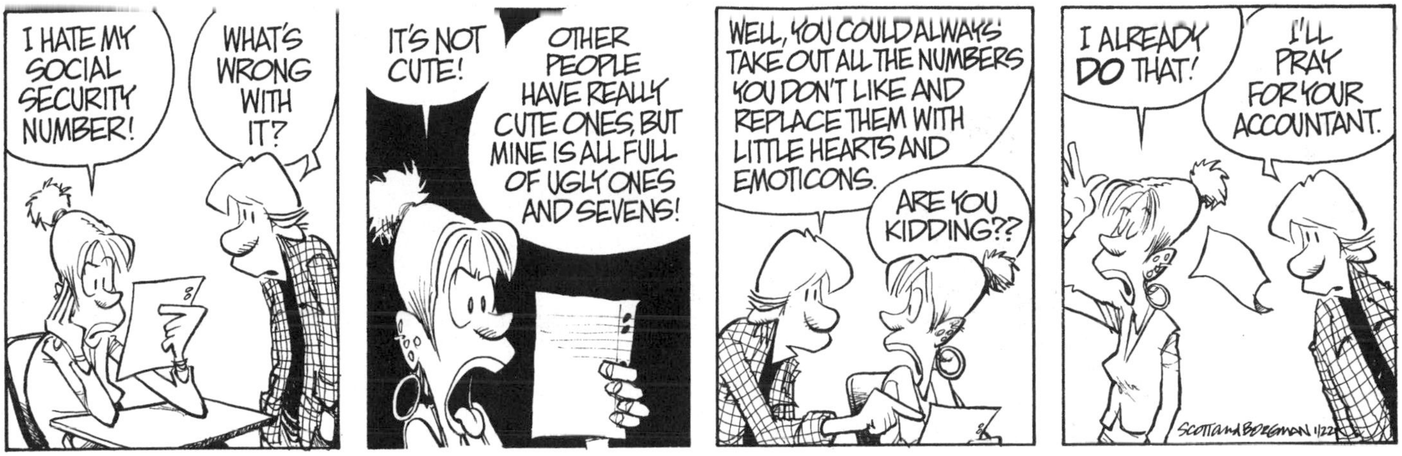
I HATE MY SOCIAL SECURITY NUMBER!
WHAT'S WRONG WITH IT?
IT'S NOT CUTE!
OTHER PEOPLE HAVE REALLY CUTE ONES, BUT MINE IS ALL FULL OF UGLY ONES AND SEVENS!
WELL, YOU COULD ALWAYS TAKE OUT ALL THE NUMBERS YOU DON'T LIKE AND REPLACE THEM WITH LITTLE HEARTS AND EMOTICONS.
ARE YOU KIDDING??
I ALREADY DO THAT!
I'LL PRAY FOR YOUR ACCOUNTANT.
SCOTT AND BORGMAN 1/22

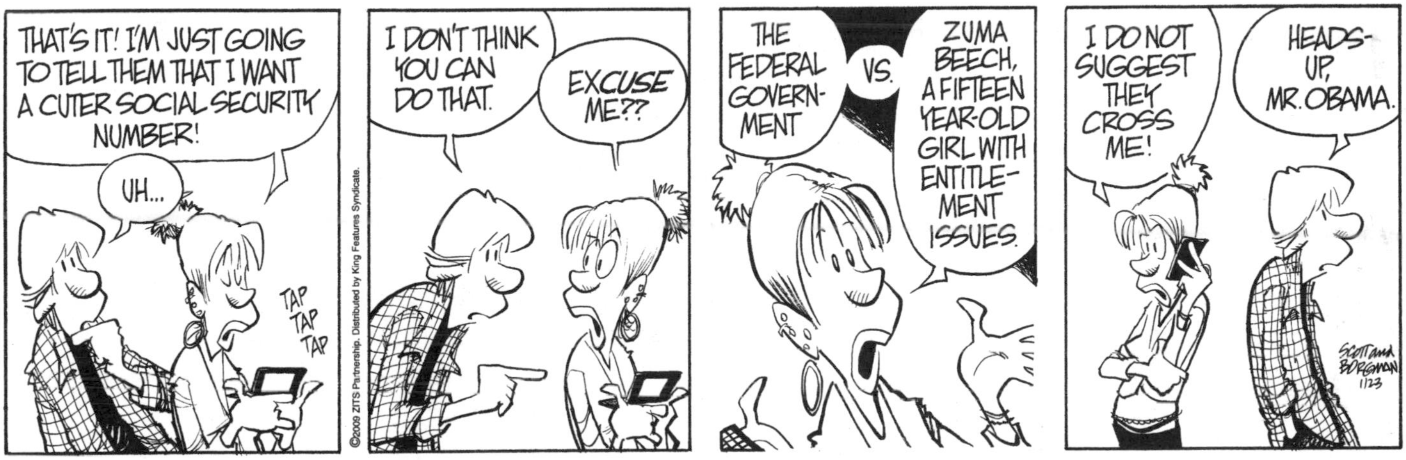
THAT'S IT! I'M JUST GOING TO TELL THEM THAT I WANT A CUTER SOCIAL SECURITY NUMBER!
UH...
TAP TAP TAP
©2009 ZITS Partnership. Distributed by King Features Syndicate.
I DON'T THINK YOU CAN DO THAT.
EXCUSE ME??
THE FEDERAL GOVERNMENT
VS.
ZUMA BEECH, A FIFTEEN YEAR-OLD GIRL WITH ENTITLEMENT ISSUES.
I DO NOT SUGGEST THEY CROSS ME!
HEADS-UP, MR. OBAMA.
SCOTT AND BORGMAN 1/23

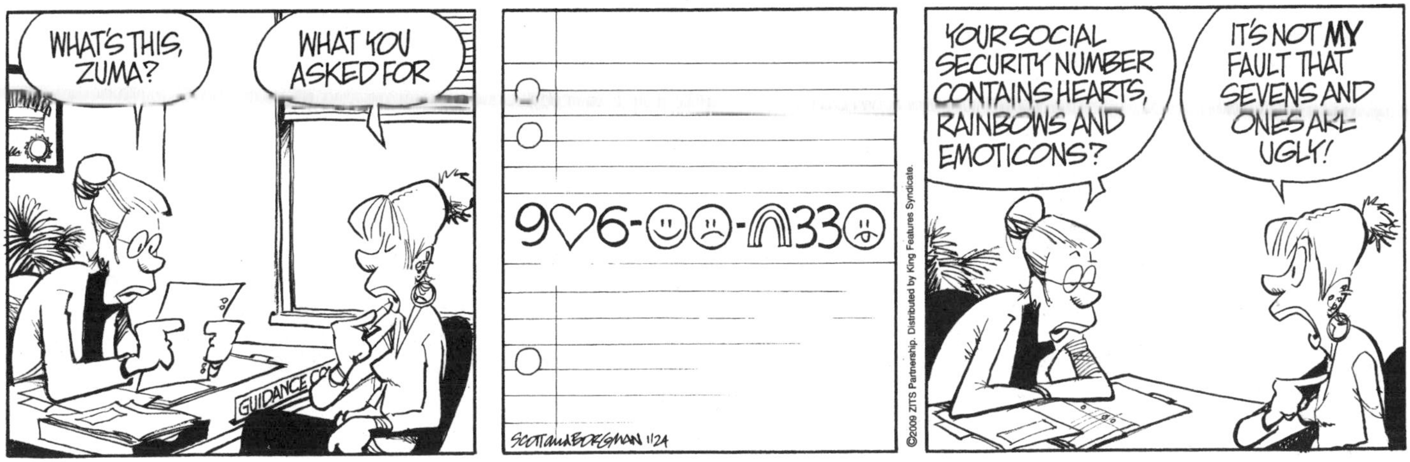
WHAT'S THIS, ZUMA?
WHAT YOU ASKED FOR
GUIDANCE CO
9♡6-☺☹-∩33☹
SCOTT AND BORGMAN 1/24
©2009 ZITS Partnership. Distributed by King Features Syndicate.
YOUR SOCIAL SECURITY NUMBER CONTAINS HEARTS, RAINBOWS AND EMOTICONS?
IT'S NOT MY FAULT THAT SEVENS AND ONES ARE UGLY!

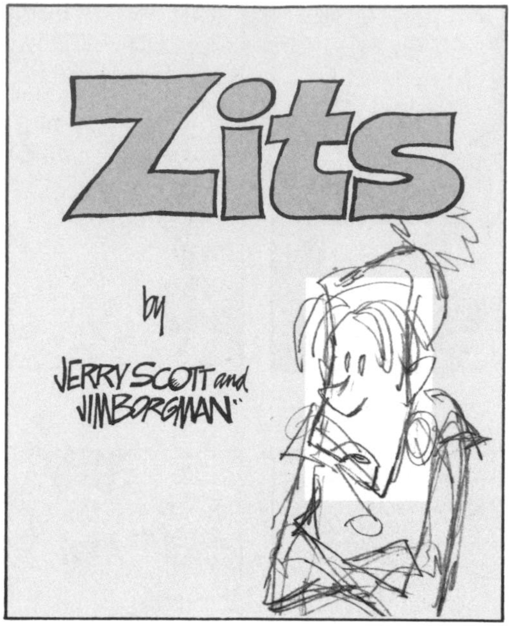

Zits
by
JERRY SCOTT and
JIM BORGMAN

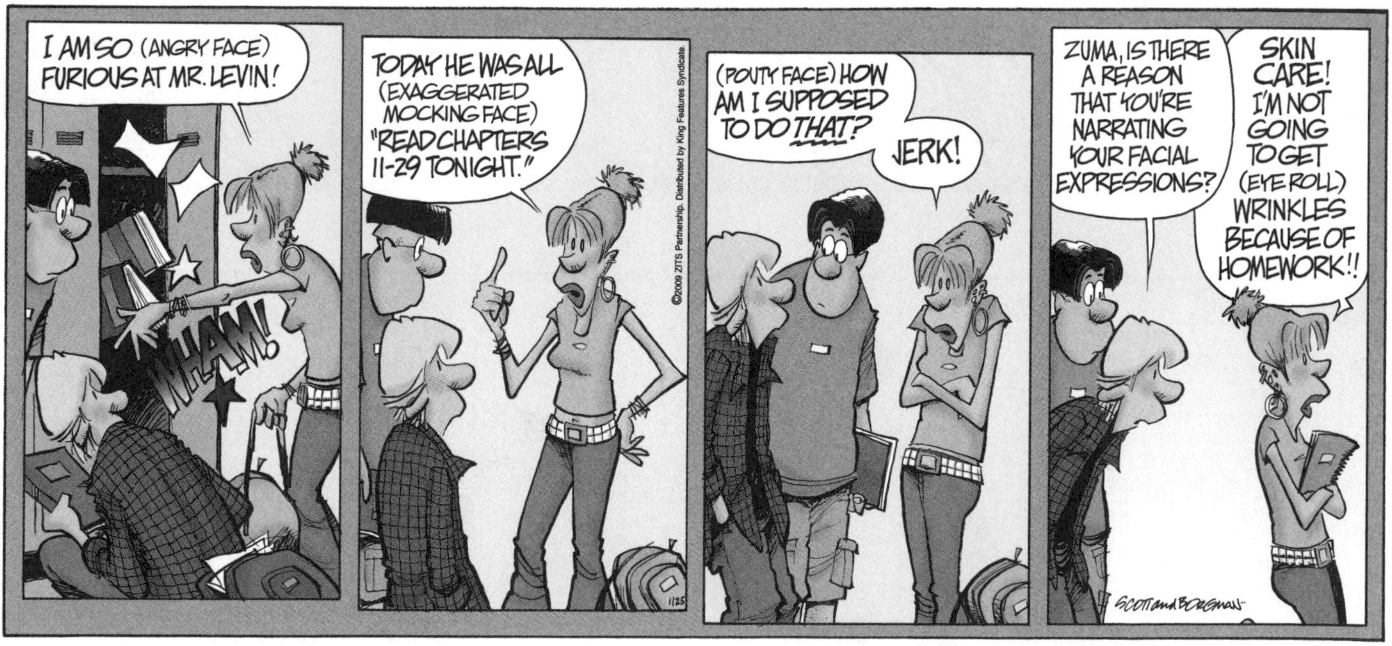

I AM SO (ANGRY FACE) FURIOUS AT MR. LEVIN!
WHAM!
TODAY HE WAS ALL (EXAGGERATED MOCKING FACE) "READ CHAPTERS 11-29 TONIGHT."
©2009 ZITS Partnership. Distributed by King Features Syndicate.
(POUTY FACE) HOW AM I SUPPOSED TO DO THAT?
JERK!
ZUMA, IS THERE A REASON THAT YOU'RE NARRATING YOUR FACIAL EXPRESSIONS?
SKIN CARE! I'M NOT GOING TO GET (EYE ROLL) WRINKLES BECAUSE OF HOMEWORK!!
SCOTT and BORGMAN

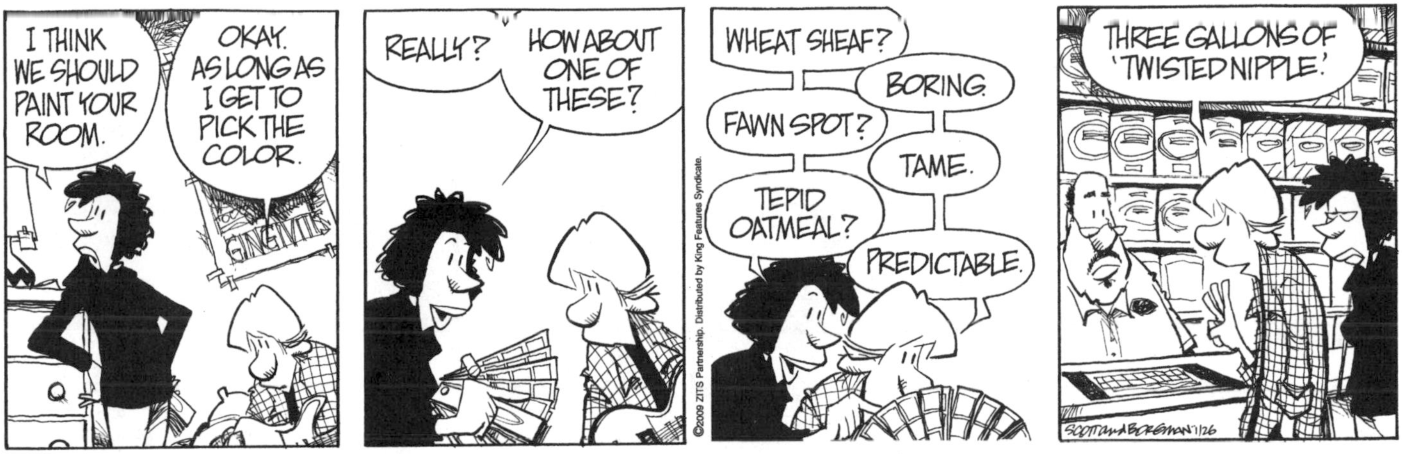
I THINK WE SHOULD PAINT YOUR ROOM.
OKAY. AS LONG AS I GET TO PICK THE COLOR.
GINGIVITIS
REALLY?
HOW ABOUT ONE OF THESE?
©2009 ZITS Partnership. Distributed by King Features Syndicate.
WHEAT SHEAF?
BORING.
FAWN SPOT?
TAME.
TEPID OATMEAL?
PREDICTABLE.
THREE GALLONS OF 'TWISTED NIPPLE.'
SCOTT and BORGMAN 1/26

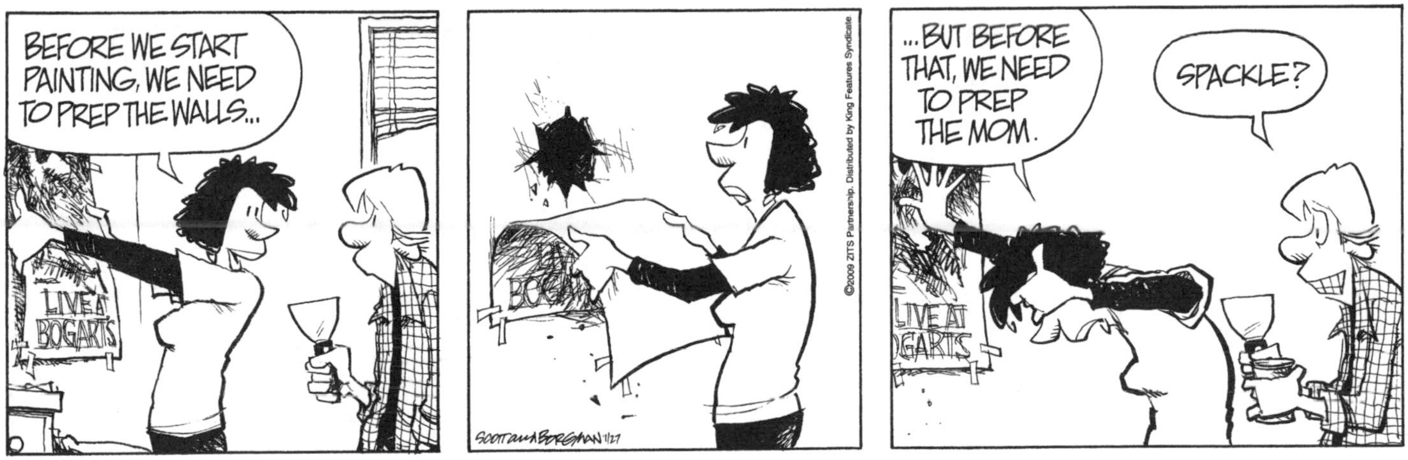
BEFORE WE START PAINTING, WE NEED TO PREP THE WALLS...
LIVE AT BOGARTS
SCOTT and BORGMAN 1/27
©2009 ZITS Partnership. Distributed by King Features Syndicate.
...BUT BEFORE THAT, WE NEED TO PREP THE MOM.
SPACKLE?

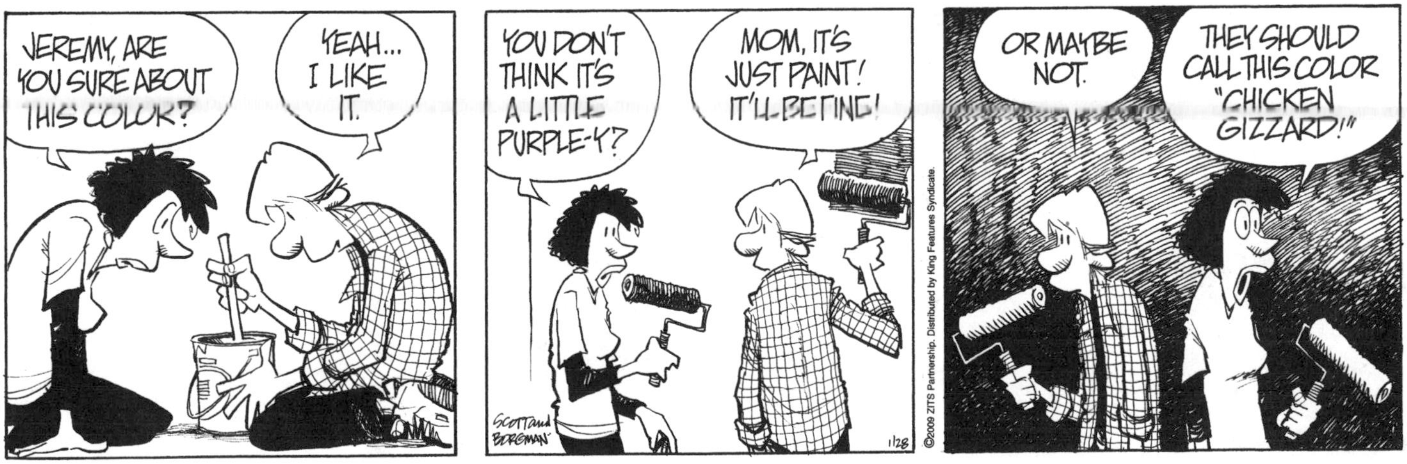
JEREMY, ARE YOU SURE ABOUT THIS COLOR?
YEAH... I LIKE IT.
YOU DON'T THINK IT'S A LITTLE PURPLE-Y?
MOM, IT'S JUST PAINT! IT'LL BE FINE!
SCOTT and BORGMAN 1/28
©2009 ZITS Partnership. Distributed by King Features Syndicate.
OR MAYBE NOT.
THEY SHOULD CALL THIS COLOR "CHICKEN GIZZARD!"

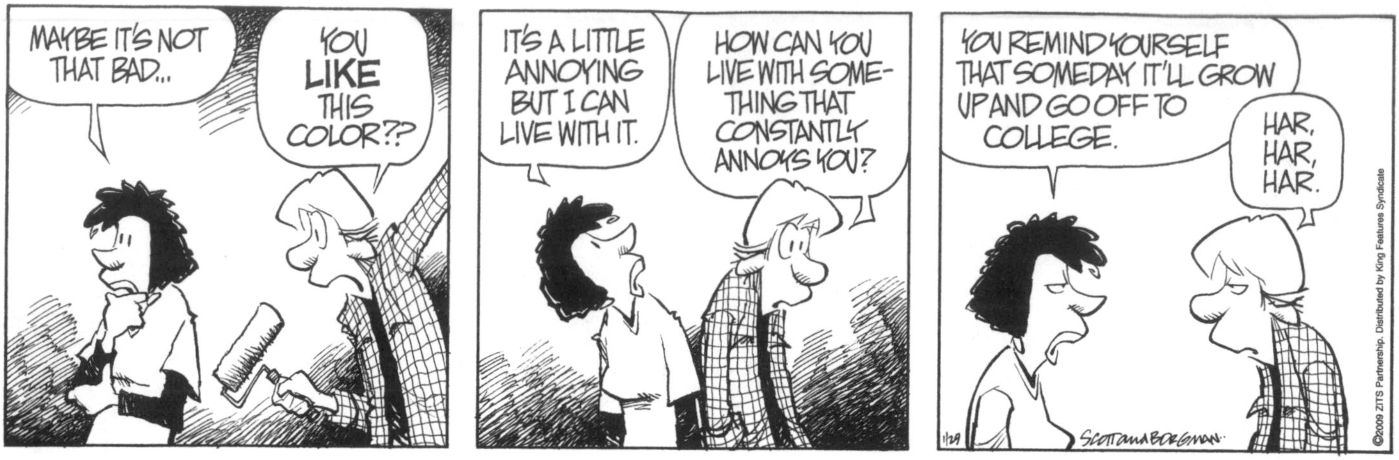
MAYBE IT'S NOT THAT BAD...
YOU **LIKE** THIS COLOR??
IT'S A LITTLE ANNOYING BUT I CAN LIVE WITH IT.
HOW CAN YOU LIVE WITH SOMETHING THAT CONSTANTLY ANNOYS YOU?
YOU REMIND YOURSELF THAT SOMEDAY IT'LL GROW UP AND GO OFF TO COLLEGE.
HAR, HAR, HAR.
1/29
SCOTT and BORGMAN
©2009 ZITS Partnership. Distributed by King Features Syndicate

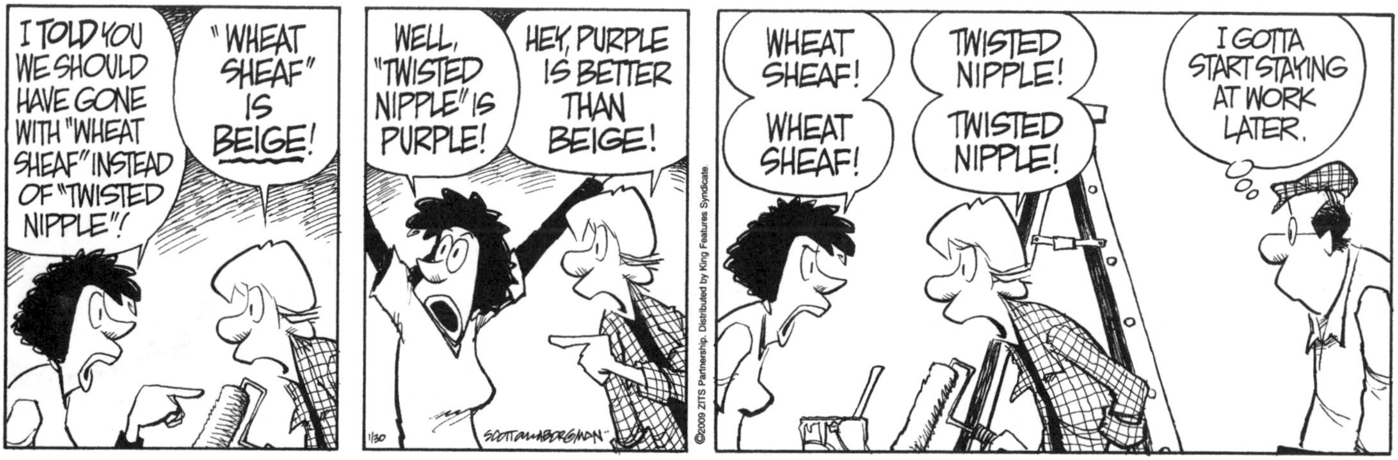
I TOLD YOU WE SHOULD HAVE GONE WITH "WHEAT SHEAF" INSTEAD OF "TWISTED NIPPLE"!
"WHEAT SHEAF" IS BEIGE!
WELL, "TWISTED NIPPLE" IS PURPLE!
HEY, PURPLE IS BETTER THAN BEIGE!
1/30
SCOTT and BORGMAN
©2009 ZITS Partnership. Distributed by King Features Syndicate.
WHEAT SHEAF!
WHEAT SHEAF!
TWISTED NIPPLE!
TWISTED NIPPLE!
I GOTTA START STAYING AT WORK LATER.

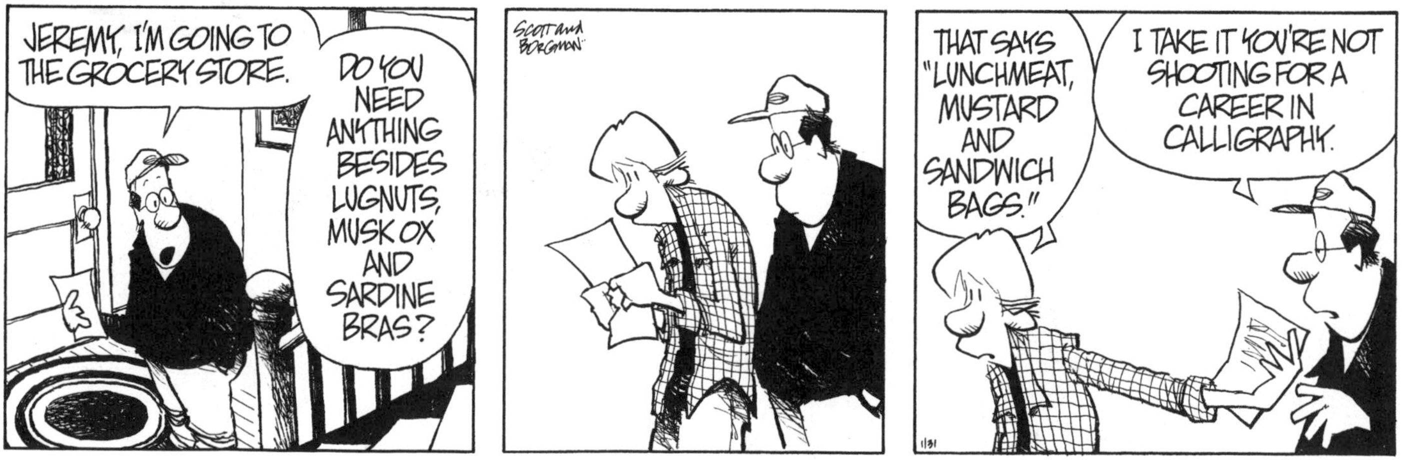
JEREMY, I'M GOING TO THE GROCERY STORE.
DO YOU NEED ANYTHING BESIDES LUGNUTS, MUSK OX AND SARDINE BRAS?
SCOTT and BORGMAN
THAT SAYS "LUNCHMEAT, MUSTARD AND SANDWICH BAGS."
I TAKE IT YOU'RE NOT SHOOTING FOR A CAREER IN CALLIGRAPHY.
1/31

Zits
JERRY SCOTT and JIM BORGMAN

OH, JEREMY!
LOOK! A BOX OF YOUR OLD PICTURE BOOKS!
HERE'S GOODNIGHT MOON, CURIOUS GEORGE, BROWN BEAR, BROWN BEAR...
(GASP!) HAROLD AND THE PURPLE CRAYON!
DO YOU REMEMBER THIS ONE?
HAROLD USES HIS CRAYON TO DRAW HIS OWN ADVENTURES!
LIKE DRAWING THE BOAT?
AND FEEDING THE VERY HUNGRY MOOSE...
...AND THE DESERVING PORCUPINE?
YEAH! AND THERE'S THE DRAGON THAT GUARDS THE APPLE TREE...
AND FINDING THE MOON...
START FROM THE BEGINNING.
©2009 ZITS Partnership. Distributed by King Features Syndicate.
SCOTT and BORGMAN

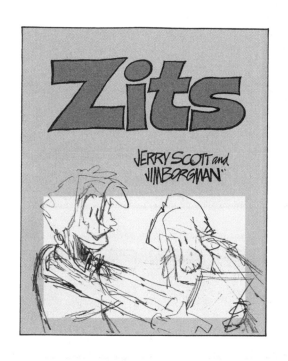

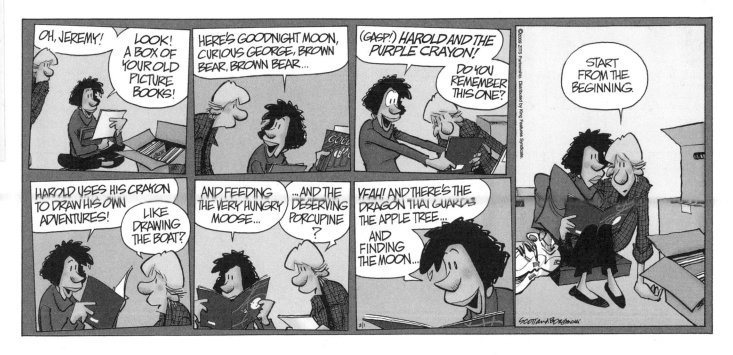

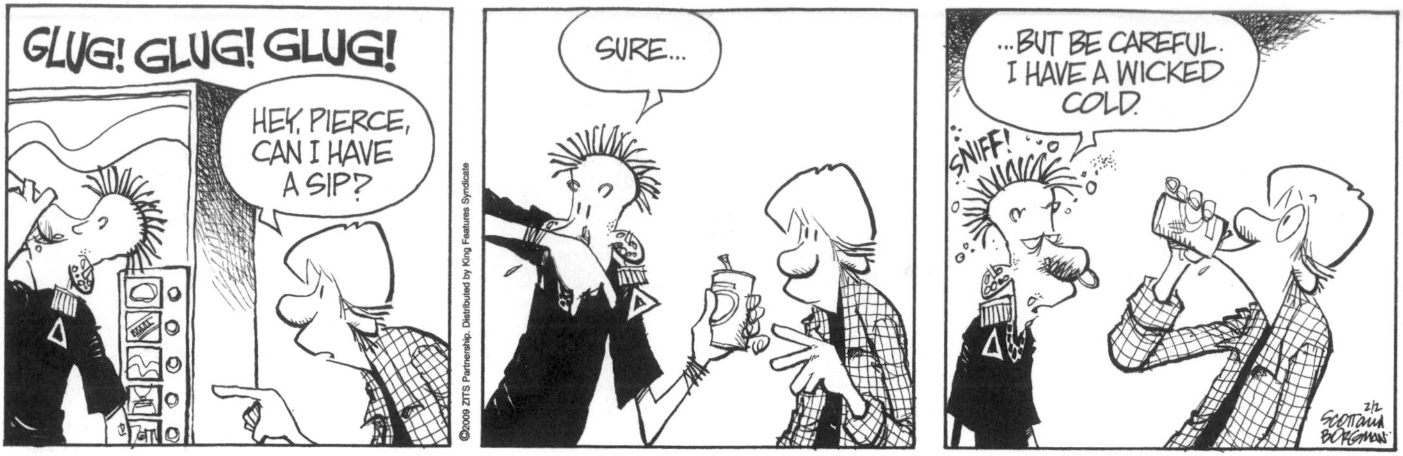
GLUG! GLUG! GLUG!
HEY, PIERCE, CAN I HAVE A SIP?
©2009 ZITS Partnership. Distributed by King Features Syndicate
SURE...
...BUT BE CAREFUL. I HAVE A WICKED COLD.
SNIFF!
2/2
SCOTT and BORGMAN

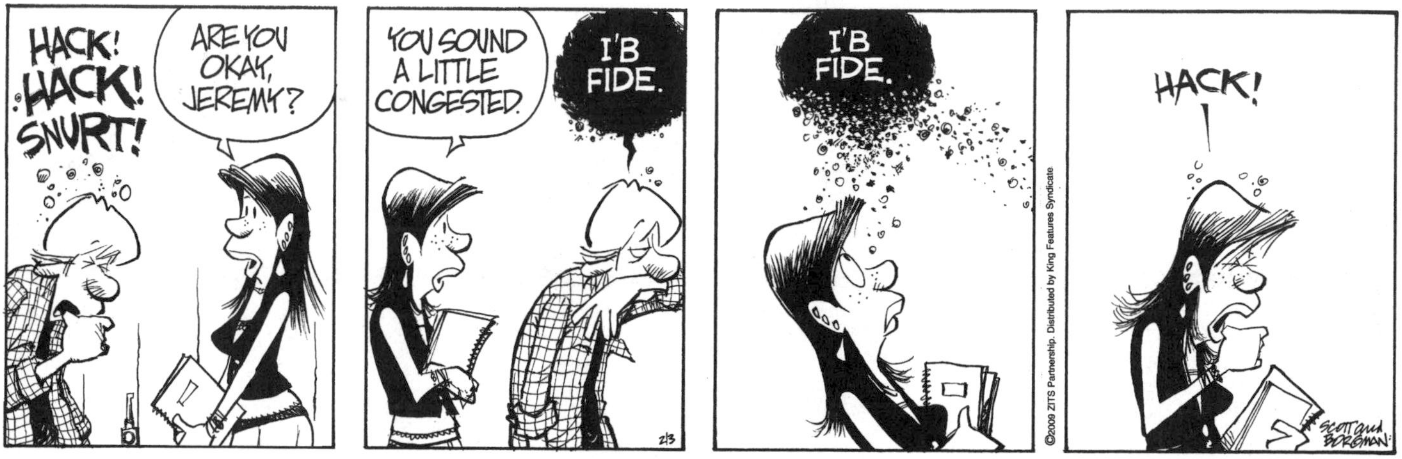
HACK! HACK! SNURT!
ARE YOU OKAY, JEREMY?
YOU SOUND A LITTLE CONGESTED.
I'B FIDE.
2/3
I'B FIDE.
©2009 ZITS Partnership. Distributed by King Features Syndicate
HACK!
SCOTT and BORGMAN

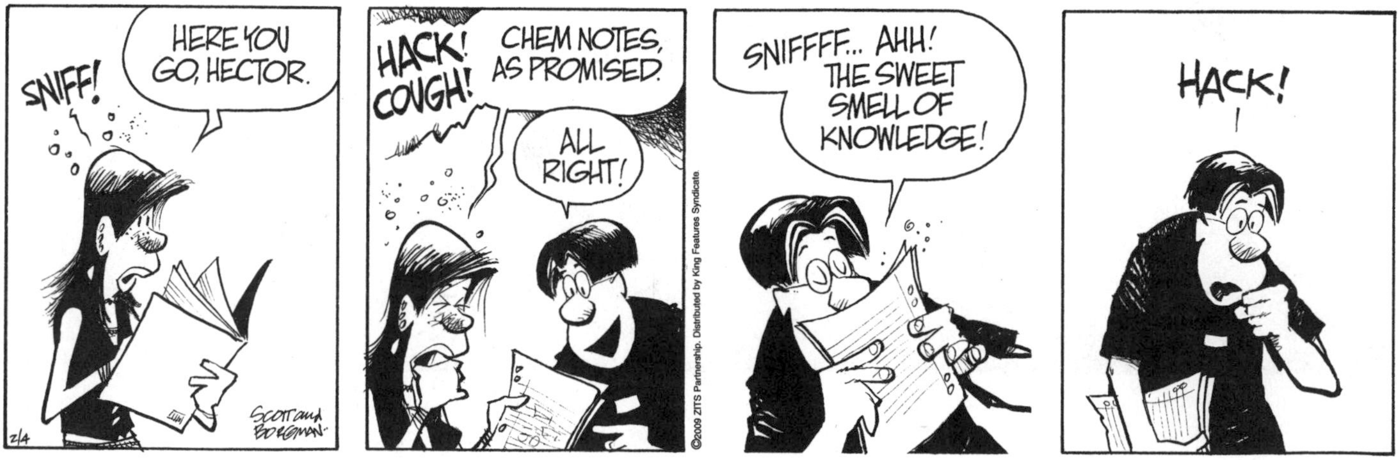
SNIFF!
HERE YOU GO, HECTOR.
2/4
SCOTT and BORGMAN
HACK! COUGH!
CHEM NOTES, AS PROMISED.
ALL RIGHT!
©2009 ZITS Partnership. Distributed by King Features Syndicate
SNIFFFF... AHH! THE SWEET SMELL OF KNOWLEDGE!
HACK!

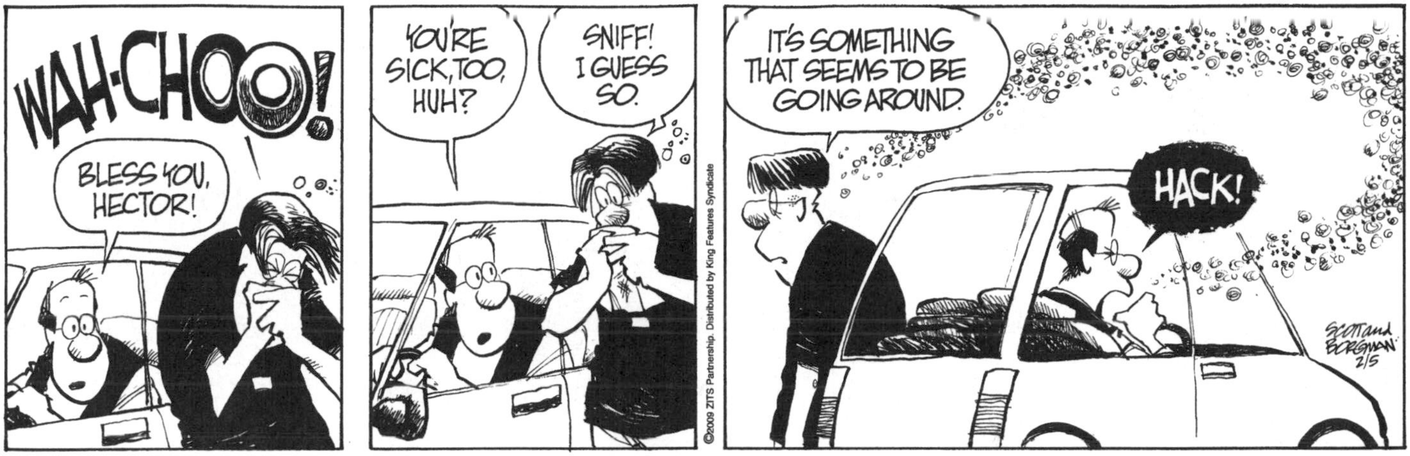
WAH-CHOO!
BLESS YOU, HECTOR!
YOU'RE SICK, TOO, HUH?
SNIFF! I GUESS SO.
©2009 ZITS Partnership. Distributed by King Features Syndicate
IT'S SOMETHING THAT SEEMS TO BE GOING AROUND.
HACK!
SCOTT AND BORGMAN 2/5

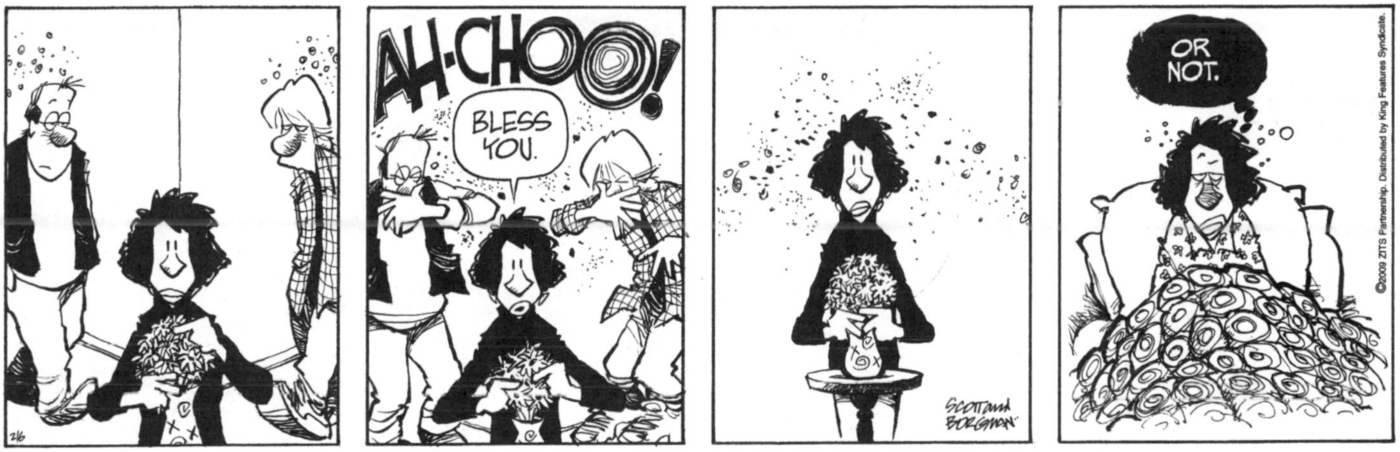
2/6
AH-CHOO!
BLESS YOU.
SCOTT AND BORGMAN
OR NOT.
©2009 ZITS Partnership. Distributed by King Features Syndicate.

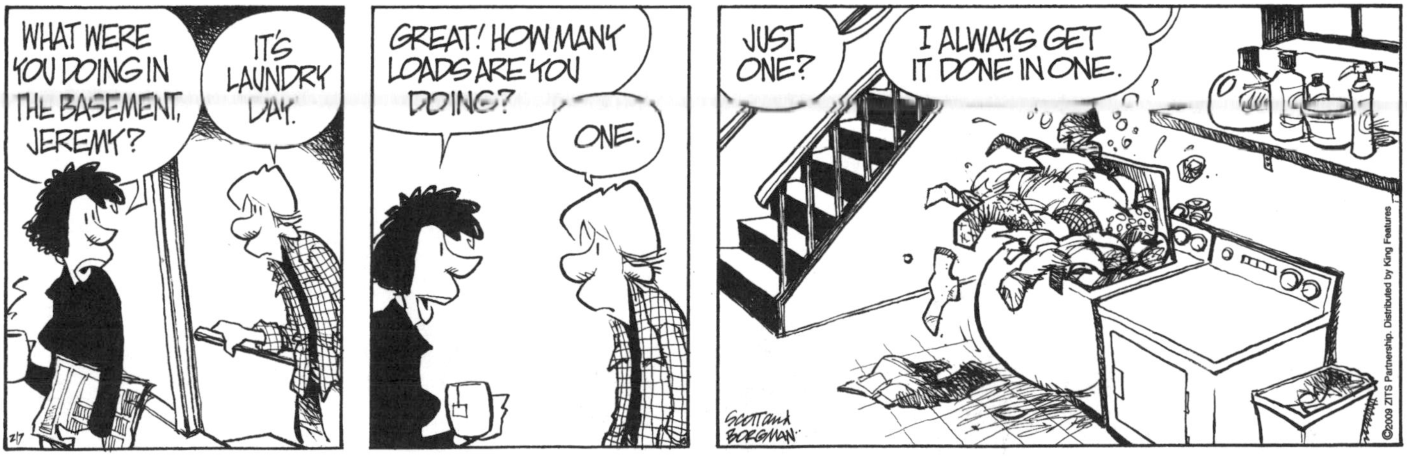
WHAT WERE YOU DOING IN THE BASEMENT, JEREMY?
IT'S LAUNDRY DAY.
2/7
GREAT! HOW MANY LOADS ARE YOU DOING?
ONE.
JUST ONE?
I ALWAYS GET IT DONE IN ONE.
SCOTT AND BORGMAN
©2009 ZITS Partnership. Distributed by King Features

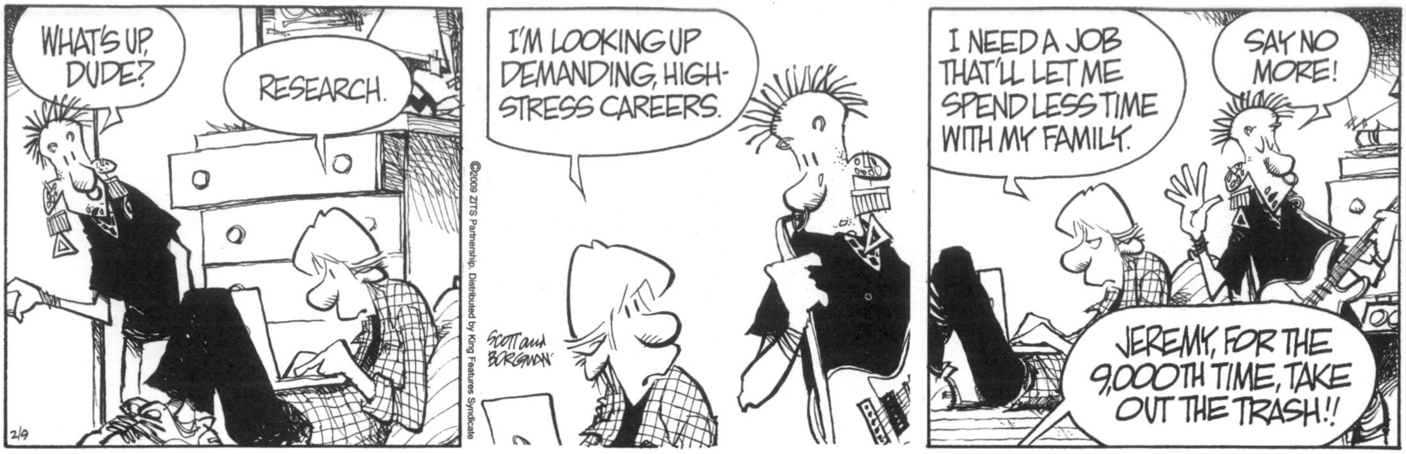
WHAT'S UP, DUDE?
RESEARCH.
©2009 ZITS Partnership. Distributed by King Features Syndicate
I'M LOOKING UP DEMANDING, HIGH-STRESS CAREERS.
I NEED A JOB THAT'LL LET ME SPEND LESS TIME WITH MY FAMILY.
SAY NO MORE!
JEREMY, FOR THE 9,000TH TIME, TAKE OUT THE TRASH!!

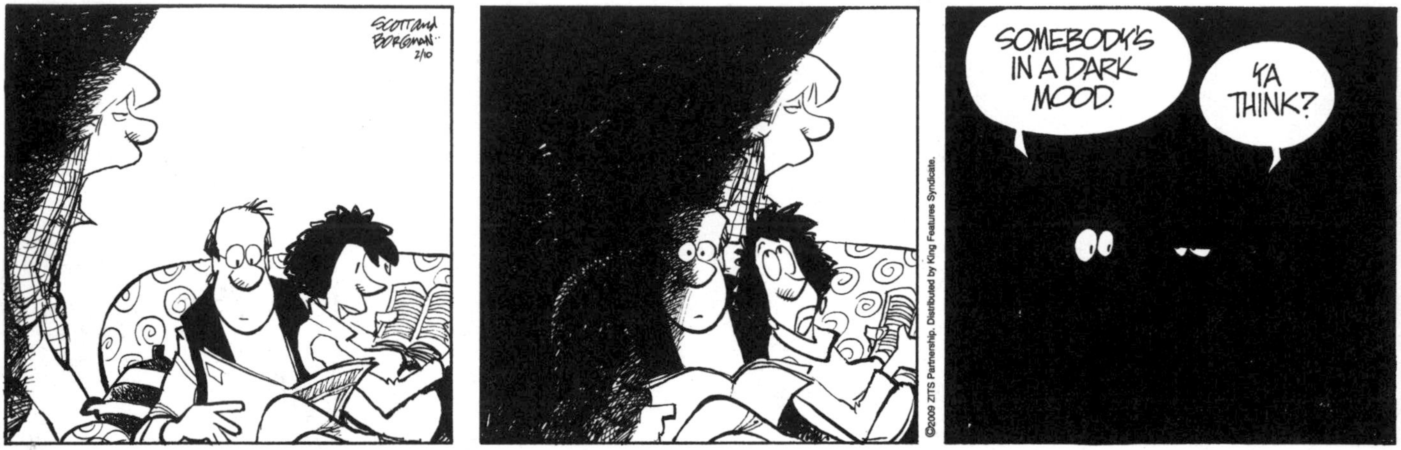
SOMEBODY'S IN A DARK MOOD.
YA THINK?
©2009 ZITS Partnership. Distributed by King Features Syndicate.

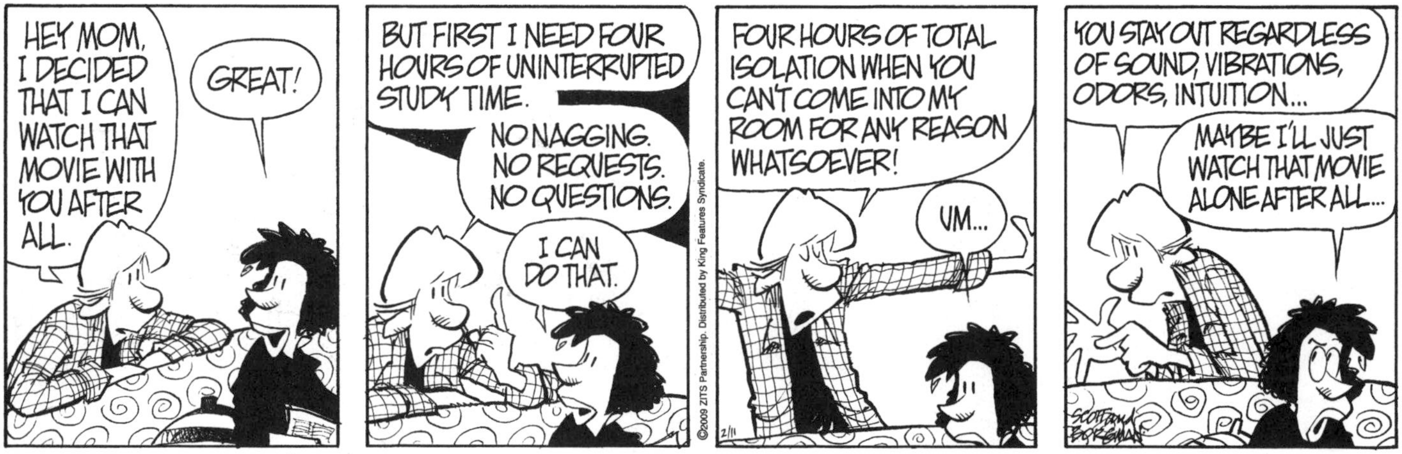
HEY MOM, I DECIDED THAT I CAN WATCH THAT MOVIE WITH YOU AFTER ALL.
GREAT!
BUT FIRST I NEED FOUR HOURS OF UNINTERRUPTED STUDY TIME.
NO NAGGING. NO REQUESTS. NO QUESTIONS.
I CAN DO THAT.
©2009 ZITS Partnership. Distributed by King Features Syndicate.
FOUR HOURS OF TOTAL ISOLATION WHEN YOU CAN'T COME INTO MY ROOM FOR ANY REASON WHATSOEVER!
UM...
YOU STAY OUT REGARDLESS OF SOUND, VIBRATIONS, ODORS, INTUITION...
MAYBE I'LL JUST WATCH THAT MOVIE ALONE AFTER ALL...

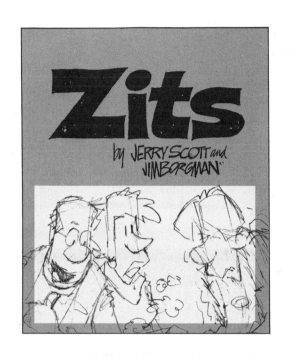

Zits
by JERRY SCOTT and JIM BORGMAN

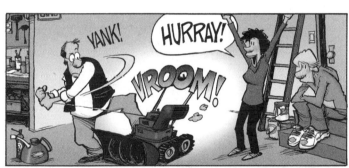

YANK!
HURRAY!
VROOM!
THAT'S WHAT I'M TALKIN' ABOUT!
(SHUDDER!)
WHAT'S WRONG, JEREMY?
NOTHING.
IT'S JUST THAT WHENEVER DAD USES A SLANG PHRASE THAT'S THE LEAST BIT CURRENT, THE WORLD SEEMS TOTALLY OUT OF BALANCE AND WEIRD.
WELL, EXCUSE ME FOR BEING JIGGY WITH THE LINGO!
BEING WHAT??
OKAY, NOW WE'RE BACK TO NORMAL!
2/8
SCOTT and BORGMAN
©2009 ZITS Partnership. Distributed by King Features Syndicate.

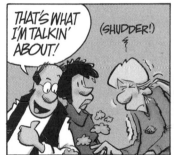

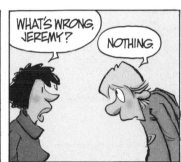

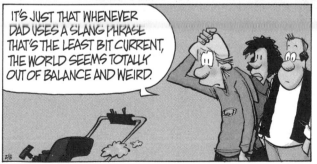

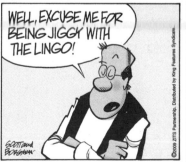

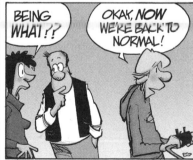

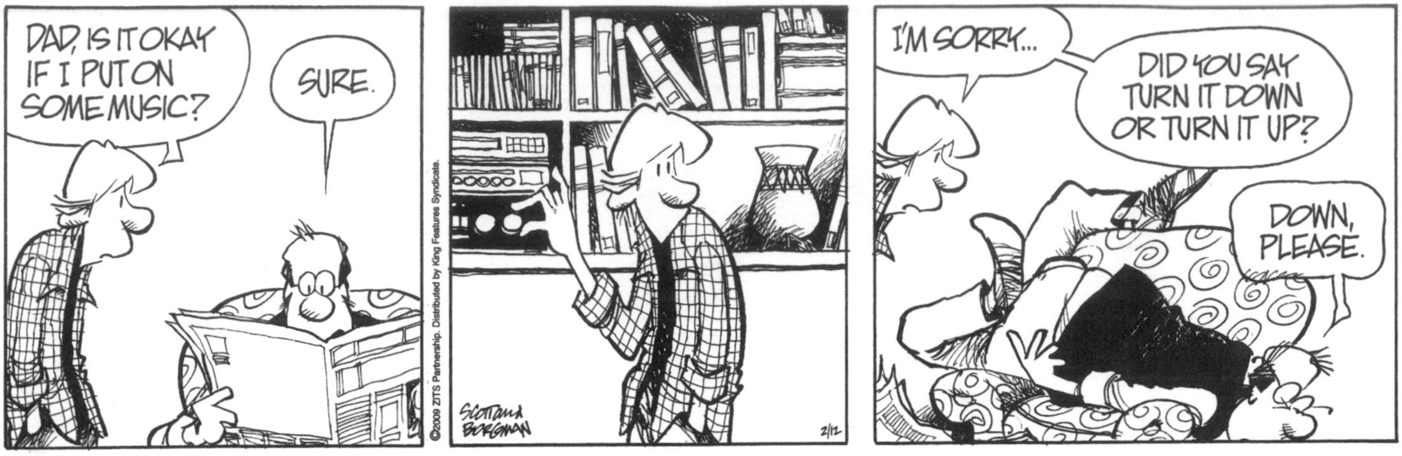
DAD, IS IT OKAY IF I PUT ON SOME MUSIC?
SURE.
©2009 ZITS Partnership. Distributed by King Features Syndicate.
SCOTT AND BORGMAN
2/12
I'M SORRY...
DID YOU SAY TURN IT DOWN OR TURN IT UP?
DOWN, PLEASE.

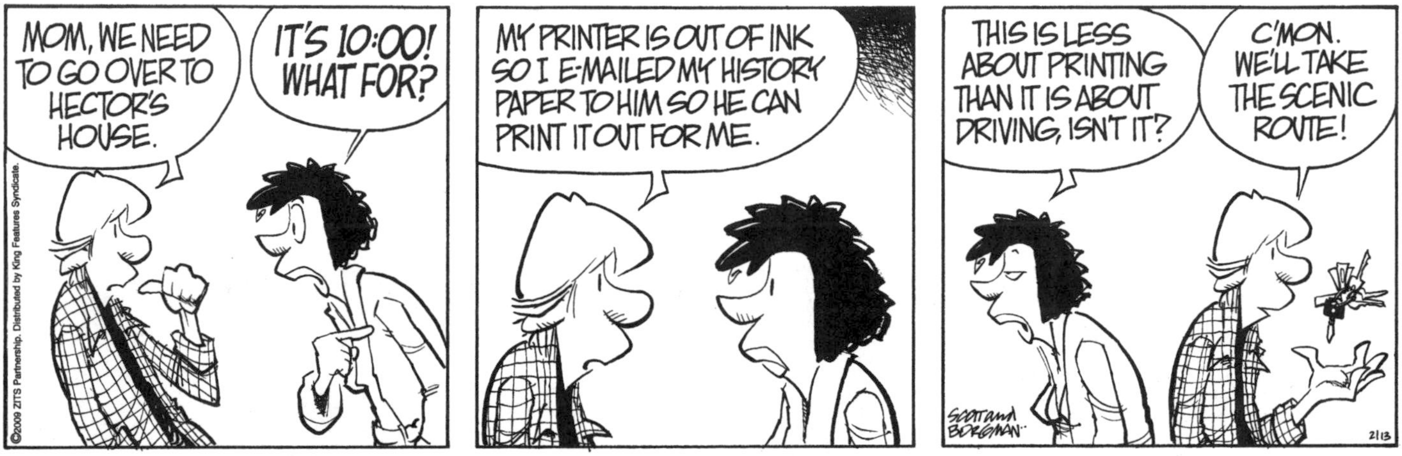
MOM, WE NEED TO GO OVER TO HECTOR'S HOUSE.
IT'S 10:00! WHAT FOR?
©2009 ZITS Partnership. Distributed by King Features Syndicate.
MY PRINTER IS OUT OF INK SO I E-MAILED MY HISTORY PAPER TO HIM SO HE CAN PRINT IT OUT FOR ME.
THIS IS LESS ABOUT PRINTING THAN IT IS ABOUT DRIVING, ISN'T IT?
C'MON. WE'LL TAKE THE SCENIC ROUTE!
SCOTT AND BORGMAN
2/13

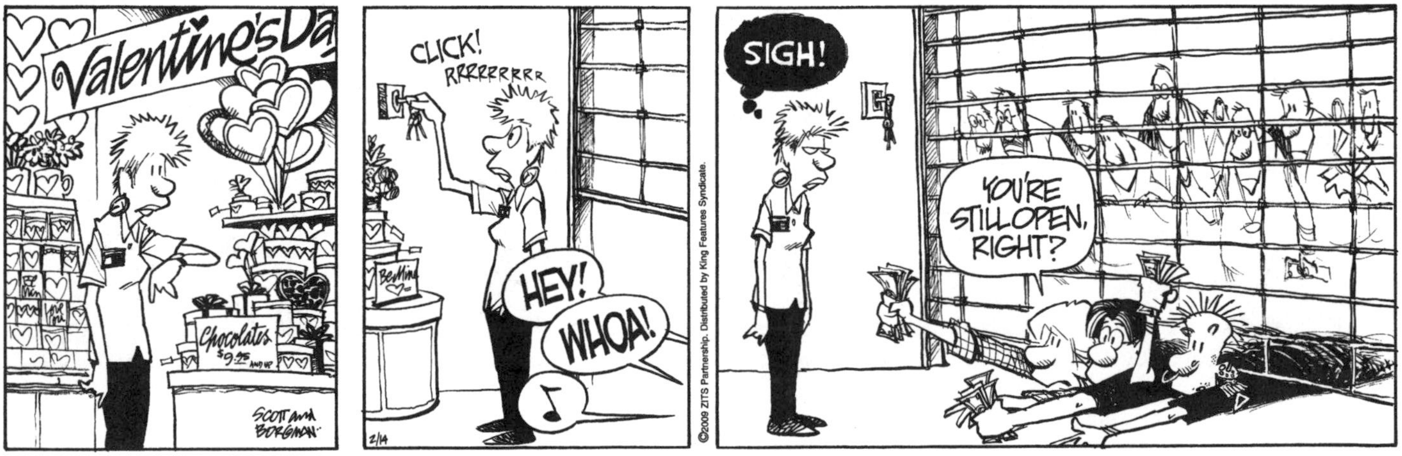
Valentine's Day
Chocolates $9.95 and up
SCOTT AND BORGMAN
CLICK!
RRRRRRRR
Be Mine
HEY!
WHOA!
2/14
©2009 ZITS Partnership. Distributed by King Features Syndicate.
SIGH!
YOU'RE STILL OPEN, RIGHT?

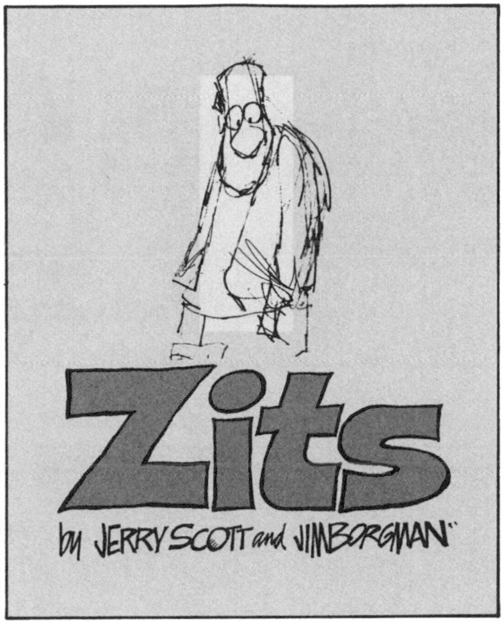
Zits
by JERRY SCOTT and JIM BORGMAN

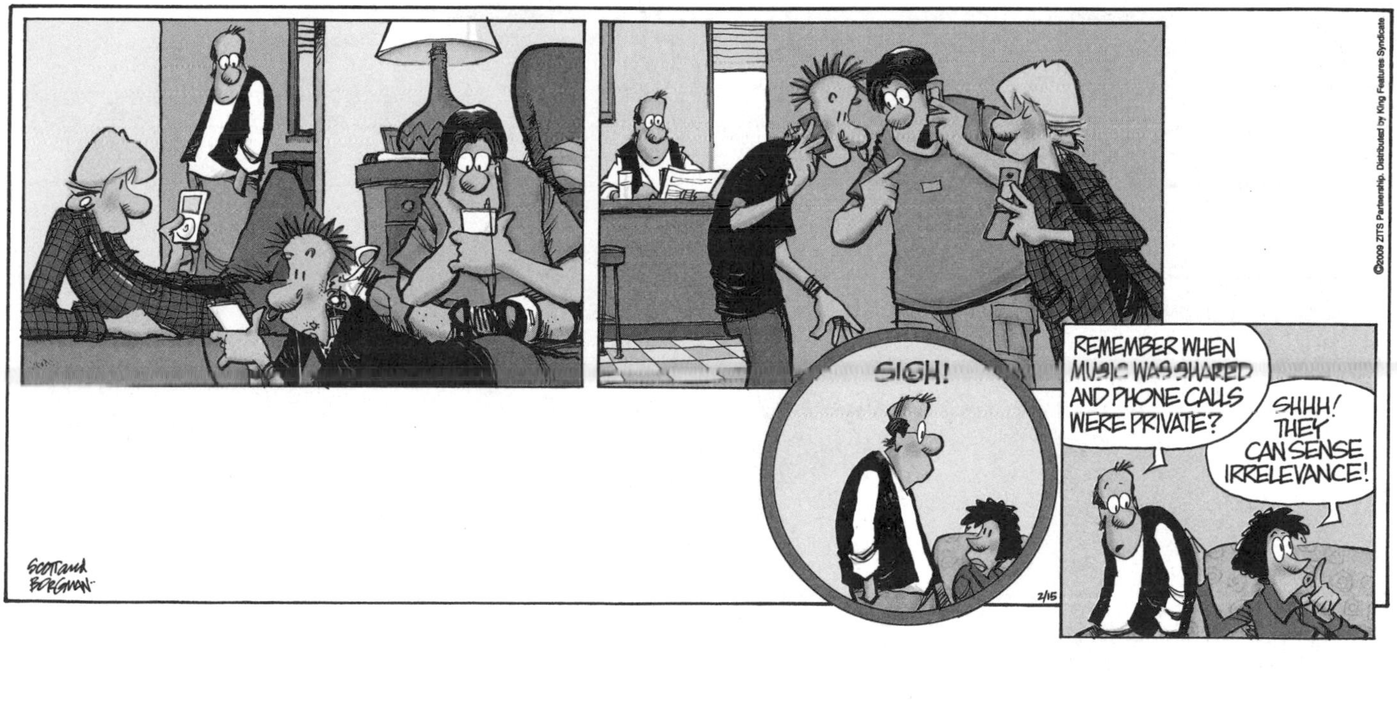
SIGH!
REMEMBER WHEN MUSIC WAS SHARED AND PHONE CALLS WERE PRIVATE?
SHHH! THEY CAN SENSE IRRELEVANCE!
SCOTT and BORGMAN
2/15
©2009 ZITS Partnership. Distributed by King Features Syndicate

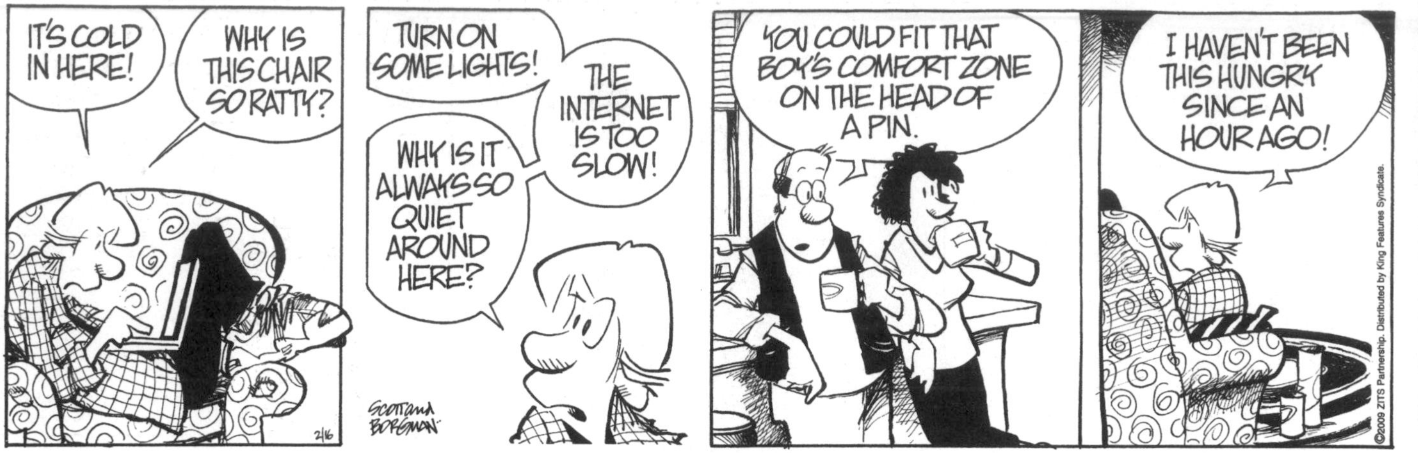
IT'S COLD IN HERE!
WHY IS THIS CHAIR SO RATTY?
TURN ON SOME LIGHTS!
THE INTERNET IS TOO SLOW!
WHY IS IT ALWAYS SO QUIET AROUND HERE?
SCOTT AND BORGMAN
2/16
YOU COULD FIT THAT BOY'S COMFORT ZONE ON THE HEAD OF A PIN.
I HAVEN'T BEEN THIS HUNGRY SINCE AN HOUR AGO!
©2009 ZITS Partnership. Distributed by King Features Syndicate.

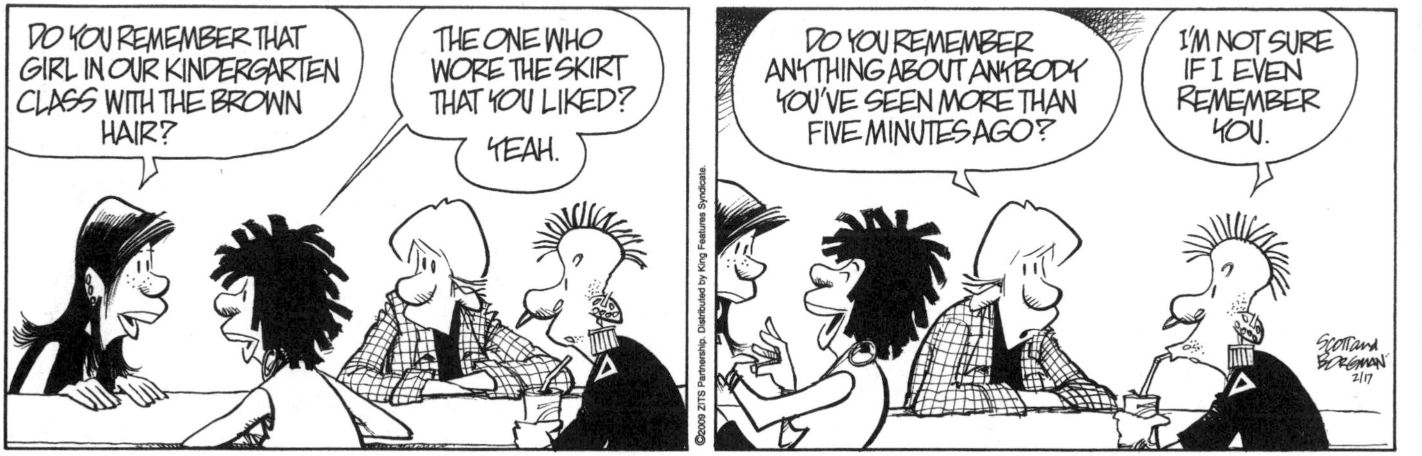
DO YOU REMEMBER THAT GIRL IN OUR KINDERGARTEN CLASS WITH THE BROWN HAIR?
THE ONE WHO WORE THE SKIRT THAT YOU LIKED?
YEAH.
©2009 ZITS Partnership. Distributed by King Features Syndicate.
DO YOU REMEMBER ANYTHING ABOUT ANYBODY YOU'VE SEEN MORE THAN FIVE MINUTES AGO?
I'M NOT SURE IF I EVEN REMEMBER YOU.
SCOTT AND BORGMAN
2/17

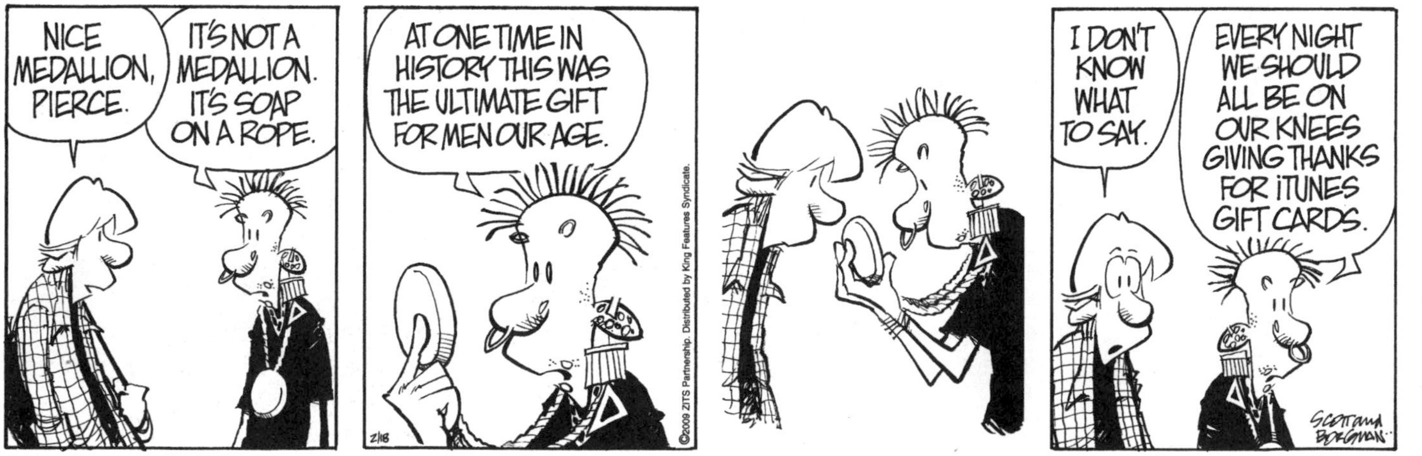
NICE MEDALLION, PIERCE.
IT'S NOT A MEDALLION. IT'S SOAP ON A ROPE.
AT ONE TIME IN HISTORY THIS WAS THE ULTIMATE GIFT FOR MEN OUR AGE.
2/18
©2009 ZITS Partnership. Distributed by King Features Syndicate.
I DON'T KNOW WHAT TO SAY.
EVERY NIGHT WE SHOULD ALL BE ON OUR KNEES GIVING THANKS FOR iTUNES GIFT CARDS.
SCOTT AND BORGMAN

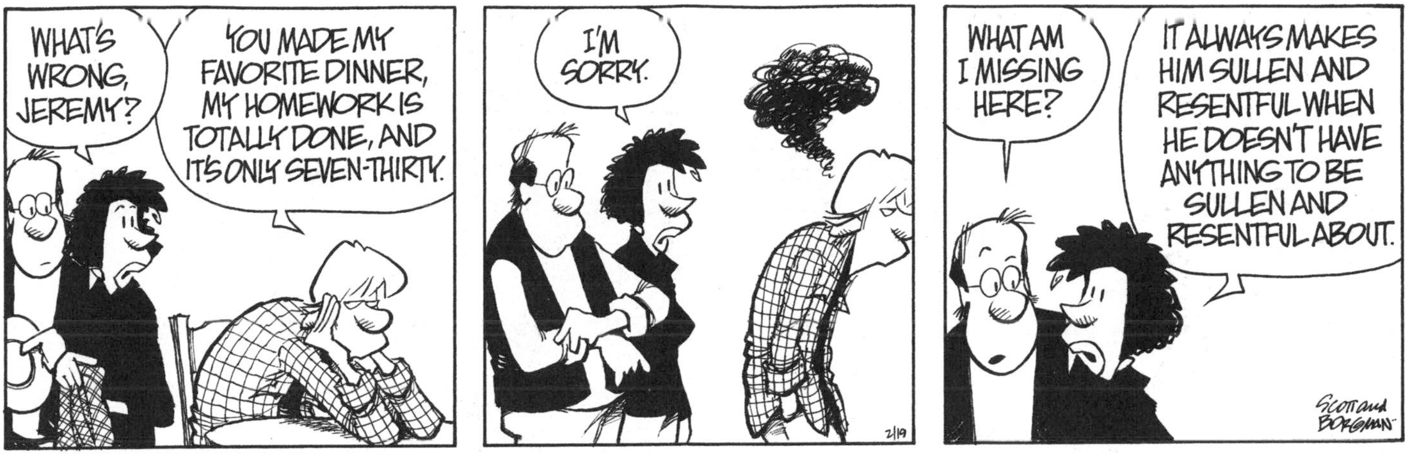
WHAT'S WRONG, JEREMY?
YOU MADE MY FAVORITE DINNER, MY HOMEWORK IS TOTALLY DONE, AND IT'S ONLY SEVEN-THIRTY.
I'M SORRY.
WHAT AM I MISSING HERE?
IT ALWAYS MAKES HIM SULLEN AND RESENTFUL WHEN HE DOESN'T HAVE ANYTHING TO BE SULLEN AND RESENTFUL ABOUT.
SCOTT and BORGMAN

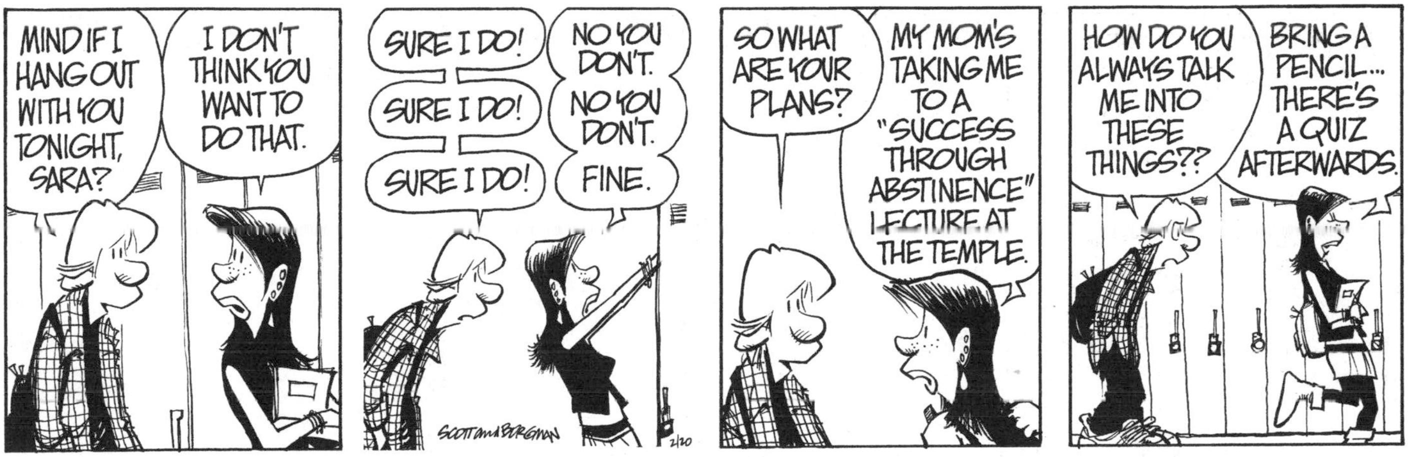
MIND IF I HANG OUT WITH YOU TONIGHT, SARA?
I DON'T THINK YOU WANT TO DO THAT.
SURE I DO!
NO YOU DON'T.
SURE I DO!
NO YOU DON'T.
SURE I DO!
FINE.
SCOTT and BORGMAN
SO WHAT ARE YOUR PLANS?
MY MOM'S TAKING ME TO A "SUCCESS THROUGH ABSTINENCE" LECTURE AT THE TEMPLE.
HOW DO YOU ALWAYS TALK ME INTO THESE THINGS??
BRING A PENCIL... THERE'S A QUIZ AFTERWARDS.

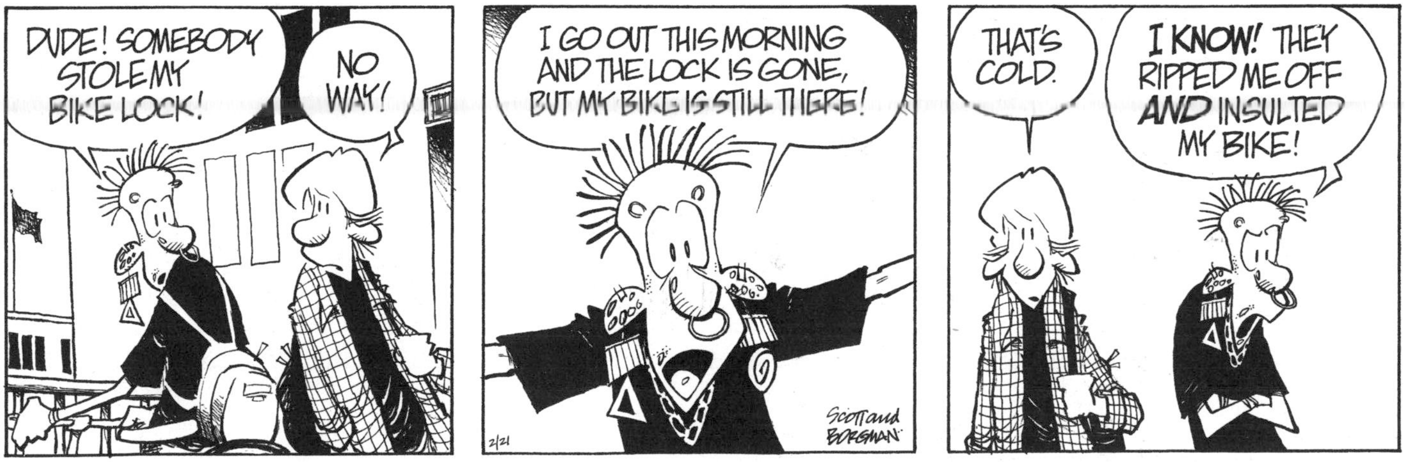
DUDE! SOMEBODY STOLE MY BIKE LOCK!
NO WAY!
I GO OUT THIS MORNING AND THE LOCK IS GONE, BUT MY BIKE IS STILL THERE!
SCOTT and BORGMAN
THAT'S COLD.
I KNOW! THEY RIPPED ME OFF AND INSULTED MY BIKE!

Zits
by
JERRY SCOTT and
JIM BORGMAN

FLICK!
WIPE! WIPE! WIPE!
SLAM!
WIPE! WIPE! WIPE!
CLICK!
2/22
WIPE! WIPE! WIPE!
FLUSH!
WIPE! WIPE!
WIPE!
ÜBERGERMAPHOBE.
MY DAD'S LIKE THIS WHEN I HAVE A COLD, TOO.... ONLY HE WEARS A SURGICAL MASK BESIDES.
SCOTT and BORGMAN
© ZITS Partnership. Distributed by King Features Syndicate.

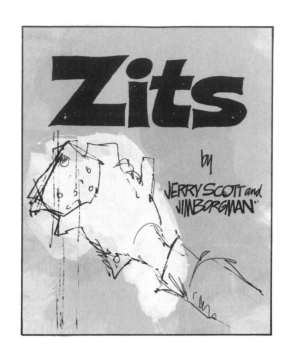

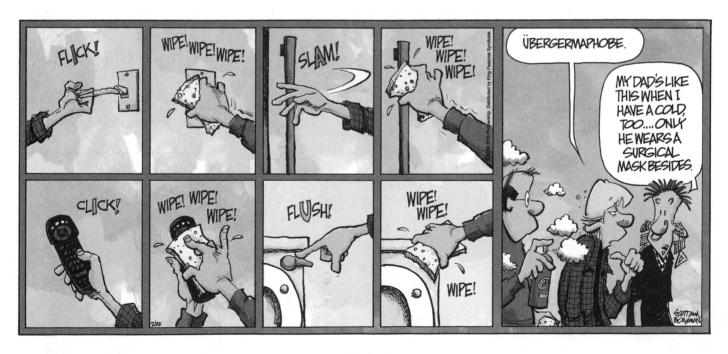

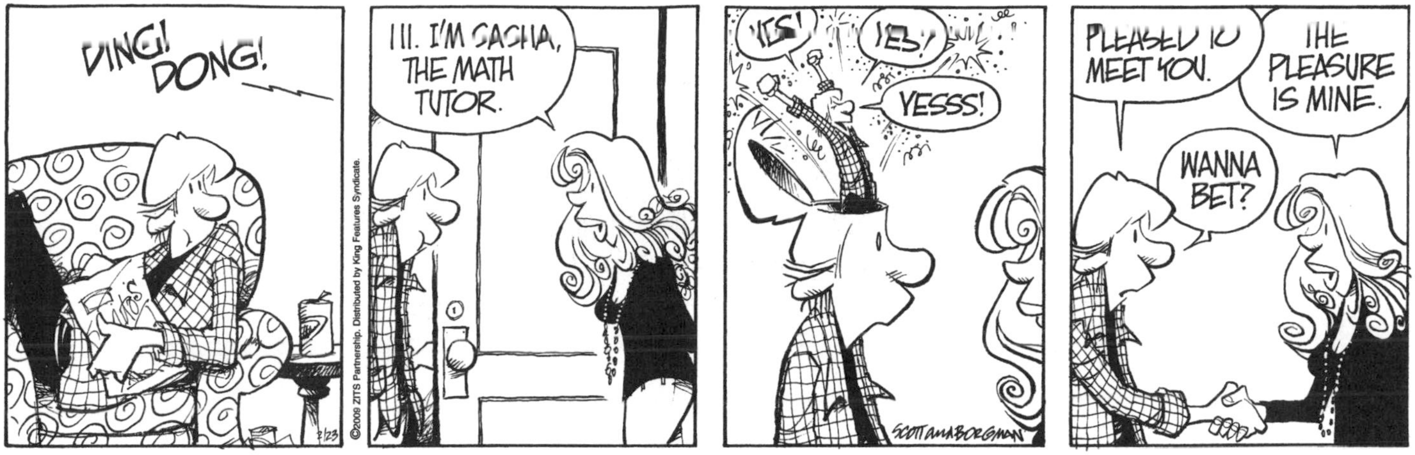
DING! DONG!
©2009 ZITS Partnership. Distributed by King Features Syndicate.
HI. I'M SASHA, THE MATH TUTOR.
YES!
YES!
YESSS!
SCOTT and BORGMAN
PLEASED TO MEET YOU.
THE PLEASURE IS MINE.
WANNA BET?

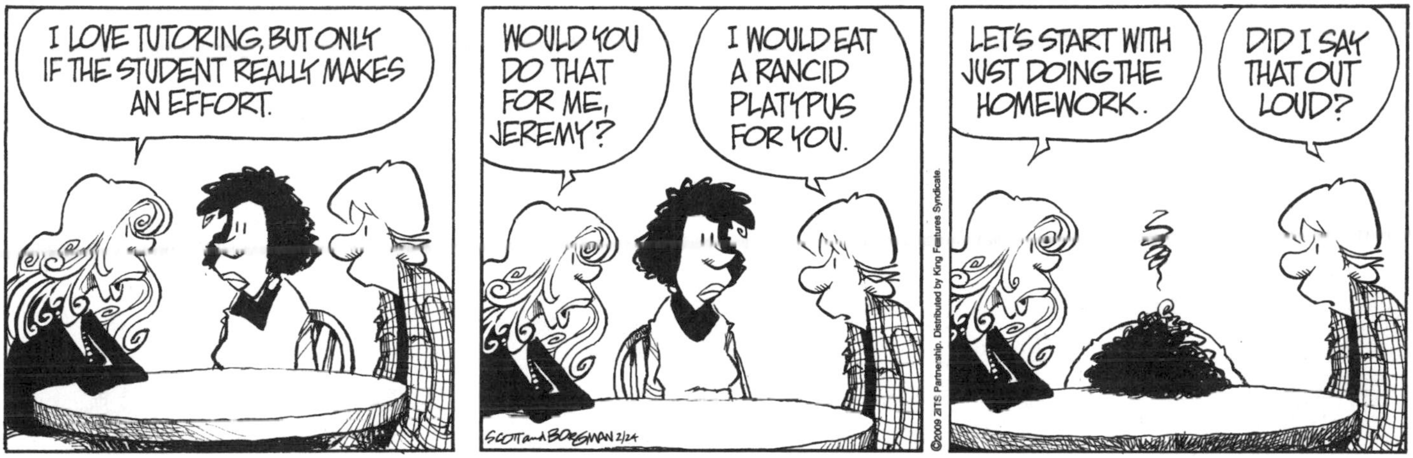
I LOVE TUTORING, BUT ONLY IF THE STUDENT REALLY MAKES AN EFFORT.
WOULD YOU DO THAT FOR ME, JEREMY?
I WOULD EAT A RANCID PLATYPUS FOR YOU.
SCOTT and BORGMAN 2/24
©2009 ZITS Partnership. Distributed by King Features Syndicate.
LET'S START WITH JUST DOING THE HOMEWORK.
DID I SAY THAT OUT LOUD?

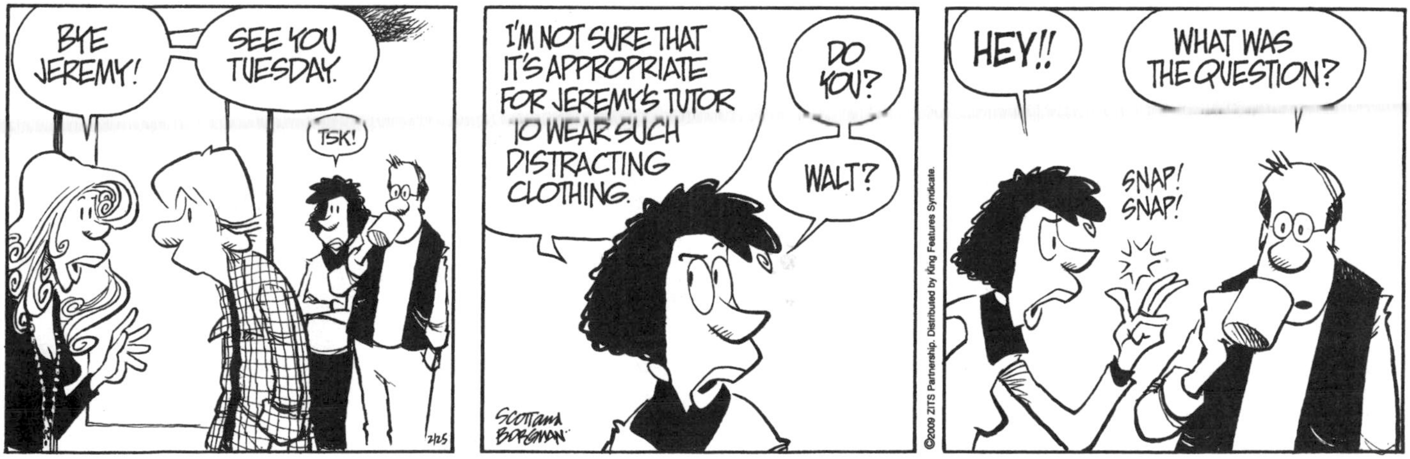
BYE JEREMY!
SEE YOU TUESDAY.
TSK!
I'M NOT SURE THAT IT'S APPROPRIATE FOR JEREMY'S TUTOR TO WEAR SUCH DISTRACTING CLOTHING.
DO YOU?
WALT?
SCOTT and BORGMAN
©2009 ZITS Partnership. Distributed by King Features Syndicate.
HEY!!
WHAT WAS THE QUESTION?
SNAP! SNAP!

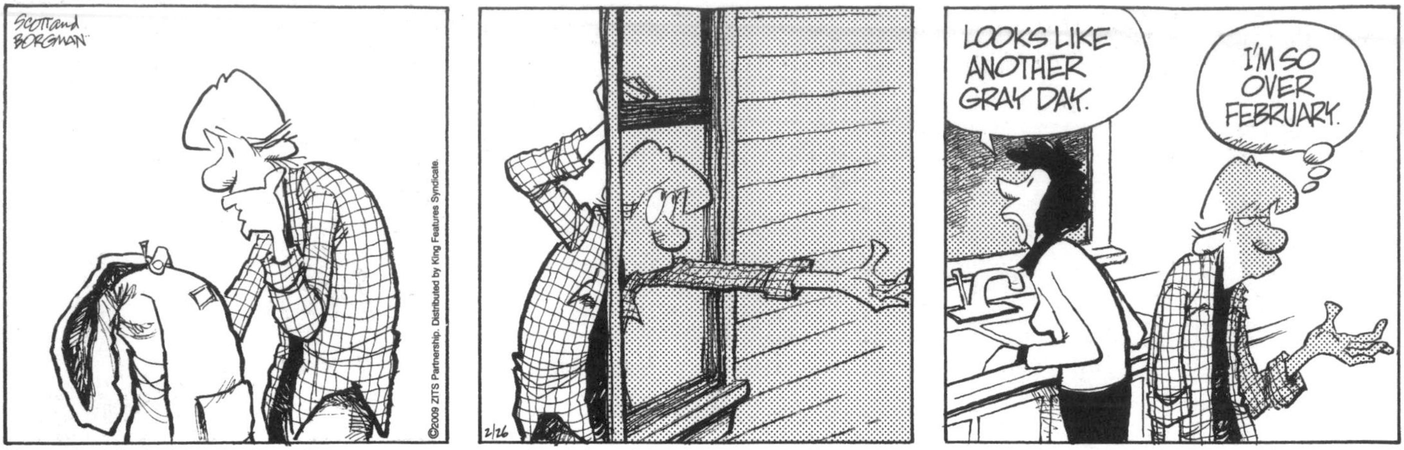
SCOTT and BORGMAN
©2009 ZITS Partnership. Distributed by King Features Syndicate.
2/26
LOOKS LIKE ANOTHER GRAY DAY.
I'M SO OVER FEBRUARY.

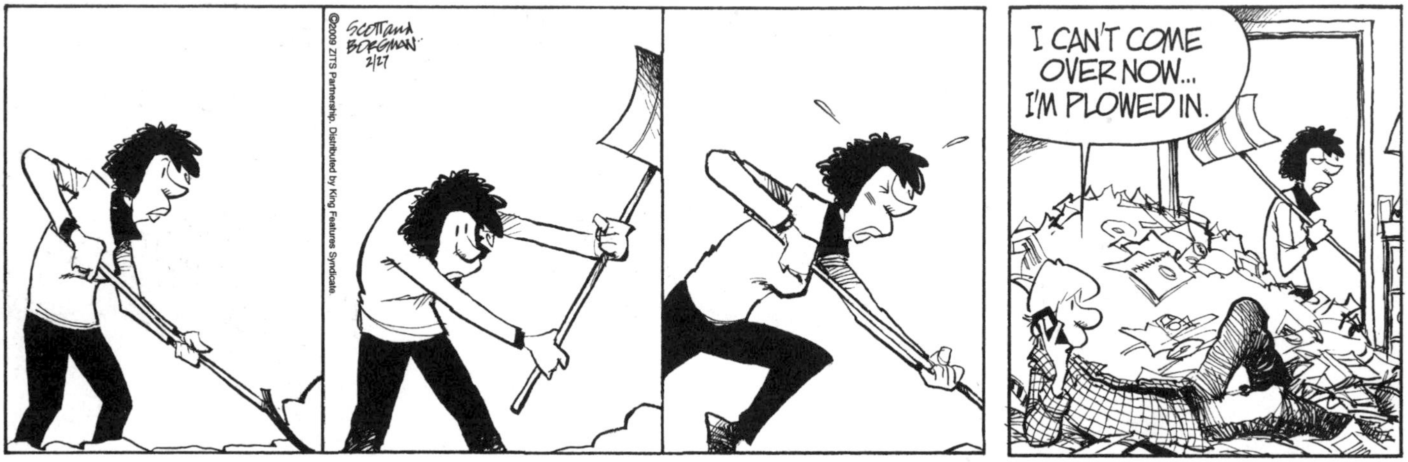
©2009 ZITS Partnership. Distributed by King Features Syndicate.
SCOTT and BORGMAN
2/27
I CAN'T COME OVER NOW... I'M PLOWED IN.

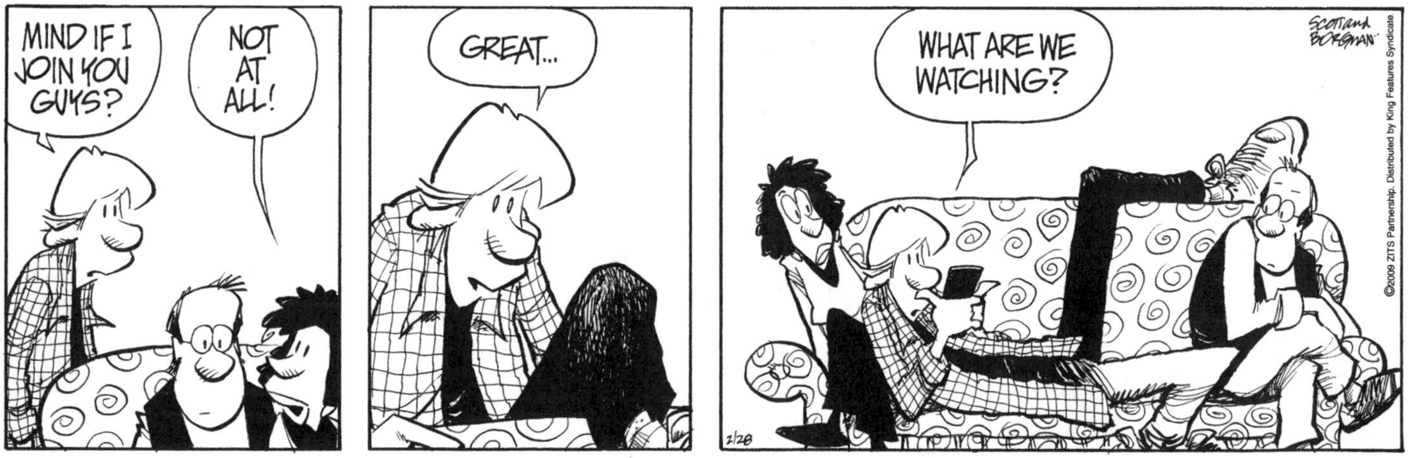
MIND IF I JOIN YOU GUYS?
NOT AT ALL!
GREAT...
SCOTT and BORGMAN
WHAT ARE WE WATCHING?
©2009 ZITS Partnership. Distributed by King Features Syndicate
2/28

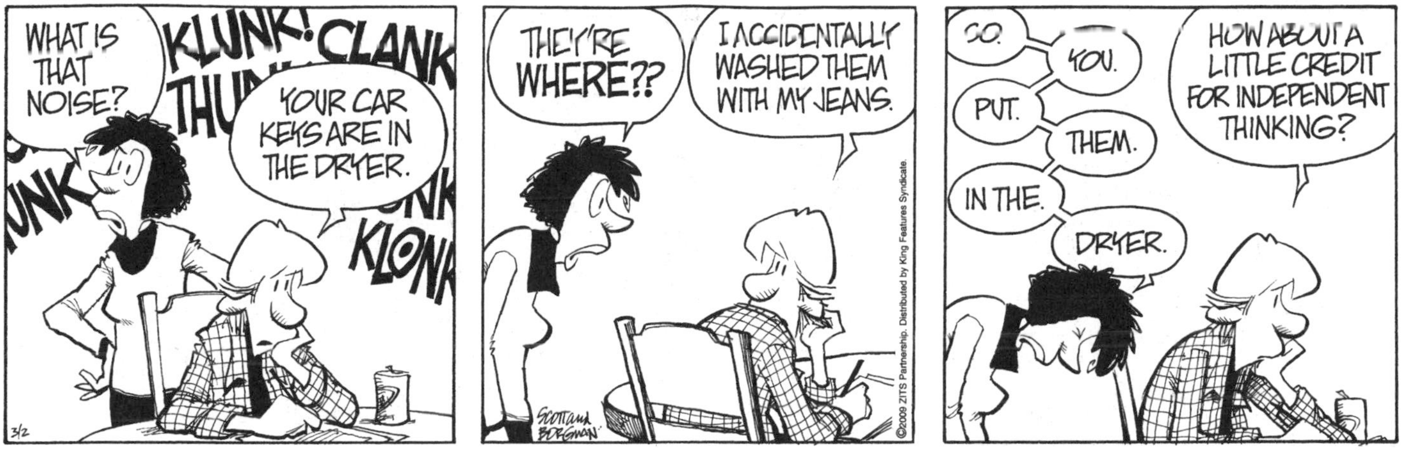
WHAT IS THAT NOISE?
KLUNK!
CLANK
YOUR CAR KEYS ARE IN THE DRYER.
KLONK
3/2
THEY'RE WHERE??
I ACCIDENTALLY WASHED THEM WITH MY JEANS.
SCOTT and BORGMAN
©2009 ZITS Partnership. Distributed by King Features Syndicate.
SO.
YOU.
PUT.
THEM.
IN THE.
DRYER.
HOW ABOUT A LITTLE CREDIT FOR INDEPENDENT THINKING?

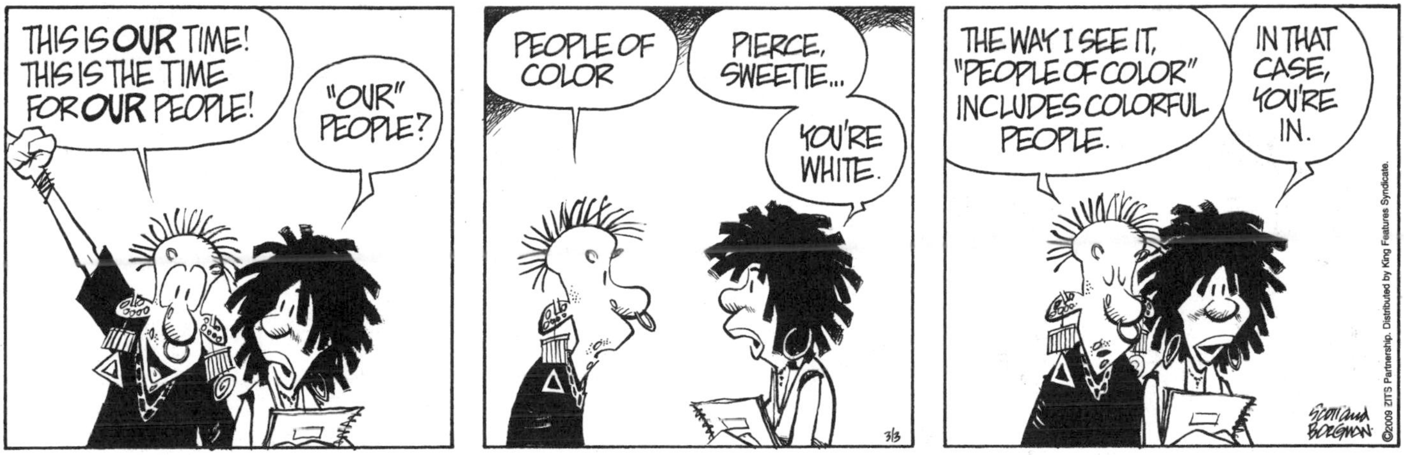
THIS IS OUR TIME! THIS IS THE TIME FOR OUR PEOPLE!
"OUR" PEOPLE?
PEOPLE OF COLOR
PIERCE, SWEETIE...
YOU'RE WHITE.
3/3
THE WAY I SEE IT, "PEOPLE OF COLOR" INCLUDES COLORFUL PEOPLE.
IN THAT CASE, YOU'RE IN.
SCOTT and BORGMAN
©2009 ZITS Partnership. Distributed by King Features Syndicate.

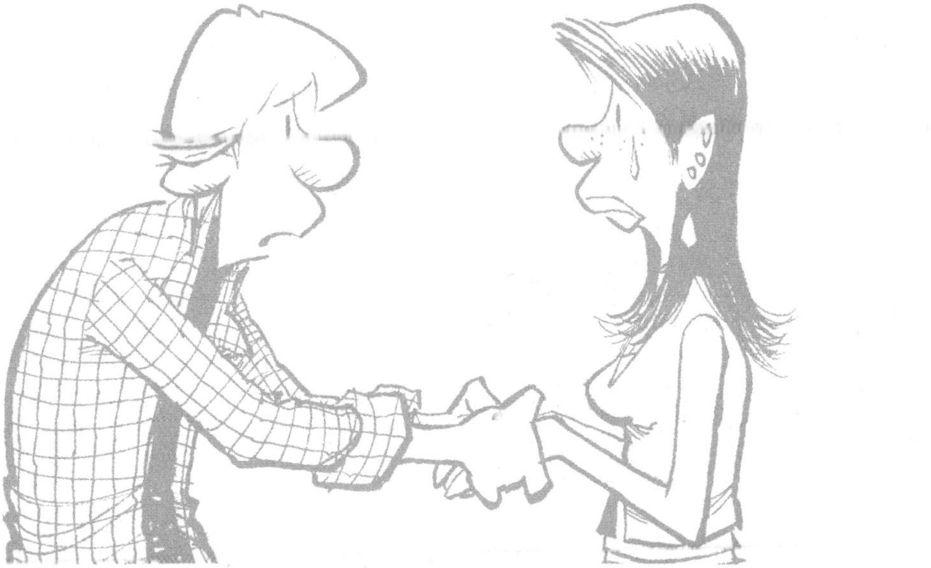

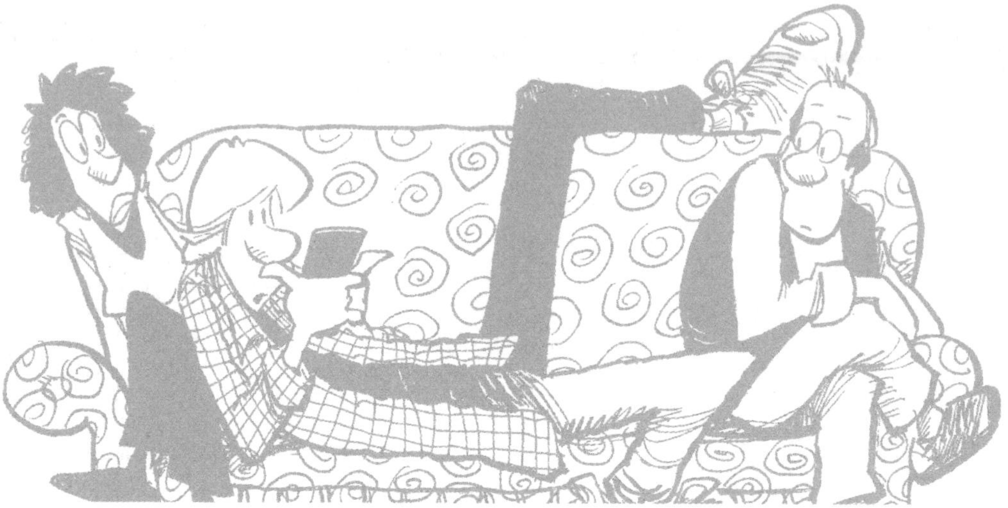

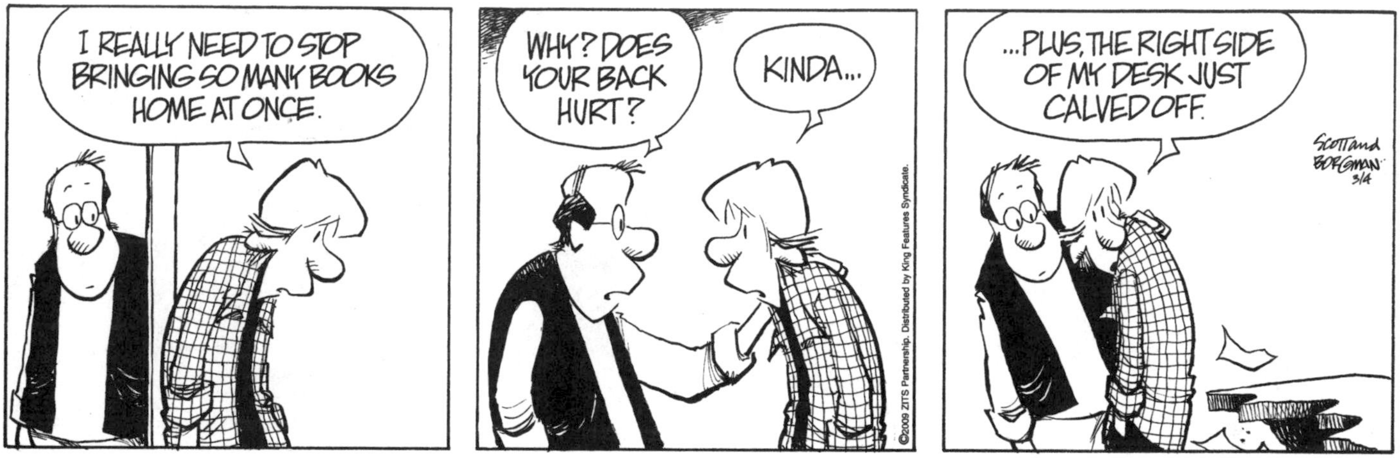
I REALLY NEED TO STOP BRINGING SO MANY BOOKS HOME AT ONCE.
WHY? DOES YOUR BACK HURT?
KINDA...
©2009 ZITS Partnership. Distributed by King Features Syndicate.
...PLUS, THE RIGHT SIDE OF MY DESK JUST CALVED OFF.
SCOTT and BORGMAN 3/4

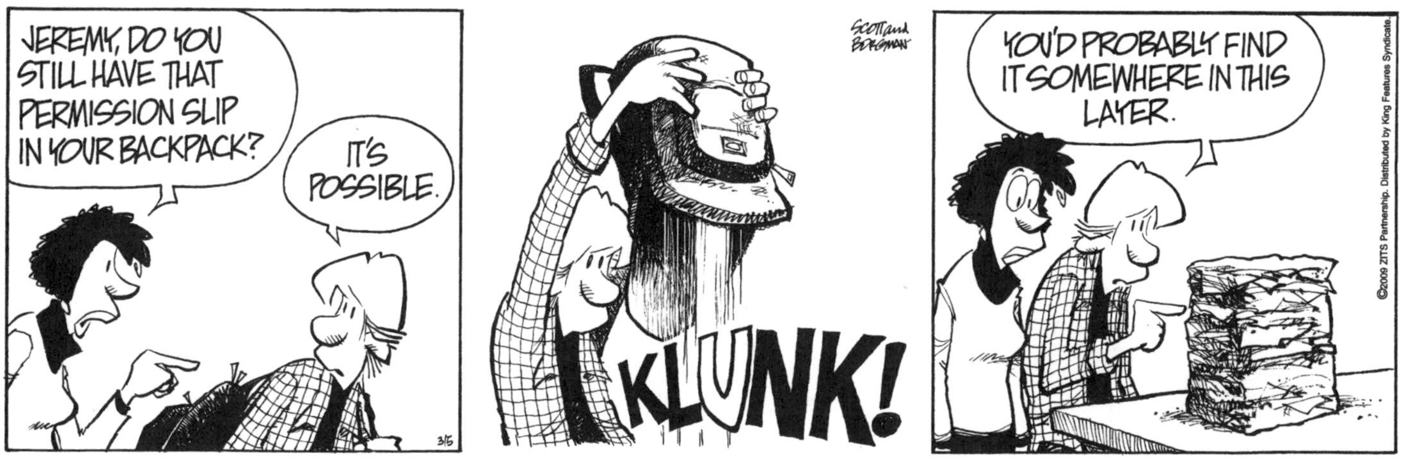
JEREMY, DO YOU STILL HAVE THAT PERMISSION SLIP IN YOUR BACKPACK?
IT'S POSSIBLE.
3/5
SCOTT and BORGMAN
KLUNK!
YOU'D PROBABLY FIND IT SOMEWHERE IN THIS LAYER.
©2009 ZITS Partnership. Distributed by King Features Syndicate.

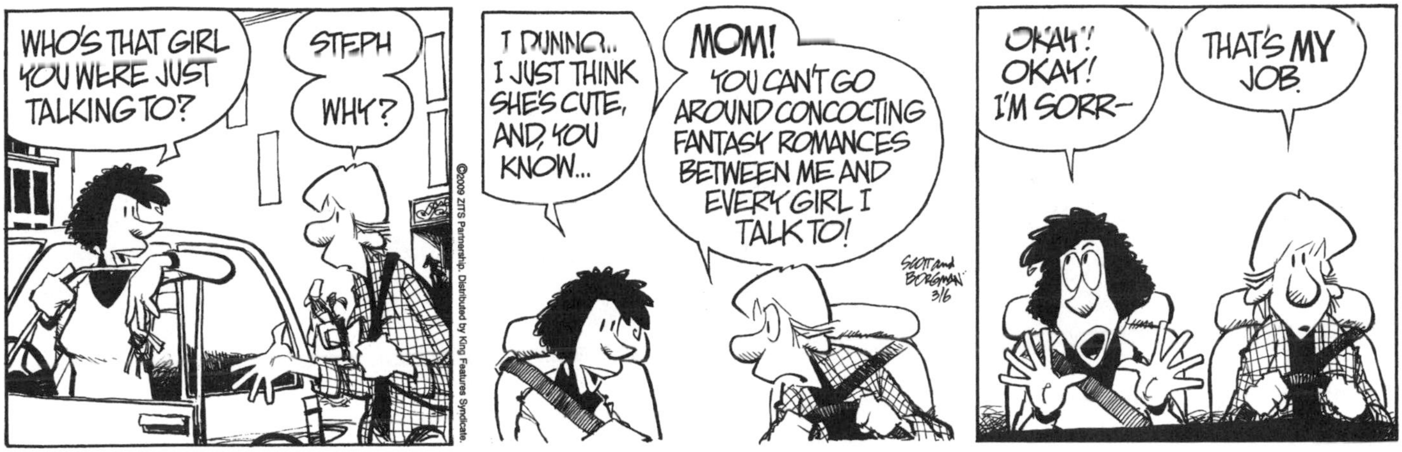
WHO'S THAT GIRL YOU WERE JUST TALKING TO?
STEPH
WHY?
©2009 ZITS Partnership. Distributed by King Features Syndicate.
I DUNNO... I JUST THINK SHE'S CUTE, AND, YOU KNOW...
MOM! YOU CAN'T GO AROUND CONCOCTING FANTASY ROMANCES BETWEEN ME AND EVERY GIRL I TALK TO!
SCOTT and BORGMAN 3/6
OKAY! OKAY! I'M SORR–
THAT'S MY JOB.

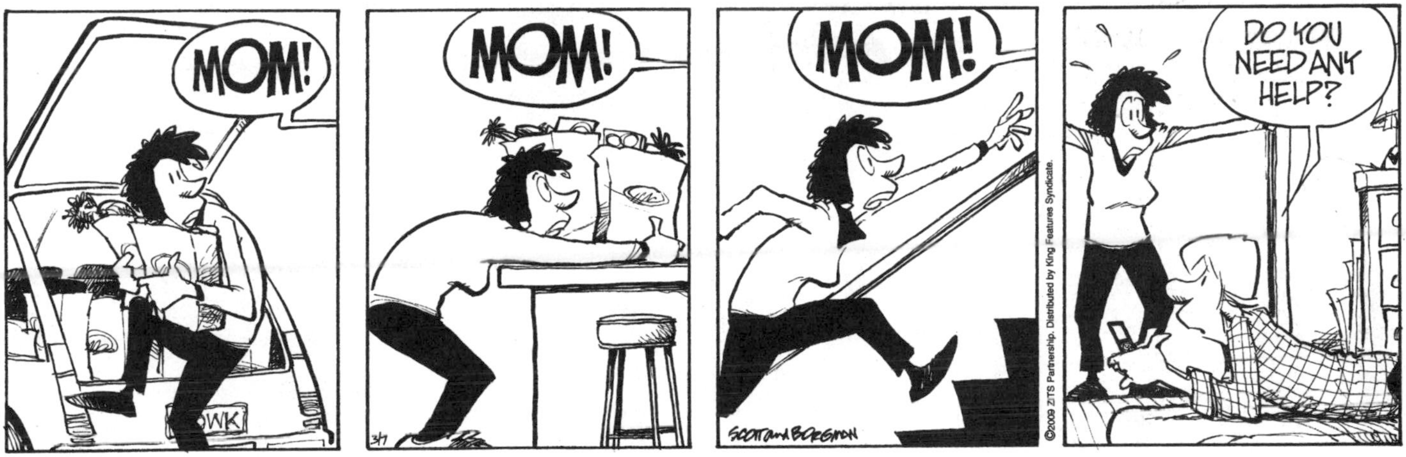
MOM!
MOM!
3/7
MOM!
SCOTT and BORGMAN
©2009 ZITS Partnership. Distributed by King Features Syndicate.
DO YOU NEED ANY HELP?

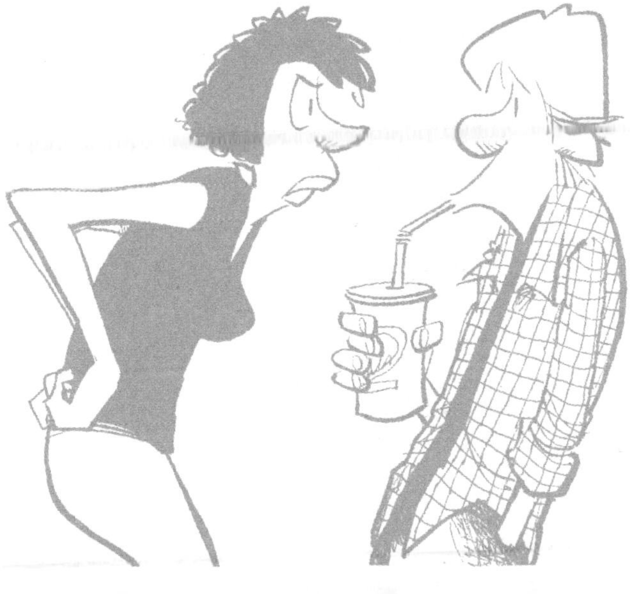

Zits
by JERRY SCOTT and JIM BORGMAN

RRRR
RRRRRRRRRR
3/1
NICE HAIR!
SCOTT and BORGMAN
©2009 ZITS Partnership. Distributed by King Features Syndicate.

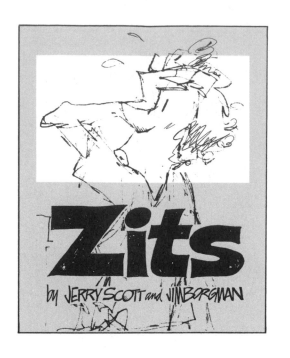

Zits
by
JERRY SCOTT and JIM BORGMAN

INSAYNE
I'M HERE
Send Menu
TAP TAP
ROCKGOD1
COME ON IN
Send Menu
TAP TAP
INSAYNE
WHERE'S THE BOOK I'M SPOSED TO PICK UP?
Send Menu
ROCKGOD1
ON THE STAIRS
Reply Menu
INSAYNE
DO I SMELL COOKIES?
Send Menu
ROCKGOD1
IN THE KITCHEN. THEY'RE AWESOME.
Reply Menu
INSAYNE
CAN I USE YOUR BATH-ROOM?
Send Menu
ROCKGOD1
B MY GUEST
Reply Menu
INSAYNE
THNX
Send Menu
INSAYNE
IT'S LATE. I GOTTA GO.
Send Menu
ROCKGOD1
C U TOMORROW
Reply Menu
SLAM!
WHAT ARE YOU STARING AT?
©2009 ZITS Partnership. Distributed by King Features Syndicate.

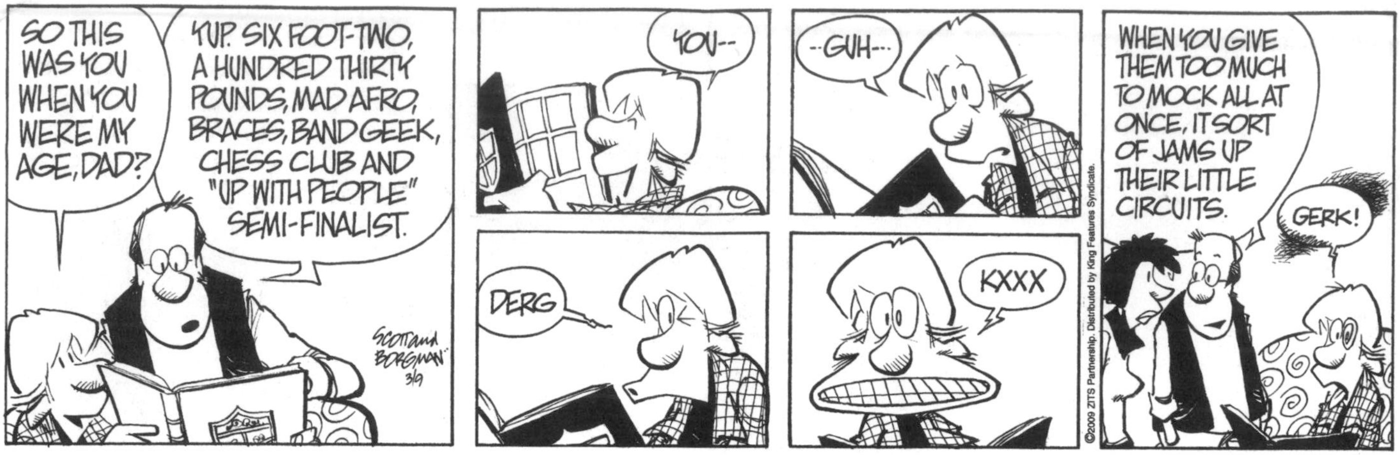
SO THIS WAS YOU WHEN YOU WERE MY AGE, DAD?
YUP. SIX FOOT-TWO, A HUNDRED THIRTY POUNDS, MAD AFRO, BRACES, BAND GEEK, CHESS CLUB AND "UP WITH PEOPLE" SEMI-FINALIST.
SCOTT and BORGMAN 3/9
YOU--
--GUH--
DERG
KXXX
WHEN YOU GIVE THEM TOO MUCH TO MOCK ALL AT ONCE, IT SORT OF JAMS UP THEIR LITTLE CIRCUITS.
GERK!
©2009 ZITS Partnership. Distributed by King Features Syndicate.

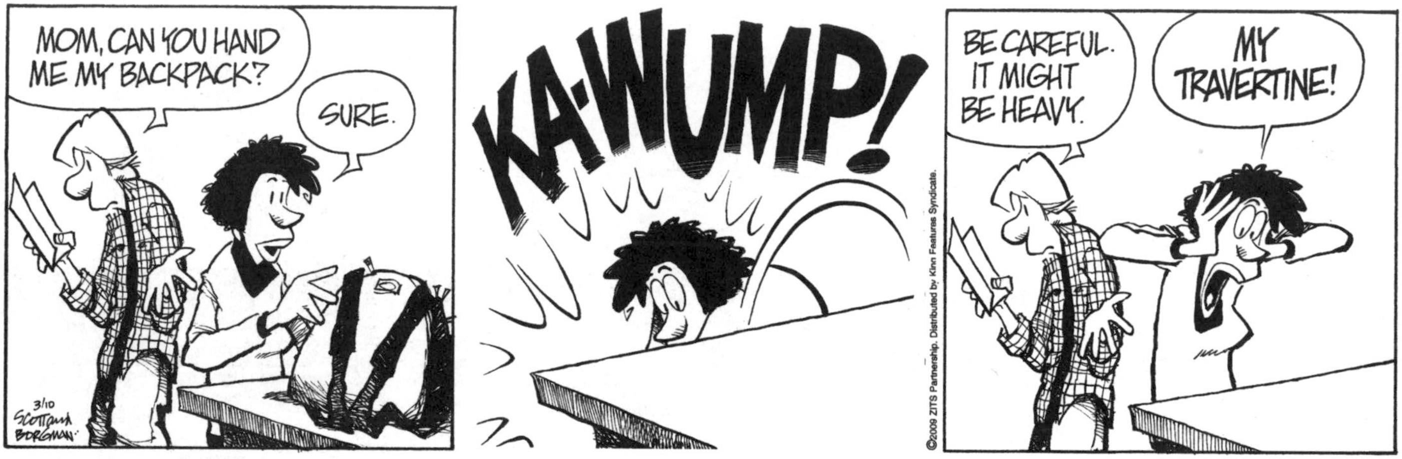
MOM, CAN YOU HAND ME MY BACKPACK?
SURE.
3/10 SCOTT and BORGMAN
KA-WUMP!
©2009 ZITS Partnership. Distributed by King Features Syndicate.
BE CAREFUL. IT MIGHT BE HEAVY.
MY TRAVERTINE!

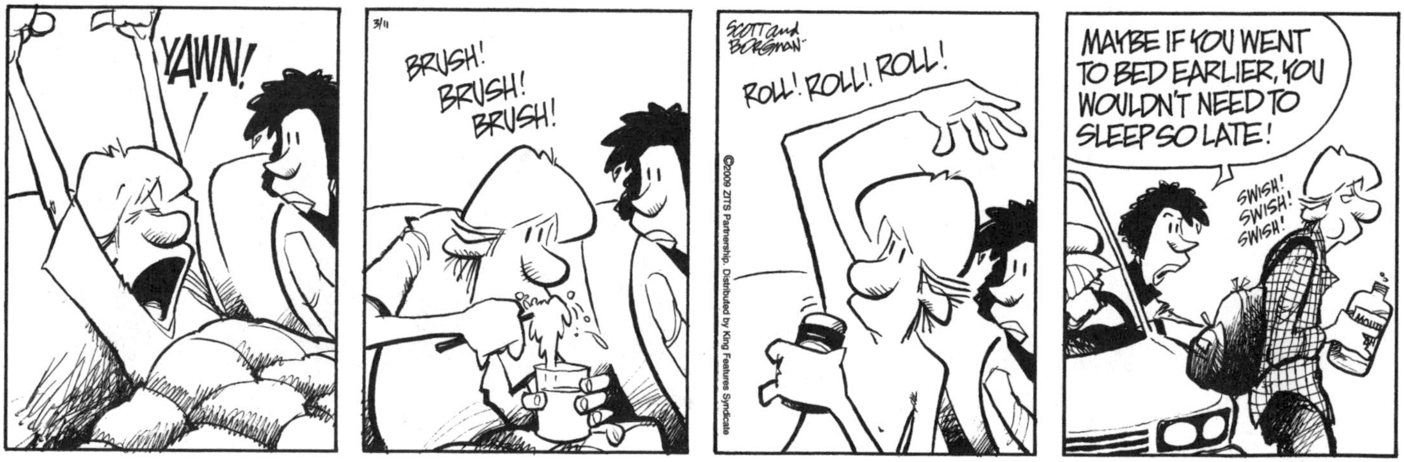
YAWN!
3/11
BRUSH! BRUSH! BRUSH!
SCOTT and BORGMAN
ROLL! ROLL! ROLL!
©2009 ZITS Partnership. Distributed by King Features Syndicate.
MAYBE IF YOU WENT TO BED EARLIER, YOU WOULDN'T NEED TO SLEEP SO LATE!
SWISH! SWISH! SWISH!

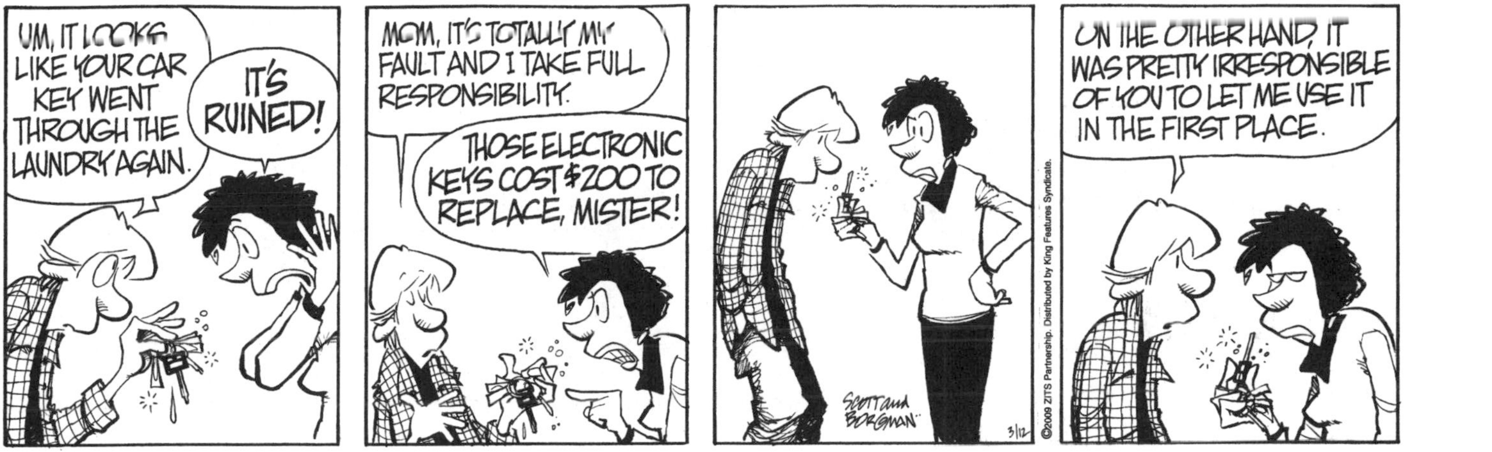
UM, IT LOOKS LIKE YOUR CAR KEY WENT THROUGH THE LAUNDRY AGAIN.
IT'S RUINED!
MOM, IT'S TOTALLY MY FAULT AND I TAKE FULL RESPONSIBILITY.
THOSE ELECTRONIC KEYS COST $200 TO REPLACE, MISTER!
ON THE OTHER HAND, IT WAS PRETTY IRRESPONSIBLE OF YOU TO LET ME USE IT IN THE FIRST PLACE.
©2009 ZITS Partnership. Distributed by King Features Syndicate.

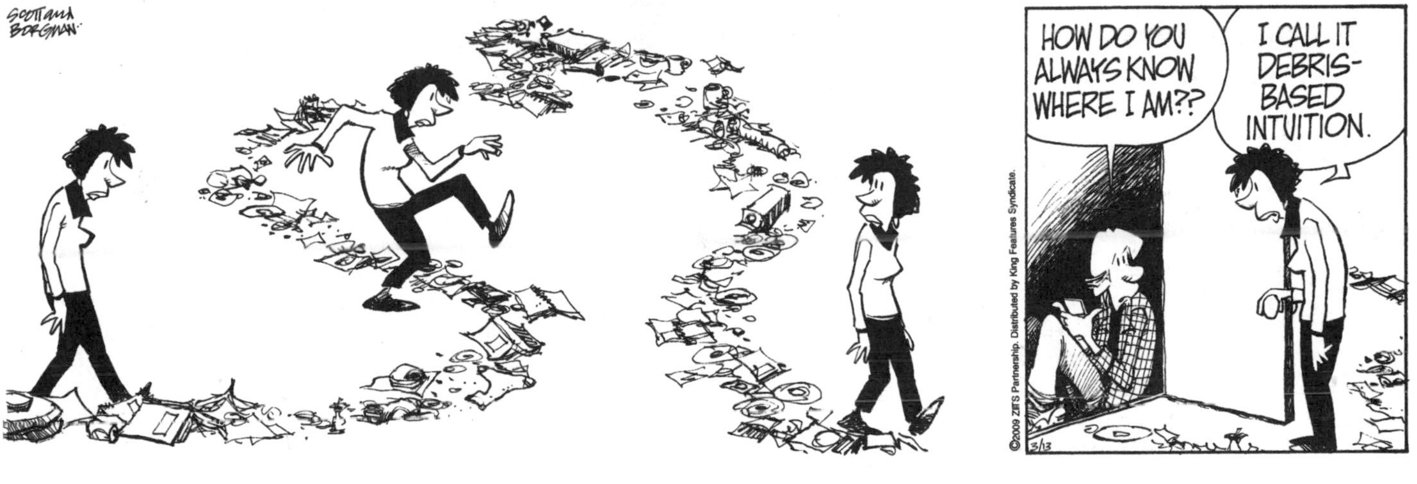
HOW DO YOU ALWAYS KNOW WHERE I AM??
I CALL IT DEBRIS-BASED INTUITION.
©2009 ZITS Partnership. Distributed by King Features Syndicate.

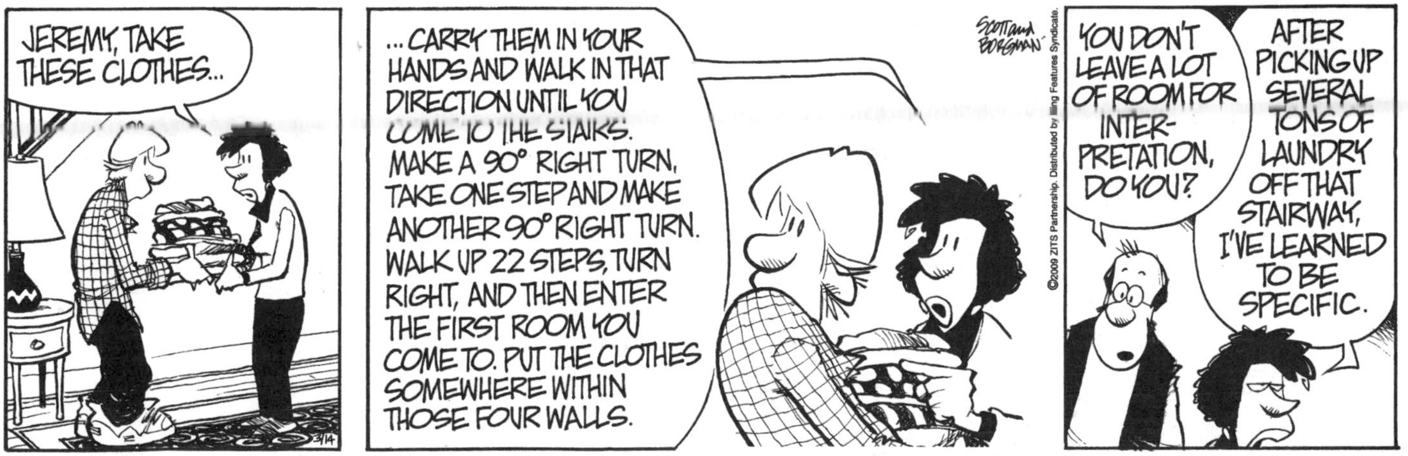
JEREMY, TAKE THESE CLOTHES...
...CARRY THEM IN YOUR HANDS AND WALK IN THAT DIRECTION UNTIL YOU COME TO THE STAIRS. MAKE A 90° RIGHT TURN, TAKE ONE STEP AND MAKE ANOTHER 90° RIGHT TURN. WALK UP 22 STEPS, TURN RIGHT, AND THEN ENTER THE FIRST ROOM YOU COME TO. PUT THE CLOTHES SOMEWHERE WITHIN THOSE FOUR WALLS.
YOU DON'T LEAVE A LOT OF ROOM FOR INTER-PRETATION, DO YOU?
AFTER PICKING UP SEVERAL TONS OF LAUNDRY OFF THAT STAIRWAY, I'VE LEARNED TO BE SPECIFIC.
©2009 ZITS Partnership. Distributed by King Features Syndicate.

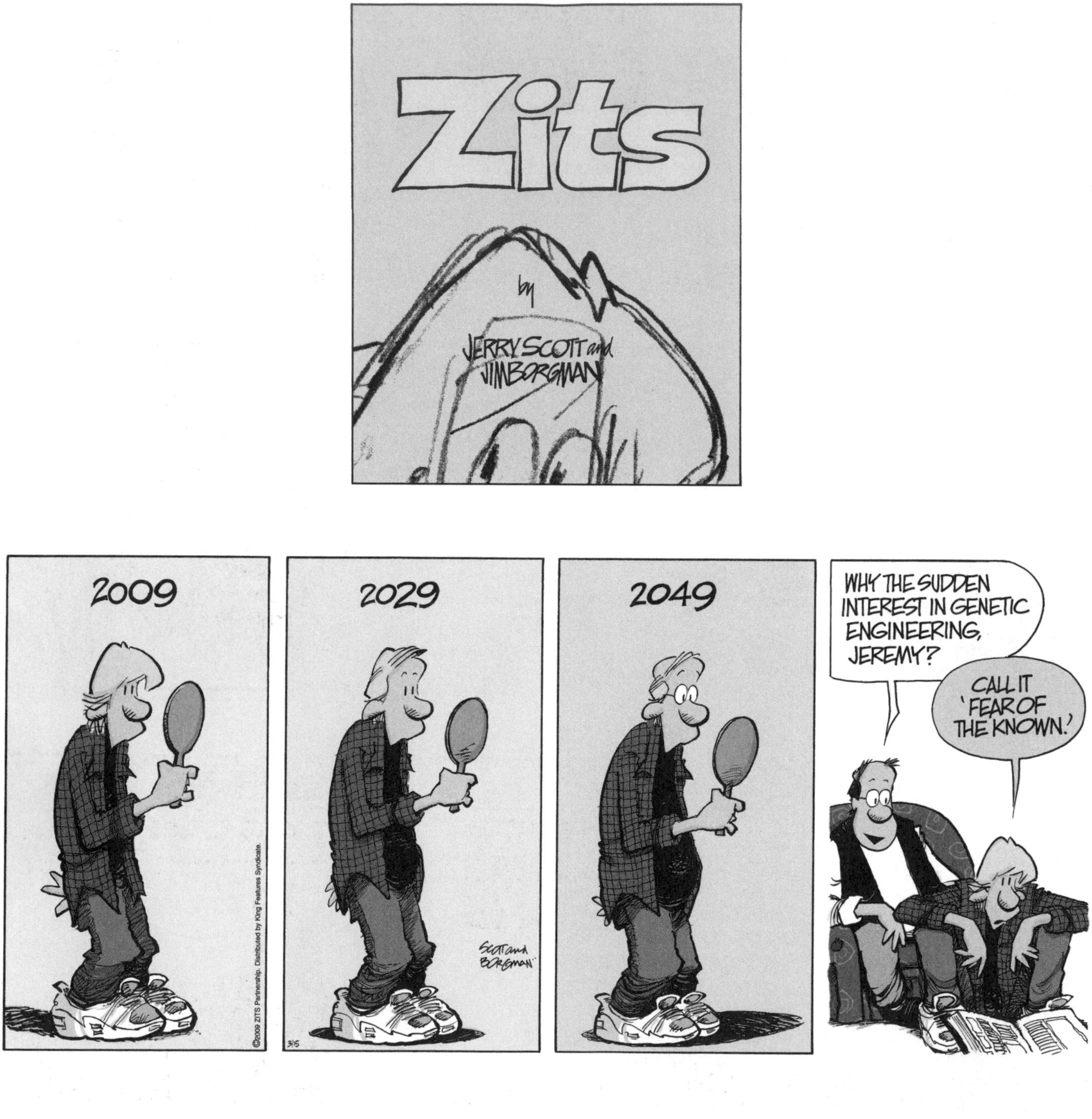
ZITS
by
JERRY SCOTT and
JIM BORGMAN
2009
2029
2049
WHY THE SUDDEN INTEREST IN GENETIC ENGINEERING, JEREMY?
CALL IT 'FEAR OF THE KNOWN.'
SCOTT and BORGMAN
3/5
©2009 ZITS Partnership. Distributed by King Features Syndicate.

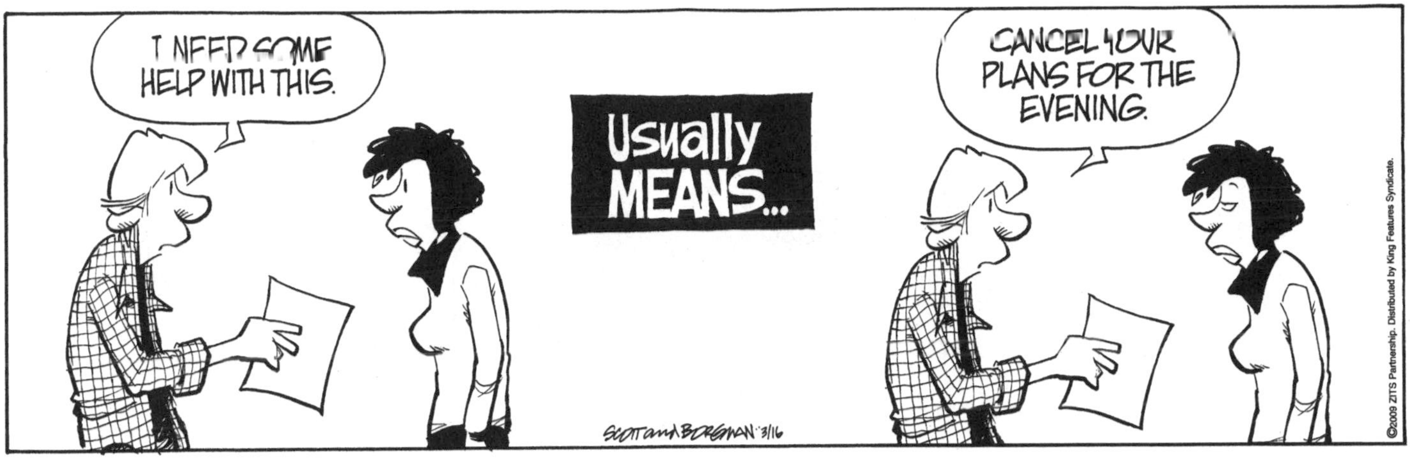
I NEED SOME HELP WITH THIS.
Usually MEANS...
CANCEL YOUR PLANS FOR THE EVENING.
SCOTT and BORGMAN 3/16
©2009 ZITS Partnership. Distributed by King Features Syndicate.

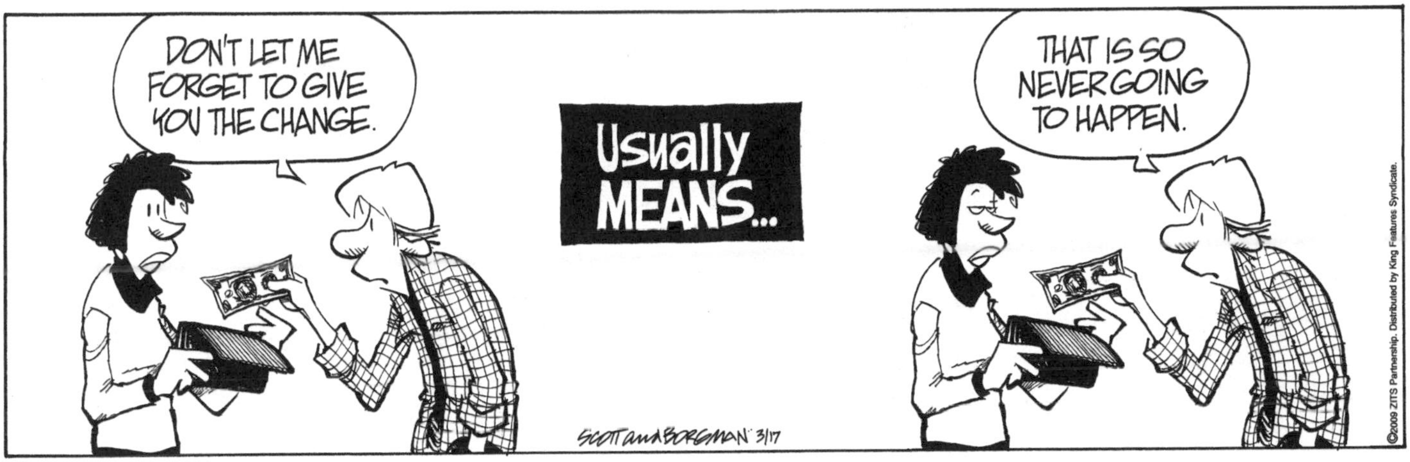
DON'T LET ME FORGET TO GIVE YOU THE CHANGE.
Usually MEANS...
THAT IS SO NEVER GOING TO HAPPEN.
SCOTT and BORGMAN 3/17
©2009 ZITS Partnership. Distributed by King Features Syndicate.

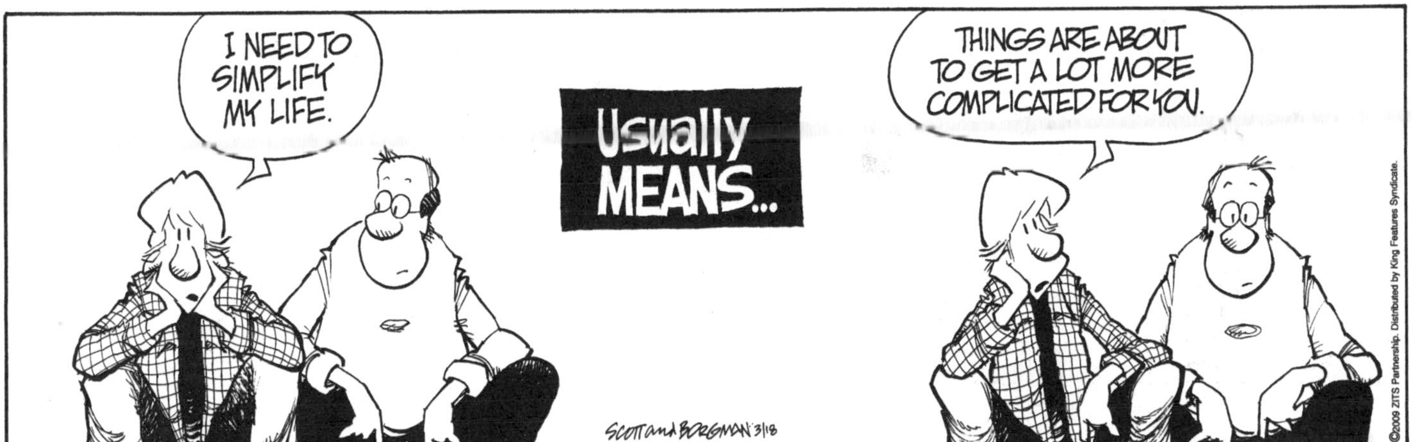
I NEED TO SIMPLIFY MY LIFE.
Usually MEANS...
THINGS ARE ABOUT TO GET A LOT MORE COMPLICATED FOR YOU.
SCOTT and BORGMAN 3/18
©2009 ZITS Partnership. Distributed by King Features Syndicate.

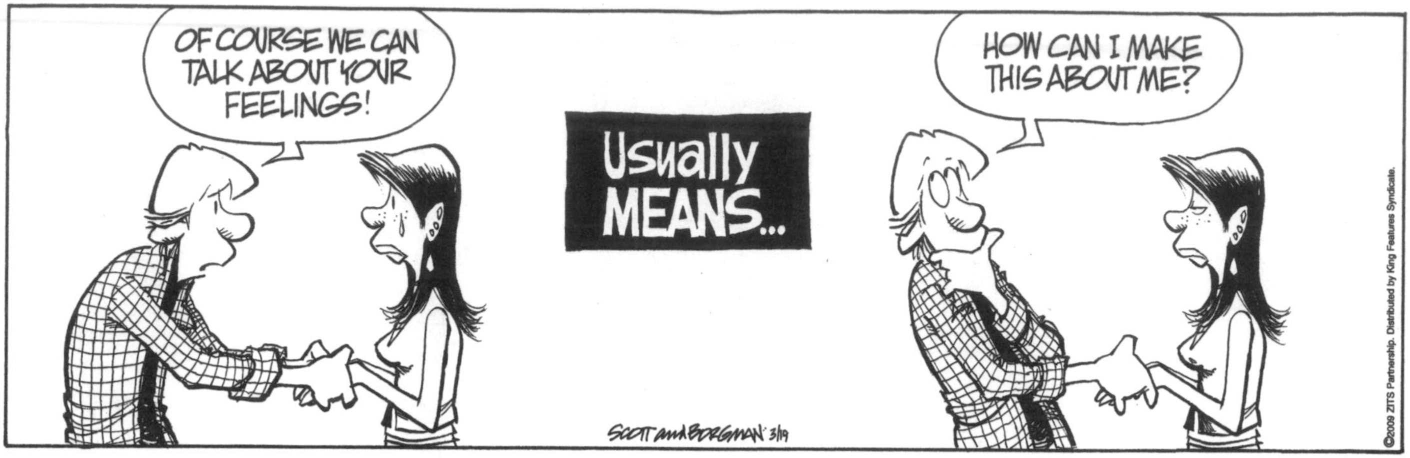
OF COURSE WE CAN TALK ABOUT YOUR FEELINGS!
Usually MEANS...
HOW CAN I MAKE THIS ABOUT ME?
SCOTT and BORGMAN 3/19

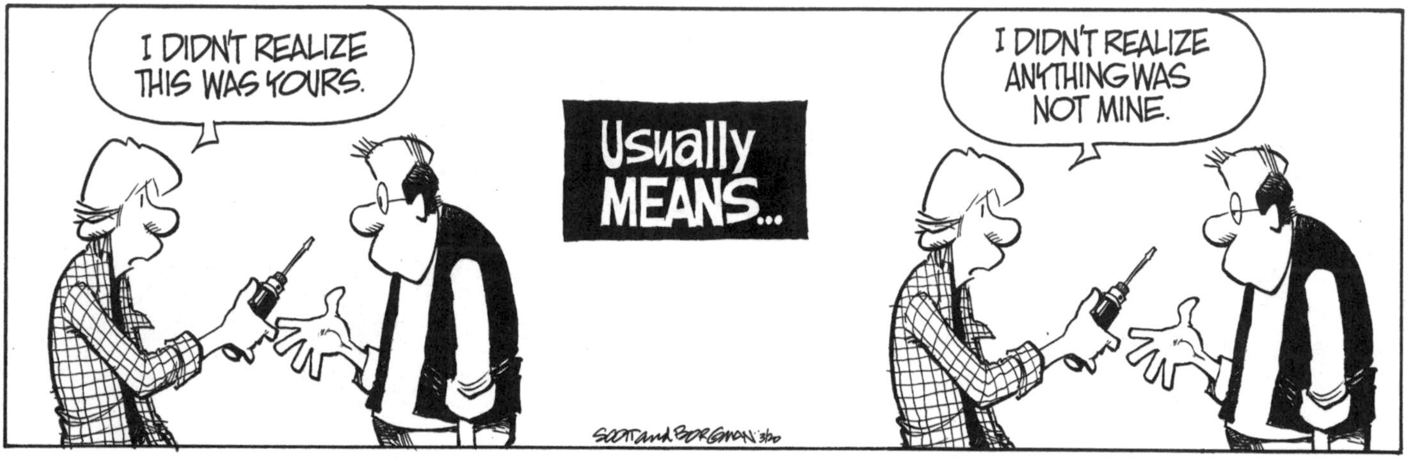
I DIDN'T REALIZE THIS WAS YOURS.
Usually MEANS...
I DIDN'T REALIZE ANYTHING WAS NOT MINE.
SCOTT and BORGMAN 3/20

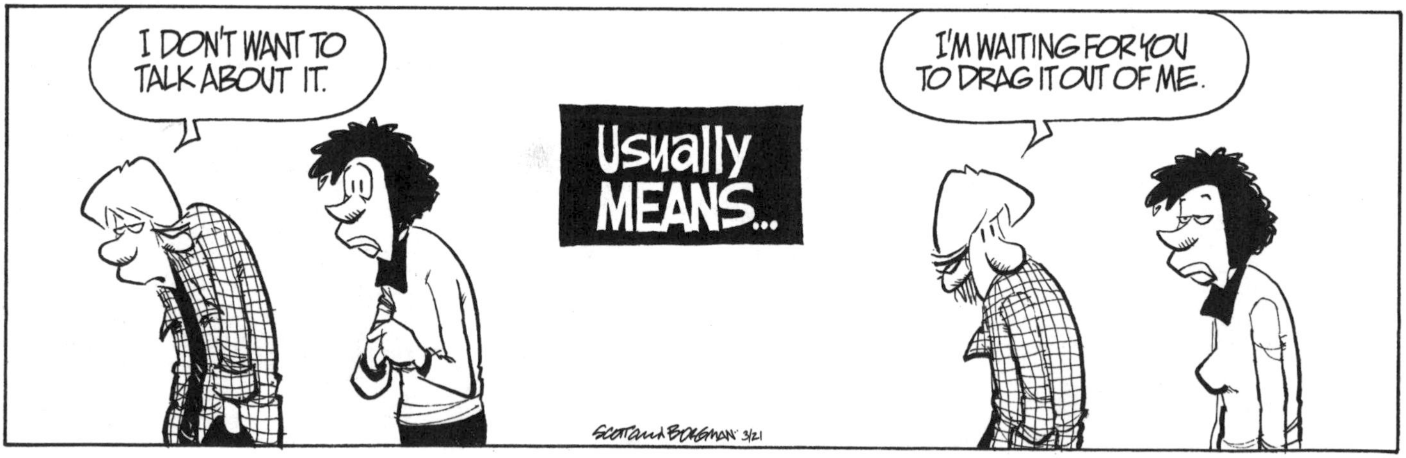
I DON'T WANT TO TALK ABOUT IT.
Usually MEANS...
I'M WAITING FOR YOU TO DRAG IT OUT OF ME.
SCOTT and BORGMAN 3/21

Zits
JERRY SCOTT and JIM BORGMAN

JINGLE!
JANGLE! KLANK!
PING! PLINK!
POING!
KLANK!
DINK-A
DINK-A
TOINK!
CHING!
DOING!
DINK!
CHANG!
KLINKITTY
KLANKITTY
PING!
POINK!
PING!
CHOING!
SCOTT and BORGMAN
©2009 ZITS Partnership. Distributed by King Features Syndicate. 3/22
PIERCE! YOUR HANDS-FREE IS SET ON "VIBRATE"!
HE KNOWS.
WOO-HOO!

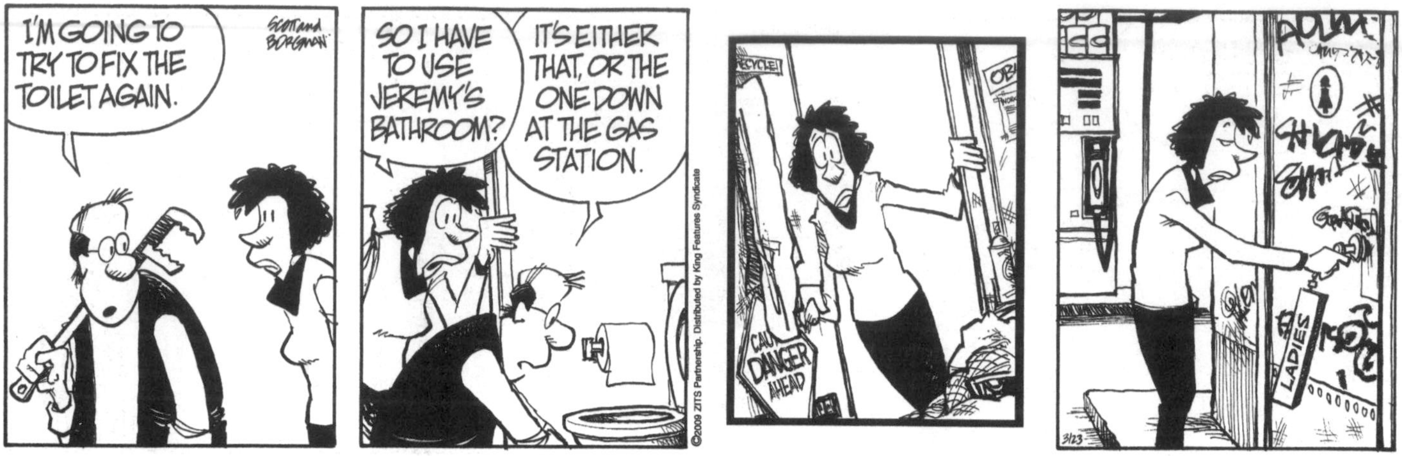
I'M GOING TO TRY TO FIX THE TOILET AGAIN.
SO I HAVE TO USE JEREMY'S BATHROOM?
IT'S EITHER THAT, OR THE ONE DOWN AT THE GAS STATION.
©2009 ZITS Partnership. Distributed by King Features Syndicate
DANGER AHEAD
LADIES

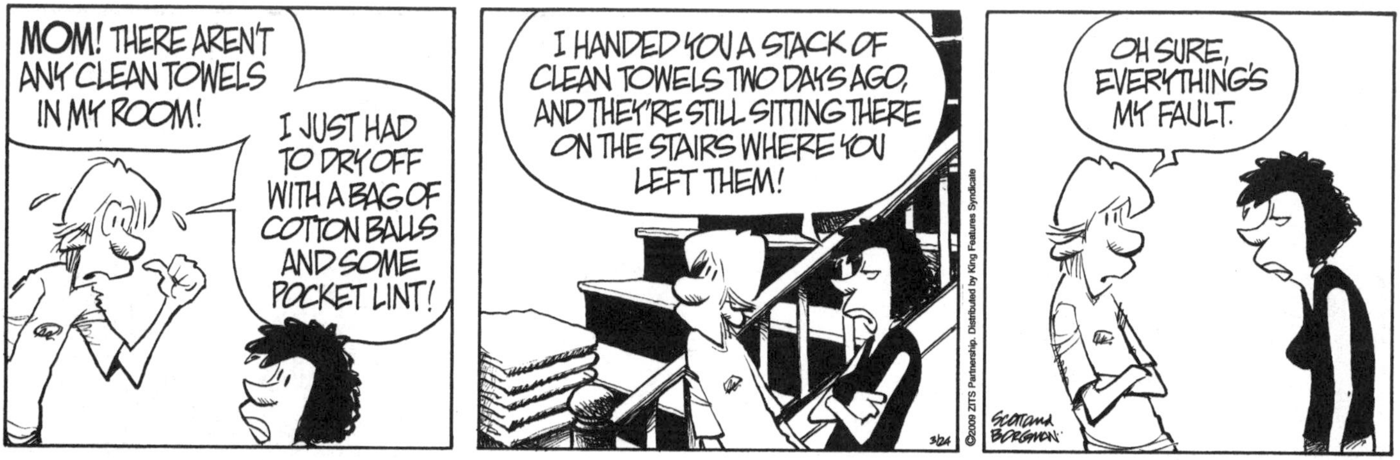
MOM! THERE AREN'T ANY CLEAN TOWELS IN MY ROOM!
I JUST HAD TO DRY OFF WITH A BAG OF COTTON BALLS AND SOME POCKET LINT!
I HANDED YOU A STACK OF CLEAN TOWELS TWO DAYS AGO, AND THEY'RE STILL SITTING THERE ON THE STAIRS WHERE YOU LEFT THEM!
©2009 ZITS Partnership. Distributed by King Features Syndicate
OH SURE, EVERYTHING'S MY FAULT.

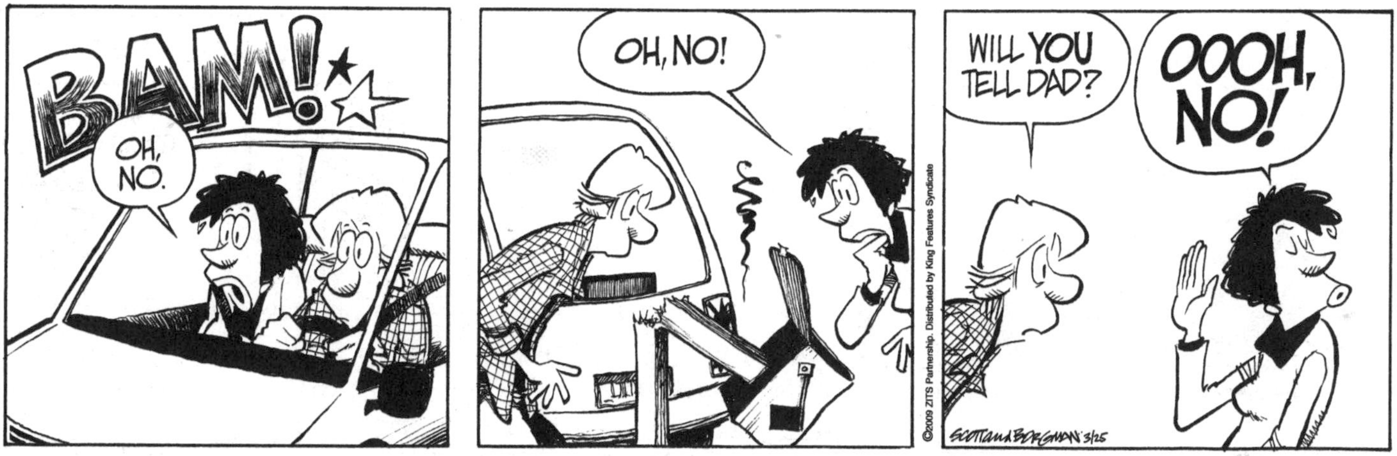
BAM!
OH, NO.
OH, NO!
©2009 ZITS Partnership. Distributed by King Features Syndicate
WILL YOU TELL DAD?
OOOH, NO!

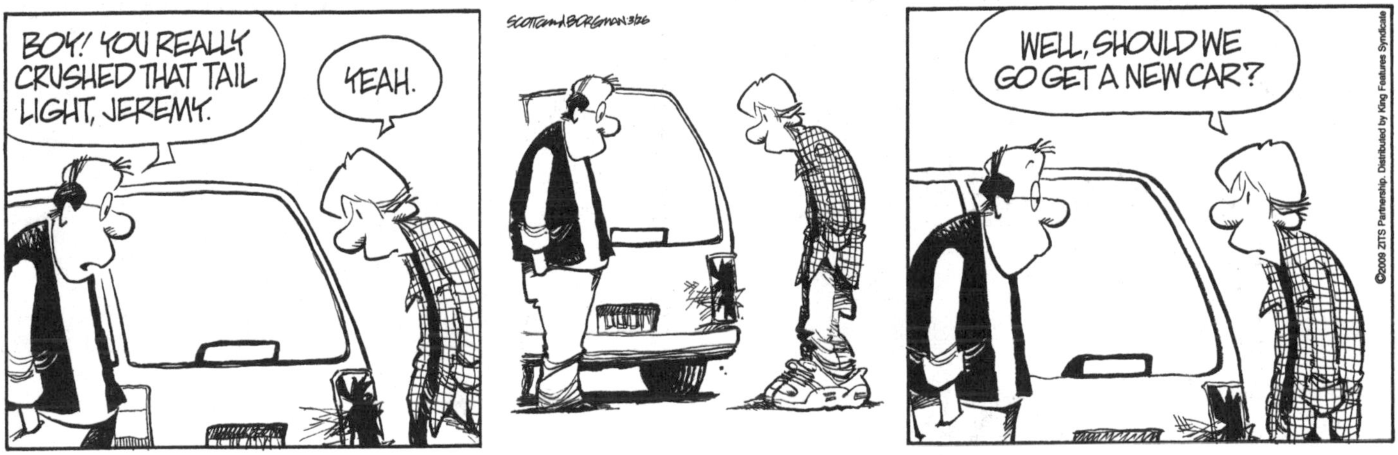
SCOTT and BORGMAN 3/26
BOY! YOU REALLY CRUSHED THAT TAIL LIGHT, JEREMY.
YEAH.
WELL, SHOULD WE GO GET A NEW CAR?
©2009 ZITS Partnership. Distributed by King Features Syndicate

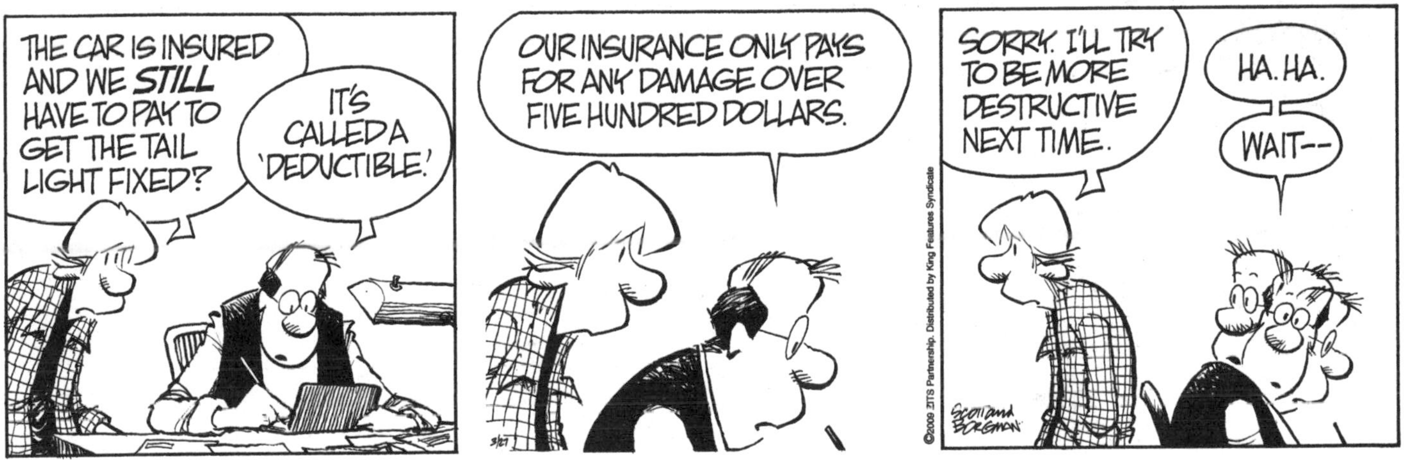
THE CAR IS INSURED AND WE STILL HAVE TO PAY TO GET THE TAIL LIGHT FIXED?
IT'S CALLED A 'DEDUCTIBLE.'
OUR INSURANCE ONLY PAYS FOR ANY DAMAGE OVER FIVE HUNDRED DOLLARS.
3/27
©2009 ZITS Partnership. Distributed by King Features Syndicate
SORRY. I'LL TRY TO BE MORE DESTRUCTIVE NEXT TIME.
HA. HA.
WAIT--
SCOTT and BORGMAN

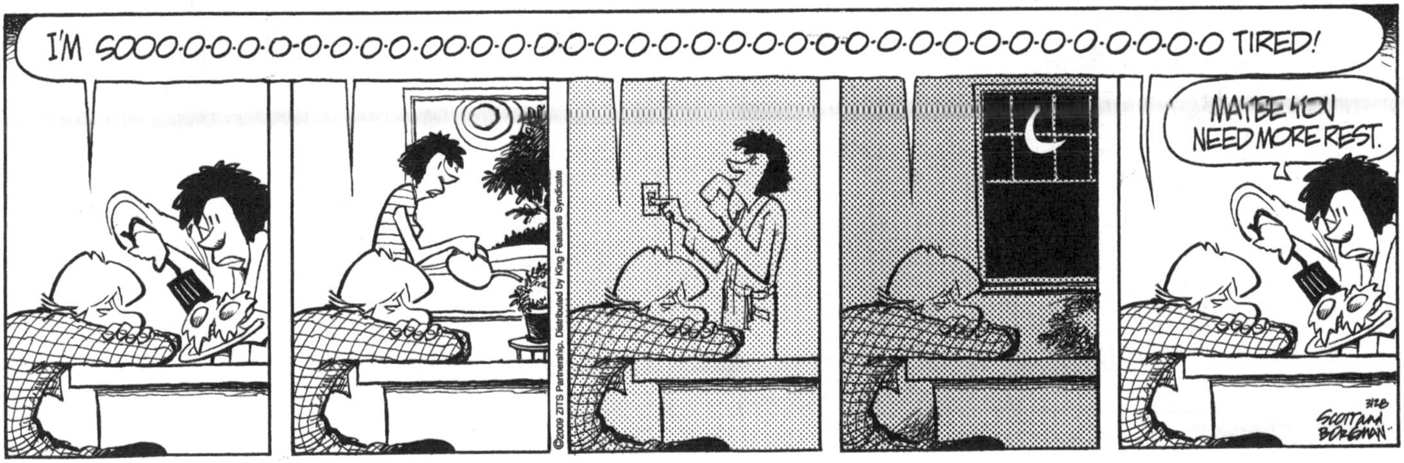
I'M SOOO-O-O-O-O-O-O-O-O-O-OOO-O-O-O-O-O-O-O-O-O-O-O-O-O-O-O-O-O-O-O-O-O-O-O-O-O-O-O TIRED!
©2009 ZITS Partnership. Distributed by King Features Syndicate
MAYBE YOU NEED MORE REST.
3/28
SCOTT and BORGMAN

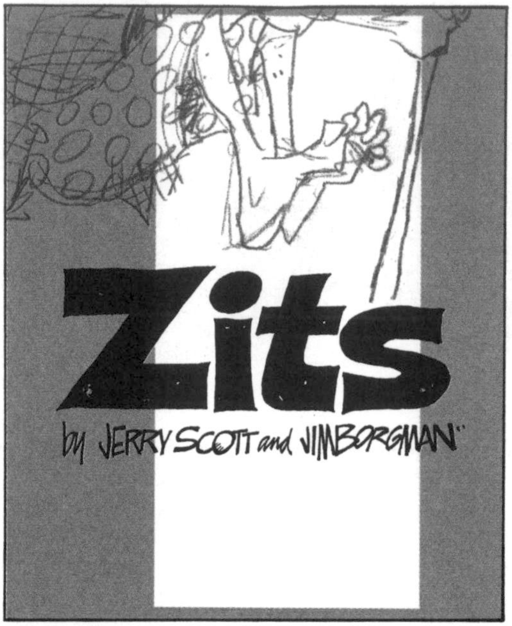
Zits
by JERRY SCOTT and JIM BORGMAN

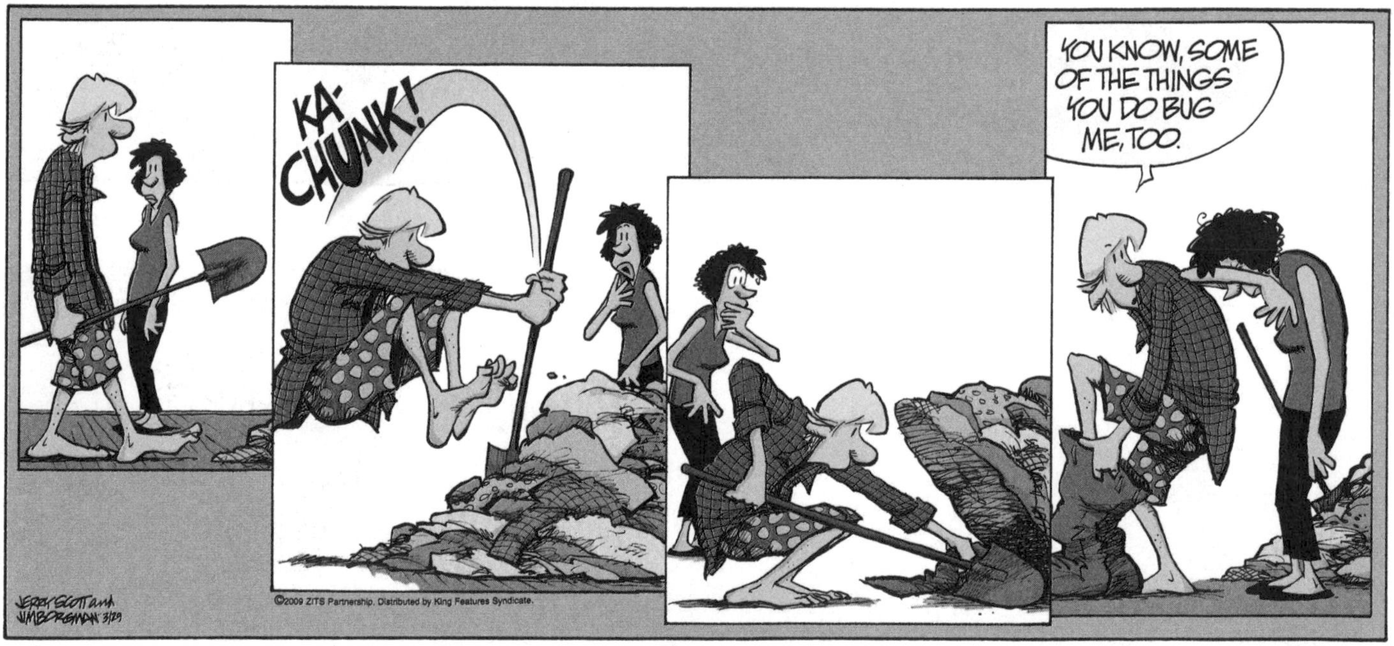
KA-CHUNK!
YOU KNOW, SOME OF THE THINGS YOU DO BUG ME, TOO.
JERRY SCOTT and JIM BORGMAN 3/29
©2009 ZITS Partnership. Distributed by King Features Syndicate.

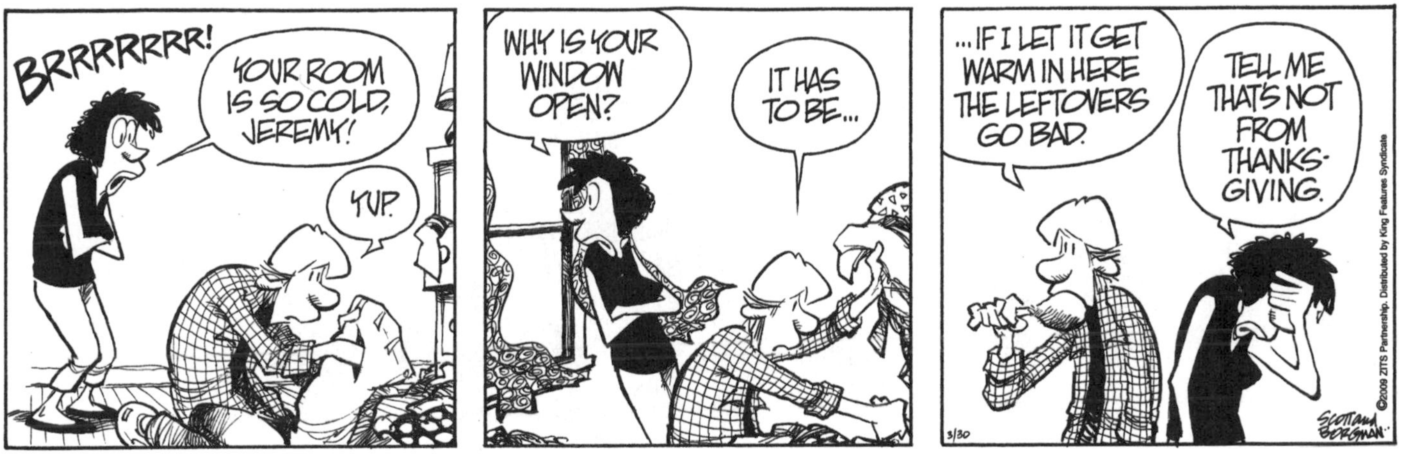
BRRRRRRR!
YOUR ROOM IS SO COLD, JEREMY!
YUP.
WHY IS YOUR WINDOW OPEN?
IT HAS TO BE...
...IF I LET IT GET WARM IN HERE THE LEFTOVERS GO BAD.
TELL ME THAT'S NOT FROM THANKS-GIVING.
3/30
SCOTT and BORGMAN
©2009 ZITS Partnership. Distributed by King Features Syndicate

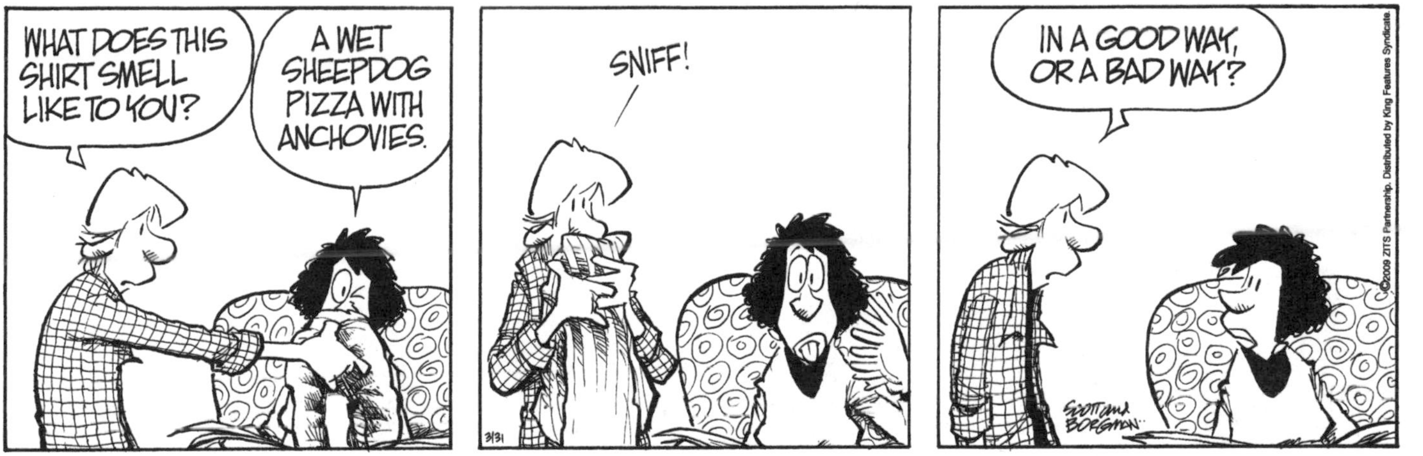
WHAT DOES THIS SHIRT SMELL LIKE TO YOU?
A WET SHEEPDOG PIZZA WITH ANCHOVIES.
SNIFF!
3/31
IN A GOOD WAY, OR A BAD WAY?
SCOTT and BORGMAN
©2009 ZITS Partnership. Distributed by King Features Syndicate.

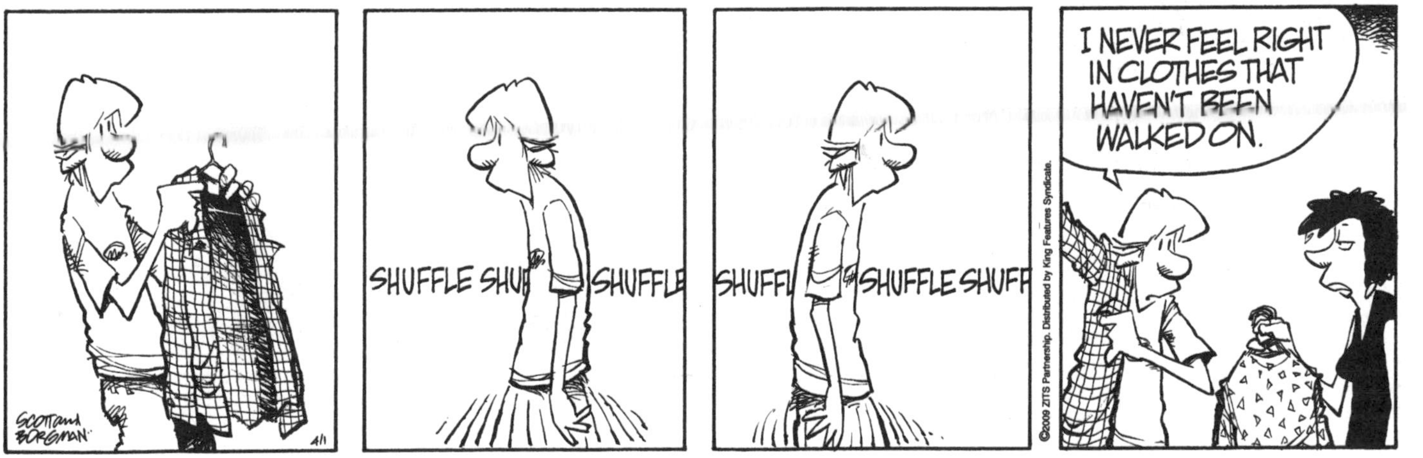
SCOTT and BORGMAN
4/1
SHUFFLE SHUF SHUFFLE
SHUFFL SHUFFLE SHUFF
©2009 ZITS Partnership. Distributed by King Features Syndicate.
I NEVER FEEL RIGHT IN CLOTHES THAT HAVEN'T BEEN WALKED ON.

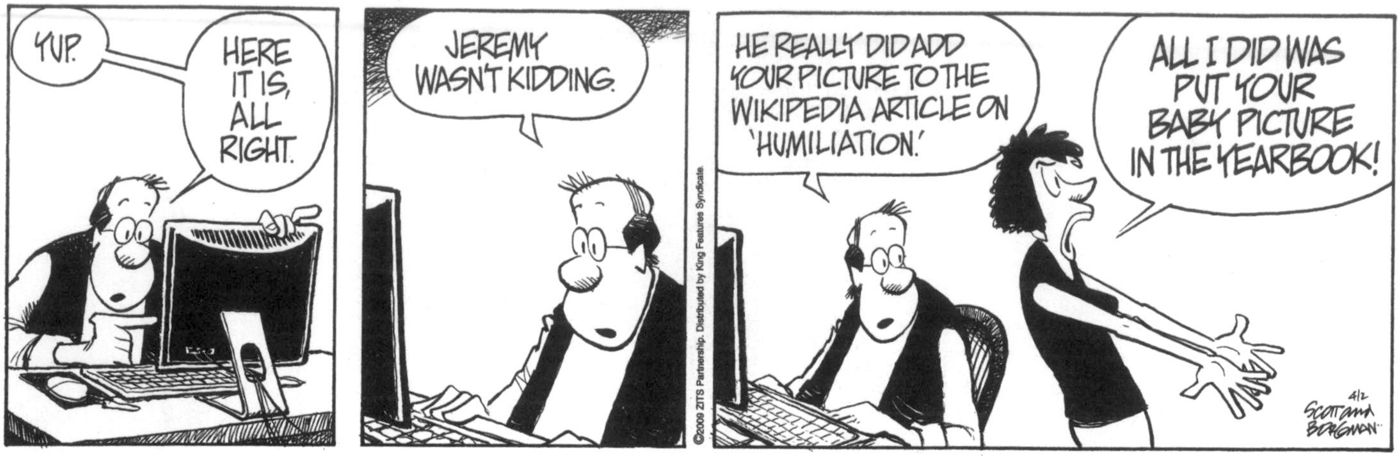
YUP.
HERE IT IS, ALL RIGHT.
JEREMY WASN'T KIDDING.
HE REALLY DID ADD YOUR PICTURE TO THE WIKIPEDIA ARTICLE ON 'HUMILIATION.'
ALL I DID WAS PUT YOUR BABY PICTURE IN THE YEARBOOK!
©2009 ZITS Partnership. Distributed by King Features Syndicate.
4/2 SCOTT and BORGMAN

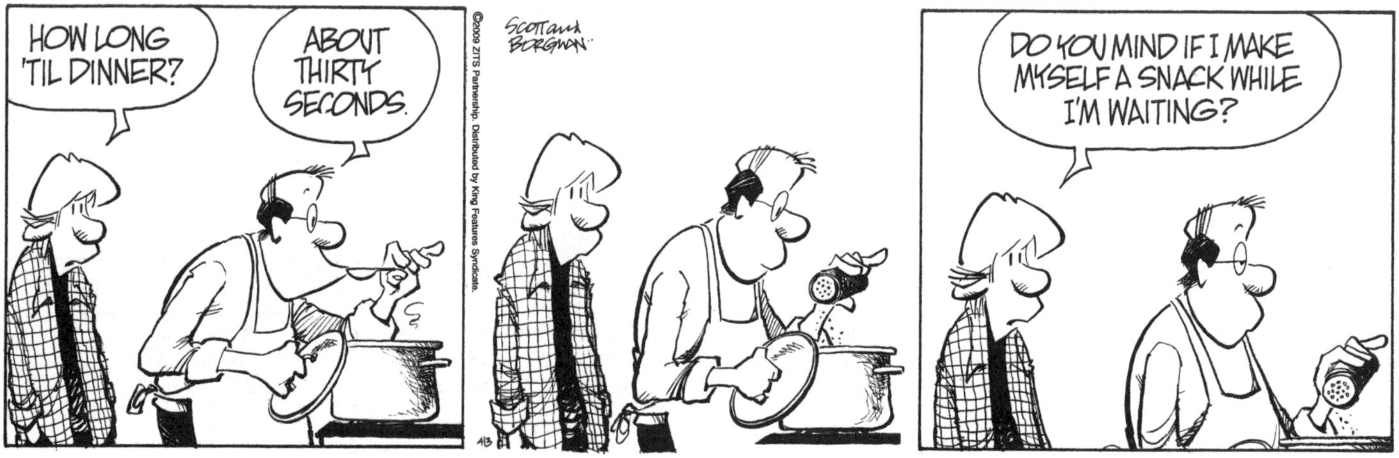
HOW LONG 'TIL DINNER?
ABOUT THIRTY SECONDS.
©2009 ZITS Partnership. Distributed by King Features Syndicate.
SCOTT and BORGMAN
4/3
DO YOU MIND IF I MAKE MYSELF A SNACK WHILE I'M WAITING?

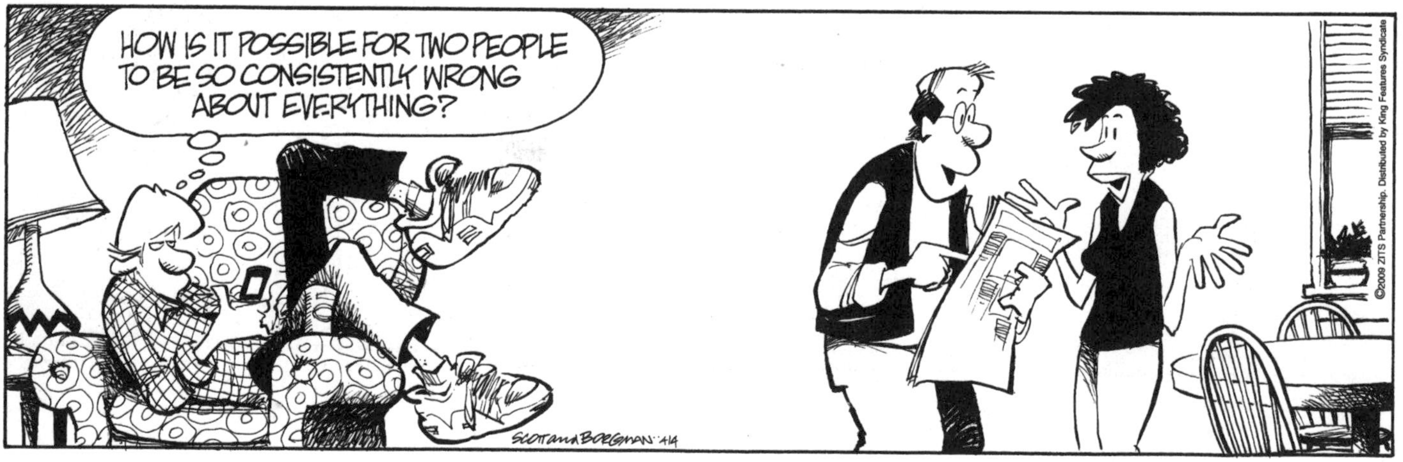
HOW IS IT POSSIBLE FOR TWO PEOPLE TO BE SO CONSISTENTLY WRONG ABOUT EVERYTHING?
SCOTT and BORGMAN 4/4
©2009 ZITS Partnership. Distributed by King Features Syndicate

Zits
by JERRY SCOTT and JIM BORGMAN

CONFUSED ABOUT WHAT YOUR KID IS TRYING TO TELL YOU? USE OUR
Teen Translator
SCOTT and BORGMAN
INSERT CONFUSING SENTENCE OR SENTENCE FRAGMENT
PUSH
AND HERE'S THE TRANSLATION:
FEED ME, FUND ME, LEAVE ME ALONE.

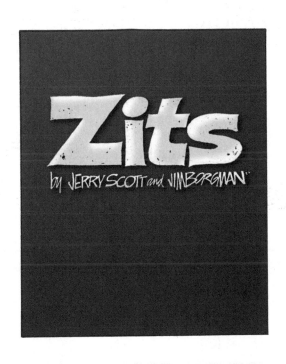

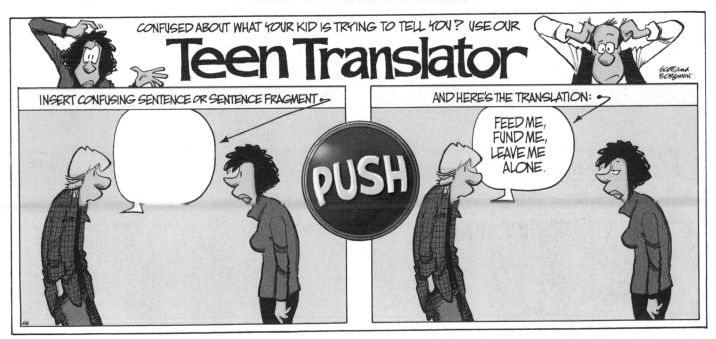

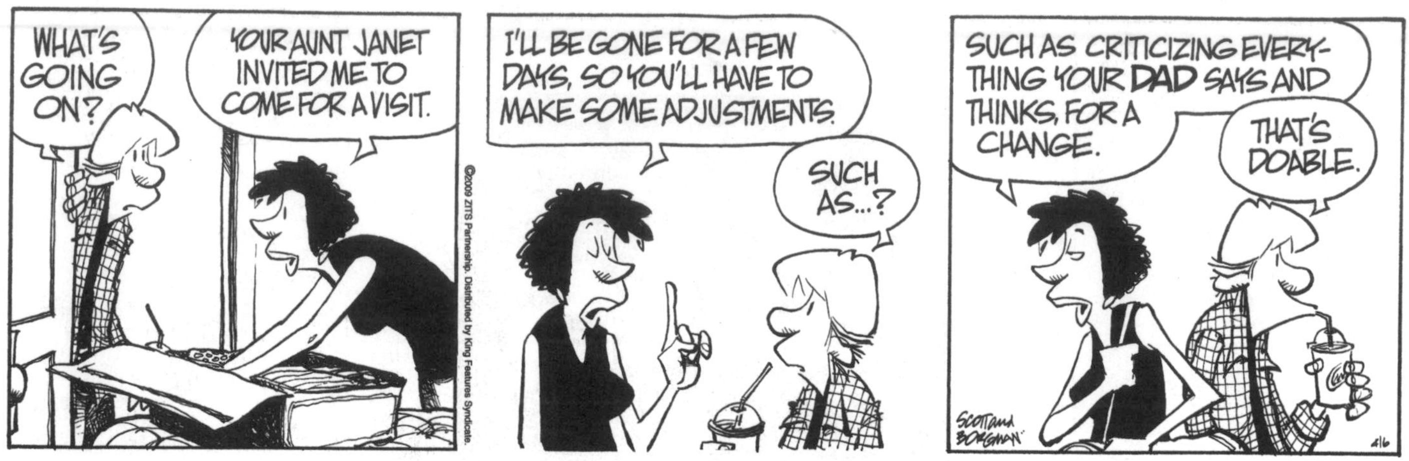
WHAT'S GOING ON?
YOUR AUNT JANET INVITED ME TO COME FOR A VISIT.
©2009 ZITS Partnership. Distributed by King Features Syndicate.
I'LL BE GONE FOR A FEW DAYS, SO YOU'LL HAVE TO MAKE SOME ADJUSTMENTS.
SUCH AS...?
SUCH AS CRITICIZING EVERYTHING YOUR **DAD** SAYS AND THINKS, FOR A CHANGE.
THAT'S DOABLE.
SCOTT AND BORGMAN
4/16

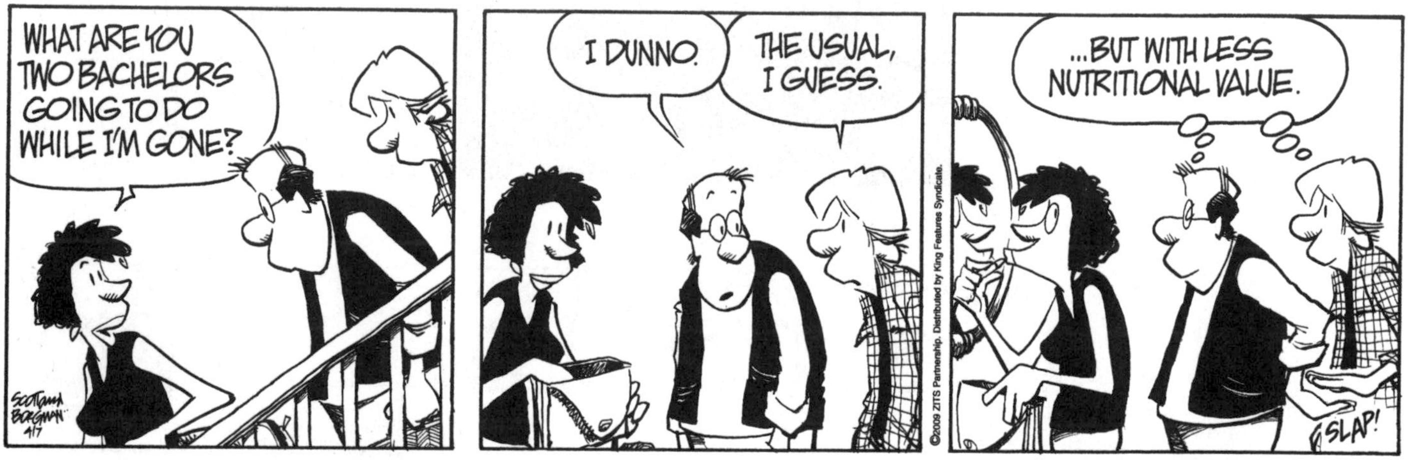
WHAT ARE YOU TWO BACHELORS GOING TO DO WHILE I'M GONE?
SCOTT AND BORGMAN 4/17
I DUNNO.
THE USUAL, I GUESS.
©2009 ZITS Partnership. Distributed by King Features Syndicate.
...BUT WITH LESS NUTRITIONAL VALUE.
SLAP!

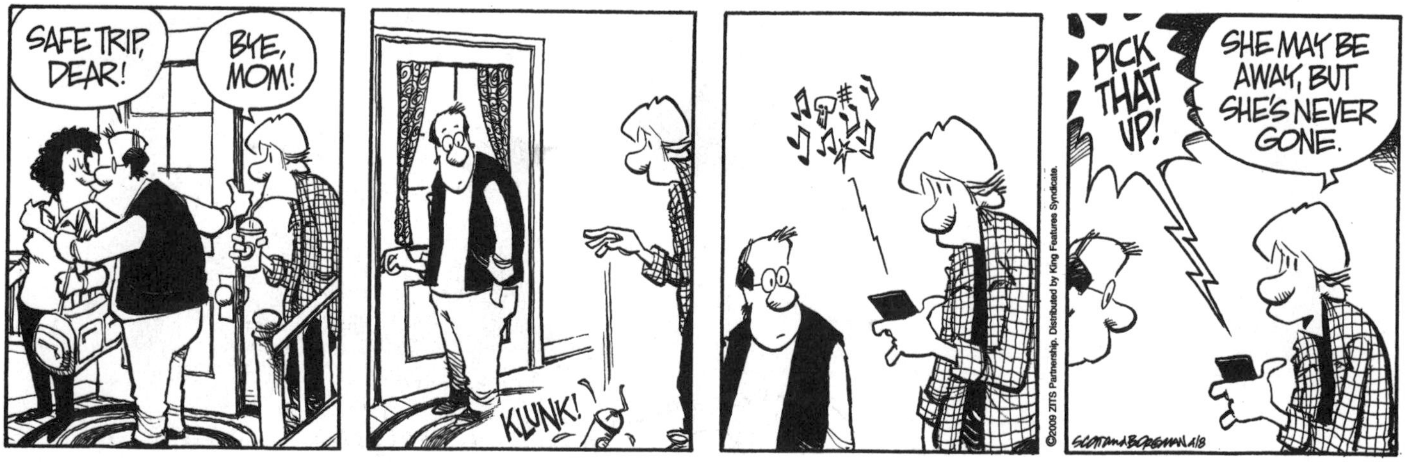
SAFE TRIP, DEAR!
BYE, MOM!
KLUNK!
©2009 ZITS Partnership. Distributed by King Features Syndicate.
PICK THAT UP!
SHE MAY BE AWAY, BUT SHE'S NEVER GONE.
SCOTT AND BORGMAN 4/18

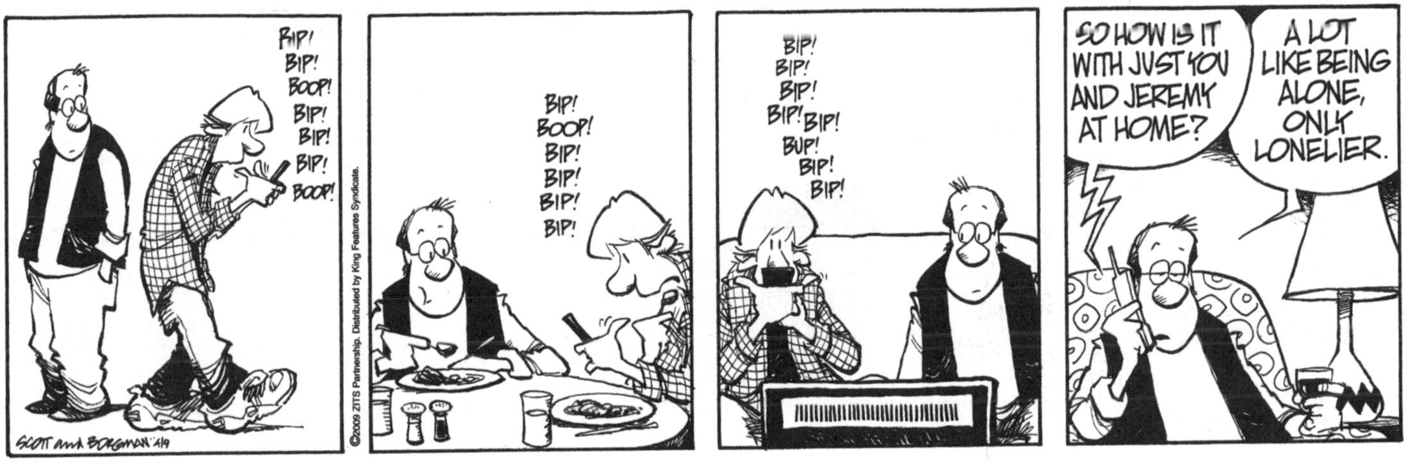
BIP! BIP! BOOP! BIP! BIP! BIP! BOOP!
SCOTT and BORGMAN 4/9
©2009 ZITS Partnership. Distributed by King Features Syndicate.
BIP! BOOP! BIP! BIP! BIP! BIP!
BIP! BIP! BIP! BIP! BIP! BUP! BIP! BIP!
SO HOW IS IT WITH JUST YOU AND JEREMY AT HOME?
A LOT LIKE BEING ALONE, ONLY LONELIER.

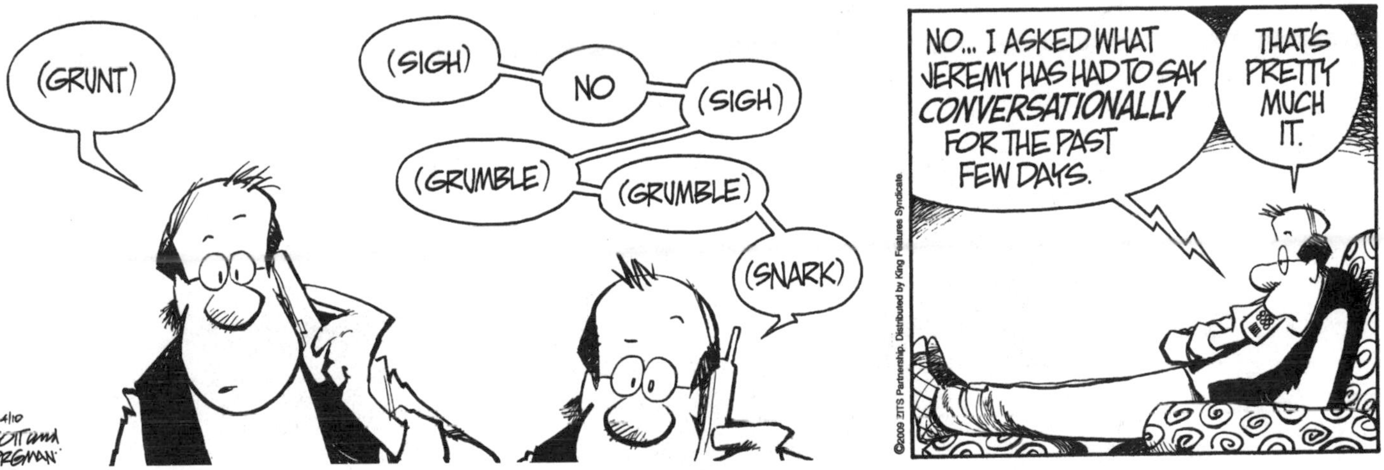
(GRUNT)
4/10 SCOTT and BORGMAN
(SIGH)
NO
(SIGH)
(GRUMBLE)
(GRUMBLE)
(SNARK)
©2009 ZITS Partnership. Distributed by King Features Syndicate.
NO... I ASKED WHAT JEREMY HAS HAD TO SAY *CONVERSATIONALLY* FOR THE PAST FEW DAYS.
THAT'S PRETTY MUCH IT.

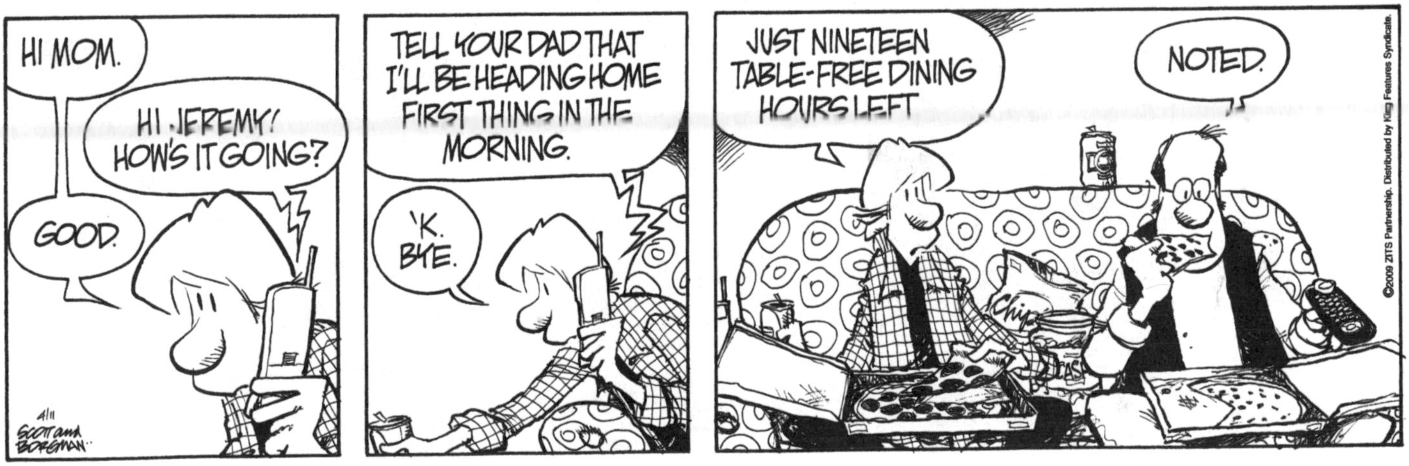
HI MOM.
HI JEREMY! HOW'S IT GOING?
GOOD.
4/11 SCOTT and BORGMAN
TELL YOUR DAD THAT I'LL BE HEADING HOME FIRST THING IN THE MORNING.
'K. BYE.
JUST NINETEEN TABLE-FREE DINING HOURS LEFT.
NOTED.
©2009 ZITS Partnership. Distributed by King Features Syndicate.

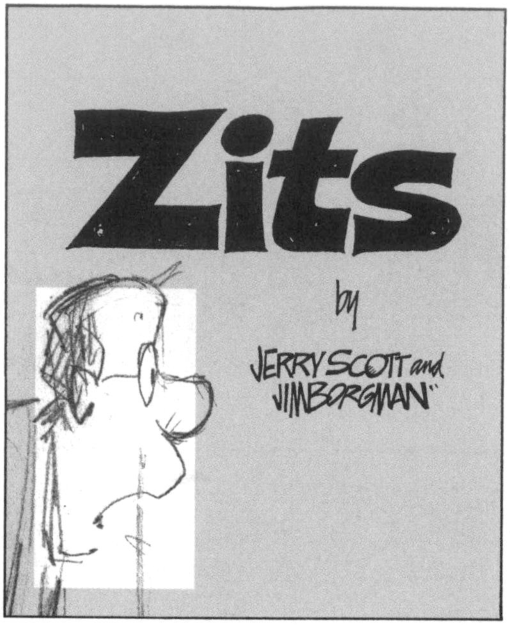
Zits
by
JERRY SCOTT and
JIM BORGMAN

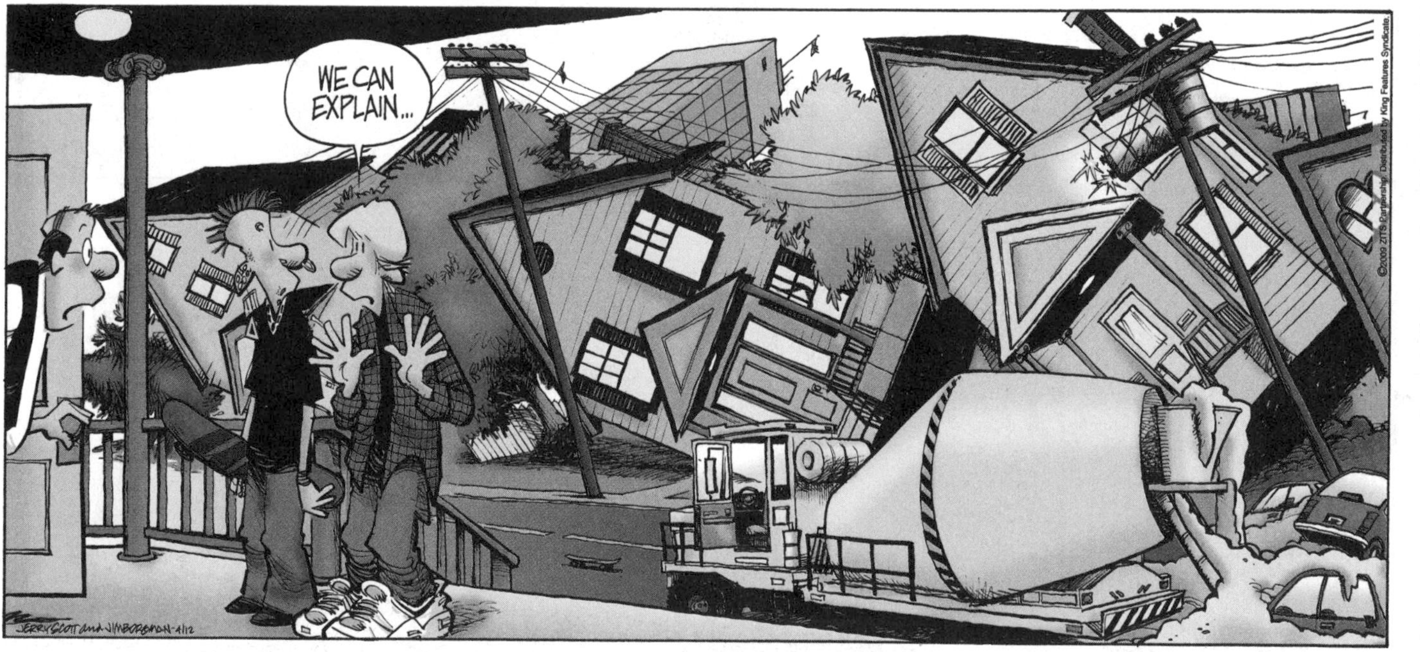
WE CAN EXPLAIN...

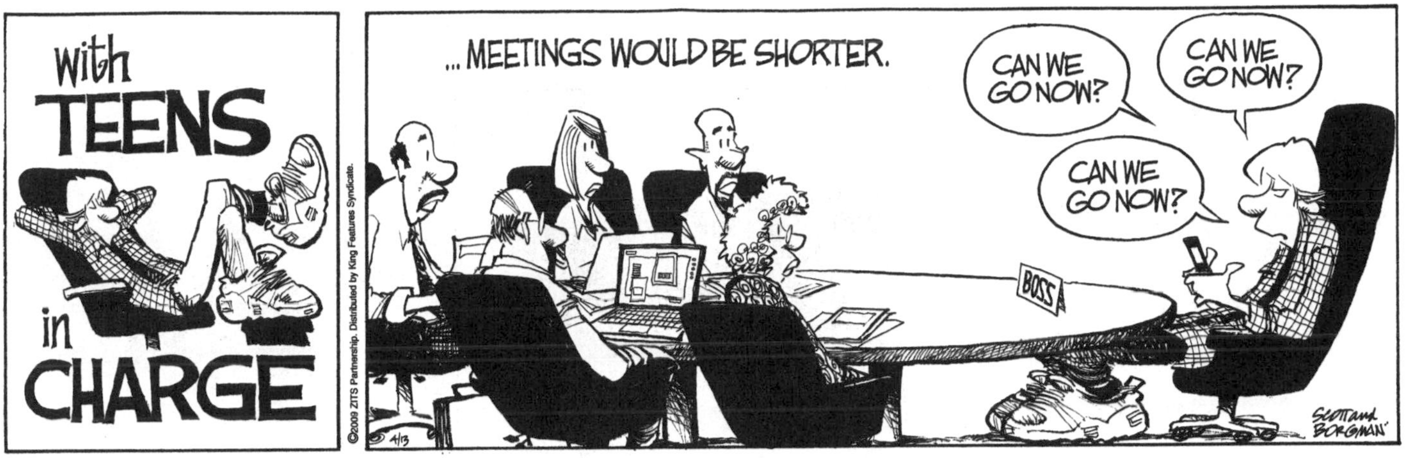

with TEENS in CHARGE
...MEETINGS WOULD BE SHORTER.
CAN WE GO NOW?
CAN WE GO NOW?
CAN WE GO NOW?
BOSS
©2009 ZITS Partnership. Distributed by King Features Syndicate.
SCOTT and BORGMAN

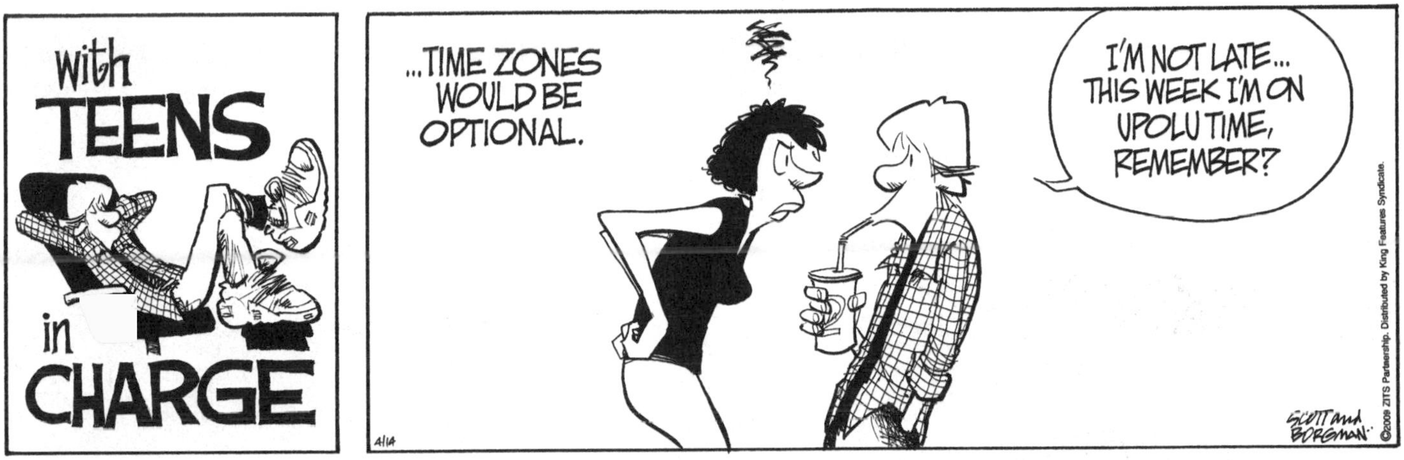

with TEENS in CHARGE
...TIME ZONES WOULD BE OPTIONAL.
I'M NOT LATE... THIS WEEK I'M ON UPOLU TIME, REMEMBER?
©2009 ZITS Partnership. Distributed by King Features Syndicate.
SCOTT and BORGMAN

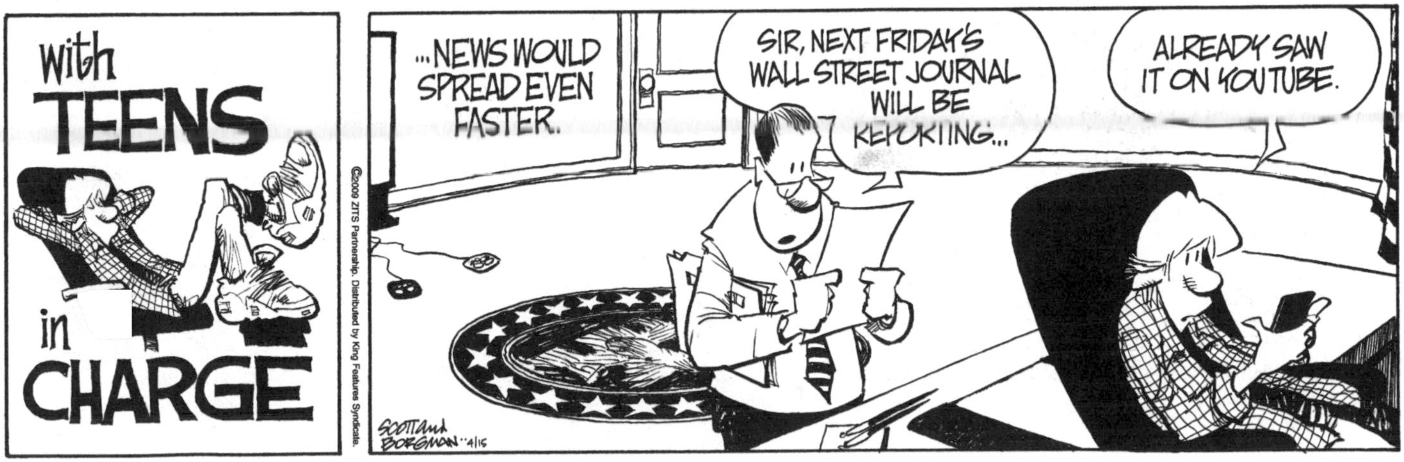

with TEENS in CHARGE
...NEWS WOULD SPREAD EVEN FASTER.
SIR, NEXT FRIDAY'S WALL STREET JOURNAL WILL BE REPORTING...
ALREADY SAW IT ON YOUTUBE.
©2009 ZITS Partnership. Distributed by King Features Syndicate.
SCOTT and BORGMAN

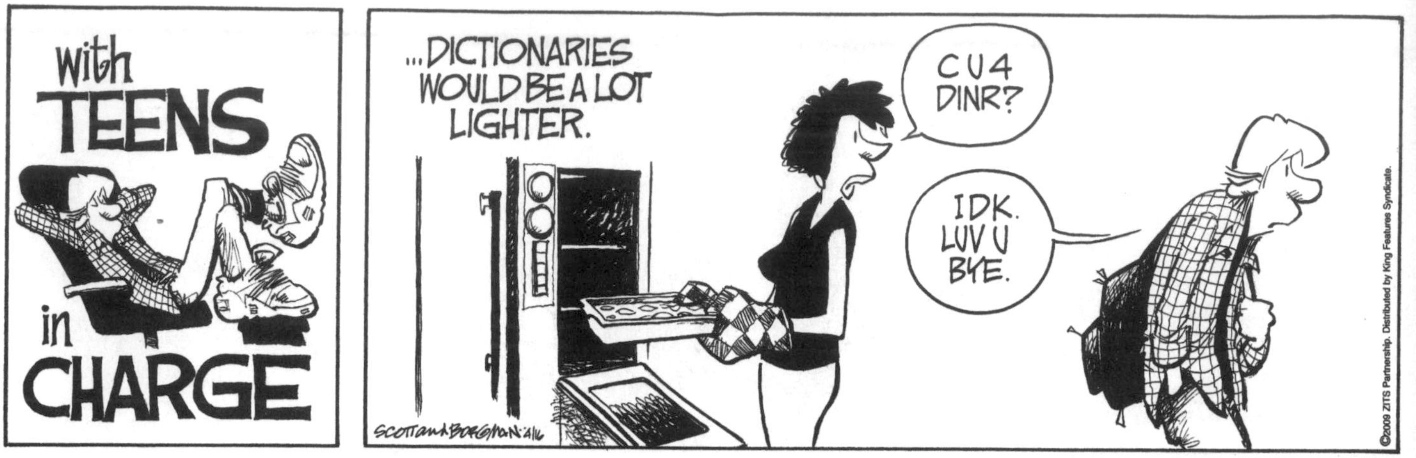
with TEENS in CHARGE
...DICTIONARIES WOULD BE A LOT LIGHTER.
C U 4 DINR?
IDK. LUV U BYE.
SCOTT and BORGMAN 4/16
©2009 ZITS Partnership. Distributed by King Features Syndicate.

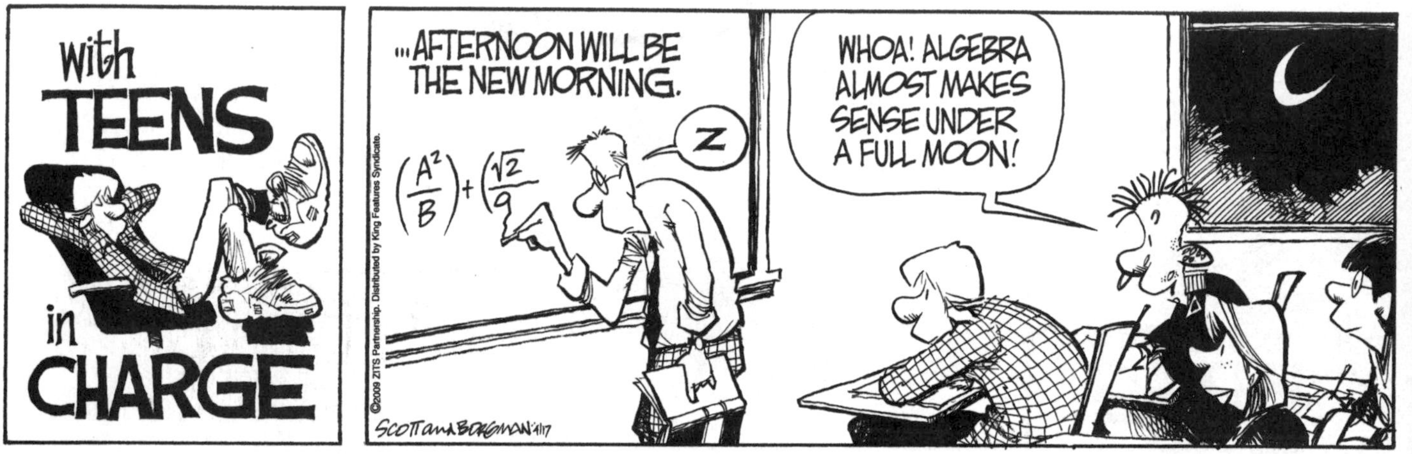
with TEENS in CHARGE
...AFTERNOON WILL BE THE NEW MORNING.
Z
WHOA! ALGEBRA ALMOST MAKES SENSE UNDER A FULL MOON!
SCOTT and BORGMAN 4/17
©2009 ZITS Partnership. Distributed by King Features Syndicate.

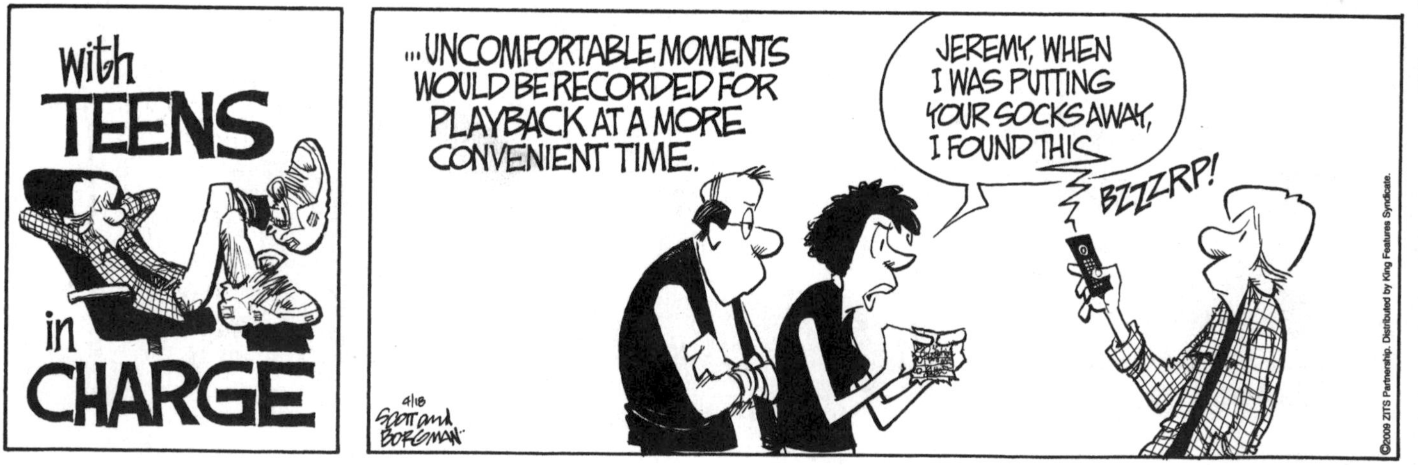
with TEENS in CHARGE
...UNCOMFORTABLE MOMENTS WOULD BE RECORDED FOR PLAYBACK AT A MORE CONVENIENT TIME.
JEREMY, WHEN I WAS PUTTING YOUR SOCKS AWAY, I FOUND THIS
BZZZRP!
4/18 SCOTT and BORGMAN
©2009 ZITS Partnership. Distributed by King Features Syndicate.

Zits
by JERRY SCOTT and JIM BORGMAN

MOM...?
...CAN WE LEAVE FIVE MINUTES EARLY AND DROP BY THE OFFICE SUPPLY STORE SO I CAN GET SOME POSTER BOARD TO MAKE AN ILLUSTRATED TIMELINE OF 14TH CENTURY EUROPEAN TRADE DEVELOPMENT ON THE WAY TO SCHOOL?
ONLY MY KID COULD UNDO FORTY MINUTES OF YOGA WITH ONE SENTENCE.
SCOTT and BORGMAN
©2009 ZITS Partnership. Distributed by King Features Syndicate.
4/19

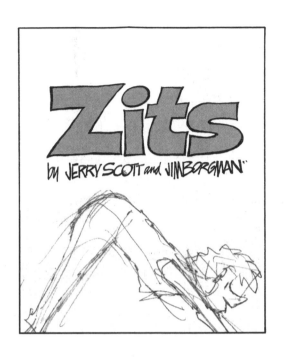

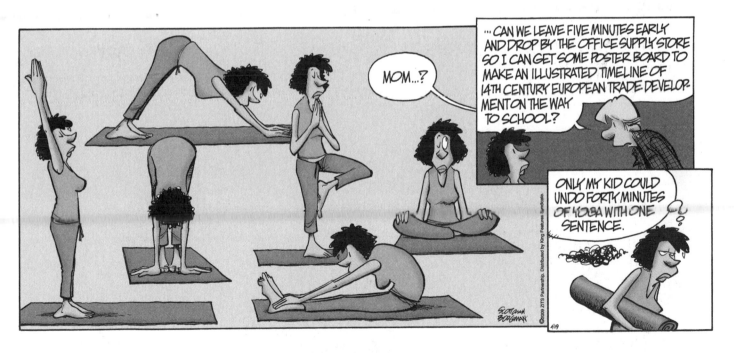